Courts and Judicial Policymaking

Christopher P. Banks
Kent State University

David M. O'Brien
The University of Virginia

PEARSON

Prentice
Hall

Upper Saddle River, New Jersey 07458

Library of Congress Cataloging-in-Publication Data

Banks, Christopher P.
  Courts and judicial policymaking / Christopher P. Banks,
David M. O'Brien.
    p. cm.
  Includes bibliographical references and index.
  ISBN 0-13-144349-6
  1. Courts—United States.   2. Judicial process—United States.
3. Justice, Administration of—United States.
I. O'Brien, David M. II. Title.
  KF8700.B36 2008
    347.73'1—dc22   2006032299

This book is dedicated
to our parents

Editorial Director: Charlyce Jones Owen
Executive Editor: Dickson Musslewhite
Assoc. Editor: Rob DeGeorge
Editorial Assistant: Jennifer Murphy
Assist. Marketing Manager: Andrea Messineo
Senior Managing Editor: Lisa Iarkowski
Production Liaison: Fran Russello
Manufacturing Buyer: Mary Ann Gloriande
Cover Design: Bruce Kenselaar
Composition/Full-Service Project Management: Shelley Creager/Techbooks
Printer/Binder: RR Donnelley & Sons Company

Credits and acknowledgments borrowed from other sources and reproduced, with permission, in this textbook appear on appropriate page within text.

Pearson Prentice Hall™ is a trademark of Pearson Education, Inc.
Pearson® is a registered trademark of Pearson plc
Prentice Hall® is a registered trademark of Pearson Education, Inc.

Pearson Education LTD. London
Pearson Education Singapore, Pte. Ltd
Pearson Education, Canada, Ltd
Pearson Education—Japan
Pearson Education Australia PTY, Limited

Pearson Education North Asia Ltd
Pearson Educación de Mexico, S.A. de C.V.
Pearson Education Malaysia, Pte. Ltd
Pearson Education, Upper Saddle River,
   New Jersey

10 9 8 7 6 5 4 3 2 1
ISBN 0-13-144349-6

Contents

Preface

The role of courts in contemporary politics—nationally and internationally—is increasingly controversial and sometimes misunderstood. Critics warn of the "judicialization of politics" and "the world-wide rule of judges." Yet, courts are central to maintaining the rule of law and "good governance." They also routinely establish law in controversial areas of public policy and may play a role in forging legal and social policy change.

Courts and Judicial Policymaking aims to explain how courts operate and the roles they play in law and politics. Part I focuses on the nature of law and its relationship to judicial politics. Chapter 1 analyzes legal systems and the sources of public and private law. Chapter 2 addresses classical and contemporary legal theories, or political jurisprudence ranging from natural law to critical legal studies, and how those theories affect law and policy. Part II considers judicial organization and administration. Chapter 3 describes the origin, structure, and administration of state and federal courts, as well as the politics of judicial reform. Chapter 4 builds on that discussion by explaining how judges become political actors as they are indoctrinated for public life and the various ways they are recruited, retained, and removed from office.

Part III (and the next four chapters), then, turns to access to courts and how formal and informal barriers affect judicial decision-making. In Chapter 5, the role legal culture and lawyers play in delivering legal services is discussed. Access to courts in terms of formal and informal barriers of justiciability (legal standing, mootness, and similar doctrines of judicial restraint or abstention) is the subject of Chapter 6, along with the different strategies interest groups employ to effectuate policy change during litigation. Chapters 7 and 8 analyze the adversarial justice and the differences between criminal procedure and civil litigation. Chapter 7 examines the role of the prosecutor, juries, and governments in prosecuting and sentencing those accused and found guilty of committing criminal offenses. By contrast, Chapter 8 considers civil litigation and the process of seeking monetary compensation for personal injuries, as well as the increasing privatization of alternative dispute resolution methods.

Part IV (Chapters 9 and 10) explores judicial policymaking and the scope and limits of judicial power. Chapter 9 details the appellate judicial process, including how scholars generally study judicial behavior, and how courts establish law and public policy in setting their agendas and writing judicial opinions. Chapter 10, then, examines controversies over the role and impact of courts, with particular attention to controversies over abortion, same-sex marriages, and public school financing cases. The different types of internal and external constraints on judicial power, along with the policymaking impact of courts, are thoroughly considered in the context of those areas of law.

Instructors and students should find *Courts and Judicial Policymaking* useful for several reasons. First, it is written from the legal and social science perspective. Second, its coverage and organization is more complete than any other text used in the subfield of law and politics, with issues ranging from "what is law?" to "how are courts social policymakers but constrained in making law?" Third, it is timely and integrates analyses from quantitative and qualitative methodologies. Fourth, it has extended discussions of key issues pertaining to the judicial process, ranging from how the judiciary has dealt with the contemporary war on terror to the increasing influence of money and hardball tactics (such as filibusters) in judicial selection and appointments. Fifth, the book brings a balanced perspective to the interaction and policymaking of the state and federal judiciaries, and how they deliver adversarial justice in criminal and civil cases. Sixth, it contains numerous visual and descriptive aids for students, including many cutting-edge charts and graphs on all aspects of the judicial process, caseloads, and opinion writing.

In addition, it has three additional pedagogical tools that will assist students and instructors. Throughout the chapters are two boxes, "Courts in Comparative Perspective" and "Controversies over Courts." The "Courts in Comparative Perspective" focuses on comparative issues of law and politics not found in other texts, such as "Constitutional Courts in Europe," "The Career Judiciary in Japan," and "Comparative Constitutional Law and Capital Punishment." The "Controversies over Courts" boxes address topics such as "How Should Judges Interpret the Constitution?," "Are State Judicial Campaigns and Elections Too Partisan?," and "Is the Federal Judiciary Too Small to Provide Equal Access to Justice?" In addition, each chapter has "Sidebars" that highlight poignant issues relating to the study of the judicial process, law, judicial politics, and social justice. For example, there are Sidebars on "Researching the Law and Judicial Decisions," "Tribal Courts," "The Poor State of Indigent Defense Systems in the States," and "The Battle over School Funding in the States."

We wish to thank the following reviewers for their valuable comments and suggestions: Marshall DeRosa, Florida Atlantic University; Roger Handberg, University of Central Florida; Gregg Ivers, American University; Susan Mezey, Loyola University—Chicago; Gerald N. Rosenberg, University of Chicago; and Jennifer A. Segal, American University.

Christopher P. Banks
Kent State University

David M. O'Brien
The University of Virginia

CHAPTER ONE

Legal Systems and Sources of Law

In the late evening on September 17, 1998, deputies from the Texas Harris County Sheriff's department went to John Geddes Lawrence's apartment in search of an armed intruder, who was reportedly "going crazy in the apartment." What they found, instead, were two men, John Geddes Lawrence and Tyron Garner, engaging in consensual sodomy, a misdemeanor under Texas's law that penalizes "deviate sexual intercourse with another individual of the same sex." After the Justice of the Peace Court found them guilty, Lawrence and Garner appealed to Harris County Criminal Court, alleging the statute violated their privacy, due process, and equal protection rights under the federal Constitution. The court rejected their claims and fined them each $200, plus court costs. Subsequently, a three-judge panel of the Texas Court of Appeals overturned their convictions, ruling that the law unconstitutionally discriminated on the basis of sexual orientation, in violation of the state constitution's Equal Rights Amendment. In March, 2001, however, Lawrence's conviction was reinstated because the panel's judgment was reversed by the full Texas Court of Appeals. That court held that the defendants' constitutional rights were not infringed, in part because the Texas legislature acted rationally in preserving public morals by enacting the homosexual conduct law. On further appeal, the Texas Court of Criminal Appeals declined review, but *Lawrence v. Texas* (2003)[1] was granted review by the U.S. Supreme Court.

Lawrence and Garner faced significant cultural and legal obstacles in challenging Texas's same-sex antisodomy law. After the Civil War, the states began prosecuting nonconformist sexual activities more stringently than heterosexual behaviors. By 1881, nearly all the states outlawed sodomy as a crime against nature. In the twentieth century, morals legislation routinely criminalized offenses such as "buggery" (the British version of sodomy), prostitution, cross-dressing, public lewdness, and obscenity. The medical profession stigmatized homosexuals as mentally deranged, describing their sexual orientations as either psychopathic or dangerous. After World War II, gays were legally classified as sexual deviants and, sometimes, even as a communist threat to national security. In the private sector, gay teachers and lawyers were discriminated against through layoffs or disbarment, and gay and lesbian literature was censored.[2]

Texas's sodomy law dates back to 1860, and, in 1973, the legislature extended its reach by specifically making homosexual sex a crime. Notably, Texas's decision to target same-sex behavior was different than that of other states, like Georgia, that criminalized both heterosexual and homosexual sodomy. The difference was important because Georgia's antisodomy law withstood constitutional challenge in another case decided by the Supreme Court, *Bowers v. Hardwick* (1986).[3] In *Bowers*, a bare majority ruled that there was no constitutional right under the Fourteenth Amendment's due process clause to engage in consensual homosexual sodomy. As a result, *Bowers* was controlling precedent and the Supreme Court could have simply dismissed the petitioners' constitutional claims in *Lawrence*.

Still, adhering to *Bowers* had to be considered against persistent countervailing pressures in the states and the global community. In the last thirty years, states became more tolerant of gay rights. By 1986, twenty-six states had repealed their criminal laws banning consensual sodomy. Although seven states in the 1970s criminalized same-sex conduct, by the late 1990s all but five had struck down or repealed their laws, either by judicial action or by legislation.[4]

Moreover, a parallel western European movement emerged outlawing discrimination on the basis of sexual orientation, which usually occurred through legislative action not through judicial decisions. In 1967, Great Britain repealed its laws criminalizing homosexual conduct. Similarly, South Africa outlawed anti-gay employment discrimination (1994), whereas Denmark, France, the Netherlands, and, most recently in 2005, Spain enacted laws permitting same-sex registered partnerships and civil marriage unions.[5] Furthermore, in *Dudgeon v. United Kingdom* (1981),[6] the European Court of Human Rights held that Northern Ireland's antisodomy ban on consensual homosexual activity violated the European Convention on Human Rights, a precedent binding forty-five countries participating in the Council of Europe. In June 2003, in *Halpern v. Attorney General of Canada* (2003)[7], the Court of Appeals for Ontario ruled that denying same-sex couples the right to marry violated the Canadian Charter of Rights and Freedoms.

By a 6:3 vote, *Lawrence v. Texas* struck down Texas's law and overturned *Bowers*. Justice Anthony Kennedy's opinion for the Court held that criminalizing homosexual conduct between consenting adults violates the Fourteenth Amendment's due process clause and the right to privacy and equal protection. Due process protection for individual liberty, he emphasized, creates "an autonomy of self that includes freedom of thought, belief, expression, and certain intimate conduct." Although *Bowers* emphasized that "for centuries there have been powerful voices to condemn homosexual conduct as immoral," Justice Kennedy highlighted the "emerging awareness" over the past fifty years that "liberty gives substantial protection to adult persons in deciding how to conduct their private lives in matters pertaining to sex." This "emerging recognition" is not only apparent in United States law, but also in foreign law. In Justice Kennedy's words, "other nations . . . have taken action consistent with an affirmation of the protected right of homosexual adults to engage in intimate, consensual conduct." Foreign precedents, including *Dudgeon*, ran counter to Justice Byron White's assertion for the majority in *Bowers* that criminal prohibitions against consensual homosexual sodomy had "ancient roots." Justice Kennedy similarly questioned Chief Justice Warren Burger's concurring opinion in *Bowers*, declaring that gay sex must be condemned pursuant to traditional norms of Judeo-Christian morality. To the contrary, Justice Kennedy emphasized, the personal autonomy of homosexuals "has been accepted as an integral part of human freedom in many other countries." Precedents—ranging from *Pierce v. Society of Sisters* (1923) and *Griswold v. Connecticut* (1963) to *Planned Parenthood of Southeastern Pennsylvania v. Casey* (1992)[8]—created a body of jurisprudence consistent with the contemporary global understanding about the scope of gay rights in Western democracies: The Fourteenth Amendment due process liberty and equal protection guarantees personal choices to engage in homosexual sexual relations in private residences.[9]

"What a massive disruption of the current social order," dissenting Justice Antonin Scalia countered, "the overruling of *Bowers* entails." For Justice Scalia, *Lawrence* wrongly overturned *Bowers* because *Bowers* was proof that democratic majorities, instead of the judiciary, have the power and legitimacy to establish legislation on the basis of moral choices. He complained that "[c]ountless judicial decisions and legislative enactments have relied on the ancient proposition that a governing majority's belief that certain sexual behavior is 'immoral and unacceptable' constitutes a rational basis for regulation." Moreover, he criticized the majority for relying on foreign law in *Lawrence* because foreign countries are not part of America's constitutional history and tradition. For Scalia, *Lawrence* was proof that the Court was acting like a superlegislature and, worse, it implied same-sex couples might have the right to marry. In that regard, in 2003 the Supreme Court of Massachusetts held that limiting civil marriage to opposite-sex couples violated the state's constitution in *Goodridge v. Department of Public Health* (2003),[10] whereas constitutional amendments barring same-sex marriages were subsequently adopted in several states and in 2006 the high courts in Georgia and New York ruled that same-sex couples are not entitled to marriage.

The controversies over *Lawrence v. Texas* highlight the importance of not only different understandings of the rule of law and the role of courts, but also of legal change and continuity and the power of judicial review in a democracy. These topics are discussed in this chapter in relation to (1) the role of law and courts in different kinds of legal systems around the world and (2) debates over the nature and sources of law. Chapter 2 extends the discussion about law and its political implications by exploring classical and contemporary jurisprudential theories of law, along with how different understandings of the rule of law affect the different kinds of roles courts play in society.

LEGAL SYSTEMS

Although *Lawrence* underscores the so-called "globalization of law," the differences among legal systems in the world should not be obscured. Every legal system is to a certain extent distinct, simply because each society and its corresponding legal norms vary. Yet generalizations about what constitutes a legal system are possible. A *legal system* refers to a set of operating institutional structures (the general framework for applying the law), legal procedures (how law is procedurally administered), and rules (the substantive content of the law).[11] No less important is how various elements of the legal system (conceptions of law, formal institutions, the legal profession, courts, and the citizenry) interact to give the law meaning, continuity, and change. Because there are innumerable legal systems in the world today, and many are of "mixed" character, scholars from various academic disciplines (comparative law, history, or legal philosophy) do not agree on how to classify legal systems or whether it is even possible to do so.

Still, a common framework typically depicts legal systems as "families of law."[12] Although legal families evolve over time and may share certain structures, procedures, or rules, a distinguishing factor among legal systems is the law's origin. Whereas, for example, *civil law systems* in the Romanic–Germanic family emphasize written civil codes constructed by legislatures, the *common law family*—including the American legal system—concentrates on the administration of law by judges and lawyers. Before the fall of the Soviet Union in 1989, in contrast to civil and common law systems, the Socialist legal family derived law from the political ideology of Marxism. Other legal families are rooted in religious sources, as in Muslim, Hindu, or Jewish jurisdictions. Some legal systems are strongly influenced by *customary law* (law based on social customs enforced by the community) or, as with "mixed" systems, the elements of more than one legal system may operate as a unified whole within a single jurisdiction. The rest of this section analyzes the major legal families and surveys the predominant legal systems in the world today.

Civil Law

Most Continental European countries have civil law systems. In the sixth century (A.D.) the Emperor Justinian sought to restore the glory of Roman law by codifying portions of it into one source, the *Corpus Juris Civilis* (CJC)—consisting of

Institutes (an introduction to basic principles), a Digest (a summary of past Roman scholarship), Codes (a compilation of past Roman legislation, edits and other laws), and Novels (a section for future legislation after the Code and Digest were completed). After the fall of the Roman Empire, the CJC was rediscovered by scholars at the University of Bologna, Italy, in the eleventh century. The rediscovery coincided with the development of the canon law by the Catholic Church and the rise of commercial law, a set of rules governing commercial relationships across the European continent. In time, the CJC (Roman civil law), canon law, and the commercial law helped to produce a common law, the *jus commune* ("law of the community") and became part of the civil law that was later "received," or adapted, in one form or another by European states. This history shaped the basic codes found in civil law countries, namely, the civil code, the commercial code, the code of civil procedure, the penal code, and the code of criminal procedure.[13]

Two variations of what became the modern civil law system took hold in France and in Germany during the nineteenth century. The French Civil Code of 1804, or *Code Napoleon*, developed under the rule of the Emperor Napoleon Bonaparte, eradicated all traces of aristocratic power in French nobility, clergy, and judiciary. It was built on *three pillars*—codes broadly protecting property, contract, and patriarchal family relationships—that formerly were under the domain of the church or the aristocracy. Because the law was based on universal ideas of natural justice (liberty and equality), it was crafted in simple terms, and it accordingly limited the need for lawyers or extensive judicial oversight. The code was thus distinctly antifeudal and antijudicial because French judges were part of the aristocratic class that had too often abused power. The bias against the judiciary is important because it laid the foundation for a tradition that institutionally isolated courts from other branches of government and reduced judges to civil servants.

Whereas the French Civil Code was inspired by revolution and strived to protect rights universally, the German Civil Code of 1896 was more technical. Proponents of the German Historical School, led by Friedrich Carl von Savigny (1779–1861), argued that legal systems must be constructed from historically derived principles of legal science. Accordingly, the German Civil Code of 1896 was a self-contained body of written law: Lawyers or judges did not have to resort to extraneous social, economic, political, or moral values to apply it. Unlike the French Code, the German Code made clear that the science of conceptualizing law (rules, legislation, and the like) was left to the realm of the lawyer and the judge not to the common person. Hence, the German Civil Code was detailed, precise, and logical. Definitions and elaborate cross-references (to all other parts of the Code) contained pragmatic guides for applying law that was virtually inaccessible to all but legal experts.

The civil law tradition remains infused in the legal systems throughout continental Europe, Asia, South America, and parts of Africa (see Table 1.1). Until recently, civil law systems did not provide for *judicial review*—the power to

TABLE 1.1   Major Global Legal Systems

Legal System	Sources of Law	Jurisdictions in Global Community		Examples
		Number	**Percentage**	
Civil Law	Written codes by legislatures	86	38	Brazil, Denmark, France, Germany, Russia
Common	Judicial decisions	43	19	Australia, Canada, Ireland, U.K., U.S.
Customary	Local customs	3	1	Andorra, Guernsey Island (U.K.), Jersey Island (U.K.)
Religious (Muslim)	Religious texts (Koran)	2	1	Afghanistan, Maldives Islands
Mixed	Combination of various legal systems	95	41	
CIV, COM		14		Philippines, Scotland (U.K.), South Africa
CIV, CUS		26		China, Japan, South Korea, Niger, Taiwan
CIV, MUS		11		Algeria, Egypt, Iraq, Libya, Morocco, Syria
CIV, MUS, CUS		4		Djibouti, Eritrea, Indonesia, Timor-Leste
CIV, COM, CUS		5		Cameroun, Sri Lanka, Zimbabwe
COM, MUS		8		Bangladesh, Pakistan, Singapore, Sudan
COM, CUS		15		Ghana, Nepal, Sierra Leone, Zambia
COM, MUS, CUS		6		Kenya, India, Malaysia, Nigeria
MUS, COM, CIV		5		Iran, Jordan, Saudia Arabia, Yemin
TAL, CIV, COM		1		Israel

Note. N = 229. All percentages are subject to rounding error. As a result of the Soviet Union's collapse in 1989, and because many significant socialist legal systems are "mixed" (e.g. China, Vietnam, Laos), the Socialist (ideological) legal family is excluded from analysis. Mulism law, and to a lesser degree, Talmudic law are identified separately from other religious-based systems because Muslim law is more permanent and widespread, whereas Talmudic law and Israel's mixed legal system are highly distinctive. Other initially religious legal systems are not as distinctive, and a number of their defining characteristics have been blended into customary or state systems.

CIV: Civil law; COM: Common law; CUS: Customary; MUS: Muslim; TAL: Talmudic.

Source: Derived from Faculty of Law, Civil Law Section, The University of Ottawa. "World Legal Systems," available from www.droitcivil.uottawa.ca/world-legal-systems/eng-monde.html (retrieved September 26, 2005).

declare legislative acts unconstitutional. The absence of judicial review is explained by the subordinate role courts play to legislatures. The nature of legal analysis in civil law systems also gives little discretion to courts in interpreting codes and legislative intent. In other words, modern civil codes are generally a systematic collection of general legal principles and laws enacted by legislative bodies. As one civil lawyer described it: "The Code . . . is a construction of the mind, designed to impose a rational and well-defined legal order on a particular society. It is the materialization of a legal philosophy at one point in time, as well as the solidification of a society's ever changing morals into a fixed set of written rules."[14] For civil law judges, then, the civil code is both the starting and the ending point for legal analysis.

The traditional civil law model has been changing, however, since the second half of the twentieth century. After World War II, new constitutional courts, along with the power of judicial review, were introduced in Europe (see In Comparative Perspective box in Chapter 2). Hence, like their American counterparts, some European constitutional courts are now playing a more dynamic role in interpreting law and making social policy.

Civil law systems are inquisitorial in operation and differ from adversarial systems, like that in the United States (see Sidebar 1.1). That is to say, legal institutions and practices are structured to arrive at legal truths under a written code or by following specific legal procedures. Lawyers, who are trained as specialists in narrowly defined areas of law, earn a formal degree in law at a university as undergraduates before they become eligible to practice. Judges are prepared to be civil servants who begin (and often end) their careers in a judicial bureaucracy. Finally, adjudication in inquisitorial civil law systems is proactive in the sense that all who play a role in litigation (especially judges) are active participants in, typically, a three-stage process that usually has a preliminary hearing, evidencing-taking, and decision-making stage, and each is structured to engage litigants and judges in an active search for facts and evidence.[15] Except for select criminal cases, there is basically no "trial" process per se, and the presence of a lay jury is rare because judges play the fact-finding role and determine the facts (and evidence) before issuing a ruling.

Sidebar 1.1

Inquisitorial and Adversarial Systems

Legal systems in the civil and common law traditions are characterized by certain traits that find expression in the way legal institutions, procedures, and rules operate or apply. The inquisitorial system is found in the civil law tradition, whereas, in the common law tradition, the adversary system controls. The main characteristics that typically distinguish one system from the other are summarized below.

Features	Inquisitorial (civil law)	Adversarial (common law)
Facts investigation	Collaborative effort with prosecutor and judge discovering facts together	Litigants opposing each other separately discover facts without judge's help
Pretrial process	Less extensive	More extensive
Trial process	More disjointed, and more costly	Singular event (after pretrial) and less costly
Judge's role	Active, engaged; more bureaucratic	Passive, neutral; less bureaucratic
Jury	Rarely used	Used often (especially in United States)
Bail	Rarely used	Used often (especially in United States)
Legal education	Undergraduate education	Professional (graduate) education
Attorney's role	More collaborative and less influential	Less collaborative and more influential
Plea bargaining or pretrial settlement	Unusual	Typical

Source: Herbert M. Kritzer, ed. *Legal Systems of the World: A Political, Social and Cultural Encyclopedia.* Vol. 1. (Santa Barbara: ABC-CLIO, 2002), 6–9; Christopher E. Smith, *Courts and Trials: A Reference Handbook* (Santa Barbara: ABC-CLIO, 2003), 40–5.

Common Law

Whereas civil law systems are based on the primacy of the legislature and a code, the common law system is based on the rule of judges. The origin of common law stems from the Norman conquest of the Anglo-Saxons in the Battle of Hastings in 1066 by King William I. After taking control, William I dispersed the land only after the fee holders swore loyalty and promised to pay sums of money to the king. Hence, for William I the problem of maintaining order and earning tax revenue was found in the creation of a feudal system that centralized royal power by devising a legal system for resolving private disputes among the landholders. Beginning in 1300, three central royal courts of justice—the Court of Exchequer, the Court of Common Pleas, and the Court of King's Bench—emerged in Westminster, and all were staffed by judges empowered to act in the King's absence. As agents for the king, the royal judges had strict instructions on how to handle local legal disputes. Access was also a privilege instead of a right: Citizens had to ask permission from a royal judge to deliver a petition in order to have the court hear the case. What developed was a highly procedural system of *writs*—or petitions requesting legal relief. To remove a trespasser from land, for example, a writ of ejectment was used. The emphasis on procedure meant that "where there is no remedy there is no wrong," and where there was no remedy there was no right.[16]

The writ system reinforced the king's power and simultaneously consolidated the royal judges' power to make unwritten law as the king's delegate. The judge was a de facto (in fact) gatekeeper of the judicial process. Over time, the process of determining the facts in disputes fell to juries, and the judge's role was only to apply the law. By the fifteenth century, the common law evolved alongside the law of equity—equity is a special set of rules permitting relief for those who suffered injustices because of the strict operation of the writs system. An equitable remedy might be found, for example, where a traditionally legal one was foreclosed, thereby violating the king's morality or fairness. A separate Court of Chancery eventually emerged to handle such cases.

Accordingly, the judge is the central figure in a common law system. The rulings of early common law judges, moreover, were "unwritten" in the sense that written law did not exist to guide the use of their discretion. Still, once a ruling was made it became binding as a legal principle or precedent for future cases. As more and more cases were decided, "a common law in the realm" was established. Notably, whereas judges had the obligation to "declare" the law on the basis of precedent, they also had the power to "make" law with precedent that if applied strictly would work an injustice for litigants in new cases. As Judge Benjamin Cardozo remarked, "the power to declare the law carries with it the power, and within limits the duty, to make law when none exists."[17] Striking the proper balance between declaring and making law was conditioned by the norm that the highest court of appeal is not bound by the precedents they set; hence, high courts have the power to reject past decisions. Precedent gives law stability and predictability but remains open to change. As it is explained further in Chapter 9, the doctrine of precedent, or *stare decisis* (let the decision stand), is a key aspect of judicial behavior in the U.S. judicial system.

Apart from England, contemporary common law legal systems include the United States, Canada, Australia, and Ireland (see Table 1.1). In the United States, the common law was adopted in conjunction with each colony's distinctive legal heritage. The reception of common law was facilitated by the writings of Sir William Blackstone (1723-1780). Blackstone held the first professorship of English Law at Oxford University, where he delivered a series of lectures later published as *Commentaries on the Laws of England* (1765-1769). The *Commentaries* received wide distribution and represented "the most ambitious and most successful effort ever made to reduce the disorderly overgrowth of English law to an intelligible and learnable system."[18] Blackstone's *Commentaries* were also influential in reinforcing an integral aspect of U.S. constitutionalism and the common law method whereby judges are the "living oracle of the law," who only "declare" the law, not make it. Indeed, in a classic statement of judicial restraint, Alexander Hamilton asserted in *Federalist* No. 78 that courts have "neither FORCE nor WILL, but merely judgment."[19]

Blackstone's declaratory theory of judicial decision making was ultimately challenged in the late nineteenth century by legal theorists from the *classical sociological* and *legal realism schools of jurisprudence* (i.e., theories about law relating to its social purpose, as explained in Chapter 2). Still, one of the great contributions of the U.S. legal system is the power of courts and judges to make law and social policy through judicial review.

The complexity of common law produced new pressures in the early nineteenth century to codify a U.S. version of the common law, principally in Massachusetts and then in New York. In 1811, Jeremy Bentham, a noted English legal reformer, went so far as to offer to write a code himself in a letter sent to President James Madison.[20] Even though Madison declined, the codification movement, led by the lawyer David Dudley Field, succeeded in enacting a Code of Civil Procedure in New York in 1848. Yet Field's efforts met harsh resistance from the eastern legal establishment, which was used to the common law style of legal research and objected to a new code-based approach. "Field Codes," however, were adopted toward the end of the century in the Dakotas, Idaho, Louisiana, Montana, and California. But the common law system survived the codification challenge and support waned by the beginning of the twentieth century.

Unlike the civil law tradition, common law systems are adversarial and lawyers have considerable power to shape and make the law through a competitive struggle to win a case. Former N.Y. Judge Jerome Frank once referred to this process as the *fight theory*. In Judge Frank's view, "the lawyer aims at victory, at winning in the fight, not at aiding the court to discover the facts." In other words, the lawyer "does not want the trial court to reach a sound educated guess, if it is likely to be contrary to his client's interest." As Frank concluded, "our present trial method is thus the equivalent of throwing pepper in the eyes of a surgeon when he is performing an operation."[21] As a result, lawyers have more control and influence in common law systems, and judges ostensibly let attorneys "fight it out." In contrast with the civil law system, the common law system lets the litigants, instead of the government, carry the burden of developing facts and defending rights.

Historically, a common law attorney's training is also different. Unlike a civil law practitioner, legal education in common law countries is generalist in scope and gained through a graduate degree after earning an undergraduate degree. Consequently, adversarial systems place great value on practical experience (i.e., apprenticeship and, later, obtaining professional experience through the "practice" of law) rather than undergraduate instruction followed by an examination and admission into a career judiciary. Judges also tend to be selected for service on the basis of their professional accomplishments instead of their formal academic achievements. Thus, all the main protagonists in the common law drama—the lawyer, the judge, and even the jury—wield enormous authority to discover, apply, and "make" law through adjudication. Not only may common law attorneys manipulate precedents through their advocacy, judges may embrace or reject the advocate's arguments on the basis of the specific facts in a case, thereby reserving the power to make law through the exercise of discretion. Moreover, juries are in a unique position to apply the facts to law as they see fit. The law's evolution in a common law system is therefore fluid, despite the constraints imposed by the doctrine of *stare decisis*.

Ideological Legal Systems

Before the fall of communism in eastern and central Europe, scholars generally agreed that socialist law ought to be considered an important third legal system. Although its origin began with the 1917 Bolshevik revolution in Russia, its impact did not become widespread until the end of World War II, when the Communist Party took control in Romania, Bulgaria, Albania, Poland, Hungary, Czechoslovakia, and eastern Germany. The People's Republic of China was also receptive and it became a foundation for Mao Tse-Tung's regime. Although the collapse of the Soviet Union in 1989 has diminished its global significance, socialist law continues to influence the legal systems not only in China but also in Russia, North Korea, Vietnam, Laos, and some other countries.[22]

Socialist legal systems borrow heavily from the civil law system in the use of codes. However, the defining characteristic is political ideology and the instrumental use of law in service of the socialist state. In other words, socialist doctrine does not embrace a Western conception of law. Law in the Western sense is the foundation of liberal democratic thought: It limits the operation of government and is a safeguard for individual rights. The rule of law, in Western democracies, helps prioritize the ordering of societal relationships, prevents arbitrary rule, and safeguards personal freedom. Conversely, socialist legal ideology denies that law as understood in the West exists and, instead, contends that law is used to enslave the populace.

Socialist ideology rejects Western liberal democratic thought on the basis of Marxist political and economic principles. With the help of Frederick Engels (1820–1895), Karl Marx (1818–1883) theorized that history is a series of alternating cycles of birth and destruction, in which one economic system is created, destroyed, and replaced by another. Feudalism, for example, was replaced by capitalism as new forms of production took hold. At the heart of socialist ideology is the belief that elites in civil society capture the means of economic production from the working class, the proletariat, and thus deprives workers from enjoying the value of their labor. For socialists, Western law supporting capitalist economic arrangements only promotes individuals' alienation and takes away personal liberty.

Marxist theory, therefore, urges the elimination of the source of the class struggle, namely individual ownership of private property and the accumulation of capital. Marx hypothesized that capitalism would be replaced by revolution, in which the proletariat could overthrow the bourgeoisie and, ultimately, restore freedom through the collective ownership of the economic means of production. When this ideal state emerged, law and government would "whither away" because there would be no need for law to maintain social control.

Marxist theory has yet to become realized in socialist legal systems. Nonetheless, Marxism found expression in a principle of socialist legality. Accordingly, the concept of law is meaningful only if it furthers the objectives of the underlying political ideology. In the former Soviet Union, the law's purpose was to ensure national security and constantly educate the masses (by force, if necessary) to advance socialist economic development.[23]

Religious Legal Systems

Throughout history, religion has influenced law across the globe. Roman Catholic canon law in continental Europe continues to loom large in the civil law tradition and, likewise, Hinduism remains an important part of Indian legal culture. The *Bible* influenced the development of Anglo-Saxon law. The *Talmud*, oral interpretations of scriptures committed to writing in Jewish law, influenced Israel's "mixed" legal system of Talmudic, civil, and common law. Muslim or Islamic law as expressed in the *Qur'an* Islam's holy book, is the touchstone for "mixed" legal systems found in Pakistan, parts of Malaysia and Indonesia, northern and eastern Africa, and much of the Middle East, including Syria, Iran, and Saudi Arabia. Indeed, a large proportion of the world's population adheres to the tenets of Islamic religion. Yet, in "pure" form it has only been in place in Afghanistan (before the U.S.-coalition-led occupation after September 11, 2001), and the Maldives Islands.

Still, many of the world's major legal systems are impacted by Islamic law. A personal commitment to the Islamic faith is holistic, involving all aspects of life. "Islam," it has been said, "is a religion, a legal system, and a lifestyle all in one."[24] Islamic law is based on the word of Allah, as revealed to the Prophet Muhammad ibn Abdullah (570–632 C.E.) by the angel Gabriel. The revelations were compiled into the *Qur'an*. Although it is Islam's most important sacred text, the *Qur'an* is supplemented by the *Sunnah*, which reports the teachings of the prophet Muhammad. Together, the *Qur'an* and the *Sunnah* constitute the center of Islamic law, the *Shariah*. As divine law, the *Shariah* cannot be changed by man. It can be interpreted by scholars but, by a command from Allah, anything less than total compliance is a violation of the whole Islamic community and subject to severe sanctions not only in this world but also in the next.

The *Shariah* identifies five pillars of personal responsibility (profession of faith, daily prayer, almsgiving, fasting, and pilgrimage to Mecca) as well as guidelines for social relations involving family, criminal, contract, and international law. During the nineteenth and twentieth centuries, nations subscribing to Islamic law were greatly affected by their contact with the West, so many of them incorporated, and then codified, modified versions of Islamic law in accordance with the civil law tradition. However, the assimilation process generated controversy, and secular Western norms increasingly clashed with those of fundamentalists advocating a return to a traditional form of *Shariah*.[25]

Saudi Arabia is an example of the effect that traditional Islamic law has had on that country's "mixed" legal system. Although sovereignty resides in the king of Saudi Arabia, as a theocracy the kingdom's institutional legal structures and procedures are based on an orthodox version of Islamic law. The political system, which operates under a constitutional framework, The Basic Law of 1992, is expected to conform to Shariah. As such, there is no separation between political and religious life. The legal process aims to reveal religious truths rather than to discover empirical facts. Shariah encourages reconciliation, and with the aid of the courts, the majority of disputes are resolved in this manner. The concept of *sulh*, "compromise, settlement or agreement between the parties," is derived from the Qur'an. Indeed, one study has reported that ninety nine percent of all civil cases end in this fashion.[26] Lawyers, as indoctrinated in *Shariah* through a university degree are of marginal assistance because acting as a Western-style advocate is disallowed in the hope that the dispute will end in *sulh*. Judges are appointed and removed by the king at the recommendation of the nation's highest court (the Supreme Judicial Council), and they play an active role in the reconciliation process. Emphasizing oral testimony instead of written documents or evidence, they work to reach amicable solutions in an informal manner. In this fashion, *kadi* justice—the law as delivered by judges construing religious doctrine—is neither adversarial (common law) nor investigative (civil law). Rather, the process is one of religious obligation, aimed at achieving a just result according to the word of Allah.

Customary and "Mixed" Legal Systems

Although few countries base their legal systems on local customs, *customary law*—rules based on social customs and enforced by community sanction—influence a considerable number of mixed legal systems. Historically, the strongest influence of customary law has been found in sub-Sahara Africa (Ethiopia, Somaliland, the Sudan, and Madagascar), where customs assisted in paying respect to ancestral beliefs, defining social obligations, or assisting in dispute resolution. Typically, customs are recognized by consensus of the social group, or tribe, often through familial or kinship ties. Accordingly, it was not unusual for African customary courts to appeal to customs in reconciling the competing interests of disputants. Strict adherence to customs, however, often yielded to the development of other legal traditions brought on by European colonization of Africa and, subsequently, African independence. Since achieving its independence from British rule in 1960, for example, Nigeria's constitutional system is organized under a variety of common law, Islamic law, and customary law influences that accommodate religious and ethnic diversity. As a result, Nigeria's judicial system has distinct courts with separate jurisdictions for handling civil disputes arising in domestic relations: The Shariah Court of Appeal applies Islamic law, whereas the Customary Court of Appeal uses customary law.[27]

The legal systems in China and Israel provide further illustrations of contemporary mixed legal systems. The legal tradition in China, for example, begins with *Confucianism*, the teachings from Kung Fu-tse or Confucius (551–479 B.C.).

Confucius, a government official and teacher who helped restore order in the Chou Dynasty in the fifth century (B.C.), espoused the principle of social harmony, as expressed through the relativism of *li*—a moral code of socially accepted behavior in order to achieve a harmonious balance between nature and man. *Li* directs persons to accept fault instead of assigning blame, which reinforces social harmony. *Li* makes "law," as understood in the West, superfluous and, hence, it is disfavorable to resort to formal sanctions through law. When social harmony is disrupted, order is restored through persuasion and conciliation, instead of through the imposition of formal edicts that can be manipulated to advance the selfish aims of those who wield power.[28]

Such traditional customs inhibited the development of law and a legal profession in premodern China. The prevailing cultural attitude was reinforced through political events that shaped China's legal system in the twentieth century. Not only did the West introduce the civil law system and the codification of law, the socialist legalist principle (borrowed from the Soviet Union) after the creation of the People's Republic of China (in 1949) was infused into the country's government during the Cultural Revolution (1966–1976) under Chairman Mao Tse-Tung. Under Mao, political power was consolidated in the Chinese Communist Party, and law became an instrument for the state. Lawyers, who were seen as bourgeois guardians of property rights, were banned from practicing, and the judicial system was denigrated as well. But since 1979, the legal profession has slowly reemerged as a result of economic modernization under Deng Xiaoping, Mao's successor, and China's entry into the World Trade Organization in 2001. Still, despite modernization, China's mixed legal system is strongly affected by cultural norms that tend to reject Western conceptions of law.

As a result, China's contemporary legal system is an amalgam of civil, customary, and socialist legal traditions. The legal process is inquisitorial and judges preside over trials in accordance with code law, as established by the National People's Congress. Moreover, in a nation of over one billion there are only approximately 100,000 lawyers. Although graduate training is available, legal education is primarily based on the civil law model of university instruction, so most lawyers are trained to be specialist bureaucrats. Corruption is also a problem, as judges are disinclined to adjudicate hard cases because of political pressure. The traditions of resolving disputes through conciliation remain strong, and China's legal system remains largely nonadversarial.

Israel's mixed legal system, incorporating Talmudic, civil, and common law elements, is also derived from a unique political and religious history. Prior to Israel's independence in 1948, its territory was under Palestinian control as part of the Ottoman Empire. Because Ottoman law contained Muslim as well as European law components, until 1948 the territory had a combination of civil law, English common law, and Muslim law. Israel became a Western democracy after independence, and its constitutional system has been constructed from codifying its basic laws and the development of an Israeli common law. Moreover, the Israeli system has a separate body of religious courts that adjudicate issues of marriage and divorce. In other domestic relations cases, Talmudic law applies only if the parties consent. Accordingly, in the words of Aharon Barak, the president of the Supreme Court of Israel, Israel stands apart from most Western legal systems because it has a "duality of civil and religious law" plus an Israeli common law tradition.[29]

THE NATURE AND SOURCES OF LAW

"Laws," Roscoe Pound once observed, "are general rules recognized or enforced in the administration of justice."[30] Pound's remark reflects the idea that law is usually thought of as a rule enacted by government and enforced through the imposition of a penalty. Those subject to law's command obey it because it is just to do so, and it is perceived as a legitimate source of governmental authority. The perception of law's legitimacy is also intertwined with law's social purpose. Hence, the law's purpose is critical to appreciating how law regulates human activity, while simultaneously maintaining social order and securing justice. Although controversial, the ruling in *Lawrence v. Texas* arguably served justice by holding that homosexuals have a constitutional right not to be discriminated against and prosecuted for engaging in consensual sexual intimacy.

Accordingly, U.S. courts apply the law to ensure that justice is done in society. In conventional terms, "justice" is understood in two ways: corrective and distributive. *Corrective justice* corrects a wrong that has harmed an innocent third party. If someone has stolen a car or vandalized public property, corrective justice is delivered by punishing the offender. *Distributive justice*, on the other hand, rectifies an inequality existing between parties because it is just to do so. In *Lawrence*, the Court administered distributive justice by using principles of constitutional due process to afford homosexuals the right to be free from criminal prosecution in situations in which heterosexuals would not be similarly punished.

The ruling in *Lawrence* registers ongoing debates about the nature and sources of law. As the preceding discussion of global legal systems illustrated, "law" includes judicial rulings, written codes, political ideology, religious faith, and often a combination of each. As in the United States and elsewhere, the nature of law's meaning is thus socially constructed by the controlling values of the government and the public. This section analyzes how the various sources of law in the United States affect common understandings of law and why the exercise of judicial review by courts is politically controversial, not only in protecting gay rights but also in other public policy areas of the law.

Whereas the political system is framed under the U.S. Constitution and its first ten amendments (the Bill of Rights), state constitutions in the fifty states also play an important role in understanding American constitutionalism. Specifically, the founding documents supply the basic structure for how government is organized and how power is divided between the legislative, executive, and judicial branches. Furthermore, as with other Western democracies (including those of Canada, Australia, and Germany), the constitutional framework is based on *federalism principles*, or sharing authority between centralized and subnational, or state, governments. Thus, law in the United States originates from a variety of federal and state institutions. In addition to federal and state constitutions, law is made by legislatures, administrative agencies, and, on occasion, the president. These various sources of law are analyzed in terms of typologies of law that broadly describe the U.S. legal systems of public and private law.

Public Law

Law affecting the government encompasses *public law*—that is, the legal relationships among governments and between governments and individuals. *Statutory law*, or legislation enacted by popular assemblies, is the major source of public law. The Americans with Disabilities Act (1990),[31] a federal statute designed to protect disabled persons from employment discrimination, is an example of statutory law. Federal and state constitutions delegate authority to legislatures to enact statutes. Article I of the U.S. Constitution, for instance, vests the U.S. Congress with broad legislative powers. Yet, because statutes are drafted in general language, they often ambiguous and require administrative and judicial interpretation. The interplay between the legislative, executive, and judicial branches in ascertaining the meaning of statutes raises important questions of separation of powers and, sometimes, of constitutional law. The distinct but interrelated subcategories of public law—constitutional law, administrative law, and criminal law—are the other principal sources of American law.

CONSTITUTIONAL LAW In 1892, before his appointment to the U.S. Supreme Court, as a state supreme court judge, Oliver Wendell Holmes, Jr., rejected a policeman's claim that a New Bedford, Massachusetts mayor improperly fired him under a state law prohibiting policemen from soliciting money for "any political purpose whatever." Judge Holmes ruled that the policeman has "a constitutional right to talk politics, but he has no constitutional right to be a policeman."[32] In one respect, Judge Holmes' decision settled the dispute at hand—the aggrieved policeman lost the case as well as his job because his free speech rights under the state constitution did not trump the mayor's power to dismiss him. But, in another respect, the outcome in *McAuliffe v. Mayor and Board of Aldermen of New Bedford* (1892) reaffirmed the legislature's power to condition the employment of public servants. In other words, Judge Holmes interpreted constitutional law to accept the legislature's authority to limit individual rights, duties, and obligations.

In the United States, constitutional rights, duties, and obligations are given final effect by the Supreme Court. Each ruling from the Court is binding as the "supreme Law of the land" under Article VI of the U.S. Constitution. Notably, though Article III vests judicial power in "one Supreme Court," the Constitution is silent on whether the Court has the authority to determine the constitutionality of legislation or official executive action. The Court asserted that power in the landmark case of *Marbury v. Madison* (1803).[33] Furthermore, as *McAuliffe* illustrates, the highest state courts enjoy similar power under their respective state constitutions.

The underlying dispute in *Marbury* raised basic questions of constitutional law and partisan politics, such as whether the Federalist Party could pack the judiciary with judgeships before the Jeffersonian Republicans assumed power after the election of 1800. By virtue of the 1801 Circuit Court Act and the District of Columbia Organic Law Act, William Marbury was commissioned by the Federalist Party's lame-duck President John Adams to become a judge. But, under the direction of President Thomas Jefferson, the formal papers making the commission official were not delivered by Secretary of State James Madison. Under a congressional statute, Section 13 of the 1789 Judiciary Act, Marbury sued for his judgeship, asking the Supreme Court to grant a writ of mandamus—a court order for the performance of a legal act—awarding the judgeship. In ruling against Marbury, Chief Justice John Marshall held that Congress could not enlarge the Court's original jurisdiction to issue the writ of mandamus through Section 13 because it violated Article III of the U.S. Constitution, the express source of the Court's original jurisdiction, and Article VI, the Supremacy Clause. The Supreme Court, therefore, ruled that Section 13 was unconstitutional and, hence, Marbury was denied his appointment. In declaring that it is the Court's duty "to say what the law is" under the Constitution, Chief Justice Marshall wrote into constitutional law the enduring principle of judicial review—that is, courts have the power to nullify legislative and executive acts that are contrary to the text of the Constitution and other federal law.[34]

Notwithstanding claims to the contrary, the Court's decisions tend to be "more provisional than final" because "the president, Congress, and the states may in various ways undercut and thwart compliance with, if not ultimately overturn, the Court's rulings."[35] If three-fourths of the states ratify a constitutional amendment, under Article V Supreme Court rulings that interpret the Constitution's text can be amended; but otherwise they remain final decisions, binding the nation and states. Accordingly, the Supreme Court has "final authority" to declare the meaning of constitutional law (see Sidebar 1.2).

Sidebar 1.2

Researching the Law and Judicial Decisions

Most sources in legal research, including the judicial opinions comprising the body of American common law, are found in public libraries, law libraries and, increasingly, on the Internet. Judicial opinions are accessed in "case reporters," or bound volumes of cases that are published and distributed by the Government Printing Office or West's Publication Corporation. Case reporters are indexed and arranged chronologically, by court and by region. Electronic, or online, access to judicial opinions can be secured by home pages of courts (e.g., the Supreme Court of the United States' Web site is www.supremecourtus.gov), or through generic legal research search engines, such as Findlaw (www.findlaw.com), or fee-based online data bases, such as Westlaw (www.westlaw.com) or Lexis–Nexis (www.lexisnexis.com). Some electronic reporting systems, such as Westlaw and Lexis–Nexis, include "unpublished opinions" as well as opinions that are published or distributed in printed volumes of West's reporters (unpublished opinions are discussed further in Chapters 3 and 9).

Cases contain official and unofficial "citations" to a court opinion and include reference to the volume, page, and date of the case. *Official citations* are the formal citations of reported cases that are cited as precedents in judicial opinions or lawyer's briefs and memoranda. The official citation to a U.S. Supreme Court opinion is *Brown v. Board of Education*, 347 U.S. 483 (1954), which means it can be located in volume 347 of the United States Reports on p. 483. Yet the same case, *Brown*, can be located by accessing *unofficial citations,* or supplemental references to the same case that use different reporters. Thus, *Brown* can also be found in volume 74, on p. 686, of the Supreme Court Reporter, at 74 S. Ct. 686 (1954), or volume 98, p. 873, of the Lawyer's Edition, at 98 L. Ed. 873 (1954), all of which are located in West's Reporting system.

For federal courts: U.S. Courts of Appeals cases are reported in the West's Federal Reporter (*Buckley v. Valeo*, 519 F.2d 821 [D.C. Cir. 1975]), and U.S. District cases are found in West's Federal Supplement series (*Eaton v. Solon*, 598 F. Supp. 1505 [N.D. Ohio 1984]). State courts are reported similarly, with the official citation naming the court issuing the opinion (e.g., Ohio Supreme Court) and the unofficial citation naming the region (Pacific Reporter, Southwestern Reporter, Southern Reporter, Northeastern Reporter). For example, the Ohio Supreme Court decided *DeRolph v. State of Ohio*, 93 Ohio St. 3d 628, 758 N.E. 2d 1113 (2001).

ADMINISTRATIVE LAW   Although the U.S. Constitution omits any reference to a government bureaucracy, the realities of governing made it necessary for administrative agencies to be created. On the federal and state level, the legislature creates the law, but administering it requires the creation of agencies to implement legislative policy. Executive agencies are a formidable presence in Washington D.C., as well as in most state capitals. They are distinct because they possess delegated legislative authority and are typically staffed through a combination of merit-based civil service opportunities and executive appointments. In the federal government, there are numerous executive departments, including Commerce, Defense, Energy, Labor, Education, Justice, and Transportation. In addition, there are a number of independent agencies and government corporations (which compete with private enterprise), as well as a host of other boards, commissions, and advisory committees that perform specialized bureaucratic tasks and a range of services. The Environmental Protection Agency, the Federal Communications Commission, the Nuclear Regulatory Commission, the Securities and Exchange

Commission, and the United States Postal Service are familiar examples of independent agencies and government corporations that have been delegated the power to regulate environmental protection, public broadcasting, nuclear energy and safety, financial securities in the marketplace, and the nation's postal service.

Under the federal Administrative Procedure Act[36] and identical state laws, administrative agencies are key sources of primary law because they are empowered to promulgate administrative regulations. Federal regulations are published in *The Federal Register* and are accessible through the *Code of Federal Regulations*. Moreover, agencies have quasi-judicial characteristics because they can resolve disputes with the public or other agencies with formal and informal agency hearings.

A recurring constitutional issue affecting the source and type of law originating from administrative agencies in the modern post-New Deal era is the amount of judicial deference courts owe to agencies. The growth of the institutional presidency and the expanding role of the federal government since World War II has placed increasing pressure on courts to act as guardians of the administrative state. The battleground for testing the constitutional limits of agency power is in the realm of statutory interpretation, in which courts evaluate legislative intent and the meaning of statutes. Agencies, such as the Environmental Protection Agency, must construe and apply the meaning of legislation, such as The Clean Air Act and its amendments. As a result, when agencies promulgate rules and regulations, or render decisions through adjudication, they are making law as a delegate to the legislative branch and an agent of the executive. In *Chevron, U.S.A., Inc. v. Natural Resources Defense Council, Inc.* (1984),[37] the Supreme Court established guidelines that frame judicial review of agency statutory interpretation: If Congress's legislative intent is clear, then courts should defer to the agency's construction of the statute; but if the intent is ambiguous, then courts will only overturn an agency's action if the agency's interpretation of the statute is unreasonable. In short, courts should generally defer to agencies' interpretations of ambiguous statutes. Still, the judiciary retains significant control over agency regulation and public policy. For example, in *Food and Drug Administration v. Brown & Williamson Tobacco Corporation* (2000),[38] the Supreme Court applied *Chevron's* standards of judicial deference to rule that the Food and Drug Administration's (FDA) improperly construed the Food, Drug, and Cosmetic Act when it assumed power to regulate tobacco products. As a result, the FDA could not enact regulations governing the dissemination and accessibility of tobacco products because the FDA exceeded its authority granted by Congress.

CRIMINAL LAW   *Criminal law* deals with the use of governmental power to enforce violations of federal and state penal codes. The legal culpability for committing a crime is defined under statutory law that covers different kinds of illegal behavior, ranging from traffic offenses to capital murder. Generally, crimes are categorized in accordance with the harm they cause. Felonies, such as arson, rape, aggravated assault, and grand larceny are serious offenses, punishable by lengthy prison sentences. Misdemeanors involve less property or bodily harm and include minor offenses such as disorderly conduct, possession of marijuana (in small amounts), loitering, and public intoxication. Misdemeanors are punished less severely, usually with shorter incarceration (less than one year) or restitution.

"[If] the Government becomes a lawbreaker," Justice Louis Brandeis once said, "it breeds contempt for the law."[39] Perhaps more than any other aspect of American jurisprudence, courts must ensure that those accused of a crime are treated fairly and swiftly. As Justice Brandeis recognized, courts are obliged to strike a balance between individual freedom and public safety in criminal law. From the time of arrest until sentencing or acquittal, courts use their discretion to afford criminal defendants substantive and procedural rights under the Constitution.

In *Gideon v. Wainright* (1963),[40] for example, a landmark case guaranteeing the right to counsel for indigent defendants, the Supreme Court protected Clarence Gideon's right under the Sixth Amendment to have an attorney appointed for him at trial. The rulings in *Mapp v. Ohio* (1961),[41] which upholds the exclusionary rule excluding evidence from an unreasonable search or seizure under the Fourth Amendment, and *Miranda v. Arizona* (1966),[42] which requires the police to give defendants the "*Miranda* warnings" in order to prevent violations of the Fifth Amendment guarantee against self-incrimination, are other often cited examples of cases expanding defendants' rights. Because the accused are presumed innocent and the government has the burden of proving guilt beyond a reasonable doubt, courts pay careful attention to whether rules of legal procedure and evidence are fairly applied in accordance with constitutional requirements. Under the Sixth Amendment, defendants are entitled to "a speedy and public trial, by an impartial jury." Hence, by having the right to a "speedy" and "public" trial with an "impartial jury," courts create legal standards to guarantee that the government respects those rights. *Batson v. Kentucky* (1986),[43] for example, held that the prosecution cannot use *peremptory challenges*—procedural requests to exclude persons from jury service—to exclude Blacks from juries because racial considerations violate the defendant's right to an impartial jury. The Court's rulings pertaining to the process of arraignment, bail, and the introduction of evidence at trial are further examples of procedural law that have significant consequences for the prosecution and defense in criminal law. These subcategories of public law are supplemented by others that find expression in other areas of social policy, such as bankruptcy law and tax law.

Private Law

Private law regulates the private affairs of citizens. It is the primary mechanism by which individuals resolve their personal disputes. It defines personal obligations to other citizens, groups, or business entities. At the same time, it also gives citizens vested interests in remaining safe from physical or material harm. The law regulating corporate behavior is private law, as is the law establishing the rules governing civil marriage, divorce, and child custody. The personal assets and liabilities of a person's estate are distributed in accordance with the law of probate, another subunit of private law. These typologies and others, as listed in Table 1.2, are also considered civil law.

Civil law, as used here, has a different connotation from that of the civil law (code-based) European tradition, and it is most easily understood in contrast to criminal law. In criminal law, the government has an interest in the prosecution of offenders who commit crimes. By contrast, in civil law the government's interest usually extends to only providing citizens with the means of resolving a private dispute. In contract law, for example, a person who breaches a contract might have to pay money damages to the person who suffered a loss.

TABLE 1.2   Types of Law

Public Law	Subject Matter
Constitutional law	Interpretation of constitutional documents
Administrative law	Enforceability of agency action or regulation
Criminal law	Enforcement of public moral code through sanction
International law	Maintaining stability of various legal relationships between nation and states
Taxation law	Collection of public revenues
Bankruptcy law	Discharge or reorganization of corporate and individual debt due to financial hardship
Antitrust law	Facilitation of free market competition between business competitors
Private Law	
Contract law	Enforceability of private agreements
Tort law	Imposition of liability for unreasonable acts between private individuals that proximately cause harm
Corporation law	Maintaining stability of various legal relationships affecting private enterprise and business corporations
Probate law	Facilitation of transfer of property upon death or disability
Family law	Maintaining stability of various legal relationships affecting families, including marriage, dissolution, and child custody
Property law	Facilitation of the various legal relationships affecting the possession and transfer of real (land) or personal (tangible items) property

Source: Derived from Lawrence M. Friedman, *American Law: An Introduction.* 2d ed. (New York: W.W. Norton & Co., 1998), 163–79; Kermit L. Hall, *The Magic Mirror: Law in American History* (New York: Oxford University Press, 1989), 7–8.

CONTRACT LAW   The modern law of contracts is an integral part of the common law tradition. In the United States, as it became easier to sell goods in a regional market economy, contract law underwent a major transformation in the late eighteenth century. Under prior doctrine, contracting parties could avoid performing their agreements if it could be shown that the terms were patently unfair. The emerging doctrine, often referred to as the *will theory* of contracts, instead recognized that the law should honor agreements that are based on the intent of the parties. The inherent fairness of the exchange became less important than the fact that the contracting parties made an agreement. Accordingly, the "convergence of wills"[44] became a basis for modern contract law. Because the intent to make a binding contract determined its enforceability, agreements that were reached in principle but not yet performed—so-called *executory contracts*—became enforceable as well. In short, under will theory, contract law was revolutionized: In making contracts, parties could rely on the certainty that their agreements would be legally binding documents.

Will theory had enormous consequences. One effect was to transform the judicial function: Courts began to share the responsibility with legislatures in determining statutory law. Hence, "[a]ntebellum judges dethroned the English common law by Americanizing it,"[45] a process hastened by the judiciary's rising stature as agents of economic lawmaking in all aspects of capitalism, including contract, antitrust, labor, bankruptcy, and commercial law. By the outbreak of the Civil War, contract law had become the predominant area and source of private law. A corresponding legal change occurred in the law of torts as well, particularly in the states.

Between the midnineteenth and the early twentieth centuries, state courts were at the forefront of preserving the sanctity of private agreements. Federal courts also helped lay the basis for the expansion of capitalism and the sustained protection of private property by affirming Congress's power to enforce public contracts and, later, at the beginning of the twentieth century, by preventing states from passing laws that would deny individuals the "liberty of contract." Two decisions, *Fletcher v. Peck* (1810) and *Trustees of Dartmouth College v. Woodward* (1819),[46] interpreted Article I, Section 10 of the U.S. Constitution, which bars states from impairing the obligations of contracts, to hold that states could not deny the validity of public as well as private contracts—specifically, the land grant given to investors by the Georgia legislature in *Fletcher* and the English royal charter that devolved into an agreement with the state of New Hampshire to set up a college in *Dartmouth College*. Moreover, in *Allgeyer v. Louisiana* (1897)[47] the Fourteenth Amendment's due process clause was broadly construed to create a "liberty of contract" that protected "all contracts which may be proper, necessary, and essential" to a citizen's right to "be free in the enjoyment of all his faculties." The principle was, then, used to nullify a New York labor law regulating the number of hours bakery workers could work in *Lochner v. New York* (1905).[48] These early decisions underscored the vital role that federal and state courts played in developing the law of contracts as well as general economic liberty principles of constitutional law.

TORT LAW   The origins of *tort law*, which affords remedies for injury, can be traced back to the Civil War. The subject matter of *torts,* private civil wrongs, was not recognized as a separate source or category of law until 1850. Before then, most legal claims seeking relief for harm caused by noncriminal acts that did not arise from contract law—such as injury to a person's reputation (slander or libel), a threat to do bodily harm (assault), or a harmful touching (battery)—were typically adjudicated under the common law system of writs in specific causes of actions, such as "trespass" (direct conduct) or "trespass on the case (indirect conduct)." Advances in technology and industrialization after the Civil War exposed the difficulties of litigating newly discovered tort claims—often caused by steamboats, railroads, and industrial accidents—with the arcane rules of common law pleading (i.e., technical compliance with civil rules of procedure, as established in early English common law). Nonetheless, a law of torts emerged and eventually modern tort law expanded to include fault-based conceptions of legal liability, like *negligence*, and related issues of harm forseeability, such as *proximate cause.*[49]

Under common law pleading, tort claims did not have to prove fault or intentional conduct because the rules of strict liability applied; that is, all the injured plaintiff had to show was that the defendant committed the act in question, without regard to fault. Yet, in *Brown v. Kendall* (1850)[50] the Supreme Court of Massachusetts helped revolutionize the law of torts by holding, in the words of Chief Justice Lemuel Shaw, that

> the plaintiff must come prepared with evidence to show either that the [defendant's] intention was unlawful or that the defendant was in fault; for if the injury was unavoidable, and the conduct of the defendant was free from blame, he will not be liable.

The controlling standard of legal liability for the tort of negligence, he wrote, was that the parties exercise "ordinary care," or "that kind and degree of care, which prudent and cautious men would use, such as is required by the exigency of the case, and such as is necessary to guard against probable danger." In other words, a plaintiff could only win if there was proof that the defendant did not use ordinary care. Moreover, Chief Justice Shaw added there would be no liability if the plaintiff helped cause the accident; in other words, there was no "contributory negligence."

In most instances, the new standards for tort liability generally permitted corporate and business defendants to escape liability and, accordingly, promoted the development of capitalism in the midnineteenth and the early twentieth centuries. By fashioning rules based on fault liability and intentional conduct, courts rewrote tort law by creating precedents that transferred the cost of having accidents from employers to insurance companies and, sometimes, to injured plaintiffs. The early common law decisions laid the basis for distinguishing three general types of torts that, today, structure modern tort law: intentional torts, negligence, and liability without fault or strict liability. *Intentional torts* are those causing harm by intentional conduct. Familiar examples include assault and battery, trespass on land, and false imprisonment. *Negligent torts* involve the imposition of liability without regard to legal intent. *Strict liability torts* are similar to the common law torts of trespass in the sense that liability is imposed without regard to legal intent or fault. Simply engaging in the activity is enough, typically because it is abnormally dangerous or hazardous. The most common example, however, is product liability litigation—lawsuits that determine that manufacturers are strictly liable for injuries caused by the defective products they make, such as a defective braking system on an automobile or a faulty gas tank on a jet.

The imposition of tort liability remains a contentious public policy issue pitting the trial bar against the insurance industry and business interests. By writing the rules governing tort liability, judges and legislators alike determine the legal standards by which individuals and corporations are tested and held financially liable. Over the past generation, extensive efforts have been taken to "reform" tort law, a struggle that has yet to be resolved but that still finds expression in new laws attempting to limit plaintiff attorneys' fees. (The impact of the tort reform movement on courts is further considered in the context of the litigation process in chapter 8).

SELECTED READINGS

Cardozo, Benjamin N. *The Nature of the Judicial Process.* New Haven: Yale University Press, 1921.

David, Rene, and John E. C. Brierley. *Major Legal Systems in the World Today.* 3d ed. London: Stevens and Sons Ltd., 1985.

Eskridge, William N., Jr. *Equality Practice: Civil Unions and the Future of Gay Rights.* New York: Routledge, 2002.

Friedman, Lawrence M. *American Law in the 20th Century.* New Haven: Yale University Press, 2002.

Gillman, Howard. *The Constitution Besieged: The Rise and Demise of Lochner Era Police Powers Jurisprudence.* Durham: Duke University Press, 1993.

Glenn, Patrick H. *Legal Traditions of the World: Sustainable Diversity in Law.* New York: Oxford University Press, 2000.

Guarnieri, Carlo, and Patrizia Pederzoli. *The Power of Judges: A Comparative Study of Courts and Democracy.* Translated by C.A. Thomas. London: Oxford University Press, 2002.

Hall, Kermit L. *The Magic Mirror: Law in American History.* New York: Oxford University Press, 1989.

Horwitz, Morton J. *The Transformation of American Law (1780-1860).* Cambridge: Harvard University Press, 1976.

Howard, A.E. Dick. *The Road for Runnymede: Magna Carta and Constitutionalism in America.* Charlottesville: University Press of Virginia, 1968.

Kritzer, Herbert M., ed. *Legal Systems of the World: A Political, Social and Cultural Encyclopedia.* Volume 1. Santa Barbara: ABC-CLIO, 2002.

Merryman, John Henry. *The Civil Law Tradition: An Introduction to the Legal Systems of Western Europe and Latin America.* 2nd ed. Stanford: Stanford University Press, 1985.

Rakove, Jack. *Original Meanings: Politics and Ideas in the Making of the Constitution.* New York: Knopf, 1996.

Shapiro, Martin. *Courts: A Comparative and Political Analysis.* Chicago: University of Chicago Press, 1981.

Tate, C. Neil, ed. *Governments of the World: A Global Guide to Citizen's Rights and Responsibilities,* 4 Vols. New York: Thompson, 2006.

Vogel, Frank E. *Islamic Law and Legal System: Studies of Saudi Arabia.* London: Brill, 2000.

Konrad, Zweigert, and Hein Kotz. *An Introduction to Comparative Law.* 3rd ed. Translated by Tony Weir. New York: Oxford University Press, 1998.

NOTES

1. *Lawrence v. Texas,* 539 U.S. 558 (2003).
2. William N. Eskridge, Jr., *Gaylaw: Challenging the Apartheid of the Closet* (Cambridge: Harvard University Press, 1999): 16–56, 59, 80–82; Daniel R. Pinello, *Gay Rights and America Law* (Cambridge: Cambridge University Press, 2003), 8.
3. *Bowers v. Hardwick,* 478 U.S. 186 (1986).
4. Paul M. Smith, Mitchell Katine, and Ruth E. Harlow, "Brief of Petitioners" in *Lawrence v. Texas* (No. 02-102, January 16, 2003), 21, 22 n. 15 (listing judicial opinions and legislative repeals of same-sex restrictions), available from www.findlaw.com (retrieved May 22, 2003).
5. Lee Walzer, *Gay Rights on Trial: A Reference Handbook* (Santa Barbara: ABC-CLIO, 2002); The International Lesbian and Gay Association, "World Legal Survey (last updated September 30, 2003)," available from www.ilga.org (retrieved September 2, 2003).
6. *Dudgeon v. United Kingdom,* 45 Eur. Ct. H.R. (1981).
7. *Halpern v. Attorney General of Canada,* 60 O.R. (3d) 321 (2003).
8. *Planned Parenthood of Southeastern Pennsylvania v. Casey,* 505 U.S. 833 (1992); *Griswold v. Connecticut,* 381 U.S. 479 (1963); *Pierce v. Society of Sisters,* 268 U.S. 510 (1923).
9. *Lawrence v. Texas,* 539 U.S. 558 (2003), 536, 562, 571–72, 576.
10. *Goodridge v. Department of Public Health,* 440 Mass. 309 (2003).
11. See Lawrence M. Friedman, *The Legal System: A Social Science Perspective* (New York: Russell Sage Foundation, 1975), 11–16.
12. See, e.g., Konrad Zweigert, and Hein Kotz, *An Introduction to Comparative Law.* 3rd ed. Translated by Tony Weir (New York: Oxford University Press, 1998); Rene David and John E. C. Brierley, *Major Legal Systems in the World Today.* 3rd ed. (London: Stevens and Sons, Ltd., 1985).

13. John Henry Merryman, *The Civil Law Tradition: An Introduction to the Legal Systems of Western Europe and Latin America.* 2nd ed. (Stanford: Stanford University Press, 1985), 13; Martin Shapiro. *Courts: A Comparative and Political Analysis* (Chicago: University of Chicago Press, 1981), 128–29; James T. McHugh, *Comparative Constitutional Traditions* (New York: Peter Lang, 2002), 18–19.

14. Philippe Bruno, "The Common Law from a Civil Law Perspective," In *Introduction to Foreign Legal Systems,* edited by Richard A. Danner and Marie-Louise H. Bernal (New York: Oceana Publications, Inc., 1994), 2, 8. See also Aharon Barak, "A Judge on Judging: The Role of a Supreme Court in a Democracy" *Harvard Law Review* 116 (2002), 16, 25.

15. Merryman, *The Civil Law Tradition*, 111–13.

16. David and Brierley, *Major Legal Systems in the World Today*, 316–17.

17. Benjamin N. Cardozo, *The Nature of the Judicial Process* (New Haven: Yale University Press, 1921), 124.

18. Daniel J. Boorstin, *The Americans: The Colonial Experience* (New York: Vintage Books, 1958), 201. See also A. E. Dick Howard, *The Road for Runnymede: Magna Carta and Constitutionalism in America* (Charlottesville: University Press of Virginia, 1968), 117–25, 129–32.

19. *The Federalist Papers* (No. 78), edited by Clinton Rossiter (New York: Mentor, 1999), 433.

20. Zweigert and Kotz, *An Introduction to Comparative Law*, 242.

21. Jerome Frank, *Courts on Trial: Myth and Reality in American Justice* (Princeton: Princeton University Press, 1973), 85.

22. David and Brierley, *Major Legal Systems in the World Today*, 169–80; James Feinerman, "Introduction to Asian Legal Systems," In *Introduction to Foreign Legal Systems*, edited by Richard A. Danner and Marie-Louise H. Bernal, (New York: Oceana Publications, Inc., 1994), 98.

23. David and Brierley, *Major Legal Systems in the World Today*, 159–88, 191–224.

24. Joshua White, "Mohammed and Madison: A Comparison of the Qur'an and the U.S. Constitution," *Journal of Transnational Law and Policy* (Spring 2002), 310. See generally Kathleen M. Moore, "Islamic Law" in *Legal Systems of the World: A Political, Social and Cultural Encyclopedia, Volume 1*, edited by Herbert M. Kritzer (Santa Barbara: ABC-CLIO, 2002): 755.

25. Sam Souryal, "The Religionization of a Society: The Continuing Application of Shariah Law in Saudi Arabia," *Journal for the Scientific Study of Religion* 26 (1987), 431.

26. Frank E. Vogel, *Islamic Law and Legal System: Studies of Saudi Arabia* (London: Brill, 2000), 154. See generally Walid Iqbal, "Courts, Lawyering and ADR: Glimpses into the Islamic Tradition," *Fordham Urban Law Journal* 28 (2001), 1039–40.

27. McHugh, *Comparative Constitutional Traditions*, 144. See also David and Brierley, *Major Legal Systems in the World Today*, 548–76; A. N. Allott, "African

Law." In *An Introduction to Legal Systems,* edited by J. Duncan M. Derret (New York: Praeger Publishes, 1968), 145.

28. H. Patrick Glenn, *Legal Traditions of the World: Sustainable Diversity in Law* (New York: Oxford University Press, 2000), 279–305; James T. McHugh, *The Essential Concept of Law* (New York: Peter Lang, 2001), 24–27; David and Brierley, *Major Legal Systems in the World Today*, 518–21.

29. Aharon Barak, "Some Reflections on the Israeli Legal System and Its Judiciary," *Electronic Journal of Comparative Law* (April 2002).

30. Roscoe Pound, "The Decadence of Equity," *Columbia Law Review* 5 (1905), 28.

31. 42 U.S.C. § 12101 et seq. (1990).

32. *McAuliffe v. Mayor and Board of Aldermen of New Bedford*, 155 Mass. 216 (1892).

33. *Marbury v. Madison*, 5 U.S. 137 (1803).

34. See generally Paul W. Kahn, *The Reign of Law: Marbury v. Madison and the Construction of America* (New Haven: Yale University Press, 2003).

35. David M. O'Brien, *Constitutional Law and Politics, Volume 1: Struggles for Power and Governmental Accountability.* 6d ed. (New York: W.W. Norton & Co., 2005).

36. 5 U.S.C. Section 550, et seq. (2000).

37. *Chevron, U.S.A., Inc. v. Natural Resources Defense Council, Inc.*, 467 U.S. 837 (1984).

38. *Food and Drug Administration v. Brown & Williamson Tobacco Corporation*, 529 U.S. 120 (2000).

39. *Olmstead v. United States*, 277 U.S. 438, 485 (1928) (Brandeis, J., dissenting).

40. *Gideon v. Wainright*, 372 U.S. 335 (1963).

41. *Mapp v. Ohio*, 367 U.S. 643 (1961).

42. *Miranda v. Arizona*, 384 U.S. 436 (1966).

43. *Batson v. Kentucky*, 476 U.S. 79 (1986).

44. Howard Gillman, *The Constitution Besieged: The Rise and Demise of Lochner Era Police Powers Jurisprudence* (Durham: Duke University Press, 1993), 49; Morton J. Horwitz, *The Transformation of American Law, 1780–1860* (Cambridge: Harvard University Press, 1976), 160–61.

45. Kermit L. Hall, *The Magic Mirror: Law in American History* (New York: Oxford University Press, 1989), 109.

46. *Trustees of Dartmouth College v. Woodward*, 127 U.S. 518 (1819); *Fletcher v. Peck*, 10 U.S. 87 (1810).

47. *Allgeyer v. Louisiana*, 165 U.S. 578 (1897).

48. *Lochner v. New York*, 198 U.S. 45 (1905).

49. Kermit L. Hall, William M. Wiecek, and Paul Finkelman, *American Legal History: Cases and Materials,* 2nd ed. (New York: Oxford University Press, 1996), 179.

50. *Brown v. Kendall*, 60 Mass. 292 (1850).

CHAPTER TWO

The Politics of Law and Jurisprudence

In upholding Georgia's sodomy law, in *Bowers v. Hardwick* (1986) Justice Byron White observed that "[t]he law is constantly based on notions of morality, and if all laws representing essentially moral choices are to be invalidated under the Due Process Clause, the courts will be very busy indeed."[1] Although the Supreme Court's deference to "morals legislation" in *Bowers* was reversed in *Lawrence v. Texas* (2003),[2] the Court's initial reluctance to use its authority to strike down statutes that represent majority will illustrates an important issue of constitutional law, judicial policymaking, and, broadly speaking, jurisprudence.

Jurisprudence refers to legal theory and theoretical questions about the nature of law, legal systems, the social impact of law, and the relationship of law to justice and morality. In addition to disclosing the connections law has to morality in constitutional jurisprudence, *Lawrence* illustrates the study of jurisprudence by raising fundamental questions of classical legal theory. In an *amicus curiae* ("friend of the court") brief filed by Public Advocate of the United States and several other conservative organized interests, classical *natural law theory* was invoked in arguing that nullifying Texas's criminal statute would be contrary to "the divine source of rights upon which this nation was founded." Under this view, the "original substantive content of liberty" of the Fifth and Fourteenth Amendments were "established by the creator" and the laws of nature.[3] Although the Supreme Court did not accept the Public Advocate's argument, the Court has adopted some *natural law principles* in some of its historic rulings.

In sum, as law evolves over time, classical and contemporary theories of jurisprudence address fundamental questions about the meaning of law and how it regulates public and private relationships in legal culture. Although it is not an exhaustive list, these questions include the following: (1) What is the origin of law?, (2) what is law's substantive meaning?, (3) what is the relationship of morality to law?, (4) in what ways is law "just?", and (5) how does the law change or evolve while preserving the stability of a political or legal system? At bottom, these are questions of legal philosophy. They elucidate the ideas and reasoning behind law's purpose, application, or normative content. Jurisprudential theory also addresses the legitimate exercise of power in order to work toward the just distribution of resources in a political society. Theories of jurisprudence thus support principles of democratic accountability, legitimacy, equality, and justice. Classical schools of jurisprudence are considered next because they are the touchstone for analyzing the law's general meaning in relation to the judiciary's "proper" role.

CLASSICAL THEORIES OF JURISPRUDENCE

Natural Law

Natural law is thought of in divine terms as God's law. The earliest statement of natural law theory can be traced to Greek philosophy. A Greek orator, Demosthenes, described it as follows: "Every law is a discovery, a gift of God, a precept of wise men."[4] Both Plato (428–348 B.C.) and Aristotle (384–322 B.C.) spoke of universal truths that could be discovered, either as abstractions (Plato) or as empirical observations (Aristotle). Grotius (1583–1645 B.C.), a Roman statesman and philosopher, built on the Greek idea of rationality by describing law as "right reason in agreement with nature," a contribution that allowed Roman conceptions of law, as expressed in *jus gentium*, to become universally applied beyond the borders of Rome.

In the Middle Ages, Christian theology adopted principles of natural law as well. St. Thomas Aquinas (1224–1274 A.D.) was an important legal theorist because he made a distinction between divine law (God's universal law) and natural law (laws of nature capable of human discovery by reason). Put differently, faith in God alone was not enough to understand the nature of the world. Instead, reason could lead to the discovery of the laws of nature, and, hence, government could play a distinct role in creating law. As a result, his work legitimized the idea that it was possible for mankind to create law that reflected those revealed by God in Holy Scripture, and law could order human behavior in accordance with fixed principles consistent with God's will.[5]

By the time of the American founding, the classical view of natural law was increasingly under sharp attack from skeptics who questioned its validity. In his *Commentaries on the Laws of England*, William Blackstone (1723–1780) suggested that there was no legal authority to obey any law that was contrary to an immutable natural law. For Blackstone, the law of nature,

> being co-equal with mankind and dictated by God himself, is of course superior in obligation to any other. It is binding over all the globe, in all countries, and at all times: no human laws are of any validity, if contrary to this; and such of them as are valid derive all their force, and all their authority, mediately or immediately, from this original.[6]

Accordingly, the colonists derived from natural law theory important natural rights arguments. But, the concept of natural rights is distinct from natural law because it defines the relationship that individuals have with government instead of explaining law's origin and whether there is a duty to respect law. In this regard, the writings of Thomas Hobbes (1588–1679) and John Locke (1632–1704) had a profound effect.

In the *Leviathan* (1651), Hobbes, an English philosopher, argued that men in a prepolitical state of existence ("a state of nature") seek security and freedom by forming a social contract establishing an absolute monarch. The English philosopher John Locke made a somewhat similar argument in his *Second Treatise of Government* (1690). Locke theorized that men agree to enter into a social contract establishing government, but their consent is predicated upon the condition that the sovereign serves the public good and protects certain fundamental natural rights, such as the right to property. The social contract thus became a model for limited government under majority rule. Moreover, in Locke's theory, government plays a key role in acting as an "umpire" in resolving individual disputes arising from the distribution of property in society. By articulating a theory of limited government that is based on consent and that also respects individual natural rights, Locke greatly influenced the thinking of Thomas Jefferson (1743–1826) when he served as the principal draftsman of the Declaration of Independence in 1776.

Relying on Locke's theory, Jefferson drafted the Declaration of Independence on the basis of the principles of popular sovereignty, consent, and natural rights: Governments "derive their just powers from the consent of the governed"; "all men are created equal [and] that they are endowed by their Creator with certain unalienable Rights [such as] Life, Liberty and the pursuit of Happiness"; and "whenever any Form of Government becomes destructive of these ends, it is the Right of the People to alter or to abolish it." A decade later, the U.S. Constitution also registered these principles. Indeed, the Constitution not only represents the idea of limited government, but it embraces natural rights theory by virtue of its written Bill of Rights. For example, the First Amendment protects the freedom of religion, assembly, and free speech. The Fourth Amendment ensures that the police cannot conduct unreasonable searches and seizures of persons or property without a signed arrest or search warrant based on probable cause. The Fifth Amendment safeguards several individual rights, including the right against self-incrimination and to protect due process. The Sixth Amendment guarantees a speedy and public trial in a criminal case along with a right to counsel, and the Eighth Amendment prevents excessive bail and imposes a ban on cruel and unusual punishments. Fundamental right of the equal protection of the law, moreover, was added when the Fourteenth Amendment was ratified by Congress in 1868.

Notably, the Supreme Court also looked to natural law principles as a basis for some of its early rulings. In *Calder v. Bull* (1798),[7] the *ex post facto* clause of Article I, Section 10, which forbids the passage of a law that would penalize an act after the fact, did not nullify a state law allowing for the right to maintain a civil appeal in a will contest. There, Justices Samuel Chase and James Iredell debated the Court's power to exercise judicial review in overturning a state law. Whereas Justice Chase argued that the Court possessed such authority, Justice Iredell countered that the Court did not have the power to strike the law down even if it violated principles of natural law. In other cases, the Court appealed to natural law principles in asserting that blacks did not enjoy constitutional rights in *Dred Scott v. Sandford* (1857).[8] In *Bradwell v. Illinois* (1873),[9] the Court ruled that women could not practice law because it was "in the nature of things" for them to remain relegated to the "domestic sphere as that which properly belongs to the domain and functions of womanhood." More recently, Justice Clarence Thomas used natural law theory and the Declaration of Independence to criticize the rationale in *Brown v. Board of Education* (1954),[10] the landmark case ending racial discrimination in public schools, and to endorse a "color-blind" Constitution. Justice Thomas's use of natural law, however, is an exception to the Court's general approach to deciding cases based on positive or written law.

Legal Positivism

English legal philosophers Jeremy Bentham (1748–1832) and John Austin (1790–1859), whose respective writings comprise the core of classical legal positivism, argued that law is best conceived of in scientific and objective terms— that is, empirically discovered by reason and free from moral judgments about what the law should be. Both objected to English common law and its assumption that it was possible for judges to create rights through law-based moral interpretation. Instead, legal positivism assumes that law only creates an obligation to obey, and rights emerge only when there is a breach of a legal duty. Bentham's theory maintained that law is based on a principle of utility that takes into account law's purpose. For Bentham, law is not simply a command or an order because the law has to achieve the greatest happiness for the greatest number of people in order to benefit the community. As a result, people obey or disobey the law because they seek pleasure or fear pain. Exercising the choice to follow the law brings pleasure because the law against murder benefits the majority; whereas, the decision to flout the law, in committing the act of murder, results in severe punishment for the few who violate the criminal prohibition. A legal command preventing murder, therefore, reaps the greatest happiness for the greatest number of people who are obliged to follow the rule. By contrast, for Austin, law is simply the command or the order of a sovereign (a person or institution with supreme lawmaking power) backed by a sanction.

Unlike Austin's view, Bentham's theory suggested that multiple sovereigns (as created by constitutions, legislatures, and courts) can regulate obedience because law is an imperative—something that has to be obeyed—as well as an empirical fact that affects behavior. Because the failure to perform a legal obligation risks punishment, compliance with law on the basis of a utilitarian calculation of experiencing pleasure or pain, determines the law's validity. People adhere to law as a command, regardless of whether it comes from one source. In this regard, both Bentham and Austin envisioned a strict separation between law and morality because law, as an "is," could not be law at all if the decision to obey it rests on its moral content (i.e., to obey only it if it is a "good" law). Accordingly, Bentham was particularly critical of natural law and its corollary doctrine of natural rights, which he referred to as "nonsense upon stilts."[11] He disagreed, for example, that the Declaration of Independence afforded citizens natural rights.

Although natural law theorists struggle with the positivist criticism that morality must be separated from law, positivists grapple with the objection that people will not, and should not, obey the law if it is immoral. H. L. A. Hart, who is considered one of the most influential legal positivists in the twentieth century, addressed the problem in *The Concept of Law*.[12] Hart did not believe that the law is a series of commands, or habitual responses, to coercive orders. Instead, law is a set of rules established by social convention: the union of what Hart called primary and secondary rules. *Primary rules* create legal duties that lay down the legal guidelines for social conduct. A primary rule obliges citizens to conform to legal standards pertaining to making a valid contract or to complying with criminal law or the law of torts. *Secondary rules* are procedural rules that confer power. In particular, they control how primary rules are identified (the rule of recognition), altered (the rule of change), and ultimately enforced (the rule of adjudication). Secondary rules, such as a law that vests an official with the power to perform a civil marriage, enable the law to be understood and carried out, either by citizens or by officials. Of the secondary rules, the most critical is what Hart termed *the rule of recognition*, which validates the criteria and social practices of what people understand to be law and ensures that officials who are in charge of applying the law are doing so under a set of legal standards that are commonly shared in society. In Hart's ideal paradigm, therefore, a legal system does not exist simply because there is a pressure to conform to a set of external commands from a sovereign. Rather, the system operates under an "internal aspect" as well, which is a shared assumption that the law imposes certain duties and obligations that are accepted by society. The internal view facilitates compliance with the law because, in complex legal systems, those who apply the law and those who are subject to it share a common perspective about controlling legal standards.

Although Hart's theory may provide a better explanation for why people obey a law than Austin's or Bentham's, it did not completely overcome the natural law criticism that positive law must have moral content. On that point, Hart acknowledged that a legal system of social rules was not a "suicide club." Morality is expressed in social norms that reflect a "minimum content of natural law"— the basic ideas shared by all about the minimal legal protections for human survival, such as rules against murder and serious property crimes. In other words, there is an inherent overlap between moral and legal behavior. Whereas Hart insisted that law is not derived from morality, and although he tried to maintain a separation between the two concepts, he conceded that morality plays a role in constructing social rules.

The separation between law and morality remains a significant issue in legal theory as well as in the politics of constitutional jurisprudence. Robert Bork, a former appellate judge in the District of Columbia circuit and President Ronald Reagan's unsuccessful appointee to the U.S. Supreme Court in 1987, adopted a positivist view. He argued that judges only have the freedom to consider the law's morality from the standpoint of enacted law. For Bork, the morality of the community is expressed in the positive law (i.e., statutes, rules, and precedents). Hence, judges act illegitimately when they impose their own views of morality because "[i]n a constitutional democracy, the moral content of law must be given by the morality of the framer or the legislator, never by the morality of the judge."[13]

By contrast, Ronald Dworkin, a leading late twentieth century liberal thinker, criticized legal positivism by attacking the presumption that judges may ignore law and its moral foundations. In books such as *Taking Rights Seriously* (1977), *Law's Empire* (1986), and *Freedom's Law* (1996),[14] Dworkin advocated the use of morality through the application of legal "principles." In Dworkin's view, a legal principle "is one which officials must take into account, if it is relevant, as a consideration inclining in one direction or another" during adjudication. As such, principles are more flexible than rules and, accordingly, moral considerations are a necessary part of legal interpretation because value judgments have to be made by judges in deciding how legal principles apply in cases. Although judges look to positive law, they must also weigh whether the outcome best fits the underlying purposes of the political system and its "constitutional morality." For Dworkin, determining the proper "fit" between the positive law and the controlling legal principle also has the advantage of reducing the discretion by judges because the application of legal principles always leads to one "right" answer during the process of interpretation.[15]

In sum, whereas Judge Bork and philosopher Hart denied a connection between law and morality, Dworkin embraced it. The implications of these contrasting views are illustrated by *Lawrence v. Texas* (2003). Like Dworkin, Justice Kennedy's opinion in *Lawrence* ruled that homosexuals have a substantive right of privacy under the Fourteenth Amendment, regardless of Texas's criminalization of homosexual sodomy on moral grounds. Dissenting Justice Scalia disagreed, sharply charging that the Court's ruling "effectively decree[d] the end of all morals legislation." In Scalia's view, the Court overstepped its authority by replacing the moral judgment of the Texas legislature with its own moral conception. He explained as follows:

> One of the most revealing statements in today's opinion is the Court's grim warning that the criminalization of homosexual conduct is "an invitation to subject homosexual persons to discrimination both in the public and in the private spheres." It is clear from this that the Court has taken sides in

the culture war, departing from its role of assuring, as neutral observer, that the democratic rules of engagement are observed. Many Americans do not want persons who openly engage in homosexual conduct as partners in their business, as scoutmasters for their children, as teachers in their children's schools, or as boarders in their home. They view this as protecting themselves and their families from a lifestyle that they believe to be immoral and destructive. The Court views it as "discrimination" which it is the function of our judgments to deter. So imbued is the Court with the law profession's anti-anti-homosexual culture, that it is seemingly unaware that the attitudes of that culture are not obviously "mainstream"; that in most States what the Court calls "discrimination" against those who engage in homosexual acts is perfectly legal . . .

This passage reveals that for Justice Scalia there is a clear separation between law and morality and judges must respect that boundary by not using their authority to write their own moral viewpoints into law.

Sociological Jurisprudence and Legal Realism

Sociological jurisprudence and legal realism developed in the late nineteenth and early twentieth centuries as a progressive response to laissez-faire economic theory and legal formalism. Harvard Law School Dean Roscoe Pound (1870–1964), a leader in sociological jurisprudence, argued that social justice must be achieved through "law in action" instead of through a formalistic adherence to "law in books." Law's evolution was a reflection of social progress, and, hence, he assumed law should be dynamically applied to fit society's needs through academics and judges that are "social engineers." Deductive reasoning, or a "mechanical jurisprudence," he maintained, was deficient because it does not recognize the different legal interests of individuals who seek social justice in the legal system. The "task of the sociological jurist," he explained, was "to attain a pragmatic [and] sociological legal science."[16]

Pound's early writings captured the attention of legal realists, a group of scholars with an influential presence in leading law schools (Columbia, Yale, and Harvard) in the 1920s and 1930s. Legal realism, or the skepticism that law is logically and predictably derived from the application of formal rules, shared the sociological view that judges make law in accordance with its practical consequences. Legal realism also criticized the casebook method of legal instruction and formalistic reasoning that was the standard in law schools after 1870. Realist theory exposed the political reality of the judicial lawmaking and questioned the belief that law is a predictable creation of formal doctrinal rules deduced from logical reasoning. As a "fact" and a "rule" skeptic, legal realists questioned whether law could be "found" or "discovered" by judges by applying the law. Supreme Court Justice Oliver Wendell Holmes, Jr., and Judge Jerome Frank were among the most visible in the early legal realist movement.

Oliver Wendell Holmes, Jr. (1841–1935), a wounded Civil War soldier who served on the Massachusetts Supreme Court (for twenty years) and the U.S. Supreme Court (for thirty years), argued the law cannot be explained in terms of simple logic. "The life of the law has not been logic," he wrote in *The Common Law* (1880), "it has been experience." Holmes maintained that law is the embodiment of human history but is also the sum of social values of the prevailing, dominant majority. In his famous 1897 essay, "The Path of the Law," he used the perspective of a "bad man" to demonstrate that law is a result of a prediction of what a court will do in deciding a case. For Holmes, the bad man "cares only for the material consequences [that enable] him to predict" what the law will do to him if he is caught breaking it, with little concern for "axioms or deductions." Yet the bad man will want to know "what … [the] courts are likely to do in fact." Hence, the law is nothing more than "prophecies of what the courts will do in fact."[17] By casting aside logic, Holmes's prediction theory laid the foundation for the realist critique that the law is much more than principles deduced from case law. He also strongly implied that law can never realistically be determinate, or certain, in its application.

Some of the implications of Holmes's ideas are elaborated by Jerome N. Frank (1889–1957), an appellate judge and scholar. Frank's book, *Law and the Modern Mind* (1930), advocated *rule skepticism* the idea that formal rules cannot be discovered by the judge using deduction as the basis for legal reasoning. Frank challenged the view that judges reason syllogistically and that legal outcomes result by first finding a legal principle and then applying it to a set of facts. Instead, "[j]udicial judgments, like other judgments, doubtless, in most cases, are worked out backward from conclusions tentatively formulated." A backwards-reasoning process thus proceeds from "a judge's hunches" and the "hunch-producers" are "multitudinous and complicated" factors that invariably consist of that particular judge's perception of what the facts and law are in any given case. Basically, the law is indeterminate because judicial decision making is post-ad hoc rationalizations of what a judge initially thinks the result should be. In Frank's words, "the law may vary with the personality of the judge who happens to pass upon any given case."[18]

Judge Frank's description of judicial decision making led to other theories that jurisprudence would only become "real" if the legal community accepted psychological explanations as to why law was uncertain. Once that first step is taken, then lawyers and judges could use methods of social science to predict legal behavior. Making predictions through rigorous social inquiry, in other words, would improve the law by making it responsive to the reality of social life. Indeed, the subtext of what Frank argued in *Law and the Modern Mind* was for a brief time actually implemented (but with little lasting success) at Columbia, Yale, and Johns Hopkins in the 1920s and 1930s. Also, Frank continuously pressed for legal reform by arguing that lawyers should be trained in clinical education in order to make them more relevant to the social purpose of law and human experience. Still, the reform efforts to incorporate social science into the legal process never came to fruition. The onset of World War II and the rise of Nazi Germany, when put against Frank's suggestion that the law is nothing more than a judge's personal hunch, combined to cause the popularity of realism to wane.[19]

In sum, sociological and realist jurisprudence envisioned lawyers and judges as either innovative social engineers or pragmatic "hunch" law makers. An important legacy of these theories of jurisprudence is that they became the touchstone for developing the policy science and legal process schools of legal thought that emerged in the 1940s and 1950s. Policy science, which emphasized the integration of interdisciplinary studies (social sciences) in the development of legal policy, suggested that the political and moral values of Western liberal democracies—freedom, toleration, and equality—could be universally shared across the globe. Process jurisprudence assumed that the legal process was the elaboration of legal principles that were rationally discovered from the kind of normative and political values that are, by consensus, at the core of the democratic process. Policy science and legal process, though, were too ambitious in their attempt to conceptualize and apply law into these terms and, hence, both were ultimately unsuccessful.[20] Nonetheless, contemporary paradigms of jurisprudence developed from these foundations of classical thinking.

CONTEMPORARY THEORIES OF JURISPRUDENCE

Classical sociological, realist, policy science, and legal process theories of jurisprudence tried to develop a common framework to explain judicial behavior within the context of achieving law's social purpose. They were augmented by new divergent approaches after World War II. Law and economics, feminist legal thought, and critical legal studies collectively represent the contemporary challenge to the belief that such consensus might be found. By measuring the achievements of law through rational economic perspectives, the "Chicago school of law and economics" celebrated individual self-interest along with law's instrumental purpose in securing social ends. Feminist jurisprudence, along with critical theories of law and race, likewise question whether liberalism may reconcile competing notions of gender and race in an increasingly multicultural society. Ultimately, these theories maintain that law is manipulated for political reasons and to institutionalize the unequal distribution of social and economic resources.

Economics in Law and Pragmatism

The jurisprudence of law and economics holds that economic principles apply to legal arrangements affecting markets and noneconomic social behavior. Originating in the University of Chicago law school in the late 1930s, the theory presumes that individual freedom is best achieved in unregulated markets and that the legal process should be determined by the rational behavior of individuals seeking to maximize their material self-interests.

Richard Posner, a leader of the law and economics school and a federal appeals court judge on the Seventh Circuit, maintains that "the science of human choice" allows individuals to be "rational maximizer[s] of [the] ends in life" to obtain what is desired most through voluntary exchange. In Posner's view, resources are allocated efficiently and wealth is maximized only if free exchange is permitted. Because economic self-interest (not selfishness) is driving behavior, human satisfaction is maximized only when highly valued resources are obtained through barter. An "efficient" breach of contract occurs, for example, if one party agrees to perform the terms of a contract but fails to do so because a third party is willing to pay more for the same service that is rendered. Still, the breach is efficient if the nonperforming party is willing to compensate the victim of the breach for the damage suffered by not having the contract performed. In economic terms, none of the parties suffered because of the breach, and the happiness of the original parties to the contract is maximized by having the contract remain in force.

Hence, law is conceptualized in terms of a cost–benefit analysis and the related concepts of utility, value, and marketplace. The value of a resource is gauged by the maximum (or, conversely, the minimum) amount a consumer is willing to pay for it. In ordinary economic terms, such an arrangement is either *Pareto optimal* (when one person's economic position is not improved at the expense of another) or *Pareto superior* (when at least one person's economic position is better but only when no one else's situation is made worse). Significantly, the Pareto efficiency principles are only meaningfully applied when it is possible to measure economic behavior objectively and then to compare the effects of any changes made to the economic status quo. As such, they are difficult to translate into legal matters because a modification in the terms of the transaction invariably produces some economic or social hardship on someone (either the parties involved directly or the third parties involved indirectly). With this in mind, Posner's innovation was to adopt an economic analysis in law that overcomes this limitation through the so-called *Kaldor-Hicks criteria*, a standard that fully compensates those who lose in a situation in which another gains. By compensating the loser for any damage that is suffered at the expense of those who profit, Pareto principles remain intact because efficacy is promoted by the utility of maintaining a legal arrangement between those who stand to win or those who stand to lose when the harmony of an economic relationship is threatened.[21]

More recently, Posner has applied economic analysis to other contemporary jurisprudential thought. In *Law, Pragmatism, and Democracy* (2003), Posner argued that economic analysis is an element of "everyday pragmatism," a form of instrumental reasoning that assists judges in adjudication. Pragmatism is an "argument for judges trying to decide cases in a way that will promote efficiency." In other words, judges use the law as a tool to achieve the best outcome. In a democracy, self-interested politicians compete for votes from largely apathetic "consumers" in a power struggle between dominant interest groups that closely resembles the free marketplace. In comparing the political system to an economic market, a pragmatic judge reaches the proper result in deciding cases. Posner thus defends the decision in the disputed 2000 election in *Bush v. Gore* (2000) as pragmatic.[22] In Posner's view, the Court weighed the practical consequences of not deciding the election against judicial intervention and concluded that the Court needed to act in order to avert a constitutional crisis.[23]

Feminist Jurisprudence

Feminism jurisprudence, or the study of how law perpetuates gender inequality, emerged from the struggle to achieve equality during the 1960s civil rights movement. Feminist jurisprudence embraces several schools of thought. *Equality theory*, often linked to liberal feminism, insists that legal institutions discriminate against women on the basis of gender difference. As a result, equality theorists, such as Justice Ruth Bader Ginsburg and Wendy Williams, argue women must be treated in the same way as men because they are similarly situated.[24] *Difference theory*, identified with thinkers such as Carrie Menkel-Meadow and Robin West, holds that women have too many biological, psychological, or social differences to be satisfactorily compared with males; thus, law ought to be tailored to accommodate gender differences. *Dominance theory* asserts that equality and difference thinkers ignore the women's perspective because they are preoccupied with understanding legal arrangements from the male point of view.[25]

Some theorists, such as Catherine MacKinnon and Andrea Dworkin have argued that men subjugate women with oppressive laws and exploit women. MacKinnon, for one, argued that sexual violence against women is a recurring manifestation of male patriarchy and the basis for rape and pornography. MacKinnon helped draft state legislation to protect women from erotic exploitation and from sexual violence, but in *American Booksellers Association v. Hudnut* (1981)[26] a federal appeals court ruled that the law violated the First Amendment because it improperly regulated the content of the ideas. Because the law defined pornography as the "graphic sexually explicit subordination of women" through media (pictures or words) that "dehumanizes" them as "sexual objects," the court struck it down. *Hudnut*, however, remains controversial because it, arguably, reaffirms the radical feminist's claim that law is an extension of male domination. Yet, for others, *Hudnut* merely confirm the values underlying individual freedom.[27]

Finally, *postmodern feminism* denies women can be identified as having one voice or a single gender experience. *Postmodern feminism* is closely linked with critical race feminists, such as Angela Harris and Kimberle Crenshaw. A common assumption of critical race theory is that most of the founders of the women's movement were white, relatively affluent, heterosexual, and college educated. As a result, they were not representative of all women and could not speak authoritatively about the experiences of black, Hispanic, and Latino women.[28]

Critical Legal and Race Perspectives

Contemporary critical perspectives of law originated in the 1980s from the New Left and the critical legal studies movement. Subsequent to the first Critical Legal Studies (CLS) Conference in January 1977, the intellectual leaders of the CLS— David Trubek, Mark Tushnet, Morton Horwitz, Roberto Unger, and Duncan Kennedy—advanced a critique of law and legal reasoning: Judges use deductive reasoning and formal rules, but the results they reach are based on personal preferences. Consequently, CLS *theory* maintains that there is no separation between law and politics. CLS theorists thus agree with the legal realist claim that law is indeterminate but with one key difference: Unlike legal realism, CLS holds that the rule of law does not exist precisely because of law's uncertainty. The CLS derives its skepticism from history, sociology, and political science in maintaining that all legal institutions are political and beset by contradictions that make the law unjust. Legal regimes are value laden but operate under the pretense of an objective (value-free) jurisprudence that empowers elites at the expense of the disadvantaged and the larger community. From the CLS point of view, law is a coercive instrument of power that is used to repress individual freedom.[29]

The thrust of CLS, therefore, has socialist or neo-Marxist overtones. In *Legal Education and the Reproduction of Hierarchy* (1983), Harvard law professor Duncan Kennedy reasoned that traditional legal education should be abolished and replaced by an ultra-egalitarian system of legal instruction. In Kennedy's view, law school is a constant struggle to achieve power and status that perpetuates stratification and dominant role playing. Accordingly, he posited that all sources of inequality and hierarchy must end and be replaced by reforms, such as law school admissions by lottery, the termination of grading systems, and the equalization of all salaries in law schools.

Similarly, Mark Tushnet, a former law clerk to Justice Thurgood Marshall and Georgetown University law professor, argued that the contradictions of law prove it is wholly political and in need of reform. In *The New Constitutional Order* (2003), Tushnet provided a "descriptive sociology" of the prevailing structure of political institutions, claiming America has entered into a new constitutional order—namely, the Reagan–Bush regime, which replaced the former political system defined by the New Deal and Great Society social programs. The new conservativism is characterized by divided government, elevated polarization in Congress, and a conservative policy orientation. Its constitutional structure is basically a device for private market interests to use law to further its own objectives, and the judiciary does little to resist to the interests forged by the new regime. Tushnet concludes that "democratic experimentalism" is "the most promising candidate" for creating a new constitutional order, mainly because it is a style of governing which works from the ground-up: Nonexperts at the local level would experiment with finding practical solutions to policy problems in coordination with national officials, who merely superintend the process rather than control it.[30]

The future of CLS is uncertain because scholars describe the theory as "moribund," and its adherents as "nihilistic," locked in a "jurisprudence of despair." The limits of CLS are further exposed by the development of competing critical theories. Critical race theory (CRT), a movement that coalesced after its first conference at the University of Wisconsin Institute for Legal Studies in July, 1989, is one example. Like CLS, CRT is deeply skeptical of liberalism, but it does not share CLS's premise that law does not exist. Instead, CRT attacks liberal legalism for masking the reality of discrimination by using benign "color-blind" solutions. For CRT theorists, color-blind remedies only addresses blatant acts of racism and not the underlying and persistent forms of racism.[31]

CRT has tried to rewrite conventional accounts of civil rights history, arguing that the advancement of civil rights was in fact a failure. Former Harvard law professor Derrick Bell, for one, asserts that *Brown v. Board of Education* (1954), the landmark desegregation ruling, only advanced Southern economic interests and generally benefited an elite white culture more interested in preserving its image as a liberator of the free world and an enemy of Communism. In other words, *Brown* reflected an "interest convergence," the mutual interests of whites in racial tolerance and economic self-interest and blacks in equality.[32]

CRT theorists generally claim that racism is socially constructed to serve the interests of the majority and that it is a function of prevailing legal thought and cultural norms. CRT principles of *intersectionality*—the idea that individuals and classes all share the same attitudes and interests—and *antiessentialism*—which rejects the claim that all persons of a particular group uniformly fit into a discrete class—are used to show the limitations of battling racial bias by treating all members of a minority group in the same fashion by a process of reduction. In other words, law only counters discrimination by first acknowledging that racism oppresses in different ways, depending upon a group's race or ethnicity. And efforts to enact legal reform only succeed if there is a complete understanding of the unique history, attitudes, and perspectives of different groups suffering discrimination in a complex multicultural and racially diverse society.

Richard Delgado, a Latino University of Colorado law professor and leader in the CRT movement, uses "legal storytelling" and "counterstorytelling" to convey the discriminatory impact of racial bias. The dominant group, argues Delgado, uses its own narratives as "the prevailing mindset [to] justify the world as it is, that is, with whites on top and browns and blacks at the bottom." The oppressed minority therefore must employ its own "[s]tories, parables, chronicles, and narratives," because they are "powerful means for destroying [the dominant group's] mindset—the bundle of presuppositions, received wisdoms, and shared understandings against a background of which legal and political discourse takes place."[33] Whereas stories disrupt the status quo, counterstories also challenge conventional wisdom. Engaging in narrative is but one method to break down the dominant hierarchies of wealth and power. In *Justice at War* (2003), Delgado lets his alter ego, "Rodrigo Crenshaw," tell stories about the difficult experiences that minorities have encountered with law enforcement in the Bush Administration's war against terrorism.[34]

Whether CRT is an effective reform movement is far from certain. All of the contemporary theories of jurisprudence, however, offer a critique that underscores the politics of law. As a result, they demonstrate the close connection legal theory has to the development of public policy by litigants, lawyers, and judges.

Controversies over Courts

How Should Judges Interpret the Constitution?

There is disagreement on and off the bench over how the Constitution should be interpreted. But that should not be surprising, for the Constitution is a legal and political document that does not say how it should be interpreted. Its "majestic generalities," as Justice Benjamin Cardozo put it, like the guarantees for "free speech," "due process," and "the equal protection of the law," invite rival interpretations and competing conceptions. They also must be applied in new, unforeseen ways in light of changing social, economic, and technological changes.

In response, some scholars and judges—notably, Judge Robert H. Bork and Justices Antonin Scalia and Clarence Thomas—have championed the position that constitutional interpretation should be confined to the text and "original intent" of the framers in order to limit judicial discretion and to reconcile judicial review with democratic governance.[a] By contrast, Justices Thurgood Marshall and William J. Brennan, Jr., among others, have countered that the Constitution is a "living document" that embodies substantive values or a "constitutional morality" that guarantees protection for "human dignity" from the majoritarian forces of democracy.[b] Still others maintain that constitutional interpretation involves not only examining the text, its historical context, and substantive values, but also consideration of the pragmatic consequences of rival interpretations and applications of constitutional guarantees.[c] These competing positions are illustrated and elaborated below.

ORGINALISM: THE LESSER EVIL—JUSTICE ANTONIN SCALIA[d]

The principal theoretical defect of nonoriginalism, in my view, is its incompatibility with the very principle that legitimizes judicial review of constitutionality. Nothing in the text of the Constitution confers upon the courts the power to inquire into, rather than passively assume, the constitutionality of federal statutes. That power is, however, reasonably implicit because, as [Chief Justice John] Marshall said in *Marbury v. Madison*, (1) "[i]t is emphatically the province and duty of the judicial department to say what the law is," (2) "[i]f two laws conflict with each other, the courts must decide on the operation of each," and (3) "the constitution is to be considered, in court, as a paramount law." Central to that analysis, it seems to me, is the perception that the Constitution, though it has an effect superior to other laws, is in its nature the sort of "law" that is the business of the courts—an enactment that has a fixed meaning ascertainable through the usual devices familiar to those learned in the law. If the Constitution were not that sort of a "law," but a novel invitation to apply current societal values, what reason would there be to believe that the invitation was addressed to the courts rather than to the legislature? One simply cannot say, regarding that sort of novel enactment, that "[i]t is emphatically the province and duty of the judicial department" to determine its content. Quite to the contrary, the legislature would seem a much more appropriate expositor of social values, and its determination that a statute is compatible with the Constitution should, as in England, prevail.

If the law is to make any attempt at consistency and predictability, surely there must be general agreement not only that judges reject one exegetical approach (originalism) but that they adopt another. And it is hard to discern any emerging consensus among the nonoriginalists as to what this might be. Are the "fundamental values" that replace original meaning to be derived from the philosophy of Plato, Locke, Mills, or Rawls, or perhaps from the latest Gallup poll? . . . As the name *nonoriginalism* suggests (and I know no other, more precise term by which this school of exegesis can be described), it represents agreement on nothing except what is the wrong approach.

At an even more general theoretical level, orginalism seems to me more compatible with the nature and purpose of a Constitution in a democratic system. A democratic society does not, by and large, need constitutional guarantees to insure that its laws will reflect "current values." Elections take care of that quite well. The purpose of constitutional guarantees—and in particular those constitutional guarantees of individual rights that are at the center of this controversy—is precisely to prevent the law from reflecting certain changes in original values that the society adopting the Constitution thinks fundamentally undesirable. Or, more precisely, to require the society to devote to the subject the long and hard consideration required for a constitutional amendment before those particular values can be cast aside.

I also think that the central practical defect of nonoriginalism is fundamental and irreparable: The impossibility of achieving any consensus on what, precisely, is to replace original meaning, once that is abandoned. The practical defects of originalism, on the other hand, while genuine enough, seem to me less severe. While it may indeed be unrealistic to have substantial confidence that judges and lawyers will find the correct historical answer to such refined questions of original intent as the precise content of "the executive Power," for the vast majority of questions the answer is clear. The death penalty, for example, was not cruel and unusual punishment because it is referred to in the Constitution itself; and the right of confrontation by its plain language meant, at least, being face-to-face with the person testifying against one at trial. For the nonoriginalist, even these are open questions.

THE CONSTITUTION: A LIVING DOCUMENT—JUSTICE THURGOOD MARSHALL[e]

I do not believe that the meaning of the Constitution was forever "fixed" at the Philadelphia Convention. Nor do I find the wisdom, foresight, and sense of justice exhibited by the framers particularly profound. To the contrary, the government they devised was defective from the start, requiring several amendments, a civil war, and momentous social transformation to attain the system of constitutional government, and its respect for the individual freedoms and human rights, that we hold as fundamental today. When contemporary Americans cite "The Constitution," they invoke a concept that is vastly different from that which the framers barely began to construct two centuries ago.

For a sense of the evolving nature of the Constitution we need look no further than the first three words of the document's preamble: "We the People." When the Founding Fathers used this phrase in 1787, they did not have in mind the majority of America's citizens. "We the People" included, in the words of the framers, "the whole Number of free Persons." On a matter so basic as the right to vote, for example, Negro slaves were excluded, although they were counted for representational purposes—at three-fifths each. Women did not gain the right to vote for over [one] hundred and thirty years.

[N]early seven decades after the Constitutional Convention (in *Dred Scott v. Stanford* [1857]), the Supreme Court reaffirmed the prevailing opinion of the framers regarding the rights of Negroes in America. It took a bloody civil war before the thirteenth amendment could be adopted to abolish slavery, though [it could] not [preclude] the consequences slavery would have for future Americans.

While the Union survived the civil war, the Constitution did not. In its place arose a new, more promising basis for justice and equality, the Fourteenth Amendment, [which ensures] protection of the life, liberty, and property of all persons against deprivations without due process and guarantee[s] equal protection of the law. And yet almost another century would pass before any significant recognition ... of the rights of black Americans to share equally even in such basic opportunities as education, housing, and employment and to have their votes counted ... equally. In the meantime, blacks joined America's military to fight its wars and invested untold hours working in its factories and on its farms, contributing to the development of this country's magnificent wealth and waiting to share in its prosperity.

The men who gathered in Philadelphia in 1787 could not have envisioned these changes. They could not have imagined, nor would they have accepted, that the document they were drafting would one day be construed by a Supreme Court to which had been appointed a woman and the descendent of an African slave. "We the People" no longer enslave, but the credit does not belong to the framers. It belongs to those who refused to acquiesce [to] outdated notions of "liberty," "justice," and "equality" and [those] who strived to better [those ideas].

CONSTITUTIONAL ASPIRATIONS AND CONTEMPORARY RATIFICATION—JUSTICE WILLIAM J. BRENNAN JR.[f]

[T]he Constitution embodies the aspirations to social justice, brotherhood, and human dignity that brought this nation into being. The Declaration of Independence, the Constitution, and the Bill of Rights solemnly committed the United States to be a country [in which] the dignity and rights of all persons were equal before all authority. In all candor we must concede that part of this egalitarianism in America has been more pretension than realized fact. But we are an aspiring people with faith in progress. Our amended Constitution is the lodestar of our aspirations. Like every text worth reading, it is not crystalline. The phrasing is broad and the limitations of its provisions are not clearly marked. Its majestic generalities and ennobling pronouncements are both luminous and obscure.

There are those who find legitimacy in fidelity to what they call "the intentions of the framers." In its most doctrinaire incarnation, this view demands that justices discern exactly what the Framers thought about the question under consideration and simply follow that intention [to resolve] the cases before them. It is a view that feigns self-effacing deference to the specific judgments of those who forged our original social compact. But in truth, it is little more than arrogance cloaked as humility. It is arrogant to pretend that from our vantage we can gauge accurately the intent of the framers on [the] application of principle[s] to specific, contemporary questions. All too often, sources of potential enlightenment such as, records of the ratification debates provide sparse or ambiguous evidence of the original intention.

Typically, all that can be gleaned is that the framers themselves did not agree about the application or meaning of particular constitutional provisions and hid their differences in cloaks of generality. Indeed, it is far from clear whose intention is relevant—that of the drafters, the congressional disputants, or the ratifiers in the states—or even whether the idea of an original intention is a coherent way of thinking about a jointly drafted document drawing its authority from a general assent of the states. And apart from the problematic nature of the sources, our distance of two centuries cannot but work as a prism refracting all we perceive. One cannot help but speculate that the chorus of lamentations calling for interpretation faithful to "original intention"—and proposing nullification of interpretations that fail this quick litmus test—must inevitably come from persons who have no familiarity with the historical record.

Perhaps most importantly, proponents of this facile historicism justify it as a depoliticization of the judiciary, the political underpinnings of such a choice should not escape notice. A position that upholds Constitutional claims only if they were within the specific contemplation of the framers in effect establishes a presumption of resolving textual ambiguities against the claim of constitutional right. It is far from clear what justifies such a presumption against claims of right. Nothing intrinsic in the nature of interpretation—if there is such a thing as the "nature" of interpretation—commands such a passive approach to ambiguity. This is a choice no less political than any other; it expresses antipathy to claims of the minority to rights. Those who would restrict claims of right to the values of 1789, specifically articulated in the Constitution, turn a blind eye to social progress and eschew adaptation of overarching principles to changes of social circumstance.

The view that all matters of substantive policy should be resolved through the majoritarian process has appeal under some circumstances, but I think it ultimately will not do.... It is the very purpose of a Constitution—and particularly of the Bill of Rights—to declare certain values transcendent, beyond the reach of temporary political majorities.... Faith in democracy is one thing, blind faith is quite another. Those who drafted our Constitution understood the difference. One cannot read the text without admitting that it embodies substantive value choices; it places certain values beyond the power of any legislature.

The Constitution on its face is, in large measure, a structuring text, a blueprint for government.... As augmented by the Bill of Rights and the Civil War Amendments, this text is a sparkling vision of the supremacy of the human dignity of every individual. This vision is reflected in the very choice of democratic self-governance: The supreme value of a democracy is the presumed worth of each individual. And this vision manifests itself most dramatically in the specific prohibitions of the Bill of Rights, a term which I henceforth will apply to describe not only the original first eight amendments, but the Civil War Amendments as well. It is a vision that has guided us as a people throughout our history, although the precise rules by which we have protected fundamental human dignity have been transformed over time in response to both transformations of social condition and evolution of our concepts of human dignity.

CONSTITUTIONAL PRAGMATISM—JUSTICE STEPHEN BREYER[g]

[T]he real-world consequences of a particular interpretive decision, valued in terms of basic constitutional purposes, play an important role in constitutional decision making. To that extent, my approach differs from that of judges who would place nearly exclusive interpretive weight upon language, history, tradition, and precedent. In truth, the difference is one of degree.

Virtually all judges, when interpreting a constitution or a statute, refer at one time or another to language, to history, to tradition, to precedent, to purpose, and to consequences. Even those who take a more literal approach to constitutional interpretation sometimes find consequences and general purposes relevant. But the more "literalist" judge tends to ask those who cannot find an interpretive answer in language, history, tradition, and precedent alone to rethink the problem several times before making consequences determinative. The more literal judges may hope to find, in language, history, tradition, and precedent, objective interpretive standards;

they may seek to avoid an interpretive subjectivity that could confuse a judge's personal idea of what is good for that which the Constitution demands; and they may believe that these "original" sources more readily will yield rules that can guide other institutions, including lower courts. These objectives are desirable, but I do not think the literal approach will achieve them, and, in any event, the constitutional price is too high.

Judges can, and should, decide most cases, including constitutional cases, through the use of language, history, tradition, and precedent. Judges will often agree as to how these factors determine a provision's basic purpose and the result in a particular case. And where they differ, their differences are often differences of modest degree. Only a handful of constitutional issues—though an important handful—are as open in respect to language, history, and basic purpose. . . . Moreover, history, tradition, and precedent remain helpful, even if not determinative.

Those more literalist judges who emphasize language, history, tradition, and precedent cannot justify their practices by claiming that is what the framers' wanted, for the framers did not say specifically what factors judges should emphasize when seeking to interpret the Constitution's open language. Nor is it plausible to believe that those who argued about the Bill of Rights, and made clear that it did not contain an exclusive detailed list, had agreed about what school of interpretive thought should prove dominant in the centuries to come. Indeed, the Constitution itself says that the "enumeration" in the Constitution of some rights "shall not be construed to deny or disparage others retained by the people." Instead, justification for the literalist's practice itself tends to rest upon consequences. Literalist arguments often seek to show that such an approach will have favorable results, for example, controlling judicial subjectivity.

Judges who reject a literalist approach deny that their decisions are subjective and point to important safeguards of objectivity. A decision that emphasizes values, no less than any other, is open to criticism on the basis of (1) the decision's relation to the other legal principles (precedents, rules, standards, practices, institutional understandings) that it modifies and (2) the decision's consequences, that is, the way in which the entire bloc of decision-affected legal principles subsequently affects the world. The relevant values, by limiting interpretive possibilities and guiding interpretation, themselves constrain subjectivity; indeed, the democratic values that I have emphasized themselves suggest the importance of judicial restraint. An individual constitutional judge's need for consistency over time also constrains subjectivity.

[T]he Constitution's language is almost always nonspecific. History and tradition are open to competing claims and rival interpretations. Nor does an emphasis upon rules embodied in precedent necessarily produce clarity, particularly in borderline areas or where rules are stated abstractly. Indeed, an emphasis upon language, history, tradition, or prior rules in such cases may simply channel subjectivity into a choice about: Which history? Which tradition? Which rules?

The literalist approach will then produce a decision that is no less subjective but which is far less transparent than a decision that directly addresses consequences in constitutional terms.

Notes

[a]See Raoul Berger, *Government by the Judiciary: The Transformation of the Fourteenth Amendment* (Cambridge: Harvard University Press, 1977); Robert H. Bork, *The Tempting of America* (New York: Free Press, 1989); Harry V. Jaffa, *Original Intent and the Framers of the Constitution* (Washington, D.C.: Regnery Gateway, 1994); and Antonin Scalia, *A Matter of Interpretation: Federal Courts and the Law* (Princeton: Princeton University Press, 1997). But also see and compare Leonard Levy, *Original Intent and the Framers' Constitution* (Chicago: Ivan Dee, 2000); and Jack Rakove, *Original Meanings: Politics and Ideas in the Making of the Constitution* (New York: Knopf, 1996).

[b]See, e.g., Charles Black, Jr., *A New Birth of Freedom: Human Rights, Named and Unnamed* (New York: Grosset/Putnam, 1997); Ronald Dworkin, *Taking Rights Seriously* (Cambridge: Harvard University Press, 1977); and Ronald Dworkin, *Freedom's Law: The Moral Reading of the American Constitution* (Cambridge: Harvard University Press, 1996).

[c]See, e.g., Richard A. Posner, *The Problematics of Moral and Legal Theory* (Cambridge: Belknap Press, 1999); Richard A. Posner, *Law, Pragmatism, and Democracy* (Cambridge: Harvard University Press, 2003); and Justin Lipkin, *Constitutional Resolutions: Pragmatism and the Role of Judicial Review in American Constitutionalism* (Durham: Duke University Press, 2000).

[d]Excerpted from Justice Antonin Scalia, "Originalism: The Lesser Evil," *University of Cincinnati Law Review* 57 (1989): 894.

[e]Excerpted from Justice Thurgood Marshall, "Remarks," at the Annual Seminar of the San Francisco Patent and Trademark Law Association (Maui, Hawaii, May 16, 1987), as excerpted in David M. O'Brien, *Judges on Judging* (Washington, D.C.: C.Q. Press, 2004).

[f]Excerpted from Justice William J. Brennan, Jr., "The Constitution of the United States: Contemporary Ratification," delivered at the Text and Teaching Symposium, Georgetown University, October 12, 1985.

[g]Excerpted from Justice Stephen Breyer, "Our Democratic Constitution," *New York University Law Review* 77 (2002): 245.

THE RULE OF LAW AND THE JUDICIAL PROCESS

John Adams, who drafted the 1780 Massachusetts Constitution, argued that it is better to have a "government of laws and not of men."[35] Inspired by the writings of the English philosopher James Harrington, the "Constitution or Form of Government for the Commonwealth of Massachusetts" was an illustration of the value Adam attached to rule of law and separation of powers. For Adams, isolating legislative, executive, and judicial power structurally prevents the undue concentration of authority. Along with the concepts of representation and federalism, the separation of powers became a model for the U.S. Constitution.

Although U.S. courts are constrained by the rule of law, this chapter has shown that the judiciary has the discretion to make public policy. As reactive institutions, however, courts render judgments only at the request of the parties and may not initiate lawsuits. Courts perform several roles, the most important of which are acting like mediators of conflict, creators of legal expectations, guardians of the Constitution, and problem solvers.

Traditionally, courts have been forums for reconciling conflict. As arbiters of private and public disputes, they not only provide security by preventing vigilantism, but help to set priorities in public policy and distribute societal resources among competing interests. In the U.S., courts perform this function through an adversary process. In courts, parties reach settlements either informally (before a trial) or formally (after a trial).

Courts also play a role in creating and ordering legal expectations. Although citizens know that legislatures ostensibly make law, they are aware that courts refine the law and establish rights. Indeed, courts routinely convey their understanding of the scope of legal duties and rights by resolving disputes and creating social change. In this regard, the published opinion of a court is valuable in orienting the behavior of litigants and enables citizens to know the probable consequences of their social actions. Adherence to the rule of law enhances the capacity of the judiciary to create norms that citizens rely upon. The Supreme Court's decision in *Planned Parenthood of Southeastern Pennsylvania v. Casey* (1992)[36] is illustrative. There, in an unusual joint opinion by Justices Sandra Day O'Connor, Anthony Kennedy, and David Souter, the Court employed the doctrine of *stare decisis* to uphold *Roe v. Wade*, the 1973 ruling legalizing abortion. The decision to affirm *Roe's* "central holding" exhibits the Court's reluctance to upset legal and social expectations. In the words of the plurality opinion in *Casey*:

> [F]or two decades of economic and social developments, people have organized intimate relationships and made choices that define their views of themselves and their places in society, in reliance on the availability of abortion in the event that contraception should fail. The ability of women to participate equally in the economic and social life of the Nation has been facilitated by their ability to control their reproductive lives. . . . The Constitution serves human values, and while the effect of reliance on *Roe* cannot be exactly measured, neither can the certain cost of overruling *Roe* for people who have ordered their thinking and living around that case be dismissed.

In addition to concluding that the social cost of overruling *Roe* was too great, the Court pragmatically recognized that reversing *Roe* would significantly damage the public's confidence in the Court as a institution. In other words, the Court's institutional legitimacy depends on fulfilling the legal expectations that courts create by demonstrating a commitment to the rule of law.

Judicial review exemplifies what Alexander Hamilton thought was the judiciary's responsibility to act as "faithful guardians of the Constitution."[37] In defending the judiciary's power to evaluate the constitutionality of legislation, he observed that courts safeguard the values underlying the Constitution by exercising the authority to overrule laws originating from "occasional ill humors in the society." Because the Constitution provided for judicial independence by granting life-tenure (on the condition of "good behavior") and fixing judicial compensation, Hamilton believed that the judiciary was a bulwark against legislation threatening to compromise constitutional rights and the rule of law.

Moreover, one of the most important trends in U.S. courts is the growing acceptance of therapeutic jurisprudence, or "problem-solving" courts. Problem-solving courts are specialized courts that assist underage offenders, defendants accused of domestic violence or drug crimes, or those with mental health problems. Such courts are non-adversarial, and try to solve the underlying problems that contributed to the crime, instead of focusing on assigning guilt or innocence. Their development signals that certain aspects of the traditional adversary model of justice are in flux, at least at the trial court level. The rise of problem-solving courts underscores that increasingly trial judges are less of dispassionate observers and more of collaborators. At bottom, such courts encourage litigants to reach brokered settlements, instead of simply presiding at trials.

The idea of problem-solving courts first emerged from the operation of a drug court in Dade County, Florida in 1989. In response to the problems of recidivism and prison overcrowding brought on by the "war" on drugs, the court began to manage its docket by imposing sentences requiring long-term monitoring instead of incarceration. The court's success encouraged others to adopt similar programs. In general, problem-solving courts have at least three characteristics: (1) intensive judicial monitoring, requiring offenders to report to the court regularly on the status of their efforts in drug treatment, securing employment, completing restitution and the like; (2) aggressive professional outreach, involving judicial efforts to create a symbiotic relationship with off-site professionals, such as social workers or social scientists; and (3) community engagement, involving judicial efforts to establish a relationship with community leaders and lay persons and encouraging them to participate actively in the justice system).[38]

Advocates of problem-solving courts argue that they are more efficient and humane method of justice, and reduce the burden of managing elevated caseloads. Their promise is demonstrated by reports showing that over 1,500 problem-solving courts are in operation and that they effectively reduce recidivism. Other courts are experimenting with adopting the therapeutic justice in the areas of mental illness, domestic violence, and other so-called "quality of life" crimes like prostitution and shoplifting. Still, they remain controversial. Critics counter that the advantages of therapeutic justice are offset by judges having to assume the time-intensive role of a collaborator, and further politicize the judicial process.

In Comparative Perspective

Constitutional Courts in Europe

Historically, European states rejected the institution and power of "American-style" judicial review. European judges may still not invalidate or refuse to enforce national laws as unconstitutional. European courts remain subordinate to the legislature. The French law of August 16, 1790, which remains in force, for instance, stipulates that "Courts cannot interfere with the exercising of legislative powers or suspend the application of the laws."

In the aftermath of World War II, however, separate constitutional courts were created and set apart from national judiciaries in several countries in Western Europe. They were modeled after the constitutional court of the Austrian Second Republic (1920–1934), which was established in 1920 as a result of Hans Kelsen, drafter of the constitution and an influential legal philosopher. No other country proceeded to establish a constitutional court, though, until after World War II. Then, most western European countries gradually established constitutional courts as a result of the bitter experiences of fascism having taken hold in Germany and Italy, as an institutional precaution against that occurring again, and as a consequence of the American occupation of those countries after the war. Austria's constitution of 1945 preserved its constitutional court, and others were established in Italy (1948), the Federal Republic of Germany (1949), France (1958), Portugal (1976), Spain (1978), and Belgium (1985).

After the collapse of the former Soviet Union in 1989, constitutional courts were likewise established in the former communist countries of central and eastern Europe, including the Czech Republic, Hungary, Poland, Romania, Russia, Slovakia, the Baltics, and the countries of the former Yugoslavia.

A new European model of constitution judicial review thus emerged. In contrast to the U.S. Supreme Court and federal judiciary, which have general jurisdiction over issues of constitutional and statutory law, regular courts in Europe still have no jurisdiction over constitutional matters. Only constitutional courts may decide constitutional issues. That was an innovation, but it is not all that separates the European model of judicial review from the American one. European constitutional courts are (1) formally detached from the national judiciary, (2) have exclusive jurisdiction over constitutional disputes, and (3) are authorized to exercise review over and issue opinions on the constitutionality of legislation.

Unlike the U.S. federal judiciary's jurisdiction over only "actual cases and controversies," European constitutional courts may exercise both abstract and concrete review of legislation. Some also have jurisdiction based on individuals' constitutional complaint procedures.

Abstract constitutional review of legislation is initiated by elected officials or national and regional governmental bodies with respect to legislation that has been recently adopted but that either (a) has not yet been put into force, as in France; or (b) that has not yet been enforced, or has been suspended, pending review by the constitutional court, as in Germany, Italy, and Spain. The executive and legislative branches in Germany, France, and Spain; the federal states or regional governments in Germany, Italy, and Spain; and an ombudsman in Spain may file suits challenging the constitutionality of legislation before constitutional courts. In short, before controversial legislation goes into effect the constitutional court must pass on its constitutionality, and thereafter the legislation may be revised.

By contrast, *concrete constitutional review* arises from challenges to legislation in the courts when regular judges are uncertain about the constitutionality or the application of a statute or ordinance. In such cases, regular judges refer the constitutional question or complaint to the constitutional court for resolution. Once the constitutional court renders its ruling, the case is remanded back to the referring judge, who then must decide the case in light of the constitutional court's decision.

In addition, in Germany and Spain individuals (and in Spain the ombudsman) may file constitutional complaints after they have exhausted all other remedies. Notably, once the process of constitutional review has been initiated, constitutional courts must consider the matter and render a decision. Unlike the U.S. Supreme Court, they have no discretionary jurisdiction or power to deny cases review.

The jurisdiction and operation of the constitutional courts in France, Germany, Italy, and Spain are summarized in the following table.

	France	Germany	Italy	Spain
Court and date of creation	Constitutional Council (1958)	Federal Constitutional Court (1949)	Constitutional Court (1956)	Constitutional Court (1978)
Jurisdiction				
Abstract review	Yes	Yes	Yes	Yes
Authority to initiate review	President, Presidential Assembly, or Senate	Federal and lander (state) governments or $^1/_3$ of the Bundestag	National government (against regional laws); regional governments (against national laws)	Prime minister, president of Parliament, fifty deputes or senators; executives of autonomous regions, and ombudsmen
Laws referred	National	Federal and lander legislation	National and regional legislation	National and regional legislation
Laws must be referred	Within fifteen days of adoption	Within thirty days of adoption	Within thirty days of adoption	Within ninty days of adoption
Concrete review	No	Yes	Yes	Yes
Authority to initiate concrete review		Judiciary and individuals	Judiciary	Judiciary, ombudsmen, and individuals

Western European constitutional courts also bear only a family resemblance and differ with respect to their composition, judges' qualifications for appointment, and term limits on judicial service. In general, constitutional judges are either appointed by political bodies, as in France, or subject to some combination of nomination and election, as in Italy and Spain. Moreover, unlike appointments to the U.S. Supreme Court, western European constitutions establish precise quotas for the appointment of professional/career judges, professors, et cetra. In the Federal Republic of Germany, for example, the sixteen-member constitutional court must always contain at least six former federal judges. In Italy, five of the fifteen judges on its constitutional court must be representatives of the federal judiciary, but in Spain only two of its twelve judges must be representatives. Some of the differences in the composition and requirements for appointment to the constitutional courts in France, Germany, Italy, and Spain are highlighted in the following table.

	France	**Germany**	**Italy**	**Spain**
Number of judges	Nine	Sixteen	Fifteen	Twelve
Appointing bodies	Named by President (3), Presidential Assembly (3), Presidential Senate (3)	Elected by Bundestag (8) Bundesrat (8) (by 2/3 majority)	Named by national government (5), elected by Parliament (5) (2/3 majority)	Named by national government (2), judiciary (5), elected by Congress (4), Senate (4) (by 2/3 majority)
Length of tenure	Nine years	Twelve years	Nine years	Nine years
Age limit	None	Forty year Minimum; 68 year maximum	None	None
Requisite qualifications	None	6/16 must be federal judges; All must be qualified to be judges.	All must be judges with twenty years experience.	May be judges, professors, lawyers, or civil servants with at least fifteen years experience

Likewise, constitutional courts in central and eastern Europe differ in their recruitment of judges and term limits. Under the Hungarian constitution of 1989, the eleven judges on its constitutional court are elected by a two-thirds vote of the National Assembly; in Bulgaria four of its twelve-member constitutional court are named by, respectively, the National Assembly, the president, and the Supreme Court of Appeals; whereas as in Poland (after 1997), the fifteen judges on its constitutional court are elected by the lower House of the Parliament and serve only eight years, whereas those in Hungary and Bulgaria enjoy tenures of nine years.

Finally, unlike the U.S. Supreme Court but like the European Court of Justice, constitutional courts in some countries, such as France and Italy, must render only unanimous decisions, dissenting opinions are prohibited by law. In other countries, like Germany and Spain, dissenting opinions are permitted but remain infrequent.

SELECTED READINGS

Bork, Robert H. *The Tempting of America*. New York: Free Press, 1989.

——————. *Coercing Virtue: The Worldwide Rule of Judges*. Washington, DC: AEI, 2004.

Breyer, Stephen. *Active Liberty: Interpreting Our Democratic Constitution*. New York: Knopf, 2005.

Cotterrell, Roger. *The Politics of Jurisprudence: A Critical Introduction to Legal Philosophy*. Philadelphia: University of Pennsylvania Press, 1992.

Corwin, Edward S. *The 'Higher Law' Background of American Constitutional Law*. Ithaca: Cornell University Press, 1968.

Crenshaw, Kimberle, Neil Gotanda, Gary Peller, and Kendall Thomas, eds. *Critical Race Theory: The Key Writings that Formed the Movement*. New York: The New Press, 1995.

Duxbury, Neil. *Patterns of American Jurisprudence*. Oxford: Clarendon Press, 1995.

Dworkin, Ronald. *Law's Empire*. London: Fontana Press, 1986.

——————. *Taking Rights Seriously*. Cambridge: Harvard University Press, 1977.

——————. *Justice in Robes*. Cambridge: Belknap, 2006.

Farber, Daniel A., and Suzanna Sherry. *Desperately Seeking Certainty: The Misguided Quest for Constitutional Foundations*. Chicago: University of Chicago Press, 2002.

Frank, Jerome. *Law and the Modern Mind*. New York: Brentano's Publishers, 1930.

Freeman, M. D. A. *Lloyd's Introduction to Jurisprudence*. 7th ed. London: Sweet & Maxwell, Ltd., 2001.

George, Robert P., ed. *Natural Law, Liberalism, and Morality*. Oxford: Oxford University Press, 2000.

Hart, H. L. A. *The Concept of Law*. New York: Oxford University Press, 1961.

Kenney, Sally, William M. Reisinger, and John C. Reitz, eds. *Constitutional Dialogues in Comparative Perspective*. London: Macmillan, 1999.

Lipkin, Justin. *Constitutional Resolutions: Pragmatism and the Role of Judicial Review in American Constitutionalism*. Durham: Duke University Press, 2000.

MacKinnon, Catherine A. *Feminism Unmodified: Discourses on Life and Law*. Cambridge: Harvard University Press, 1987.

Posner, Richard A. *Law, Pragmatism, and Democracy.* Cambridge: Harvard University Press, 2003.

Rumble, Wilfrid E., Jr. *American Legal Realism.* Ithaca: Cornell University Press, 1968.

Scalia, Antonin. *A Matter of Interpretation: Federal Courts and the Law.* Princeton: Princeton University Press, 1997.

Sunstein, Cass. *Radicals in Robes: Why Extreme Right-Wing Courts Are Wrong for America.* New York: Basic Books, 2005.

Tushnet, Mark. *The New Constitutional Order.* Princeton: Princeton University Press, 2003.

Twining, William. *Globalisation and Legal Theory.* Evanston: Northwestern University Press, 2001.

Vermeule, Adrian. *Judging Under Uncertainty.* Cambridge: Harvard University Press, 2006.

Vogel, Frank E. *Islamic Law and Legal System: Studies of Saudi Arabia.* London: Brill, 2000.

NOTES

1. *Bowers v. Hardwick*, 478 U.S. 186 (1986), 196.

2. *Lawrence v. Texas*, 539 U.S. 558 (2003).

3. "Brief, *Amicus Curiae* of Public Advocate of the United States, Conservative Legal Defense and Education Fund, Lincoln Institute for Research and Education, Help and Caring Ministries, Inc., and Citizens United Foundation in Support of Respondent" 2003 *U.S. Briefs* 102 (February 18, 2002), available from www.lexis.com (retrieved June 16, 2004).

4. As quoted in Edward S. Corwin, *The 'Higher Law' Background of American Constitutional Law* (Ithaca: Cornell University Press, 1988), 5.

5. Edgar Bodenheimer, *Jurisprudence: The Philosophy and Method of the Law* rev. ed. (Cambridge: Harvard University Press, 1974), 3–30; David Van Drunen, *Law and Custom: The Thought of Thomas Aquinas and the Future of the Common Law* (New York: Peter Lang, 2003), 30–37.

6. *Blackstone's Commentaries on the Laws of England in Four Volumes,* edited by Wayne Morrison (London: Cavendish, 2001), 41.

7. *Calder v. Bull*, 3 U.S. 386 (1798).

8. *Dred Scott v. Sandford*, 60 U.S. 393 (1857).

9. *Bradwell v. Illinois*, 83 U.S. 130 (1873).

10. *Brown v. Board of Education*, 347 U.S. 483 (1954).

11. George P. Fletcher, *Basic Concepts of Legal Thought* (New York: Oxford University Press, 1996), 146. See generally M. D. A. Freeman, *Lloyd's Introduction to Jurisprudence*, 7th ed. (London: Sweet & Maxwell, Ltd. 2001), 199–221; H. L. A. Hart, *Essays on Bentham: Studies in Jurisprudence and Political Theory* (Oxford: Clarendon Press, 1982).

12. H. L. A. Hart, *The Concept of Law* (Oxford: Oxford University Press, 1961).

13. Robert H. Bork, "Tradition and Morality in Constitutional Law." In *Judges on Judging: Views from the Bench,* edited David M. O'Brien (Washington, DC: CQ Press, 2004), 164.

14. Ronald Dworkin, *Taking Rights Seriously* (Cambridge: Harvard University Press, 1977); Ronald Dworkin, *Freedom's Law: The Moral Reading of the American Constitution* (Cambridge: Harvard University Press, 1996); Ronald Dworkin, *Law's Empire* (London: Fontana Press, 1986).

15. Dworkin, *Taking Rights Seriously*, 22, 26; Dworkin, *Freedom's Law,* 1-38; Dworkin, *Law's Empire*, 176-224.

16. Roscoe Pound, "The Need of a Sociological Jurisprudence," *Green Bag* 19 (1908), 611-12.

17. Oliver Wendell Holmes, Jr., "The Path of the Law," *Harvard Law Review* 10 (1896), 42-43.

18. Jerome Frank, *Law and the Modern Mind* (New York: Brentano's Publishers, 1930), 101-11.

19. Neil Duxbury, *Patterns of American Jurisprudence* (New York: Oxford University Press, 1995), 135-62.

20. Duxbury, *Patterns of American Jurisprudence*, 161-299. See, e.g., Harold D. Laswell and Myres S. McDougal, "Legal Education and Public Policy: Professional Training in the Public Interest," *Yale Law Journal* 52 (1943), 203-95.

21. Richard A. Posner, *The Economics of Justice* (Cambridge: Harvard University Press, 1981), 65-66, 75, 88-99.

22. *Bush v. Gore*, 531 U.S. 98 (2000).

23. Richard A. *Posner Law, Pragmatism, and Democracy* (Cambridge: Harvard University Press, 2003), 78-80, 188-203, 296-99, 322-56. See generally *Bush v. Gore: The Question of Legitimacy,* edited by Bruce Ackerman (New Haven: Yale University Press, 2002).

24. William J. Turnier, Pamela Johnston Conover, and David Lowery, "Redistributive Justice and Cultural Feminism," *American University Law Review* 45 (1997), 1295.

25. Turnier, Conover, and Lowery, "Redistributive Justice and Cultural Feminism," 1285.

26. *American Booksellers Association v. Hudnut*, 771 F.2d 323 (7th Cir. 1981).

27. Katharine T. Bartlett, "Feminist Legal Methods," *Harvard Law Review* 103 (1990), 829; Denise Schaeffer, "Feminism and Liberalism Reconsidered: The Case of Catharine MacKinnon," *American Political Science Review* 95 (2001), 699-708; Cass R. Sunstein, "Pornography and the First Amendment," *Duke Law Journal* 1986 (1986), 589. See generally Catherine A. MacKinnon, *Feminism Unmodified: Discourses on Life and Law* (Cambridge: Harvard University Press, 1987).

28. Kathryn Abrams, "The Constitution of Women," *Alabama Law Review* 48 (1997), 867-74; Turnier, Conover, and Lowery, "Redistributive Justice and

Cultural Feminism," 1298–99; Patricia A. Cain, "Feminism and the Limits of Equality," *Georgia Law Review* 24 (1990), 804–5, 829–40.

29. See, e.g., Duncan Kennedy. "Form and Substance in Private Law Adjudication," *Harvard Law Review* 89 (1976), 1689–1778; Roberto Mangabeira Unger, "The Critical Legal Studies Movement," *Harvard Law Review* 96 (1983), 560–675; Mark V. Tushnet, "Following the Rules Laid Down: A Critique of Interpetivism and Neutral Principles" *Harvard Law Review* 96 (1983), 781–827.

30. Mark Tushnet, *The New Constitutional Order* (Princeton: Princeton University Press, 2003), ix–x, 1–7, 111–12, 167–72. See also Duncan Kennedy, *Legal Education and the Reproduction of Hierarchy: A Polemic Against the System* (Cambridge, England: Afar, 1983).

31. Richard Delgado and Jean Stefancic, *Critical Race Theory: An Introduction* (New York: New York University Press, 2001), 1–9, 15–35. Criticisms of CLS are found in Duxbury, *Patterns of American Jurisprudence*, 421–509; Tushnet, *The New Constitutional Order*, ix; Freeman, *Lloyd's Introduction to Jurisprudence*, 1335–39.

32. Derrick A. Bell, Jr., "Brown v. Board of Education and the Interest-Convergence Dilemma," *Harvard Law Review* 93 (1980), 518. See generally Kimberle Crenshaw, Neil Gotanda, Gary Peller, and Kendall Thomas, eds. *Critical Race Theory: The Key Writings that Formed the Movement* (New York: The New Press, 1995).

33. Richard Delgado, "Storytelling for Oppositionists and Others: A Plea for Narrative," *Michigan Law Review* 87 (1989), 2411.

34. Richard Delgado, *Justice At War: Civil Liberties and Civil Rights During Time of War* (New York: New York University Press, 2003).

35. See David McCullough, *John Adams* (New York: Simon and Schuster, 2001), 100–03, 220–25.

36. *Planned Parenthood of Southeastern Pennsylvania v. Casey*, 505 U.S. 833 (1992), 856.

37. *The Federalist Papers* (No. 78). Clinton Rossiter, ed. (New York: Mentor, 1963), 438.

38. See generally "Justice in Jeopardy" *Report of the American Bar Association on the 21st Century Judiciary* (July 2003), 47–50, available from www.abanet.org/ home.html (retrieved December 10, 2003); David Rottman and Pamela Casey, "Therapeutic Justice and the Emergence of Problem-Solving Courts," *National Institute of Justice Journal* (July 1999), available from www.ncsconline.org/ (retrieved December 10, 2003); Bruce J. Winick, "Therapeutic Justice and Problem-Solving Courts," *Fordham Urban Law Journal* 30 (2003), 1055–90.

CHAPTER THREE

Judicial Organization, Structure, and Administration

The federal courts, charged U.S. House Representative Tom Feeney (R-Fla), "are a child of Congress, whether they like it or not. If we wanted to," he explained, "we could give judges no discretion whatsoever in sentencing." As sponsor of the Feeney Amendment to Congress's PROTECT Act,[1] the law establishing a nationwide Amber Alert system for victims of child abductions, the freshman legislator countered a criticism that his amendment was retaliatory and aimed at intimidating judges. For many federal judges, Feeney's bill smacked of political retribution because, as the former Florida House Speaker, he sharply criticized the Florida Supreme Court's decision requiring vote recounts in the 2000 presidential election that was reversed in *Bush v. Gore* (2000).[2] In turn, California District Judge Dickran M. Tevrizian, Jr. claimed that Feeney's amendment was a "power grab by one branch of government over another branch."[3]

The Feeney amendment was politically controversial because it enhanced prosecutorial discretion at the expense of judicial power. Specifically, it greatly restricted judges from using their power to show leniency from federal sentencing guidelines. The amendment changed prior law by requiring judges to explain their departures in writing. Not surprisingly, federal judges considered the Feeney amendment a political attack on judicial independence.

The Supreme Court's rulings in *Blakely v. Washington* (2004)[4] and *United States v. Booker* (2005),[5] however, undercut legislative authority over crime control policy. The rulings invalidated Washington's sentencing guidelines (*Blakely*) and rendered the federal sentencing guidelines merely advisory (*Booker*) on the grounds that fixed sentences violated the defendants' sixth amendment right to a fair trial. In short, the Court repelled a political attack on federal judges' discretion in sentencing.

The political struggle to define the limits of judicial authority in administering criminal sentencing policy illustrates interbranch conflict over judicial architecture. *Judicial architecture* refers to the organization and administration of court operations, including judicial structure, administration, budgeting, rule

57

making, staffing, education, and discipline.[6] The interplay between these elements is necessarily political because the judiciary's relationship to the external political environment (other political branches, organized interest groups, and the public at large) often registers ideological struggles over the direction of public policy. Partisan debates over these issues also influence a judiciary's institutional identity and internal operations, such as whether there is sufficient funding and resources to manage caseloads efficiently.

This chapter focuses on the basic issues of the politics of judicial architecture: the structure, organization, and administration of courts. First, a brief history of the origins of U.S. courts provides a basis for examining the modern structure and organization of state judiciaries and that of the federal judicial system, as well as the problems of caseload management. Finally, this chapter discusses judicial reforms and concludes that courts are aggressively adopting new strategies for reform in order to become more accessible to the public and to administer justice more efficiently.

THE ORIGINS OF U.S. COURTS

The history of U.S. courts begins with the struggle for independence. Before the constitutional convention in Philadelphia in 1787, the states were in the forefront of experiments to limit governmental power by separating institutions and imposing checks and balances. As a result, there emerged a diverse network of independent judiciaries across the now fifty states that resemble, but are distinct from, the federal judiciary. The federal judiciary was created only after the ratification of the Constitution. Yet, the structure and organization of state and federal judiciaries remains largely the same as that which took shape during the founding period.

Before the American Revolution, town, county, and representative assemblies were sources of colonial law. Colonial governments typically consisted of a governor (appointed by the Crown), an appointed council, and an elected assembly. Of the three institutions, the assembly had most of the people's allegiance because the governor and courts were viewed as symbols of the Crown. The divisions of authority, however, were blurred because the governor shared legislative powers and the councils often served as high courts. Accordingly, colonial legal institutions consisted of a confusing and sometimes overlapping layer of courts that included superior courts and county or local courts, each with varying jurisdiction over specific criminal and civil matters.[7]

Colonists grew increasingly hostile over England's attempt to assert more formal control through magisterial rule. The lack of separated institutions was perceived as a source of political corruption and destructive of personal freedoms. In 1775, the colonies responded by calling special conventions for the purpose of drafting constitutions, based on the principle of consent and separate legislative and judicial branches. Several 1776 constitutions added bills of rights, established rotating terms of office, and required annual elections. Others also made explicit reference to the principle separation of powers, and most removed the power to appoint judges from governors and placed it instead in the legislature. Following the lead of Virginia, six states identified the judiciary as a distinct branch of government. Most states as well granted judges tenure on the basis of "good behavior." Although the extent of the judiciaries' power remained largely untested in practice, the highest courts in some states (Virginia, Pennsylvania, and Massachusetts) asserted the power of judicial review—the power to declare legislation and other official acts unconstitutional.[8]

The Articles of Confederation, drafted in 1777 and approved by the Continental Congress in 1781, however, did not establish a separate national judiciary. Congress was the "last resort of appeal," but, with few exceptions, congressional power was only effective if nine of the thirteen states approved of legislative action.[9] The Articles failed as a constitutional document. The lack of a federal coercive sanction against state laws was a structural defect that James Madison thought was "mortal to the ancient Confederacies, and [a] disease of the modern."[10] Madison's experience in the Continental Congress and the Virginia Assembly in the 1780s convinced him of the need for centralization and a national veto over state laws because dominant majorities often put their interests ahead of the nation. Although Madison's proposal for a "council of revision," with the power to strike down state laws, was ultimately rejected at the Constitutional Convention, he realized the political system required a strong central government in order to curb factionalism, conduct foreign relations, regulate commerce, and protect natural rights. State legislatures also acted unpredictably, passing laws favoring debtor relief at the expense of the creditors in an uncertain economy struggling with the problem of paying Revolutionary war debts. State courts, on the other hand, tended to protect creditors and the mercantile class, forcing many farmers and debt-ridden citizens to face foreclosures.

The nation under the Articles was thus fatally beset by problems. Those favoring an invigorated centralized government, including Madison, Alexander Hamilton, and John Dickinson, met in Annapolis, Maryland at a convention in September 1786. Although only five states and twelve delegates attended, the occasion was used to call for a second convention to convene in Philadelphia in May, 1787 for the purpose of considering remedies to meet the "exigencies of the Union."[11] By early 1787, it was clear that a new model of governance was required.

Most of the fifty-five delegates to the Constitutional Convention were lawyers, revolutionary war heroes, and political statesmen. James Madison, a nationalist from Virginia, advanced the "Virginia Plan" to set the Convention's agenda and to replace the Articles. In addition to establishing a legislature and giving it the power to veto state laws, the Virginia Plan proposed creating an executive, a national judiciary, and a council of revision that could veto laws from Congress. But, in maintaining the Articles should be revised and not replaced, William Patterson's "New Jersey Plan" countered that all states must be represented equally.

By June, the differences over the key issue of representation caused the Convention to deadlock. The stalemate was broken by John Dickinson. The compromise divided Congress into a bicameral institution elected by the states and the people. The states were represented in the Senate by allowing the legislatures of each state to select its senators. In contrast, the House of Representatives' membership was determined through popular elections held in the states. The judiciary, on the other hand, consisted of a Supreme Court staffed by justices serving life terms after presidential appointment and Senate confirmation. Although there was some disagreement over whether the justices should be selected through legislative election or executive appointment, after the compromise the latter method was chosen with the Senate's "advice and consent."[12]

Besides judicial appointments, the nature and scope of the Court's jurisdiction and power was also debated. On July 17, the Convention rejected Madison's proposal for a congressional veto over state laws. The ensuing deliberation produced Article VI, the Supremacy Clause, and its mandate that federal and state courts are bound under the law established by the Constitution. Accordingly, the framers understood that federal courts could exercise judicial review over acts of the federal and state governments, although it was less clear whether state courts could use the same power to nullify national law.[13]

The 1789 Judiciary Act

Following the Constitution's ratification, the First Congress swiftly enacted the Judiciary Act of 1789, which laid the foundation for the federal judiciary. The act established the federal courts' organizational structure and jurisdiction. State judiciaries were left untouched and retained their jurisdiction over cases not otherwise raising issues under federal law. Just as significantly, with the exception of diversity cases (in which citizens of one state sue another for monetary damages exceeding a certain amount), the act ensured that virtually all federal questions—questions involving the interpretation of the Constitution and federal law—fall primarily to state courts, not to the federal judiciary. That decision reflected a political compromise because Anti-Federalists feared the creation of a federal judiciary and favored state courts. Thus, the act generally limited federal courts' jurisdiction to admiralty, forfeitures, and penalties, federal criminal law, and cases in which the national government is a plaintiff. The restrictions on federal judicial power meant that the state courts, which were more numerous, would play a central role as the principal trial courts.

Although significant jurisdictional limitations were initially placed on federal courts by the Judiciary Act of 1789, Congress's decision to create lower federal courts in the first place was a key political victory for the Federalists, who feared that otherwise all trials would occur in state courts. Congress created thirteen district (trial) courts, one in each state, and three appellate or circuit courts in three geographical regions (eastern, southern, and middle). District courts heard mostly admiralty cases and were presided over by a single judge in quarterly sessions during each year. Circuit courts were specially convened to hear cases twice a year in each circuit's district. Their main function was to adjudicate diversity and criminal cases, but they also could hear appeals in certain cases from district courts. However, Congress did not authorize any judgeships in circuit courts. Instead, they were staffed by two Supreme Court justices who traveled to the location where the circuit court was held with a district judge, becoming a three-judge court. The practice became known as "riding circuit." Although it was physically demanding and unpleasant for most justices, the measure was practical because justices had very few cases in the first decades of the new republic. It also contributed to the process of nation building at a time when many citizens were unfamiliar with, or even deeply distrustful of, the national government. Still, the justices resented the practice because they thought of themselves as "traveling postboys," who were placed in the uncomfortable position of having to hear the appeals of cases they originally heard while serving on circuit courts.[14]

The Judiciary Act of 1789 established the Supreme Court's membership at six (one chief justice and five associate justices). In addition to authorizing federal courts to make procedural rules and appoint clerks, the act established the Court's appellate jurisdiction. Section 13 specified that the Court enjoyed original jurisdiction—a court's power to act like a trial court and hear cases in the first instance—in accordance with the U.S. Constitution's Article III. But, more controversially, it purported to extend the Court's original jurisdiction beyond "all Cases affecting Ambassadors, other public Ministers and Consuls, and those in which a State shall be Party" by giving it the power to issue writs of prohibition and mandamus in certain cases. This latter provision was contentious and Chief Justice John Marshall in *Marbury v. Madison* (1803),[15] the landmark ruling establishing the Court's power of judicial review, later nullified Section 13 to the extent that it vested the Court with original jurisdiction to grant writs of mandamus. Moreover, Section 25 of the Judiciary Act empowered the Court to hear appeals from the highest state court rulings that either invalidated federal law or upheld state law in opposition to federal law. By bringing state court judgments under federal appellate review, Section 25 was essentially an important restatement of the principle found in the Supremacy Clause of Article VI of the U.S. Constitution.[16]

The Growth of the Federal Judiciary

Before the Civil War the country rapidly expanded westward, and a number of new states and territories became part of the union. The growth increased the federal courts' responsibilities and caseloads. Congress accordingly enacted legislation that added more circuits and judges in response to rising litigation, but not without political controversy. Thomas Jefferson's election in 1800 caused the lame-duck Federalist Party to attempt to retain control over the federal courts by passing the Judiciary Act of 1801, known as the "Midnight Judges Act." The

1801 act ended circuit riding by constructing six circuits and sixteen new circuit court judgeships. The judgeships were filled with "midnight judges" or appointments made shortly before the transfer of power by the outgoing Federalist President, John Adams.

The incoming Jeffersonian Republican Party, though, promptly repealed the law and replaced it with the Judiciary Act of 1802. The 1802 act reduced the scope of federal jurisdiction and kept the number of circuits but abolished the circuit court judgeships. The 1802 act, furthermore, reinstituted the practice of circuit riding but reduced some of its burdens by assigning one justice to each circuit and permitting circuit courts to convene with the presence of only one district judge.

Besides the 1802 act, the Republicans targeted two Federalist judges—District Court Judge John Pickering and Supreme Court Justice Samuel Chase—for impeachment. Although Pickering was convicted, Chase was acquitted, a result that signaled that the federal courts had achieved some independence from the political branches despite the overtly partisan attack. The political conflict underscored the judiciary's importance as a key agent of legal policy change. The skirmish between the Republicans and the Federalists presaged future battles over the ideological control of the federal judiciary, and rising caseloads presented persistent problems. The difficulties were compounded by the acquisition of the Louisiana Purchase and the emergence of the modern business corporation, which both produced more commercial and maritime activity that expanded the role of federal courts. Congress responded to the caseload pressures with piecemeal measures increasing the number of circuits and judgeships. By 1863, the size of the federal judiciary had grown to ten circuits, and the total number of justices on the Supreme Court rose to ten, its highest level.

By 1861 President Abraham Lincoln warned in his first inaugural address that "the country has outgrown our present judicial system." Of particular concern were the limitations of circuit courts and a backlog of Supreme Court cases. At least eight newly admitted states could not convene circuit courts with Supreme Court justices in attendance. Between 1860 and 1880, the Court's docket rose from 310 to 1,212 cases, and the Court was obliged to decide all of them. Moreover, lower federal courts faced similar pressure. From 1873 to 1890, the caseloads of district and circuit courts increased from 29,013 to 54,194 cases. As Justice Felix Frankfurter observed, the prevalence of federal litigation indicated that the "fear of rivalry with state courts and respect for state sentiment were swept aside by the great impulse of national feeling born of the Civil War." In other words, the prior conviction that federal courts were largely "subsidiary courts" gradually was replaced by an acceptance of judicial "national administration."[17]

The federal courts' growing prominence underscored the need for an intermediate tier of courts to relieve the Supreme Court's workload. Relief finally came with the Circuit Court of Appeals Act of 1891, or the Evarts Act, named after Senator William M. Evarts (R-N.Y.). Besides eliminating the justices' circuit riding, the Evarts Act restructured the federal courts' organization. It retained the circuit courts but abolished their appellate jurisdiction and created a new set of inter-mediate courts, the circuit courts of appeals. Organized in nine geographical cir-cuits, each new circuit court of appeals was originally staffed with a circuit court judge, a district court judge, or a Supreme Court justice assigned to the circuit. It convened, though, with a quorum of two judges. In practice, the Evarts Act allowed the circuit courts of appeals to absorb the Court's caseload. Moreover, in certain cases the circuit courts of appeal could certify appeals to the Court for review or, conversely, the Court had the option to grant review by writ of *certiorari*—the order transferring the appellate record from the lower court. With subsequent legislation, the Judicial Code of 1911, Congress abolished the old circuit courts and exclusively assigned circuit court judges to the new circuit courts of appeals.

Although the reconfiguration of circuit courts helped ease the Supreme Court's caseload, its litigation volume continued to rise in the early twentieth century. The increase encouraged President William H. Taft to assert, in his second annual address in 1910, that "[n]o man ought to have, as a matter of right, a review of his case by the Supreme Court." Rather, "[h]e ought to be satisfied by one hear-ing before a court of first instance and one review by a court of appeals."[18] Roughly a decade later, Taft had the rare opportunity to translate this principle of judicial reform into action after his confirmation as chief justice. As president and later chief justice, Taft maintained that the state courts of last resort and the federal circuit courts both played a vital role in deflecting the bulk of federal appellate litigation away from the nation's highest court. In his view, the Supreme Court was overburdened by frivolous appeals and argued that it ought to be a final arbiter for only those cases having great social and legal significance. Accord-ingly, Chief Justice Taft actively lobbied Congress to restrict the Court's manda-tory jurisdiction that led to the Judiciary Act of 1925, the next major legislation affecting the federal judiciary's operation.

The 1925 legislation, also known as the "Judge's Bill," was drafted by a com-mittee of justices before it was sent to Capitol Hill. A milestone in judicial admin-istration, it extended the Court's power to manage its docket and to set most of its agenda through discretionary review and the *certiorari* process. By letting the Court "decide what to decide," Congress shifted a substantial portion of the Court's docket to the circuit court of appeals by giving the Court discretionary jurisdiction and the power to deny review. The Judge's Bill did not completely eradicate direct Court review in certain instances, however. But Congress incre-mentally expanded the Court's discretionary jurisdiction. In 1988, The Judicial Improvements and Access to Justice Act finally virtually removed all remaining nondiscretionary appeals from the Court docket (see Table 3.1).

Subsequently, Congress also added more judges, courts, and administrative apparatuses in response to expanding caseloads. Federal caseloads in the district and circuit courts of appeals particularly experienced sharp increases after 1960.[19] As a result, Congress established federal magistrates at the district court level in order to reduce caseloads and created two new appellate courts (the Eleventh Circuit and the U.S. Court of Appeals for the Federal Circuit, in 1980

Year	Key Event or Legislation	Impact
1967	Act of 1967	Established Federal Judicial Center
1968	The Federal Magistrates Act	Creates federal magistrate judgeships
1978	Bankruptcy Act of 1978	Creates bankruptcy courts, later made into subunits of U.S. District Courts by 1984 Amendment and judicial decision
1980	Act of 1980	Splits Fifth Circuit and creates Eleventh Circuit from part of former Fifth Circuit
1982	Federal Courts Improvement Act of 1982	Creates U.S. Court of Appeals for Federal Circuit
1988	Act to Improve the Administration of Justice of 1988	Eliminated nearly all of U.S. Supreme Court nondiscretionary appellate jurisdiction

Source: Derived from Federal Judicial Center, "Timeline for Landmark Judicial Legislation," available from www.fjc.gov (retrieved October 6, 2005); David M. O'Brien, *Constitutional Law and Politics: Civil Rights and Liberties,* 6th ed., Vol. 2. New York: W.W. Norton, 2005, 111–13.

and in 1982, respectively). In addition, Congress took a number of steps in the twentieth century to improve judicial administration, most notably with the creation of the Administrative Office of U.S. Courts (1939) and the Federal Judicial Center (1969). These agencies are the basis for the modern judiciary in providing administrative support and research for the federal courts.

CONTEMPORARY JUDICIAL FEDERALISM: STATE AND FEDERAL COURTS

The U.S. has two judicial systems, a dual system of state and federal courts (see Figure 3.1 and Table 3.2). This system of *judicial federalism* stands in contrast with unitary judicial systems elsewhere around the world (see the In Comparative Perspective box in this chapter). Although there are a number of specialized courts on the state and national levels, U.S. courts are predominantly hierarchical in structure and geographically based. Both judicial systems have primarily three levels. In many cases, state and federal courts share concurrent jurisdiction, but jurisdiction not expressly given to the federal courts remains the province of the state courts. Furthermore, state courts handle the bulk of the nation's judicial business, in part because they are larger and more diverse as compared to the federal judiciary.

Although judicial power is divided between the two systems of courts, Article III and the Supremacy Clause in Article VI gives the Supreme Court appellate jurisdiction over appeals of state supreme court rulings that conflict with federal

FIGURE 3.1 The United States Court System.

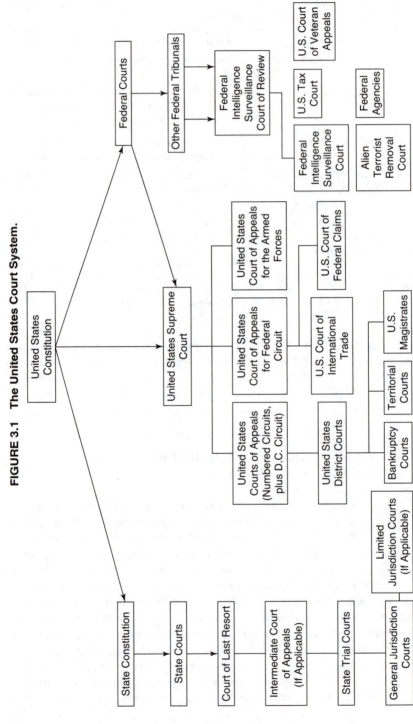

Source: Derived from Judicial Conference of the United States, *Long Range Plan for the Federal Courts* (December, 1995), 55.

TABLE 3.2   A Comparison of the State and Federal Judiciary

Court System	Geographical Boundaries	Judicial Officers	Aggregate Caseload
Federal	13 Circuits, 94 Districts	876	415,122
State	50 States	29,373	100 million

Note. "Aggregate caseload" includes cases filed in state trial courts, those in U.S. district courts (civil and criminal), and those in U.S. courts of appeals. It excludes about 1.6 million cases filed in U.S. bankruptcy courts and roughly 9,000 petitions filed to U.S. Supreme Court.

Source: Administrative Office of U.S. Courts, "Judicial Business of the United States Courts 2004 (Caseload Highlights)," available from www.uscourts.gov/judbus2004/front/caseload.pdf (retrieved October 19, 2005); Administrative Office of U.S. Courts, "Federal Judicial Vacancies" (Authorized Judgeships)," available from www.uscourts.gov/judicialvac.html (retrieved October 19, 2005); National Center for State Courts, *Examining the Work of State Courts, 2004* (Williamsburg: National Center for State Courts, 2005).

law. Although state courts are bound by federal law, in those areas of constitutional law in which the Court declines review or in which a state court has based its decision on its own state constitution, the Court will not review or overturn a state court decision, even if it is inconsistent with prevailing federal law. But, since the Court's ruling in *Michigan v. Long* (1983),[20] those state court judgments must be based on "adequate and independent state grounds" and state supreme courts must make a "plain statement" that they are resting their decision on their state constitution, not the Supreme Court's rulings or the Constitution. Otherwise, the Supreme Court presumes that state courts are interpreting federal law and reverse state court decisions with which it disagrees.

State courts play a vital role in the administration of justice in construing their own constitutional provisions and bills of rights. Although most state supreme courts adjudicate issues of state constitutional law in "lockstep" (affording the same amount of freedom) with the Supreme Court's rulings, studies show that state supreme courts are active in expanding individual rights in certain cases, such as the free exercise of religion (First Amendment), jury trial (Sixth Amendment), and search and seizure (Fourth Amendment). A "new judicial federalism" has been prevalent since the late 1970s, a time when the Supreme Court became more conservative.[21]

State Judiciaries

State courts decide the bulk of the nation's litigation. Generally, state judiciaries' consist of an appellate court of last resort, which sits as the highest judicial body; an intermediate court of appeals; and a set of general and limited jurisdictional trial courts (Figure 3.2). General jurisdiction trial courts handle a broad range of civil and criminal cases, whereas limited jurisdictional courts have more specialized caseloads.

The evolution of state judiciaries is closely tied to the diverse legal cultures and traditions of the states. Early state court organization drew from the multitiered

FIGURE 3.2   **State Court Organization.**

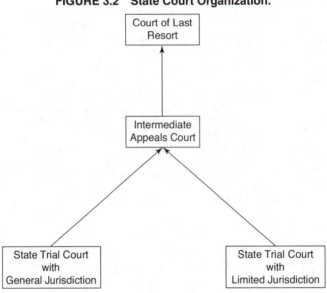

judicial systems of the colonial era. Those models often blurred the distinction between some legislative, executive, or judicial functions. Between the Civil War and the early twentieth century, reformers strove to make courts more autonomous and to simplify their operations. The reform movement, which coalesced in the 1950s, was thus designed to improve professionalism and administration. Also, judicial reformers sought to alter methods of judicial selection (further discussed in chapter 4), and to achieve court unification. "Court unification" consisted of the structural reorganization of courts. It fostered five interrelated trends: (1) trial court consolidation; (2) centralized management; (3) centralized rulemaking; (4) centralized budgeting; and (5) state, rather than local, financing.[22]

The politics of state court unification also caused division within the legal profession because the status quo was threatened. Attorneys and judges, for example, wanted to maintain individual control over case scheduling and management procedures.[23] Moreover, streamlining judicial operations intensified struggles between intergovernmental departments over the allocation of resources. Despite these difficulties, in the second half of the twentieth century state courts improved case management by increasing their staff and research support, adopting new technologies, and centralizing administrative control over their dockets.

The most progress was in state trial court consolidation. Twelve state judiciaries (including the District of Columbia and Puerto Rico) consolidated their trial courts into "unified" single-court formats, combining general and limited jurisdiction courts. Another fourteen nonunified states have identified some type of court reorganization as a priority for future strategic plans: Arizona, Colorado, Delaware, Georgia, Maine, Maryland, Nevada, New Hampshire, Ohio, Pennsylvania,

Texas, Utah, Virginia, and West Virginia.[24] Still, there is a lack of uniformity even within unified court systems (see Figure 3.3). For example:

- California, Illinois, Iowa, Minnesota, and Puerto Rico have three layers of courts (trial, intermediate appeal, and court of last resort);

- Connecticut, Kansas, Missouri, and Wisconsin have three layers of courts, but with a separate limited jurisdiction (a probate or municipal) court as part of the general jurisdiction court at the bottom level;

- The District of Columbia and South Dakota have two layers of courts (trial and court of last resort); and,

- North Dakota has two layers of courts, but with a separate limited jurisdiction (municipal) court as part of the general jurisdiction court at the bottom level.[25]

FIGURE 3.3   California's Unified Court System.

Supreme Court
(Court of Last Resort, Seven Justices sit en banc)
• Mandatory Jurisdiction in criminal capital and disciplinary cases
• Discretionary Jurisdiction in civil, non-capital criminal, administrative agency, juvenile, original proceeding, and interlocutory decisions

↑

Courts of Appeal
(Intermediate Appellate Court, 105 Justices sit in panels in six districts)
• Mandatory Jurisdiction in civil, non-capital criminal, administrative agency, and juvenile cases
• Discretionary Jurisdiction in administrative agency, original proceedings, and interlocutory decisions

↑

Superior Court
(General Jurisdiction Court, Fifty-eight Counties, 1,498 Judges, 417 Commissioners and Referees)
• Tort, Contract, Real Property ($25,000/no maximum) cases, along with miscellaneous civil cases
• Exclusive domestic relations, estate, mental health, and civil appeals jurisdiction
• Felony DWI/DUI cases, with exclusive criminal appeals jurisdiction
• Exclusive juvenile jurisdiction
• Jury trial except in appeals, domestic and juvenile cases

Source: National Center for State Courts, *State Court Caseload Statistics, 2004: Supplement to Examining the Work of State Courts, 2004* (Williamsburg: National Center for State Courts, 2005), 12.

FIGURE 3.4 Ohio's Nonunified Court System.

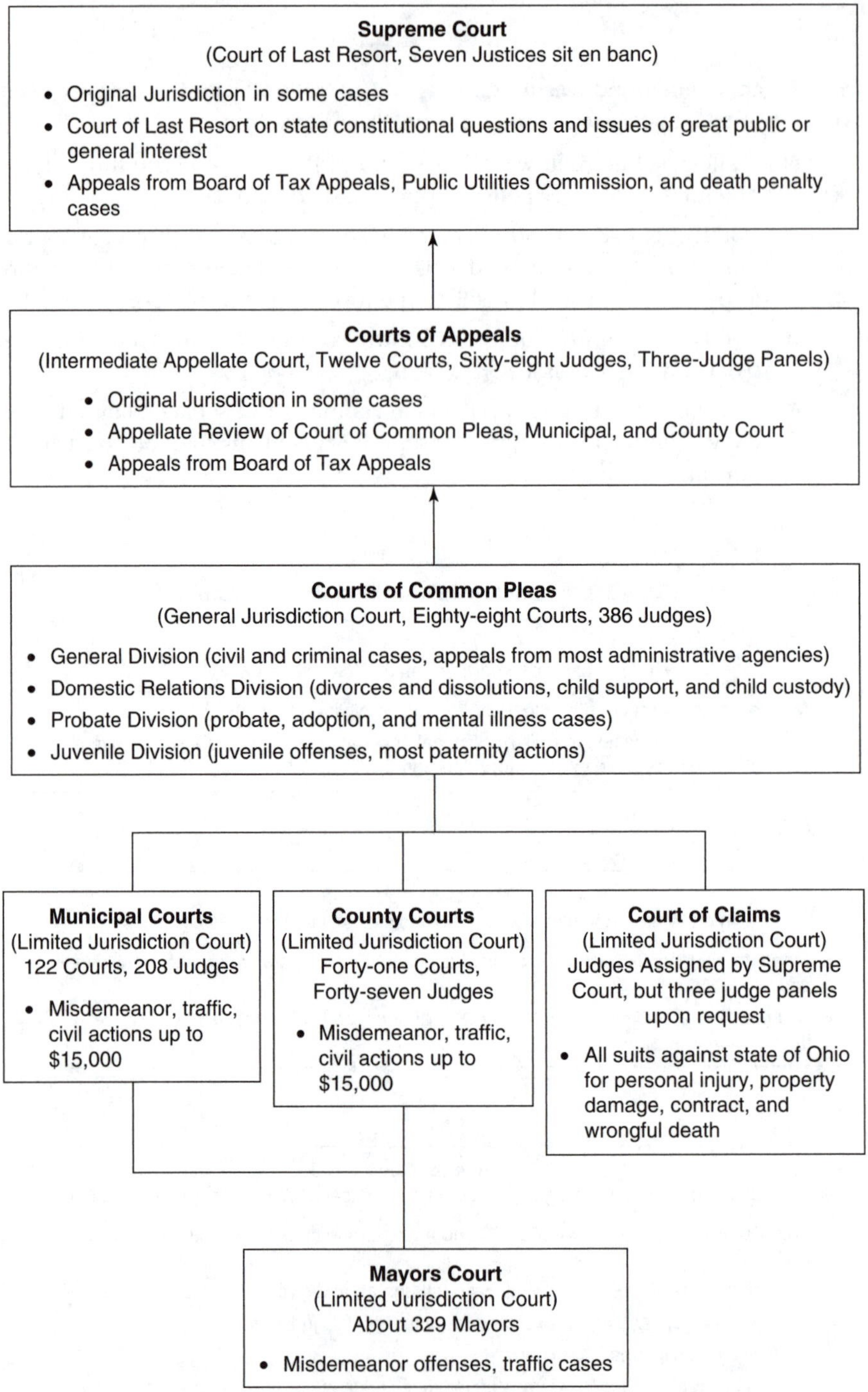

Supreme Court
(Court of Last Resort, Seven Justices sit en banc)

- Original Jurisdiction in some cases
- Court of Last Resort on state constitutional questions and issues of great public or general interest
- Appeals from Board of Tax Appeals, Public Utilities Commission, and death penalty cases

Courts of Appeals
(Intermediate Appellate Court, Twelve Courts, Sixty-eight Judges, Three-Judge Panels)

- Original Jurisdiction in some cases
- Appellate Review of Court of Common Pleas, Municipal, and County Court
- Appeals from Board of Tax Appeals

Courts of Common Pleas
(General Jurisdiction Court, Eighty-eight Courts, 386 Judges)

- General Division (civil and criminal cases, appeals from most administrative agencies)
- Domestic Relations Division (divorces and dissolutions, child support, and child custody)
- Probate Division (probate, adoption, and mental illness cases)
- Juvenile Division (juvenile offenses, most paternity actions)

Municipal Courts
(Limited Jurisdiction Court)
122 Courts, 208 Judges

- Misdemeanor, traffic, civil actions up to $15,000

County Courts
(Limited Jurisdiction Court)
Forty-one Courts, Forty-seven Judges

- Misdemeanor, traffic, civil actions up to $15,000

Court of Claims
(Limited Jurisdiction Court)
Judges Assigned by Supreme Court, but three judge panels upon request

- All suits against state of Ohio for personal injury, property damage, contract, and wrongful death

Mayors Court
(Limited Jurisdiction Court)
About 329 Mayors

- Misdemeanor offenses, traffic cases

Source: Supreme Court of Ohio, "Structure of the Ohio Judicial System," available from www.sconet.state.oh.us/introduction/structure/ (retrieved October 20, 2005).

While all nonunified state court systems are unique, their bottom tier of trial courts is composed of a network of general and limited jurisdictional courts that handle a wide range of legal disputes, such as probate, juvenile, family, small claims, traffic violations, and the like. Nonunified court systems, as shown by Figure 3.4, thus represent the prototypical state judicial system. Moreover, regardless of whether the court system is unified or not, a few states deliver localized justice

Sidebar 3.1

Tribal Courts

Native American and Alaska native tribal courts exist independently of the state and federal judiciaries. Located on reservations, they decide civil and criminal disputes. Following the Supreme Court's 1883 decision in *Ex Parte Crow Dog*,[a] holding that federal courts do not have the power to review criminal cases involving acts committed on Indian land, the Bureau of Indian Affairs, which monitors the national government's relationship with native Americans, created the "Court of Indian Offenses" to adjudicate disputes between tribal members in accordance with federal law. With the passage of the Indian Reorganization Act in 1934, however, the tribes were encouraged to create their own laws and justice systems. Of the more than 560 federally recognized tribes, approximately twenty-five tribal courts model their judicial systems on the Code of Federal Regulations, and about 275 tribes operate their own formal tribal court systems. Most tribal courts receive funding from the Department of Interior to operate their judicial systems, but many use their own revenues as well.

Tribal trial procedure is identical to the legal process of state or federal courts. The scope of a tribal court's authority follows precedent established by the U.S. Supreme Court. Early court rulings, in *Cherokee Nation v. Georgia* (1831)[b] and *Worcester v. Georgia* (1832),[c] established that tribes were "domestic dependent nations" and that state law did not control inside an Indian reservation. But, it makes a difference whether the person accused is a tribal member. In criminal actions, tribal courts cannot determine the guilt of a person who is not a member of the tribe, even if a tribe member was harmed. Tribal courts have more authority in civil actions and may decide certain cases involving nontribal members if there was a consensual relationship or agreement with the tribe.

The contours of tribal court jurisdiction remain matters of controversy. Since 1978, the Supreme Court has whittled away at tribal sovereignty by expanding the right of states to regulate affairs inside Indian lands and by limiting the ability of tribal courts to regulate the activities of nontribal members. In ruling that tribal courts cannot regulate hunting and fishing activities by nontribal members on land they did not own inside the reservation, *Montana v. United States* (1981)[d] established the general rule that tribal courts' jurisdiction is confined to "what is necessary to protect tribal self-government or to control internal relations." *Nevada v. Hicks* (2001)[e] further weakened tribal sovereignty in holding that tribal courts lack jurisdiction over state law enforcement officials who go onto an Indian reservation to investigate a crime allegedly committed by a tribal member but that occurred outside the reservation. *United States v. Lara* (2004)[f] held that the Double Jeopardy Clause does not bar successive prosecutions by separate sovereigns, in this case the Indian tribe's prosecution of the nonmember for "violence to a policeman" under tribal law and the federal government's identical prosecution under federal law. The Court held that Congress intended to vest the tribe with inherent tribal authority to prosecute nonmembers for misdemeanor offenses, but its own sovereign capacity was not barred to bringing about a subsequent federal prosecution.

Notes

[a] *Ex Parte Crow Dog*, 109 U.S. 556 (1883).

[b] *Cherokee Nation v. Georgia*, 30 U.S. (1 Pet.) 1 (1831).

[c] *Worcester v. Georgia*, 31 U.S. (1 Pet.) 515 (1832).

[d] *Montana v. United States*, 450 U.S. 544 (1981).

[e] *Nevada v. Hicks*, 533 U.S. 353 (2001).

[f] *United States v. Lara*, 541 U.S. 193 (2004)

to some parts of the population. Tribal courts, for example, remain a significant aspect of the legal process in the states where they exist, especially as trial courts.

STATE COURTS OF LIMITED AND GENERAL JURISDICTION   For most citizens, the judicial process occurs in a court of limited jurisdiction. Limited jurisdiction courts routinely deal with traffic, civil, and less serious (nonfelony) criminal cases. Most are simply called *municipal* or *district courts*. Yet, at one time they were typically known as *police courts*, or *justice of the peace* courts, usually staffed by nonlawyers. In such a court, disputes between landlords and tenants might be heard, along with those involving speeding tickets, drunk driving arrests, breach of contracts, probate of wills, small claims' disputes, or even domestic violence between family members. See Table 3.3 for types of state courts.

Today, there are approximately 13,544 limited jurisdiction courts in the states. About sixty-seven percent of all filings in state courts originate from them, of those, sixty-one percent are traffic cases.[26] Many states also use limited jurisdiction courts to adjudicate other civil matters, including probate (Alabama, Michigan, Rhode Island), family (Delaware, New York, South Carolina), and juvenile (Georgia, Nebraska, Tennessee) cases. Less frequently, they deal with worker's compensation (Nebraska), tax (New Jersey), and environmental (Vermont) disputes.

Municipal judges increasingly work in conjunction with part-time small claims magistrates to adjudicate claims in specialty courts or subunits of the full court that offer "therapeutic justice" to litigants involved in probation, mental health, drug abuse, or domestic violence cases. Typically, caseloads in these courts consist of misdemeanor filings, preliminary hearings in felony cases, and small

TABLE 3.3 Type of State Courts

Courts of Last Resort		Intermediate Appellate		General Jurisdiction		Limited Jurisdiction	
Most Common	Other	Most Common	Other	Most Common	Other	Most Common	Other
Supreme	Court of Appeals	Court of Appeals	Appellate	Superior	Probate	Municipal	Magistrate
	Court of Criminal Appeals		District Court of Appeals	District	Juvenile	District	Juvenile
	Supreme Judicial		Court Civil Appeals	Circuit	Court of Common Pleas	Probate	Family
			Court of Criminal Appeals		Family	Justice of Peace or Justice	County or District
			Intermediate Court of Appeals		Court of Claims		Probate, Surrogates or Orphans
			Appellate Court		Water		Civil or Criminal
			Tax		Workers' Compensation		Alderman or Mayors
			Court of Special Appeals		Tax		City, Town, or Village
			Appellate Division of Supreme Court		Court of First Instance		Chancery

(continued)

TABLE 3.3 (Continued)

Courts of Last Resort		Intermediate Appellate		General Jurisdiction		Limited Jurisdiction	
Most Common	Other	Most Common	Other	Most Common	Other	Most Common	Other
			Appellate Term of Supreme Court		Judicial District		Small Claims
			Commonwealth		Circuit Court and Family Court	Workers'	Compensation
					Court of Chancery	Traffic	
					Superior		Environmental
					Supreme		General Sessions
					County		Court of Tax Review
							Court of Claims
							Housing or Land
							City and Parish Courts

Source: National Center for State Courts, *State Court Caseload Statistics, 2004: Supplement to Examining the Work of State Courts, 2004* (Williamsburg: National Center for State Courts, 2005), 3–59.

TABLE 3.4   State Trial Court Docket

Subject Matter	All Trial Courts	General Jurisdiction	Limited Jurisdiction
Traffic	54.6	42.0	60.7
Civil	17.0	23.0	14.0
Criminal	20.6	18.6	21.6
Domestic	5.7	12.3	2.4
Juvenile	2.2	4.2	1.2

Note. N = 100.1 million cases filed in 2003. All figures are reported as percentages and are subject to rounding error.

Source: National Center for State Courts, *Examining the Work of State Courts, 2004: A National Perspective from the Court Statistics Project* (Williamsburg: National Center for State Courts, 2005), 14.

claims.[27] Depending on the court's jurisdiction and the nature of the proceeding, it may or may not be possible to request a jury trial. Moreover, a disgruntled litigant is not likely to have the option to appeal an adverse judgment.

Other state trial courts have general jurisdiction. They are commonly referred to as the *superior*, *district*, or *circuit court*. In the United States, there are approximately 2,044 general jurisdiction state courts. Their dockets primarily consist of serious criminal and civil cases. The right to a jury trial may be offered, but it generally depends on the kind of dispute and whether it involves a serious civil or criminal action. These courts share some similarities with limited jurisdiction courts. Some states, for example, give them authority over some specialized areas, such as probate (Indiana and Tennessee), family (Vermont), tax (Arizona and Oregon), and even water (Colorado and Montana) claims.[28] Still, there are important differences as well. In general jurisdiction courts, litigants are afforded more procedural rights because the risk of liberty and out-of-pocket loss is greater. Furthermore, litigants generally may appeal, which is often not possible in specialty courts.

The prevalent type of disputes in state trial courts' dockets is shown in Table 3.4. About a third of state trial court filings begin in general jurisdiction courts. Of those, roughly forty-two percent are traffic cases and the rest involve civil (twenty-three percent), criminal (ninteen percent), domestic (twelve percent), and juvenile (four percent) matters.[29] Traffic cases constitute more than half of the dockets. Whereas the percentage of civil and criminal cases is virtually the same in all state trial courts, general jurisdiction courts handle considerably more civil and domestic cases than do limited jurisdiction courts. But limited jurisdiction courts have more criminal cases. Apart from traffic cases, civil and criminal cases comprise more than one-third (37.6 percent) of what all state trial courts do.[30]

In sum, trial courts of limited jurisdiction play a critical role in handling the bulk of all traffic cases and a substantial amount of the civil and the criminal docket. The fines and fees they collect also make them key sources of revenue for state government. General jurisdiction courts, on the other hand, play a different but equally important role in adjudicating serious civil and criminal matters. Accordingly, whereas limited jurisdiction courts adjudicate a slightly different type of caseload, their caseloads are less serious and perhaps cause less of a burden on the resources of state trial courts of general jurisdiction, which deal with more difficult felony cases that take a significant toll on courts and communities alike.

INTERMEDIATE APPELLATE COURTS   Appellate courts are different than trial courts because they usually decide issues of law—what the law is or should be—instead of developing facts on the record. By and large, state appeals courts correct errors committed below, such as when a trial judge wrongly instructs a jury or improperly excludes key evidence. Although correcting legal errors gives intermediate appellate courts the opportunity to make the law, it also functions to reserve for the court of last resort the most significant questions of public policy.

In general, there are two types of state appeals courts: intermediate appellate courts and courts of last resort. *Intermediate appellate courts* sit between trial courts and courts of last resort, but they are known a variety of other names (as shown in Table 3.3). States vary on whether intermediate appellate courts must hear mandatory appeals or whether they have discretion in deciding the kinds of cases they address. Two states (Iowa, and Mississippi) with intermediate courts and three without them (Nevada, Delaware, and Wyoming) have exclusively mandatory appellate jurisdiction. The remaining states have mandatory appeals, but many also afford at least some discretion to intermediate courts. Indeed, Louisiana, Michigan, California, and Virginia, intermediate courts have discretionary jurisdiction in fifty percent or more of their docket.[31]

The most common arrangement consists of one court of last resort with discretionary jurisdiction, sitting above an intermediate appeals court with mandatory jurisdiction. At least half the states have such a system. All of the intermediate courts organized this way decide cases by panels of three randomly selected judges instead of by one judge ruling on the case. Five states (Alabama, Indiana, New York, Pennsylvania, and Tennessee) have bifurcated intermediate court of appeals, with two different appellate courts having separate jurisdiction over criminal, civil, or tax cases.[32]

In thirty-nine states and Puerto Rico, there are intermediate appellate courts, and only eleven states plus the District of Columbia do without them. Judicial districts without them are among the ones with the smallest populations. That is understandable because as first-level appellate review courts, intermediate appeals courts play a key role in reducing the court of last resort's caseload. In this sense, state intermediate appellate courts operate as "screening devices" for upper level courts.[33]

Because their caseloads principally originate from subordinate courts, it is not surprising that state intermediate appellate courts also predominately handle civil (forty-seven percent) and criminal (forty percent) mandatory appeals; the balance consists of administrative agency, juvenile, and miscellaneous appeals.[34] Typically, most state intermediate appellate courts affirm lower court rulings, although over eighty percent of case terminations are processed by an approximately equal number of signed judicial opinions, preargument dismissals, and summary memoranda and orders.[35] As a result, about half of the dockets of state intermediate appellate courts are cleared through a review of briefs, without summary orders and with no dissents. These courts issue opinions for only about one-third of their dockets. In short, though they guarantee the right of litigants to appeal, intermediate appellate courts enable the state's highest court to adjudicate only those cases raising important public policy questions.

STATE COURTS OF LAST RESORT   Courts of last resort usually provide a second level of review and the final opportunity for litigants to press their claims. Although there are only fifty states, there are fifty-four courts of last resort—two states, Oklahoma and Texas, have two (instead of a single) courts of last resort for civil and criminal cases. Whereas most states identify them as "Supreme Courts," some, like New York, refer to them as *Courts of appeals.*

In many respects, they resemble state intermediate appellate courts. For example, because state courts of last resort and intermediate appeals courts are collegial institutions, both dispose mostly of civil and criminal appeals in rotating panels of judges. Yet, there are significant differences. One is that courts of last resort handle fewer appeals and have greater discretion over the cases they hear. State courts of last resort, though, differ in the exercise of their discretionary jurisdiction. One study showed that high percentages of discretionary appeals granted in Rhode Island, whereas more populous states, including New Jersey (three percent) and California (one percent), have among the lowest percentage.[36]

Moreover, state courts of last resort are substantial policymakers in their own right. On average, they resolve more civil than criminal cases, but there is considerable variation in the types of cases they hear because of regional differences. Approximately ninty-six percent of the Alaska supreme court's docket consists of civil appeals, whereas in Florida and North Carolina, civil disputes comprise about forty percent and thirty percent of the caseload, respectively. About fifty percent of the civil dockets in Illinois, Michigan, and Tennessee are tort cases, but far less tort disputes are decided in Indiana, Georgia, and Oregon.[37]

Furthermore, as compared with state intermediate appellate courts, the reversal rate in many state courts of last resort tends to be higher, and a greater percentage of their dockets are terminated by pre-argument dismissals and summary orders than by judicial opinions.[38] In short, if cases make it to a state's court of last resort, only a small percentage of them are decided by written opinion and involve significant questions of public policy.

The Federal Judiciary

Congress reorganized the federal judiciary's structure, jurisdiction, and operation through piecemeal legislation. Still, the federal judiciary's original three-tiered organization has remained intact since the passage of the Evarts Act in 1891. At the apex is the Supreme Court of the United States, sitting above federal courts of appeals and district (trial) courts. There are thirteen appellate circuits: eleven numbered circuits spanning twelve geographic areas covering the fifty states,

FIGURE 3.5 Geographical Boundaries of the U.S. Courts System.

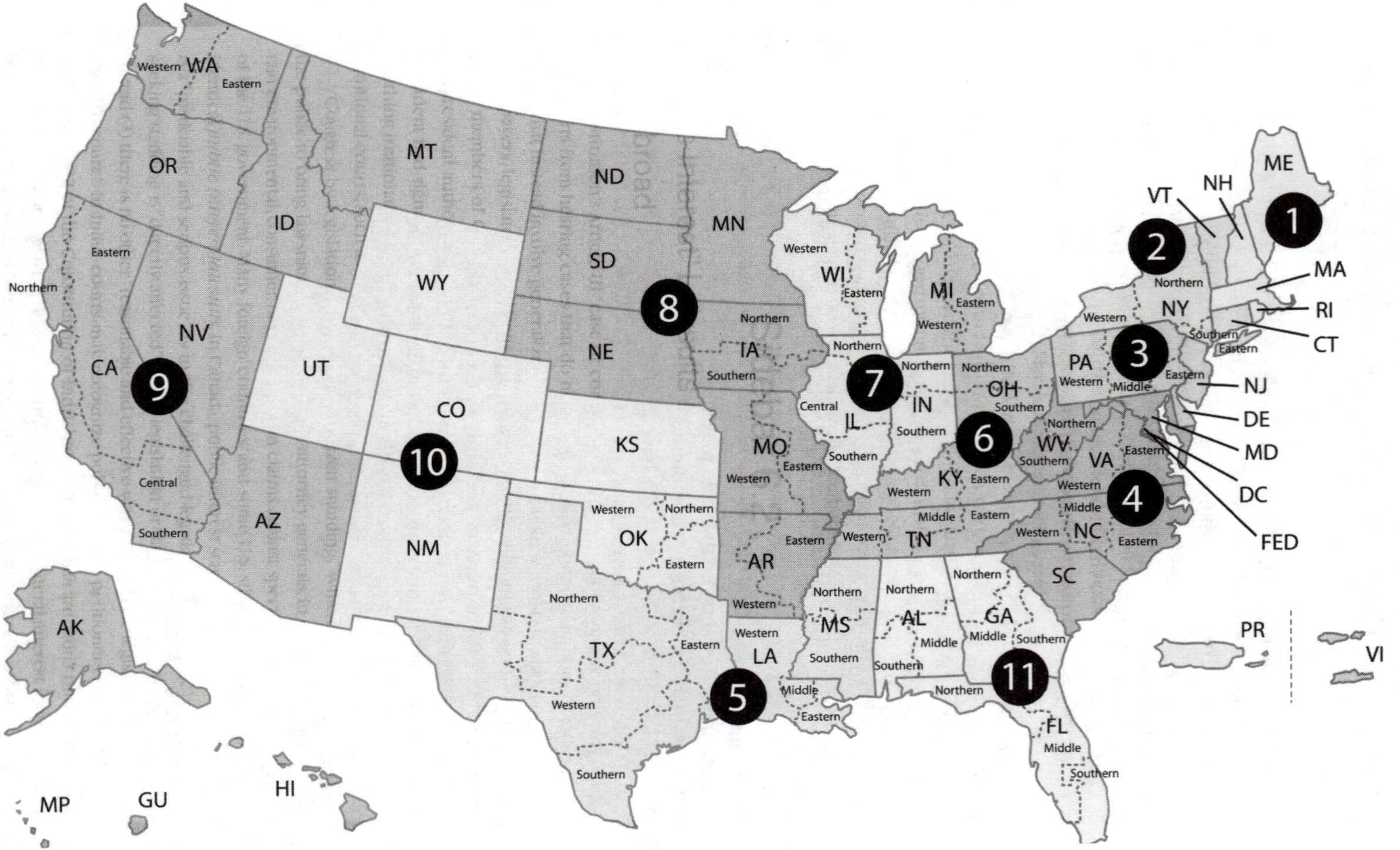

Source: Administrative Office of U.S. Courts, available from www.uscourts.gov/images/circuitmap.pdf (retrieved December 15, 2005).

one circuit for the District of Columbia Circuit, and one, the U.S. Court of Appeals for the Federal Circuit in Washington D.C., with nationwide jurisdiction over certain specialized cases. The smallest is the First Circuit (with six authorized judgeships) in the Northeast, and the largest is the Ninth Circuit (with twenty-eight judges), covering multiple Western states the size of western Europe and including twenty percent of the American population. The typical size of a federal court of appeals is between twelve and fifteen members.

See Figure 3.5 which depicts the geographical boundaries of the U.S. Court System from December 15, 2005.

U.S. DISTRICT COURTS   The U.S. district courts are the federal judiciary's trial courts. There are 678 authorized judgeships for the nation's ninety-four federal district courts, with at least one in each state. District court judges are appointed by the president and confirmed by the Senate. Although they occasionally hear cases in three-judge panels in select cases, such as reapportionment or voting rights litigation, district court judges usually decide cases alone. In addition to having authority over bankruptcy cases, district courts exercise power over disputes involving federal questions (an interpretation of the federal Constitution, statute, regulation, or treaty) and diversity cases (between citizens of different states or between U.S. citizens and those of another country, if the lawsuit claims $75,000 or more). In 2005, fifty-eight percent of all civil cases commenced in district courts were private actions raising a federal question, but only twenty-three percent were diversity cases.[39]

District courts have original and general jurisdiction. As trial courts, they adjudicate far more cases than federal appellate courts. District courts decide about 352,360 civil and criminal cases, whereas only about 62,762 appeals are handled annually by appellate courts, and less than approximately 9,000 filings are made to the U.S. Supreme Court.[40]

District court judges may sit with a jury or by themselves in a bench trial. In general, they are charged with adjudicating both the facts and the law. Accordingly, litigants present the facts through evidence and the judge decides whether to admit it into the trial on the basis of the federal code of evidence. After the litigants present the facts, the judge or jury apply the law and reach a decision. Subsequent to the trial, each litigant has the right to appeal.

The number of civil and criminal cases on the dockets of federal district courts has steadily increased along with the number of authorized judgeships since 1960 (Table 3.5). Over the last two decades, roughly eighty percent of the docket of district courts has been civil cases. A key function of the federal district court is to interpret and apply federal statutes to litigant claims: sixty-five percent of the civil docket involve the adjudication of statutory actions, whereas only thirty-five percent of the docket is represented by contract, tort, and real property claims (Table 3.6). Of the statutory actions, district court judges also spend a significant part of their time hearing civil rights issues and prisoner petitions. The latter is particularly noteworthy because they tend to drain judicial

TABLE 3.5 U.S. District Court Caseload and Docket Composition, 1960–2004

Year	Total Cases	Authorized Judgeships	Civil Cases		Criminal Cases	
			Filings	Percentage of Docket	Filings	Percentage of Docket
1960	89,112	245	59,284	66.5	29,828	33.4
1965	101,012	306	67,678	66.9	33,334	33.0
1970	127,280	401	87,321	68.6	39,959	31.3
1975	160,602	400	117,320	73.0	43,282	26.9
1980	200,461	516	171,074	85.3	29,387	14.6
1985	318,401	575	278,681	87.5	39,720	12.4
1990	265,048	575	217,013	81.8	48,035	18.1
1995	294,123	649	248,335	84.4	45,788	15.5
2000	322,262	655	259,517	80.5	62,745	19.4
2002	341,841	665	274,841	80.4	67,000	19.5
2003	323,604	680	252,962	78.1	70,642	21.8
2004	352,360	678	281,338	79.8	71,022	20.2

Note. All percentages are subject to rounding error. The 1960–1976 data are from the year ending June 30; subsequent data are from the year ending September 30.

Source: Administrative Office of U.S. Courts, *Judicial Facts and Figures* (Tables 2.11, 3.1, 4.1), available from www.uscourts.gov (retrieved October 25, 2005). The number of district courts and authorized judgeships for 2004 was obtained from Administrative Office of U.S. Courts, "Authorized Judgeships," available from www.uscourts.gov/history/contents.html (retrieved October 25, 2005).

resources by flooding the courts with frivolous writs alleging constitutional deprivations. On the other hand, there are prisoner petitions (like *habeas corpus* actions asserting illegal confinement), which are meritorious and deserve to be heard by a court. Significantly, such claims are heard by district courts that are also on the front line in routinely adjudicating matters pertaining to a variety of general offenses (seventy-six percent), including homicide, robbery, assault, and theft crimes; though, drug (twenty-eight percent) and fraud (twelve percent) offenses command most of their time. The remaining portion of the criminal docket in district courts involves immigration and other statutory violations.

As in state trial courts, most cases are disposed of by district courts before trial. About eighty-eight percent of all civil actions are terminated pretrial and almost another ten percent are ended either during or shortly after that. Only about two percent of the civil caseload are decided either during or after trial. A similar pattern appears with criminal cases, but with the important difference that a defendant's guilty plea is the basis for ending proceedings instead of a negotiated settlement. Almost ninty-six percent of those convicted plead guilty.[41]

District court judges work with other miscellaneous judicial divisions and personnel in handling their caseloads. They include the territorial courts, U.S.

TABLE 3.6 Nature of Civil Actions and Criminal Offenses in U.S. District Court, 2000–2004

Civil Cases			Criminal Cases		
Action	Total Filings	Percentage of Total Civil Docket	Offense	Total Filings	Percentage of Total Criminal Docket
Contract	193,283	14.6	*General Offenses*	250,420	75.6
Real Property	35,278	2.7	■ Homicide	1,580	.48
Tort	233,245	17.7	■ Robbery	6,237	1.9
Statutory Actions	857,759	65.0	■ Assault	3,686	1.1
■ Bankruptcy appeals and withdrawals	17,861	1.4	■ Burglary/breaking and entering	261	.08
■ Civil rights (voting, employment, housing, etc.)	202,993	15.4	■ Larceny/theft	15,775	4.8
■ Prisoner petitions (habeas corpus, civil rights, prison conditions, etc.)	282,065	21.4	■ Embezzlement	5,150	1.6
■ Forfeiture and penalty	10,596	.80	■ Fraud	39,208	11.9
■ Labor laws	83,270	6.3	■ Auto theft	803	.24
■ Securities, commodities, and exchanges	15,964	1.2	■ Forgery/counterfeiting	5,5575	1.7
■ Protected property rights (copyright, trademark, patents)	43,830	3.3	■ Sex offenses	6,111	1.8
■ Social security	84,225	6.4	■ Drugs	92,581	28.0

(continued)

TABLE 3.6 (Continued)

Civil Cases			Criminal Cases		
Action	Total Filings	Percentage of Total Civil Docket	Offense	Total Filings	Percentage of Total Criminal Docket
■ Tax suits	5,636	.43	■ Miscellaneous (drunk driving, perjury, bribery, weapons, and firearms, etc.)	73,453	22.2
■ Other statutory actions (domestic relations, insanity, probate, etc.)	89,343	6.8	*Special Offenses*	80,807	24.4
			■ Immigration	68,424	84.6
			■ Federal statutes (agriculture or conservation acts, food and drug act, customs laws, postal laws, etc.)	12,368	15.3

Note. N = 1,319,565 for civil cases. N = 331,227 for criminal cases. For statutory actions in civil cases, filings averaging less than 1,000 in any given category over the five year period were excluded as were filings from nonstatutory actions that averaged less than 1,000 filings over the five year period. All percentages in bold or in subcategories for civil cases do not equal 100 percent because of noted exclusions; also, all percentages for criminal cases are subject to rounding error. Data are from year ending September 30.

Source: Administrative Office of U.S. Courts, *2004 Annual Report of the Director* (Tables C-2A and D-2), available from www.uscourts.gov (retrieved October 25, 2005).

magistrates, and bankruptcy courts. Territorial courts are technically considered U.S. district courts and generally enjoy equivalent jurisdiction and powers. But because they are located in U.S. territories, they also operate like local courts; their judges are not Article III judges, and they serve a limited term of ten years with no guarantee of reappointment. Territorial courts sit in Guam, the Northern Mariana Islands, Puerto Rico, and the Virgin Islands.

U.S. magistrate judges, on the other hand, are appointed by district judges and serve for either eight- or four-year terms, depending upon whether they act in a full- or part-time capacity. Although they do not enjoy the prestige or reputation of Article III district judges, magistrate judges play a key role in helping district courts manage their caseloads.

Sidebar 3.2

United States Magistrates

In 1793 Congress gave circuit courts the power to appoint persons to take bail in criminal cases; they worked only part-time and were paid on the basis of fees. In 1896, Congress institutionalized the position by giving federal district court judges the power to appoint "U.S. commissioners" and established a uniform fee schedule for their services. Over the next century, the commissioners' responsibilities continued to grow to the point where further reform was necessary. In 1968, Congress enacted The Federal Magistrates Act, replacing the fee system with salaries and mandating that the former commissioners, or "magistrates," have been admitted to the bar.

Magistrate judges, as they are now called, serve either in a full-time or part-time capacity for an eight- or a four-year term, respectively. District court judges still appoint them, but the nominations are processed through a citizen's merit screening commission. Because Congress has not limited the number of times a magistrate judge can be reappointed, it is not unusual for them to stay on the bench for lengthy time periods.

Magistrates have become significant actors as the district courts' caseloads have become more voluminous. There are about 486 authorized full-time magistrates, whereas fifty-one are part-time judges and three are hybrid Clerk of Court/Magistrate Judges. Magistrates perform multiple tasks as court officers. With consent of the parties, they assign cases for trial and pretrial, issue warrants, conduct pretrial hearings, and set bail in criminal cases. They also have the power to try and sentence defendants convicted of minor crimes, subject to the right to appeal to a district court judge.

Magistrates play a vital role in managing the federal court caseload. Magistrate judges dispose of more than 941,632 matters, almost twice as many as the 1990s. Their work is significant and includes the following:

■ Disposing of nearly 8,101 Class A misdemeanors (e.g., traffic, theft, food/drug, weapons, trespass, fraud, assault).

- Disposing of over 84,808 Petty Offenses (e.g., DUI/DWI, immigration, food/drug, littering, drunk/disorderly, hunting, trespassing, theft).
- Participating in over 321,164 felony preliminary hearings (e.g., search and arrest warrants, initial appearances, arraignments, bail review).
- Performing over 44,437 miscellaneous duties (e.g., seizure/inspection warrants, calendar calls, grand juries).
- Conducting about 146,978 criminal pretrials.
- Conducting almost 272,345 civil pretrials.
- Issuing over 48,061 reports and recommendations pursuant to statute, including nearly 23,576 prisoner petitions.

Source: The Federal Judicial Center, "History of the Federal Judiciary: Landmark Judicial Legislation," available from www.fjc.gov/history/home.nsf (retrieved March 1, 2004); Administrative Office of U.S. Courts, "Magistrate Judges, Bankruptcy Judges, Can Serve Long Careers on Federal Bench," *Third Branch* (November 2003, No. 11), available from www.uscourts.gov/ttb/nov03ttb/magistrate/index. html (retrieved March 1, 2004); Federal Magistrate Judges Association, available from www.fedjudge. org/index.asp (retrieved April 16, 2006); and Administrative Office of U.S. Courts, *2005 Annual Report of the Director* (Tables S-17, M-4, M-4A, M-4B), available from www.uscourts.gov (retrieved April 16, 2006).

Bankruptcy courts are linked to federal district courts. They handle debtor–creditor claims emerging from personal and corporate bankruptcies. Although they are considered subunits of federal district courts, they are anomalous because bankruptcy judges do not have Article III status. Congress and the courts have grappled with the political and legal implications of not giving bankruptcy judges Article III status. Specifically, in 1978 Congress enacted a new bankruptcy code that created new U.S. Bankruptcy Courts as Article I legislative courts. They were vested with broad jurisdiction covering all civil actions arising under the bankruptcy code. Yet, these judges were not given Article III life tenure or salary protections, even though they are appointed by the president and confirmed by the Senate for fourteen-year terms. However, *Northern Pipeline Construction Company v. Marathon Pipe Line Company* (1982)[42] held that it was unconstitutional for bankruptcy courts to exercise jurisdiction over state law claims because the principle of separation of powers was violated when Congress vested Article III power and jurisdiction in Article I judges who lacked the status of Article III judges.

In response, Congress enacted the Bankruptcy Amendments and Federal Judgeship Act of 1984. It fixed the constitutional problems in two ways. First, while ensuring that the district courts retained jurisdiction, the law let the district courts delegate judicial power to the bankruptcy court for the purpose of handling bankruptcy litigation. Second, the act transferred the power to appoint bankruptcy judges to fourteen-year terms from the president to federal appellate courts. The changes remain important because they eliminated the Article III basis for exercising bankruptcy jurisdiction by Article I judges over "core" proceedings in bankruptcy, thereby conforming to *Northern Pipeline.*"Non-core" bankruptcy matters are referred to U.S. district courts. As a result, bankruptcy judges today are considered "units" of the district courts, and they have the status of judicial officers instead of Article III judges because they have limited tenure and no salary protection.[43]

Bankruptcy judges play a critical role in an overloaded bankruptcy system that is expanding at a rapid pace. Since 1995, the caseload has increased eighty-three percent, with over 1.6 million bankruptcy petitions flooding the system. In response, Congress enacted The Bankruptcy Abuse Prevention and Consumer Protection Act of 2005, a major reform designed to increase debtor accountability and restrict opportunistic or abusive filings. Unlike past law, for example, the act requires debtors filing consumer bankruptcies to repay some of their obligations if they have the financial ability to do so. In addition, debtors must file a certificate of credit counseling and a repayment plan as a precondition to filing a petition, and postfiling debtor education must be completed in order to receive a final decree discharging the debts. Although the act created twenty-eight new judgeships to help administer the new requirements, the rush to file bankruptcies before the act went into effect caused a sharp increase in filings: In October 2005, over 600,000 cases were filed, whereas, a year earlier, total filings equaled about 130,000.[44]

There are a number of other courts and tribunals performing federal trial functions. They have specialized jurisdiction over cases relating to public policy areas such as international trade disagreements, public contract cases, veteran benefits appeals, taxpayer disputes, and national security wiretaps. The U.S. Court of International Trade, an Article III court that sits in New York and is staffed by nine judges appointed for life, reviews civil actions pertaining to import transactions and international trade. The U.S. Court of Federal Claims, an Article I court that has sixteen judges serving fifteen-year terms, adjudicates monetary claims asserted over government contracts, tax refund lawsuits, Fifth Amendment "Takings" cases, intellectual property, and Indian tribe cases. Another Article I court, the U.S. Court of Appeals for Veteran Claims handles appeals from the federal Board of Veteran Appeals regarding entitlements, including veteran disability, survivor, and education benefits. The U.S. Tax Court, an Article I court hears cases relating to taxpayer disputes. Finally, two other courts, the Alien Terrorist Removal Court and the Federal Intelligence Surveillance Court (FIS Court) were created as part of the commitment to fight terrorism. The Alien Terrorist Removal Court uses five district court judges to determine requests by the Attorney General to remove an alien on the grounds of being a foreign terrorist. The FIS Court, created by the Federal Intelligence Surveillance Act of 1978 (FISA), reviews government applications for wiretaps of those who pose a threat to national security. The role of the FIS Court and the requirement for obtaining judicial approval of wiretaps assumed greater significance in light of President Bush's decision shortly after 9/11 to authorize, without full disclosure to Congress, the National Security Agency to conduct domestic wiretaps of American citizens and other persons suspected of communicating with terrorists abroad without utilizing the FIS Court to issue such wiretaps.[45]

U.S. COURTS OF APPEALS The U.S. circuit courts of appeals, with 179 authorized judgeships, are located in eleven regional circuit courts plus the Court of Appeals for the D.C. Circuit and the Court of Appeals for the Federal Circuit. All have general jurisdiction that typically includes a variety of civil, criminal, and administrative law appeals. But the D.C. Circuit has a high concentration of agency cases because of its location in the nation's capitol. In addition, the Court of Appeals for the Federal Circuit is unique because it is a nonregional court of appeals that exercises jurisdiction over a few topical areas of law; it has exclusive jurisdiction over patent appeals emerging from district courts and the U.S. Patent and Trademark Office.[46]

There are other appellate courts that serve specialized functions regarding administrative law, military justice, and national security. The most notable are two Article I courts, the Court of Appeals for the Armed Services and the Foreign Intelligence Surveillance (FIS) Court of Review. The Armed Service court's docket includes capital appeals from the armed forces' Court of Criminal Appeals and referrals from the Judge Advocate General. In contrast, the FIS Court of Review is a controversial "secret" court that handles appeals from another "secret" lower court, the FIS Court, in matters pertaining to the domestic surveillance of persons suspected to be threats to national security. Their proceedings are not usually disclosed to the public because they must be cautious in safeguarding the executive branch's efforts to protect the nation from domestic and external threats. For these and other reasons, the foreign intelligence review courts rarely publish opinions for their decisions. Before the 9/11 terrorist attacks on the World Trade Center in New York and on the Pentagon, the government's track record of securing approval for wiretaps on those suspected of posing a national security threat was rarely questioned or denied by the FIS Court, which rendered appeals to the higher FIS Court of Review superfluous. However, the 9/11 attacks and Congress's enactment of the USA PATRIOT Act shortly thereafter thrust both courts into the spotlight. Each for the first time published opinions that, at first, struck down a key provision of the USA PATRIOT Act, but the appellate FIS Court of Review reversed. These courts are likely to play even larger roles in the ongoing war on terrorism.[47]

Circuit court judges are appointed by the president with the Senate's confirmation. They ordinarily hear appeals in panels of three randomly selected judges. They primarily hear appeals from the district courts and other courts or administrative agencies. Although they may make law and establish a uniform body of national legal precedent, as appellate courts they screen out cases for the Supreme Court and correct errors of law at lower level. Hence, they do not generally determine "the facts" of a case, instead they defer to the jury or trial judge. Circuit courts thus dispose of cases by applying the established facts to the law that litigants cite in their briefs and oral arguments, or which is otherwise discovered by the judge or their staff (law clerks or staff attorneys) through legal research or during in-chamber deliberations, including formal conferences among judges. As collegial institutions, circuit courts engage in a dynamic process of small-group decision making that enables them to become the "courts of last resort for the great mass of federal litigants" because their decisions are final, except in the few instances that the Supreme Court agrees to grant review of their decisions.[48]

Caseload pressures and limited resources affect circuit court decisional practices. Seventh Circuit Judge Richard A. Posner reported that since 1960 the average length of oral argument has declined by at least fifty percent, typically, only about forty percent of all appeals are orally argued. Usually, litigants are given ten to twenty-five minutes to present their case, and most of the time is spent answering questions from the bench. Moreover, though circuit courts strive to issue opinions for their judgments, for reasons of economy they increasingly issue unpublished or summary decisions that simply announce the decision. As Posner and other court watchers have observed, nonpublication a practice that is becoming increasingly controversial, occurs in a vast majority of appeals (nearly eighty percent). Initially devised by the U.S. Judicial Conference as a method to ease the appeals courts' caseloads, in the 1970s all circuits established rules of procedure limiting the publication of opinions to only those cases having value as a significant precedent.[49]

However, some lawyers view unpublished opinions as legal judgments that ought to be cited, especially with online legal data retrieval systems like WestLaw and Lexis-Nexis. Not all judges agree. Before 2006, nine circuit courts allowed some sort of citation to unpublished opinions, but four circuits–the Second, Seventh, Ninth, and Federal–banned the practice, and six other circuits discouraged it. Yet, in April 2006 the Supreme Court approved an amendment to Rule 32.1 of the Federal Rules of Appellate Procedure, which permits the citation of opinions, orders, judgments, or other written dispositions that have been designated as "unpublished" or "nonprecedential" by federal courts. For some, such as Richard Frankel of Trial Lawyers for Public Justice, allowing citation of unpublished opinions is a "good first step toward improving the openness and transparency of our court system." Still, others, like Second Circuit Chief Judge John Walker, Jr., oppose the rule change because it represents a "sea change" in judicial practices that unnecessarily overburdens courts.[50]

Judicial workload statistics reveal that federal appellate courts play a vital role in establishing uniform principles of national law in civil and criminal cases as well as in reviewing agency and other specialized court decisions. In roughly the last two decades, 85.7 percent of the average federal appellate court's docket consisted of appeals from the district courts, with the remaining appeals coming from federal agencies (8.2 percent), bankruptcy courts (2.4 percent), and original (3.4 percent) proceedings. More than half of the appeals from district courts are civil actions (65.0 percent), and the remainder are criminal appeals (20.7 percent). Because a substantial portion of the district courts' civil docket involves civil prisoner petitions and criminal drug cases, the federal appeals courts similarly handle a large number of prisoner (28.7 percent) and drug (46.3 percent) appeals.[51]

TABLE 3.7 U.S. Courts of Appeals Docket Composition and Source of Appeals, 1988–2004

Year	Total Appeals	From District Courts						From Other Sources			
		Civil Appeals	Percent Total Docket	Criminal Appeals	Percent Total Docket	Federal Agencies	Percent Total Docket	Bankrptcy Appeals	Percent Total Docket	Original Proceedings	Percent Total Docket
1988	38,345	26,934	70.2	6,436	16.7	3,113	8.1	1,214	3.1	648	1.6
1989	39,927	26,997	67.6	8,399	21.0	2,794	6.9	1,100	2.7	637	1.5
1990	40,893	26,980	65.9	9,642	23.5	2,558	6.2	1,107	2.7	606	1.4
1991	43,027	28,033	65.1	10,249	23.8	2,859	6.6	1,277	2.9	609	1.4
1992	47,013	30,328	64.5	11,215	23.8	3,235	6.8	1,637	3.4	598	1.2
1993	50,224	32,374	64.4	11,862	23.6	3,928	7.8	1,388	2.7	672	1.3
1994	48,322	32,309	66.8	10,674	22.0	3,369	6.9	1,382	2.8	588	1.2
1995	50,072	34,203	68.3	10,162	20.2	3,295	6.5	1,667	3.3	745	1.4
1996	51,991	36,137	69.5	10,889	20.9	2,827	5.4	1,434	2.7	704	1.3
1997	52,319	35,414	67.6	10,521	20.1	4,412	8.4	1,158	2.2	814	1.5
1998	53,805	37,522	69.7	10,535	19.5	3,793	7.0	1,203	2.2	752	1.3
1999	54,693	36,680	67.0	10,251	18.7	3,280	5.9	1,109	2.0	3,373	6.1
2000	54,697	35,780	65.4	10,707	19.5	3,237	5.9	1,007	1.8	3,966	7.2
2001	57,464	36,046	62.7	11,281	19.3	3,300	5.7	961	1.6	5,876	10.2
2002	57,555	35,499	61.6	11,569	20.1	5,789	10.0	843	1.4	3,855	6.6
2003	60,847	34,390	56.5	11,968	19.7	9,988	16.4	902	1.5	3,599	5.9
2004	62,762	33,075	52.7	12,506	19.9	12,255	19.5	862	1.4	4,064	6.5
Total Avg.	50,820	32,864	65.0	10,522	20.7	4,355	8.2	1,191	2.4	1,889	3.4

Note. N = 863,956 (total appeals); 558,701 (civil appeals); 178,866 (criminal appeals); 74,032 (agency appeals); 20,251 (bankruptcy appeals); 32,106 (original proceedings appeals). All percentages are subject to rounding error. In 2001, the perception of a one-year deadline for filing petitions pursuant to *Apprendi v. New Jersey*, 530 U.S. 466, allegedly caused a spike in motions to seek such petitions in the U.S. Courts of Appeals.

Source: Administrative Office U.S. Courts, *Judicial Facts and Figures* (Table 1.1), available from www.uscourts.gov (retrieved October 25, 2005).

See Table 3.7 which depicts the U.S. Court of Appeals Docket Composition and Source of Appeals from 1988–2004.

In exceptional cases, a circuit court of appeals may convene *en banc* (the entire court) to reconsider a panel's ruling. The Federal Rules of Appellate Procedure permit *en banc* review if a majority of circuit judges order it, if it "is necessary to secure or maintain uniformity of the court's decisions," or if "the proceeding involves a question of exceptional importance." Ordinarily, the losing party of the appeal must request a rehearing or a rehearing *en banc* by petition. The vast majority of such petitions are denied. Despite their infrequency, *en banc* judicial opinions represent the appellate court's collective judgment and resolve intracircuit court conflicts among three-judge panels. Accordingly, *en banc* opinions reflect the political preferences of a court and may promote judicial legitimacy by helping to made federal law uniform.[52]

U.S. SUPREME COURT   At the apex of the federal judiciary is the Supreme Court of the United States. It resolves legal disputes arising from both federal and state courts. Approximately sixty-five percent of the court's docket comes from federal courts and about thirty percent from state courts. In managing its docket, the court's role has changed over time in response to its expanding caseload. Before 1925, the court's primary function was to decide cases in order to correct legal errors below, but Congress has given it discretionary jurisdiction over the cases it chooses to hear. Thus the court only grants review in cases involving "substantial questions of federal law" and intercircuit conflicts (when federal appellate courts issue conflicting decisions on the same issue). Because it has the discretion to set its agenda, the Supreme Court "assume[s] the role of super legislature"[53] and has become became the final arbiter of complex social policy issues.

The court sits with one chief justice and eight associate justices. The chief justice is also the titular head of the federal judiciary, presiding over the U.S. Judicial Conference and overseeing the Federal Judicial Center and Administrative Office of U.S. Courts (the policymaking, legal research, and administrative agencies of the federal courts, discussed in the next section). In addition to performing their regular judicial duties, each associate justice serves as circuit justice for one or more of the regional circuits. Each justice has three to four law clerks, who screen *certiorari* petitions for review, perform legal research, prepare "bench memos" (used in preparation for oral argument), and draft opinions. The justices have their own conference and robing rooms, and lawyers practicing before the court have a separate lounge. The solicitor general, a frequent litigator representing the federal government, has its own office. The court has a library, barber shop, museum, dining, and its own basketball court. The Marshal's Office is in charge of building security and public safety. Like other government institutions, it has a Web site (www.supremecourtus.gov), along with a separate public information office for access to docket information, filings, and briefs.[54]

The court has original and appellate jurisdiction. The court adjudicates cases as specified in Article III between certain parties (e.g., ambassadors, public ministers and consuls, and between two states) and grants appeals from lower courts. Filings to the court are inspected by the clerk for procedural correctness in accordance with the court's rules and then placed in one of three categories of the docket: paid cases, unpaid cases, and as original proceedings. In approximate terms, about one-quarter of the filings are put on what is somewhat ambiguously termed the "appellate docket" because they are paid cases, which require a $300 fee (and another $100 for oral argument, if granted). Most of the remaining three-quarters of the filings go on the miscellaneous docket, which includes unpaid cases or *informa pauperis* petitions (IFPs) because they come from indigents for which the filing fee is waived. A handful of cases come on original jurisdiction and these proceedings make up the rest of the court's annual caseload; they are usually heard by a special master or attorney appointed by the court to make recommendations on it should be decided. In the 2005–2006 term, the court's docket consisted of 2,025 paid cases, 7,775 IFPs, and four original cases, for a total of 9,608 filings. Notably, only a fraction of all petitions were given plenary consideration: Only eighty-three cases were decided by written opinion.

Cases come to the court in basically three ways: as a writ for certification, as a mandatory appeal, or as a petition for a writ of *certiorari*. A writ of certification is reserved for the unusual situation where a lower federal court asks the court to clarify a legal issue; very few cases come in this manner. Once but no longer, most cases came as mandatory appeals, which the court had to decide. But as discussed earlier, the court's burgeoning caseload led Congress to pass the Judiciary Act of 1925 and the Judicial Improvements and Access to Justice Act of 1988, legislation that effectively replaced mandatory appeals with petitions for *certiorari*. Although a *cert.*, as it is commonly known, represents nearly ninety-nine percent of the docket, it only operates as a tool to manage the caseload if four of nine Justices vote to grant *cert.* in an informal practice known as "the rule of four." Congress's decision to expand the court's discretionary jurisdiction distinguishes the high bench from other federal courts, and gave it the power to manage its docket in deciding what to decide, in terms of both how many cases are granted and what substantive issues are addressed.[55] As an institutional norm, the court's discretionary jurisdiction enables it to decide only those cases which are nationally significant and have broad legal, social, or political value. Notably, because of changes in the court's membership as well as in certain institutional voting practices, the court in the 1990s reduced substantially the number of cases given full consideration (with briefs and oral argument).[56] About twenty-five years ago, the court routinely confronted about 5,000 cases on its docket, and the court decided between 150 and 180 cases, about three percent of those filings. Today, the docket is considerably larger, but the court gives plenary consideration to only about eighty cases per year, less than one percent of its docket.

The court is a collegial institution, and its decisional processes are a function of tradition, norms, and formal legal practices. Much of what the court does is conducted behind closed doors. Its term begins on the first Monday of October and usually ends in late June. From October to April, the court hears oral arguments on the cases it accepts for review, but in May and June none are scheduled. During the months oral arguments are held, the court meets in conferences on Wednesdays and Fridays to discuss new filings and to deliberate on cases that were orally argued. In May and June, conferences are held on Thursdays. Throughout the term, on "opinion days" (which by tradition are not announced in advance), the justices assemble in the courtroom to communicate their decisions in front of the media and interested members of the bar and public.[57]

In the summer preceeding the beginning of a new term, the justices' law clerks undergo a training session and begin the process of screening *certiorari* petitions that flood the court throughout the year. Since 1972, except for Justice John Paul Stevens the justices have had their clerks combine their efforts in a *cert. pool* in the screening process. In addition to *cert. pool*, the justices have adopted other conventions to help manage the caseload. Before a new term, for example, the justices meet in a one to two day preterm conference to clear the 2,000 or so cases that have come in from the past term. The preterm conference is significant because about one-fourth of the docket is eliminated before the new session begins and, of those cases, four-fifths are screened out by law clerks and never evaluated by the justices.[58]

Once the justices grant cases, they hear oral arguments from the litigants, who are referred to as the *petitioner* (the party bringing the appeal) and the *respondent* (the party defending against the appeal). Upon request, an interested nonparty may present their views in *amicus curiae* ("friend of the court") briefs. Although they appear in all kinds of Supreme Court litigation, in highly visible cases, such as abortion, school prayer, or affirmative action appeals, *amicus* briefs are routinely used as a strategic device to advocate a special interest groups' policy position. After *cert.* is granted, litigants and third party *amicus* interests may engage the justices further if the court schedules oral argument. As in the federal courts of appeals, oral argument is the most publicly visible action of the court, and it is the only chance—typically thirty minutes per side—for litigants to persuade the justices directly on the case's merits. As Chief Justice William Rehnquist put it, "there is more to oral argument than meets the eye—or ear" and, in a "significant minority of cases," he said he "left the bench feeling different about the case than [he] did when he came on the bench."[59]

After oral argument, the justices meet in conference to screen *cert.* petitions and to consider the merits of the small number of cases given oral argument. Two lists are used to structure deliberations—the Discuss List (or Special List I) and Special List II (formerly called the Dead List). The size of the court's contemporary docket has made conferences into largely symbolic and nondeliberative meetings that are used to deny most petitions. For those cases granted review, a tentative consensus about their outcome is readied at conference. But it is not uncommon for justices to change their votes after hearing oral arguments and voting in conference.

Traditionally, after conference, if in the majority the chief justice assigns a justice to write the opinion for the court. If the chief justice is not in the majority, then the task falls to the most senior associate justice. Once an assignment is made, the justices' law clerks help prepare an initial draft that is then circulated among the justices for revision. The process of circulating opinions is dynamic and interactive. In the twentieth century, justices have increasingly issued concurring opinions

In Comparative Perspective

Courts in South and Southeast Asia

In contrast to the systems of judicial federal in Australia, Canada, the United States, and some other countries, the judiciaries in South and Southeast Asia are all unitary systems, though Pakistan is a federal state it, like some other countries, also has separate religious courts for disputes over Islamic law. With the exception of Singapore, all are economically developing countries and, as a result, courts confront serious problems stemming from inadequate salaries, facilities, and other resources for caseload management. Virtually all confront backlogs of cases in both high and lower courts. In addition, most of these countries are ethnically and culturally diverse and bear some legacy of colonialism.

Courts in South and Southeast Asia revolve around basically three systems: national judicial career systems; career judiciaries that are part of the national civil service system; and mixed or noncareer judiciaries, in which political parties exercise extraordinary influence over judges.

SEPARATE INDEPENDENT JUDICIAL CAREER SYSTEMS

Pakistan, Thailand, and the Philippines have separate judicial career systems, modeled along the lines of those in Japan and in western Europe. Yet, each is different. Despite a common law tradition, Pakistan remains ideologically conflicted. The 1999 coup by General Parvez Musharraf was the third time in fifty years that the military overthrew a democratically elected government. With each coup, the judiciary has come under extreme pressures. By contrast, Thailand's legal system is rooted in a combination of customary law, Buddhism, and the ancient Hindu jurisprudence of the Code of Manu. Not until the nineteenth century was the continental civil law system adopted, along with elements of the common law tradition.

Pakistan

Pakistan has a system of superior and subordinate courts combined with a third tier of special courts and administrative tribunals. The superior judiciary includes the Supreme Court, composed of the chief justice and sixteen justices; four high courts for different provinces with between six and fifty judges; and a federal Shariat court for Islamic disputes. The subordinate courts are civil and criminal district (trial) courts. Special sessions courts, along with high courts, deal with banking controversies, and quasi-judicial tribunals handle other specialized matters such as tax disputes.

Judicial appointments in Pakistan are made after a combination of civil service examinations, conducted by the Public Service Commission, followed by interviews by panels of senior high court judges for the appointments of subordinate judges. District judges may either be promoted from positions as civil judges or magistrates or from the practicing bar after ten years of experience. For superior courts—the regional high (appeals) courts and the Supreme Court—appointments are made from senior judges and lawyers by the president on the basis of consultations with the chief justice and the regional government in which an appointment is filled. These judges may be drawn from district courts or from the practicing bar if they are at least forty-five years old.

Historically, there have been reoccurring power struggles between the executive and the Supreme Court. In 1996, the Supreme Court of Pakistan issued an extraordinary decision in the "Judges' Case," *Al-Jehad Trust v. Federation of Pakistan*, (PLD 1996 SC 324). The ruling held that ad hoc judges could not be named to the court instead of filling permanent positions; acting chief justices could be appointed for a maximum of ninety days; and the senior-most judge of a high court should be appointed as chief justice, unless there were persuasive reasons for not doing so. Most important, the constitutional provision authorizing executive appointment of judges "after consultation" with the chief justice was interpreted to mean that the latter's recommendations are binding on the executive.

Tensions between the judiciary and the government again erupted over the appointment of Chief Justice Sajjad Ali Shah in 1997, and ten justices of the Supreme Court ruled that his appointment was illegal; he was forced to go on leave and subsequently retired in 1998. The following year, General Parvez Musharraf led a coup and in turn required judges to swear an oath of loyalty. Several justices refused, but in 2000 the Supreme Court upheld the imposition of military rule.

Thailand

Under Thailand's 1993 Constitution, there is a separate constitutional court, a Supreme Court, a court of appeals, and over 100 trial courts in cities and provinces along with nine provincial juvenile courts. There are also special courts with limited jurisdiction for labor, child and family, bankruptcy, and international trade disputes. Thailand has a career judicial system, except for its constitutional court. Its fifteen-member constitutional court is the sole judicial body empowered to exercise judicial review but only over laws passed by the legislature not regulations issued by the executive branch.

Five of the judges on the constitutional court are appointed on the basis of election by the Supreme Court, and two are appointed on the basis election by the administrative court. All other judges are appointed by the Senate on the recommendation of the Judicial Service Commission (JSC), which monitors written and oral examinations. The JSC is chaired by the chief justice of the Supreme Court and includes twelve others elected by law school deans, political scientists, and political parties.

Judicial candidates must be at least twenty-five years old and hold a BA in law. If they pass the examination, they are admitted to a one-internship. As civil servants, judges serve on the bench until they reach the mandatory retirement age of sixty; however, they may be reappointed to two five-year terms and serve until age seventy. Despite having a civil service judiciary, its codes of conduct are infrequently enforced and the bar association remains weak. As a result, the Thai judiciary faces serious problems in not only recruiting qualified people but also because it is considered (along with the judiciaries in Bangladesh, the Philippines, and Indonesia) one of the most corrupt in Asia.

The Philippines

The Philippines judiciary includes the Supreme Court, composed of fifteen justices, and a court of appeals, which sits in separate regional divisions and consists in a presiding justice and fifty-two associate judges. Below these courts are thirteen metropolitan and municipal trial courts; there is also a separate tax court and tribunals for family, commercial, and Shariah (Islamic) law. In total, there are 2,221 sitting judges.

The Philippines's 1993 Constitution vests the power in the president to appoint judges. In practice, since 1986 the Judicial & Bar Council has recommended nominees for judgeships, from which the president makes appointments. The Judicial & Bar Council includes the chief justice, the secretary of justice, a representative of Congress, a member of the Philippines Bar Association, a law professor, a retired justice, and a representative of the private sector. Still, the president and the legislature exercise considerable influence over judicial appointments because the president retains final authority over appointing judges, and the legislature approves the composition of the Judicial & Bar Council.

JUDICIAL CAREER SYSTEMS THAT ARE PART OF THE CIVIL SERVICE SYSTEM

Countries that include judgeships within their larger national civil service systems are Bangladesh, Nepal, Singapore, and Indonesia. Despite that commonality, there are differences.

Bangladesh

Since becoming an independent state in 1971, Bangladesh has a two-tier judicial system, along with special criminal and civil courts. The Supreme Court is at the apex but works by appellate divisions that include approximately fifty judges. It hears appeals from the appellate division with a full bench of seven judges hearing important matters. Below are district courts and magistrate courts. Other courts include (1) courts to try public servants; (2) a tribunal for crimes against women and children; (3) courts with jurisdiction over administrative, bankruptcy, environmental, labor, and family disputes; and (4) juvenile courts. There are also separate civil courts for family, labor, and environmental disputes, along with minor courts for rent control disputes, small claims, and village courts.

Bangladesh uses a slightly different appointment system for Supreme Court justices, the judges on subordinate courts. The former are appointed by the president, whereas the latter are named by the president upon the recommendation of the chief justice from the pool of higher and lower court judges.

The career path for the 746 subordinate lower court judges in sixty-one district courts and magistrates begins with passing an examination given by the Public Service Commission after completing an undergraduate BA in law. Approximately 100,000 graduates compete for the 600 to 1,000 annual vacancies. Assistant judges are recruited through this process by the Ministry of Justice, which in turn makes recommendations for their appointment to the Supreme Court, which generally acts accordingly.

However, in a historic decision the Bangladesh Supreme Court Appellate Division held in 1999 that a constitutional amendment was not necessary for ensuring the independence of the judiciary in a case brought by 200 lower court judges, who argued that they should be independent of the national civil service system. Moreover, the Court issued twelve directives that, when implemented, might strengthen the independence of the judiciary. Among the directives, the government was directed to provide a separate budget for the Supreme Court, which it has done. The government was also directed to separate the recruitment of judges from the Bangladesh civil service and to establish a Judicial Service Commission (JSC) for the appointment of judges. Although the government has yet to fully implement all of the directives, the media and bar association have promoted public debate over the importance of a separate independent judiciary removed from the national civil service system.

Nepal

Nepal's 1990 Constitution, the fifth since 1948, established a constitutional monarchy in which the king exercises power only formally, sharing power with a bicameral parliament and the prime minister appointed from the strongest party in the House of Representatives.

Nepal has one Supreme Court with jurisdiction over matters referred to it by the king's council, constitutional amendments, and civil and criminal appeals from appellate courts, an election tribunal, a labor court, an administrative court, a revenue tribunal, and a special court for corruption cases and cases involving terrorism and drug trafficking. There are sixteen courts of appeal with jurisdiction over civil and criminal appeals of decisions rendered by seventy-five district courts.

Nepal combines a judicial career and civil service system in ways that, on the one hand, minimize the external influences of the executive and legislature over judicial recruitment and, on the other hand, promote the institutional autonomy of the judiciary. Moreover, Nepal has a so-called Coordination Committee for recruiting both career and noncareer judges, thereby providing opportunities for divergent views on the bench.

In general, judicial appointments to regular courts are made by the King based on recommendations of the Judicial Council. The Judicial Council is composed of the chief justice, the Minister of Justice, two senior Supreme Court justices, and a jurist named by the King. Since 1990 the practice has been to elevate the senior associate justice to the chief justiceship. Appointees to administrative, labor, tax, and special courts are appointed by the government from regular appellate court judges, senior lawyers, experienced administrators, and tax experts.

Regular lower court judges are appointed by the Judicial Council and must have passed a judicial service test administered by the Civil Service Commission (CSC). The CSC recommends nominees to the government, which prepares a list of candidates for judicial service, subject to approval by the chief justice. The Judicial Council also makes recommendations for the appellate bench and typically solicits recommendations from the Nepal bar association, which actively monitors appointments and promotions. For appointments to appellate courts and the Supreme Court, the Judicial Council works with a Coordination Committee in order to achieve a mix of career and non-career judges on the high courts.

Singapore

After Singapore gained independence from the British Empire it retained the Judicial Committee of the Privy Council as its court of final appeal until 1994. Singapore's judges are among the highest paid not only in Asia but in the world, and its judiciary is considered one of the most reliable.

Singapore has a constitutional tribunal that decides constitutional matters, but it sits apart from the Supreme Court, high court, and court of appeals. Below these courts are subordinate courts with specialized jurisdiction. They include civil and criminal courts, juvenile and family courts, coroner's courts, and small claims courts. Singapore has a mixed career judicial appointment system. The president, on the recommendation of the prime minister, appoints the chief justice and other members of the Supreme Court, court of appeals judges, and "judicial commissioners"—members of the Supreme Court who have only limited terms but who may receive a full term appointment. These judges and justices tend to be recruited from the attorney general's office; very few come directly from private legal practice.

Recruitment for the subordinate courts is done by the Singapore Legal Service, composed of the chief justice, the attorney general, the chair of the Civil Service Commission, another member of the Supreme Court, and two additional members of the Civil Service Commission. Because subordinate judges serve limited terms and are frequently transferred to other positions within Singapore's legal services, judges enjoy little prestige apart from being civil servants.

Indonesia

Indonesia has a consolidated judicial system. Under its Supreme Court, which includes fifty-one justices and works by divisions, there are four sets of courts with different jurisdictions: (1) regular courts, composed of twenty-six appeals courts and 326 trial courts with general civil and criminal jurisdiction; (2) 305 courts with jurisdiction over religious matters; (3) military courts; and (4) courts with limited jurisdiction over disputes with the government and administrative agencies.

Judges are civil servants subject to selection, appointment, transfers, and promotion by the Ministry of Justice. However, in 2004 responsibility for judicial recruitment transferred to the Supreme Court. Still, the approximately 200 annual new judicial recruits continue to be selected by the Ministry of Justice after they have earned a BA from a law school. They must then pass written and oral examinations before admission into a one-year program at the Ministry of Justice Education and Training Center. Upon graduation, they are assigned to a district court for more training before becoming government employees as judges and beginning their judicial careers. They must retire at age fifty-five, unless they are promoted to a high court or to the Supreme Court, in which case they may retire at ages sixty and sixty-five, respectively.

PARTY-DOMINATED JUDICIAL SYSTEMS

Courts in Southeast Asia bear the imprint of the continental civil law tradition, they are combined with traditional legal cultures and socialist legal influences. Cambodia shares with Vietnam the influence of French colonialism. From 1863 to 1953, Cambodia was a French colony and French law structured its legal system. That system was destroyed during the reign of the Khmer Rouge in the late 1970s. In 1980, Vietnam reintroduced the French system along with socialist legal concepts. But the 1993 Constitution created a constitutional monarchy and ostensibly adopted the principle of separation of powers. Like Vietnam and Cambodia, before its independence in 1975 the Lao People's Democratic Republic had a judicial system modeled on that in France. Afterward, socialist legal elements were introduced. In Vietnam, the rule of law was never strong and a Confucian-inspired moral system was the guiding force. The struggle for independence from French colonialism brought the introduction of Marxist-Leninist, Chinese, and later Soviet communist legal elements.

Judges in these countries are appointed for very short (usually five-year) terms, with no employment security. They are paid very low salaries and have inadequate court facilities. They also are subject to extensive oversight by local and national party officials. Cambodia has only 249 registered members in its national bar association for a country of eleven million.

Cambodia

Unlike Lao and Vietnam, Cambodia has a separate constitutional court. Below it is the Supreme Court, an appellate court; and eighteen provincial courts, two municipal courts, and a military court. There are only 139 judges, of which less than one-half have law degrees.

Cambodian judges are formally appointed by the king in accord with recommendations of the Supreme Council of Magistracy and the Ministry of Justice. But, in practice, appointments are made on the basis of brokered deals among the leading three political parties. There are no clear established rules for judicial selection. Unlike some other judiciaries, the Supreme Court has little influence over the appointment of lower court judges.

In 2002, the prime minister issued a decree establishing a Magistrates School and laying down minimal qualifications for judicial applicants. Under the new guidelines, individuals may apply for judicial positions if they have an undergraduate law degree and are at least twenty-one years old but not older than thirty, or if they have a postgraduate degree and are fewer than thirty-eight years old. In short, the judiciary has low prestige because of low salaries, inadequate facilities, and a reputation for being ineffective, corrupt, and subject to reprisals from party officials.

Lao People's Democratic Republic

Lao has a three-tier system with the Supreme Court at the apex, three regional appellate courts, and trial courts in provinces and municipalities. There are also special military courts. Judges are civil servants but do not undergo special legal training, except for a one-year internship. There are 194 judges in the country, with nine on the supreme court, ninety-five provincial court Judges, and ninety district court judges.

Since 1993, the Ministry of Justice has appointed either practitioners or new law school graduates from the one law school in Vientiane for a one-year period of on-the-job-training in local district courts. The president of the constitutional court then evaluates them and, with the consent of the provincial authority and counterparts in the Lao Revolutionary Party at the provincial and district levels, recommends to the

Ministry of Justice their appointment as "provisional judges" before their actual appointment by the Standing Committee of the National Assembly.

Although judges are civil servants, a single political party governs all branches of government, including the judiciary. The Lao People's Revolutionary Party parallels all levels of the governmental structure, from the top down to the local "grass roots" level. Party committees monitor, and ultimately control, judges and other civil servants. In short, the Lao judiciary is subject to not only hierarchical controls and oversight within the government, but also external party pressures at regional and local levels of governance, as are judges in Cambodia and Vietnam.

Vietnam

Vietnamese courts are under the supervision of the National Assembly and the Communist Party. There is a three-tiered system of courts: the Supreme People's Court, sixty-one people's courts at the provincial level, and 620 people's courts at the district level. Since 1994, there has also been a court with limited jurisdiction over economic disputes, two other specialized courts for administrative and labor disputes, as well as a military court. The Supreme People's Court and provincial courts work by divisions for criminal, civil, economic, labor, and administrative matters.

In 2002, Vietnam undertook judicial reforms that will provide detailed guidelines for the appointment of judges. Under guidelines laid down in the Court Organization Law of 1993, judges must have a law degree and demonstrate a "judicial capacity of resolving cases" as well as four years of legal experience for appointment as a district judge, six years for appointment as a provincial judge, and at least eight years of legal experience to qualify for an appointment to the Supreme Court. Because of the lack of trained people, most judges have been selected from the military and local leaders in the Communist Party.

Vietnamese judges are subject to close internal and external supervision. The president appoints the chief justice of the Supreme People's Court and the other justices of the high court, but only with the agreement of the chief justice and the Central Committee on Judicial Selection (CJS) of the National Assembly. Lower court judges are appointed by the chief justice upon the CJS's recommendation after consulting the party committee responsible for monitoring the court on which a vacancy is filled. Likewise, promotions, transfers, and salaries are determined by the chief justice and the chief judge of a local court in consultation with the local party committee.

Source: See David M. O'Brien, "The Politics of Judicial Selection and Appointments in Japan and Ten South and Southeastern Asian Countries," in Kate Melleson and Peter Russell, eds., *Appointing Judges in an Age of Judicial Power* (Toronto: University of Toronto Press, 2006); Paula Newberg, *Judging the State: Courts and Constitutional Politics in Pakistan* (Cambridge: Cambridge University Press, 1995); Hamid Khan, *Constitutional and Political History of Pakistan* (New York: Oxford University Press, 2001); Andres Narvasa, Jr., *Judicial Power in the Philippines* (Manila: Supreme Court of the Philippines, 1997); Kevin Tan, ed., *The Singapore Legal System* (Singapore: Singapore University Press, 2nd ed., 1999); and, generally, Herbert Kritzer, ed., *Legal Systems of the World* (Santa Barbara: ABC-CLIO, 2002).

(agreeing with the result but not the majority's rationale) and dissenting opinions (disagreeing with the result and the majority's rationale). As a result, more individual opinions are issued than institutional opinions for the court's decisions.

THE POLITICS OF JUDICIAL ADMINISTRATION

Solving legal problems is complex, time consuming, and bureaucratic. Even entering a courthouse often means passing through a metal detector that is used by security officers to maintain public safety. Lawsuits are filed in the clerk of court's office, where legal papers are checked to ensure that they comply with the law and the court's rules of procedure, before they are stamped with the date and entered into the court's computer system. Courts also make available a law library for research. In the courtroom, trials are held. A judge presides, sometimes with a jury, and is assisted by a number of law clerks and staff. There is also a court reporter who transcribes the proceedings for the official record and a bailiff who tends to the jury's needs and ensures that there are no disruptions.

Once a lawsuit is filed, the clerk of court typically enters it into a computerized caseload management system that informs attorneys about the status of the case, from the beginning of the lawsuit to the final judgment. In many cases, central staff attorneys assist the judge with motions and researching the applicable law. In criminal cases, the defendant may meet with a bail bondsman, the prosecutor, and a public defender if he or she cannot afford to hire an attorney. Later, if convicted there may be meetings with probation officers, drug counselors, or mental health professionals. In civil cases, the court may have a division that encourages arbitration or mediation instead of a time consuming and costly trial because of the high rate and cost of litigation.

All of a court's resources—its building, courtroom, computers, library, staff offices, judges' chambers, and the court's security system—must be adequately funded and managed in order for the judicial process to function efficiently and effectively. Because the judiciary is an integral part of the political system, judges must interact with the legislatures and executives to secure appropriations, obtain judicial staffing, and procure new technologies. They also exercise inherent authority to make rules of procedure. In addition, as representatives of the third branch government, higher court and senior court judges oversee the activities of lawyers and other colleagues when they need to be disciplined or sanctioned for unprofessional conduct. In sum, judges are more than dispute settlers and decision makers. They must assume the management of courts and deal with other political branches and public organizations.

The rest of this chapter examines the evolution of judicial administration and the rise of what some term "bureaucratic justice."[60] Since the 1960s, burgeoning caseloads have transformed the ideal model of justice—in which litigants receive their "day" in court—into a delay-ridden process that forces courts to rely upon administrative solutions to cope with rising dockets. Bureaucratic justice has important consequences because the quality of the justice may be diminished as judges delegate their responsibilities to subordinate staff attorneys, law clerks, and administrative personnel, and accordingly spend less time on cases. The specter of rising caseloads and limited judicial resources has also prompted courts to seek political solutions to the problems posed by bureaucratic justice. After exploring the history of state judicial administration, the evolution of the federal judicial bureaucracy is considered. The chapter concludes by considering how courts respond to the political challenges they face in delivering justice in the twenty-first century.

State Court Administration

The history of state court administration is one of a series of intermittent reform movements, aiming to integrate court operations and to assert judicial autonomy from other political branches. In the nineteenth century, court reform centered on changing methods of judicial selection (as discussed in chapter 4). The Industrial Revolution led to an enormous growth in cities, businesses, and litigation. As a result, in the twentieth century demands on the nation's courts grew exponentially, but reforms were slow, uneven, often overridden by parochialism, and compounded by the decentralization of fifty independent state judiciaries.

In historical perspective, state courts functioned as loose decentralized networks. Because most judges were elected, they had considerable influence over court dispositions, and yet they were often beholden to the local community. Indeed, local attorneys often showed more leadership than did judges in managing court schedules and dockets, in part because judges were not trained no managers and typically took a dim view of caseload management. In addition, the local bar association was generally beyond reproach, and there were few if any mechanisms for promoting judicial accountability. As a result of the growing backlog of cases at the outset of the twentieth century, judicial reformers pushed to make courts more democratically accountable and to address the problems of court congestion, corruption, the lack of administration and to improve the professionalism of judges and lawyers.[61]

Roscoe Pound, the former dean of Harvard Law School, was one of the most prominent leaders of judicial reform. In a 1906 speech, "The Causes of Popular Dissatisfaction with the Administration of Justice," he urged procedural simplification of the legal process and structural changes in the courts. Pound thought it was possible to consolidate trial courts and to streamline operations. Pound's call for reform led to the founding of the American Judicature Society, which continues to promote judicial reforms and the administration of justice. Pound's speech also led to the creation of a Board of Circuit Judges in Wisconsin in 1913, the first organization to give judges the power to centralize management. Identical initiatives were commenced under the leadership of the president of the American Bar Association, Arthur T. Vanderbilt, and Judge John Parker, who jointly advocated in 1938 the adoption of resolutions giving courts the power to make rules, compile statistical records, and assign judges to cases in order to better administer justice. At least thirty states created judicial councils, but the movement died out in the 1940s because of a lack of funding. Notably, though, in 1949 the Conference of Chief Justices was founded as a forum for all of the states' chief justices to discuss policies for improving judicial administration.[62]

The creation of judicial councils and other reforms in the first half of the twentieth century led in the 1950s to a court unification reform movement. Although one goal was the consolidation of lower courts into a more unified structure, the movement also broadly addressed ways to improve judicial discipline, judicial education, court management, and budgetary control. Many states modified the process for punishing judicial misconduct by creating judicial disciplinary commissions instead of relying upon traditional procedures of impeachment and electoral recall.

Another important change was the founding of the National Judicial College in Reno, Nevada in 1964. It challenged the existing practice of allowing judges to go on the bench without any formal education (beyond a law degree) by giving them the benefit of some "on the job" experience. Although these reforms were milestones in the improvement of judicial administration, it was not until the 1970s that significant progress was made in achieving better court management. At the urging of Chief Justice Warren Burger, the Institute for Court Management (ICM) in 1970 and the National Center for State Courts (NCSC) in 1971 were created. Whereas the ICM (which was later merged into the NCSC) instituted a program to train and certify court managers, the NCSC quickly established itself as an invaluable research center for state courts. As a result, many states now use nonlegal administrators to manage the nonadjudicative functions of courts, including personnel management, accounting, and the application of new technologies. In addition, many states have worked toward budgetary unification of the financing of trial courts and appellate courts together. At least twenty-nine states are primarily state-funded, although several others remain fiscally dependent at the county or local level of government.

Although each state assigns to the highest court the responsibility for rule making, supervising attorney admissions, imposing discipline, and maintaining external relations with other branches and the public, the Conference of Chief Justices assists with setting the policy agenda for all the states. The National Center for State Courts provides logistical research support and services. Furthermore, every state centralizes judicial operations in order to manage filings and cases, either at the state or local (trial) level. Although in the majority of states the chief justice of the court of last resort acts as chief executive officer for the judiciary, some states use judicial councils, where other members of the judiciary sit on committees that establish policy, practices, and rules. A common format for governance is what Robert Tobin calls a "modified executive model," an arrangement that allows the chief justice to remain in charge of administration but also permits the state court administrator to use delegated authority to run court operations and to implement, to the extent possible, established judicial priorities.[63]

See Figure 3.6 which depicts the organization of judicial administration in the United States.

FIGURE 3.6 **The Organization of Judicial Administration in the United States.**

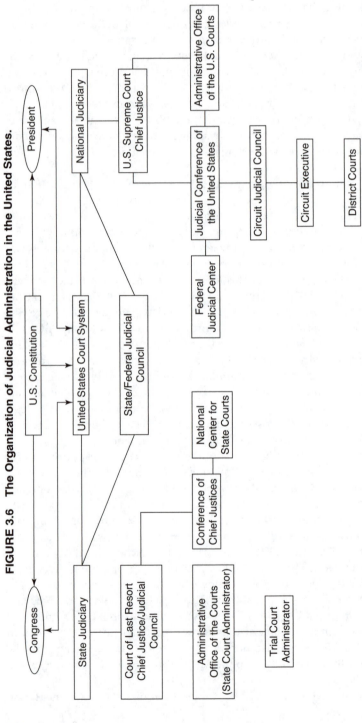

Source: Russell Wheeler, "The Administration of the Federal Courts: Understanding the Entities and Interrelationships That Make Federal Courts Work," in *The Improvement of the Administration of Justice,* 7th ed. (Chicago: Judicial Division, American Bar Association, 2001); Judicial Conference of the United States, *Long Range Plan for the Federal Courts* (December, 1995); Robert W. Tobin, *Creating the Judicial Branch: The Unfinished Reform* (Williamsburg: National Center for State Courts, 1999); Peter Graham Fish, *The Politics of Federal Judicial Administration* (Princeton: Princeton University Press, 1973).

The Administration of the Federal Judiciary

Improvements in the administration of the federal judiciary in the twentieth century occurred at roughly the same time as the judiciary in the states. Even though the basic three-tiered hierarchy of the federal judiciary was established by the end of the nineteenth century, there were a number of obstacles to managing federal courts. For example, in diversity cases Congress required federal courts to use the procedural rules as that which occurred in the states. The lack of uniform rules fostered decentralization but thwarted the development of consistent legal practices across the circuits. Moreover, the Department of Justice had statutory authority that made it the *de facto* administrator of the federal judiciary. As a result, all U.S. marshals, deputies, and attorneys, who are appointed by the president and confirmed by the Senate but under the control of the attorney general, performed a wide range of administrative services for federal courts, including executing judgments, providing courtroom space, securing utilities and supplies, and disbursing funds appropriated for the federal courts.

In addition, the federal courts generally struggled with the problems of congested caseloads. In response, Chief Justice William Howard Taft (1921–1930) initiated a number of reforms. Besides persuading Congress to enact the Judiciary Act of 1925, which expanded the court's discretionary jurisdiction and power to mange its docket, Chief Justice Taft secured funding for building the court's own courthouse on 1 First Street, directly across from the Capitol; it was completed in 1935, shortly after his death. At Taft's request, Congress also instituted the Conference of Circuit Senior Judges in 1922, an organization that permits the chief justice, in conjunction with the chief judges in the circuits, to confer annually and to assign district court judges in the circuits. The conference, whose name was changed to the Judicial Conference of the United States in 1948, was a key step toward improving judicial governance because it respected the local autonomy of district and appellate courts but encouraged coordination among the circuits. The conference, too, assumed greater significance in 1939 when Congress created the Administrative Office of U.S. Courts and transferred budgetary control and judicial statistics' preparation from the Department of Justice to it. That legislation also created circuit judicial councils in order to supervise the docket management of district courts and to act as a clearinghouse between the Judicial Conference and the circuits with respect to setting administrative and legislative priorities.[64]

A major consequence of these and other innovations was to move the federal courts away from the direct administrative control of the executive branch. Congress also gave the Supreme Court the power to promulgate the Federal Rules of Civil Procedure in 1938, which now governs the basic litigation practices in the federal judiciary. Notably, as political scientist Peter Fish observed, the ability to wrest some of the key aspects of judicial administration—rule making, budgetary control, and judicial assignments—away from the executive branch was, in part, a political response to the challenge posed to the federal courts when President Franklin D. Roosevelt's court-packing plan unsuccessfully tried to end the

Supreme Court's nullification of New Deal legislation. That plan would have added one justice for every one over the age of seventy so that the court's membership would have increased to fifteen, thereby giving F. D. R. the opportunity to name new justices who favored his economic agenda. Although the president lost his bid to rein in the Court, opposition to the plan galvanized efforts within the legal profession to increase judicial autonomy and to improve judicial operations.

A similar impetus occurred in 1969 with Congress's creation of the Federal Judicial Center (FJC), an influential source of research and training for federal court judges and judicial personnel. President Lyndon B. Johnson pushed for its creation because he believed the federal courts needed additional resources for handling rising caseloads due to the expanding size of the national government, litigation brought by the civil rights movement, and the large number of criminal law decisions handed down by the Warren Court (1953-1969) during its "due process revolution."

As in the states, the management of federal judicial operations is overseen the highest judicial officer, the chief justice of the United States. The chief justice has a crucial role in overseeing federal judicial policy, the Judicial Conference of the United States, and the Administrative Office of U.S. Courts. For its part, the Judicial Conference consists of chief judges from the courts of appeals and the Court of International Trade plus one district judge from each of the circuits. They serve for limited terms and work through committees. It meets twice a year to discuss appropriation requests to Congress, amendments to rules of procedure, the impact of proposed legislation affecting the judiciary, the assignment of judges, and miscellaneous personnel issues (such as matters of judicial disability and misconduct). As the national policymaker for the federal courts, the Judicial Conference supervises the activities of the Administrative Office, which prepares the judiciary's budget request, implements personnel compensation plans, and compiles judicial statistics.

Within the federal judicial system, the point of contact for regional and local governance is the circuit judicial councils and the chief judges of the circuits (who play a perfunctory role). The councils' composition and function has changed from their inception in 1939; they originally consisted of only court of appeals judges and primarily monitored the administration of district court business. Through a series of amendments, however, Congress broadened the membership to include an equal number of appellate and district judges. In addition to overseeing the lower courts' docket and, at times, reviewing complaints of judicial misconduct and disability, circuit judicial councils today have authority to ensure that district court operations are conducted expeditiously and to work with circuit executives, an administrative position created by the Circuit Executive Act in 1972. The circuit executive administrator provides secretarial support for the council and assists circuits with their budgets, personnel, physical plant, security, reporting, and external relations.[65]

State–federal judicial councils attempt to link federal court operations to the states. Originally created in the states as a result of an initiative of Chief Justice

Burger in 1970, their purpose was to address common problems and conflicts from between federal and state courts' operations, such as when the attendance of attorneys, witnesses, or other court personnel are needed in both federal and state courts at the same time. Although there have been numerous conferences and symposia encouraging this kind of intergovernmental judicial cooperation, the promise of the use of state–federal judicial councils has not yet been realized because they only exist in about thirty states.

Finally, two independent entities, the U.S. Sentencing Commission and the Judicial Panel on Multi-District Litigation, perform significant policymaking roles. Created by the Sentencing Reform Act provisions of the Comprehensive Crime Control Act of 1984, the U.S. Sentencing Commission is staffed by seven presidential appointments (including three federal judges). In addition to giving Congress advice on a variety of related administrative functions, the Commission promulgated the Federal Sentencing Guidelines in 1987. The guidelines define the range of sentences that federal judges may impose those convicted of violating federal law. The Judicial Panel on Multi-District Litigation consists of seven district or appeals court judges appointed by the chief justice. Its purpose is to help streamline the adjudication of complex civil cases involving products liability, intellectual property, securities regulation, and antitrust that are filed in multiple federal jurisdictions. A Multiple-District Litigation Panel (MDLP) may order that all the cases brought in different jurisdictions be transferred to a single district for pretrial proceedings, thereby expediting the litigation.

THE POLITICS OF JUDICIAL REFORM IN THE TWENTY-FIRST CENTURY

Both state and federal judicial courts are greatly affected by their relationship to the executive and legislative branches as well as to organized interests, litigants, and the public. Any sustained effort to reform the courts on the basis of improving judicial operations or promoting more democratic accountability are consequently driven by political motives and counter-responses that may compromise judicial independence. In the 2004 presidential election, for example, courts were often at the center of a number of political controversies because the electorate was polarized over public policy issues involving the war on terrorism, gay marriage, affirmative action, and religious freedom. The ruling in *Bush v. Gore* (2000),[66] which stopped the Florida vote recount, highlighted controversies over the role of federal courts. But state courts have also increasingly been at the center of electoral conflicts as evidenced by the continuing controversies over the Vermont supreme court's ruling on civil unions and the 2004 ruling by the Massachusetts supreme court that same-sex marriages may not be discriminated against.

But those are just a couple of the many issues that have polarized the electorate over the rulings of state and federal courts. Moreover, though many controversies over courts are reported by the media, many other battles garner less attention. A few examples are illustrative:

- In 2004, opponents of gay marriage outside the Supreme Court of Massachusetts urged that the best "remedy for a lunatic judiciary" was the removal of four justices who held that same-sex marriages are legal. That same month, President George W. Bush announced his support for a constitutional amendment banning same-sex marriage in order to nullify the decisions of "activist judges."

- In 2004 in the U.S. Senate, a bill titled the "Constitution Restoration Act of 2004" was introduced in order to reinforce "states rights by clarifying that the Supreme Court and district courts do not have jurisdiction to hear cases brought against a federal government or officer for acknowledging God as the sovereign source of law, liberty, or government."

- In 2005, House Judiciary Committee Chairman F. James Sensenbrenner, Jr., (R-Wis.) sent a letter to the chief judge of the U.S. Court of Appeals for the Seventh Circuit demanding that a panel's decision giving a drug offender less prison time than what was required under a mandatory sentencing law be reversed.

- In 2005, in response to the Supreme Court's ruling allowing a city in Connecticut to take residential property and turn it over to a private developer for economic redevelopment, the New Hampshire Libertarian Party began collecting signatures to ask the town to use its power of eminent domain to seize Justice David Souter's home and convert it into a hotel for public use.

These examples demonstrate that courts are subject to a variety of political controls, including (1) public criticism, (2) threats to remove recalcitrant judges by legislative impeachment or recall, (3) threats to change methods of judicial selection (e.g., term limits), (4) the enactment of "court-stripping" legislation restricting a court's jurisdiction to hear or decide certain cases, and (5) the imposition of constitutional amendments curbing judicial self-governance and independence by removing a court's authority to promulgate internal court rules and procedures. These are not the only modes of ensuring control or accountability, however. Other devices include restricting judicial appropriations, salaries, or retirement benefits or, conversely, enacting laws that monitor case management and impose oversight by the evaluation of judicial performance standards.[67]

Courts respond to political challenges in different ways, but most are centered on administrative solutions through external lobbying, internal self-examination, and reform. Sometimes courts enlist the help of outside groups interested in maintaining the integrity of the judicial process. On occasion, groups that are not directly connected to the judicial branch promote judicial reforms and defend judicial independence, as illustrated by the endorsement of the American Bar Association and the American Judicature Society for publicly financed state judicial elections because of the recent sharp increase in the costs of campaigning.

Controversies over Courts

Should the Public Finance State Judicial Elections?

During the last decade, state judicial elections have become increasingly hotly contested and costly. Appellate court judges in eight states face partisan elections. Fifteen states hold nonpartisan judicial elections, and six others conduct partisan contests. Another nineteen states hold retention elections for state judges. Over eighty-seven percent of all state and local judges stand for election in some manner. About 25,000 state judges stand for election, more than all state legislators, governors, and executive offices combined. State supreme court elections have been especially hard fought in Ohio, Michigan, Texas, and increasingly other states as well.

Campaigns for state judicial elections are increasingly expensive. The cost of state supreme court elections in 2000, for instance, totaled $45.6 million, over sixty percent more than in 1998 and double that spent in 1994. In 2002, four candidates for the Ohio state supreme court spent $6.2 million on their campaigns. In addition, four independent interest groups spent $1.83 million on television ads, and another group backed by the Ohio Chamber of Commerce spent another $1 million in support of judicial candidates. In 2004, sixty-three state supreme court justices in twenty-eight states faced reelections.

State judicial campaigns have become most costly because large corporations, such as Home Depot, Wal-Mart, insurance company AIG, the U.S. Chamber of Commerce and the Business Roundtable, as well as conservative groups, like the Law Enforcement Alliance of America (LEAA), have been spending millions of dollars on state judicial elections. A driving force behind the escalating costs and contentiousness of judicial elections has been the election of "business friendly" state judges. But state court judgeships have been targeted by interest groups in retaliation for state supreme court rulings on abortion, raising property taxes, large jury awards, and requiring equal public financing of schools.

In response to the escalating costs and increasingly hard fought campaigns for state judgeships, the American Bar Association (ABA), the American Judicature Society, and numerous other organizations have promoted the public financing of judicial campaigns and state court elections. Chief justices of seventeen state supreme courts have also called for the public financing of judicial elections. And public opinion polls repeatedly find that an overwhelming majority of voters believe that judges give campaign contributors special treatment and support public financing of judicial elections. Although seventy-four percent of the public still favors electing judges, eighty percent also support the public financing of state judicial campaigns.

In particular, the ABA has endorsed principles in support of public financing of state judicial elections, including:

1. Public financing programs must be sensitive to Constitutional limitations on states' power to regulate judicial campaign finance.
2. Public financing programs should be designed to best suit the particular needs of a particular state or territory.

3. Public financing programs are most suitable for primary and general election campaigns of high court judges, and in some cases, intermediate appellate judges.
4. Public financing programs should provide judicial candidates with full public funding in amounts sufficient to encourage participation.
5. Public financing programs should be restricted to serious candidates in contested elections who have met specified criteria indicating a certain level of support.
6. Public financing programs should be conditioned on the candidate's agreement to forego private funding and to limit their use of public funds to legitimate campaign purposes.
7. States and territories should address the impact of independent campaign expenditures and recognize the impact of general issue advocacy on public financing programs.
8. Public financing programs should distribute funds in the form of bloc grants to candidates and should also provide voter guides to the electorate.
9. Public financing programs should be funded from a stable and sufficient revenue source.
10. Public financing programs should be administered by an independent and adequately staffed entity.

Still, fewer than half (twenty-four) of the states provide public financing for state and local judicial elections. And among those, only two, Wisconsin and North Carolina, provide public financing for judicial elections. Wisconsin has the oldest publicly financed judicial election system. Wisconsin supreme court candidates are eligible for $97,000 in state money if they agree to a $215,000 spending limit; but, if one candidate refuses to accept public financing, then the publicly funded candidate is released from the spending cap. However, Wisconsin's system of financing judicial elections, which is paid for through a one dollar check-off contribution on state income tax returns, has been historically underfinanced.

In 2004, North Carolina's Judicial Campaign Reform Act of 2002 went into effect. Under that state law, all appellate-level judicial races are nonpartisan and receive public financing in the general election for qualified candidates who agree to fundraising and spending limits. Unlike Wisconsin's system, North Carolina's system is funded by a combination of income tax check-off contributions and revenues from lawyers' licensing fees. North Carolina's system for financing state court elections is considered a model for reformers nationwide. The public financing of state judicial elections are under consideration as well in a number of other states, including Idaho, Illinois, New York, and Texas.

Source: See Justice at Stake Campaign, The Brennan Center for Justice at New York University School of Law and the National Institute on Money in State Politics, *The New Politics of Judicial Elections* (New York: Justice at Stake Campaign, 2001), available from www.justiceatstake.org; American Bar Association, Standing Committee on Judicial Independence, *Public Financing of Judicial Campaigns* (Chicago: American Bar Association, 2002); and American Judicature Society, available from www.ajs.org/select11.html

The success of courts in repelling political attacks is often determined by their skills in external relations. Court appropriations are a constant political concern because judiciaries must rely to some degree on the legislative and executive budgetary processes for resources and salaries. It is not unusual, for example, for the chief justice of the United States to use the Annual Year-End Report on the State of the Federal Judiciary to lobby Congress and to draw attention to the need to bring federal judicial salaries into line with those in the private sector. Political scientists James Douglas and Roger Hartley found that courts are sometimes subjected to political retribution because legislatures use their fiscal authority as a tool to influence or protest court rulings. In addition, they found that judicial independence is compromised when states face fiscal hardships and state courts are pressured to generate fees to offset budgetary problems. They also discovered that though state judiciaries try to remain "above" politics in dealing with other branches on budgeting issues, judges realize that it is politically necessary to act as lobbyists in order to achieve funding. On rare occasions, courts may even have to resort to self-help, as illustrated by a judge's decision in Cook County, Illinois in 2003 to award to himself, and several other hundred state judges, cost-of-living increases on the grounds that the governor's 2.8 percent increase violated the state constitution's prohibition that judges' salaries may not be diminished during judicial service.[68]

Apart from repelling direct attacks by legislators, courts also use administrative processes to respond. Long range plans, conferences, symposia, and workshops are not only educational, but they help set judicial priorities in dealing with other political branches. In particular, long range plans are vital planning instruments for courts in the new millennium.

Two reports, the *2000 Ohio Courts Futures Commission Report* (OCFCR) and the *1995 Long Range Plan for Federal Courts* (LRPFC), are illustrative. The first was directed by Ohio Supreme Court Chief Justice Thomas J. Moyer and involved a three-year study by a commission of fifty-two citizens, judges, attorneys, and legal experts. Because the Ohio court system had not changed since 1851, the broad charge of the commission was to recommend reform by anticipating the needs of the judiciary over the next quarter century (by 2025). Such a plan was required in light of the state's aging population, increasing cultural diversity, and rapid technological advancements, especially as they affected the rise of alternative dispute resolution forums and reinforced the persistent criticism that Ohio legal system was confusing.

The OCFCR's "vision statements" and "action recommendations for a healthy and effective Ohio court system in the year 2025" included (1) facilitating court access by making courts more accessible to those with disabilities; simplifying courts operations, rules, and procedures; and expanding court hours and staff availability; (2) increasing public understanding and confidence in the judiciary by aggressively educating the public and political leaders in the political system about judicial operations and engaging in more public service in the community; (3) building a technological infrastructure for the judiciary by creating a statewide Court Technology Standards Committee to oversee the technological readiness of individual courts in providing information and legal services to the bar and public; (4) improving the structure, organization, and management of courts by exploring various methods to make courts more responsive to the demands of local communities as well as continuously working to raise state funding for essential court functions such as judicial compensation, the procurement of staff and personnel, equipment, facilities, and supplies; (5) enhancing court rules and processes by requiring that trial courts use an integrated case-flow management process and encouraging judges to become actively involved in docket management; (6) encouraging the use of nonadversarial alternative dispute resolution techniques, such as mediation or arbitration; (7) reforming the jury system to make the legal process more comprehensible and accessible for jurors, thereby increasing their willingness to serve on juries; and, (8) improving the judicial selection process by making it less partisan and devising programs and judicial accountability performance standards in order to ensure that judges are properly trained and qualified for judicial service.[69]

Notably, Ohio's strategy for change mirrors the approach of twenty-seven other states since the 1980s. Common themes include many of the OCFCR's main recommendations, namely to improve court access, encourage the use of alternative dispute methods and specialized courts, increase judicial competency through performance evaluations, facilitate the use of therapeutic justice, modernize the courts through technological upgrading, and earn public confidence and respect.[70] The state reports, furthermore, coincide with a comprehensive effort on the federal level to engage in long term planning.

The *Long Range Plan for the Federal Courts* (LRPFC) presents a bleaker alternative reality: a federal judicial system in "crisis" with clogged dockets, delayed justice, overworked and underpaid judges, and less collegiality and incentives for federal judges. In projecting the state of the federal judiciary in 2020, the LRPFC is similar to state long-range planning reports in emphasizing that courts must improve court access, augment court resources and judicial staff, simplify processes and rules, implement new technologies and streamlining operations, as well as make better efforts to connect with the public through educational programs. Unlike the state reports, though, the LRPFC report does not foresee the need to alter the structure of court organization without exploring other alternatives, though federal judges remain sharply divided over such matters as whether the Ninth Circuit should be split into two circuits.[71]

The long-range planning process in the state and federal courts provides a useful snapshot of the principal challenges judiciaries face in the twenty-first century. On balance, the long-range plans present a first-hand account of how courts see themselves as legal institutions operating within the constraints imposed by a dynamic external political environment. Several themes appear:

■ Courts are reiterating the established policy argument that additional resources are needed (more judges, staff, and funding) in light of increasing caseloads, fiscal uncertainty, and an institutional perception that the nature of litigation has dramatically changed in the past few decades. With more civil statutory actions on the federal level, for example, Congress has agreed to increase court staff, but that decision has enlarged the judicial bureaucracy and raised other concerns about bureaucratic justice, with more law clerks, magistrates, bankruptcy courts, and circuit executives.

■   The ongoing prospect of court delay and inefficiency, when combined with a general hostility by the public toward the legal profession especially since the 1990s, has compelled Congress to exercise more oversight over judicial operations, which in turn creates heightened demands for more judicial accountability in handling their caseload, both in terms of substance and efficiency. Additional oversight may force courts to respond accordingly and lobby for legislation and resources that preserve judicial independence.

■   There is general agreement that managerial judging has emerged in the past thirty years, along with the recognition that procedural rules and alternative dispute resolution techniques are available tools that help courts manage the caseload. These methods require judges to become more proactive during pretrial proceedings in order to exert pressure on litigants to settle the case and ease the caseload. More so than a generation ago, different options exist for bypassing trial and using court-supervised alternatives to trial (i.e., arbitration, mediation, and the like). Thus, few lawsuits today are actually disposed of by formal trial.

■   The application of the Internet and development of related technologies are key aspects of judicial administration.

■   The prevailing litigation environment and an increasing diversity in the nation's ethnic composition requires that courts make good faith efforts to be more open and participatory in dealings with the public.[72]

These developments reinforce the political reality that state and federal courts are complex bureaucracies that require greater flexibility in judging than in the past. At least in part, because of caseload demands and the complexity underlying the litigation process, today's judge cannot be simply a neutral and detached adjudicator. Rather, a judge must be an efficient manager of court resources and, at times, an engaged mediator and problem solver that delegates responsibility well in order to clear congested dockets. Appellate court judges, moreover, must be prepared to adopt a leadership role that is inherently political when lobbying for additional resources in the areas of judicial compensation, retirement benefits, administrative personnel, or new technologies. The next chapter explores some the challenges confronting courts have in performing these new roles within the context of the politics of judicial recruitment, retention, and removal.

SELECTED READINGS

Banks, Christopher P. *Judicial Politics in the D.C. Circuit Court.* Baltimore: John Hopkins University Press, 1999.

Barrow, Deborah J., Gary Zuk, and Gerard S. Gryski. *The Federal Judiciary and Institutional Change.* Ann Arbor: The University of Michigan Press, 1996.

Fish, Peter Graham. *The Politics of Federal Judicial Administration.* Princeton: Princeton University Press, 1973.

Frankfurter, Felix, and James M. Landis. *The Business of the Supreme Court: A Study in the Federal Judicial System.* New York: Macmillian Company, 1928.

Howard, J. Woodford Jr. *Courts of Appeals in the Federal Judicial System: A Study of the Second, Fifth, and District of Columbia Circuits.* Princeton: Princeton University Press, 1981.

Klien, David E. *Making Law in the United States Courts of Appeals.* Cambridge: Cambridge University Press, 2002.

O'Brien, David M. *Storm Center: The Supreme Court in American Politics,* 7th ed. New York: W.W. Norton, 2005.

Posner, Richard A. *The Federal Courts: Challenge and Reform.* Cambridge: Harvard University Press, 1999.

Songer, Donald R., Reginald S. Sheehan, and Susan B. Haire. *Continuity and Change on the United States Courts of Appeals.* Ann Arbor: The University of Michigan Press, 2000.

Stumpf, Harry P., and John H. Culver. *The Politics of State Courts.* New York: Longman, 1991.

Tobin, Robert W. *Creating the Judicial Branch: The Unfinished Reform.* Williamsburg: National Center for State Courts, 1999.

Wheeler, Russell R., and Cynthia Harrison. *Creating the Federal Judicial System,* 2d ed. Washington, DC: Federal Judicial Center, 1994.

NOTES

1. "Prosecutorial Remedies and Other Tools to End the Exploitation of Children Today," Act of 2003, P.L. 108-21, 117 Stat. 650 (2003).
2. *Bush v. Gore,* 531 U.S. 98 (2000).
3. John Gibeaut, "Opening Sentences," *American Bar Association Journal* (March, 2004), 54.
4. *Blakely v. Washington,* 542 U.S. 296 (2004).
5. *United States v. Booker,* 543 U.S. 220 (2005).
6. See generally, *The Improvement of the Administration of Justice,* 7th ed. Edited by Gordon M. Griller and E. Keith Stott, Jr. (Chicago: Lawyers Conference, Judicial Division, American Bar Association, 2002); Robert W. Tobin, *Creating the Judicial Branch: The Unfinished Reform* (Williamsburg: National Center for State Courts, 1999); Deborah J. Barrow, Gary Zuk, and Gerad S. Gryski,

The Federal Judiciary and Institutional Change (Ann Arbor: The University of Michigan Press, 1996).

7. Melvin I. Urofsky and Paul Finkelman, *A March of Liberty: A Constitutional History of the United States, Volume I: From the Founding to 1890,* 2nd ed. (Oxford: Oxford University Press, 2002), 41-58; Kermit L. Hall, *The Magic Mirror: Law in American History* (Oxford: Oxford University Press, 1989), 17-22.

8. G. Alan Tar, *Understanding State Constitutions* (Princeton: Princeton University Press, 1998): 60-93.

9. Sue Davis, *American Political Thought: Four Hundred Years of Ideas and Ideologies* (Englewood Cliffs: Prentice Hall, 1996), 91-93.

10. Letter from James Madison to Thomas Jefferson (October 24, 1787) *The Writings of James Madison*, Edited by Gaillard Hunt (New York: G.P. Putnam's Sons, 1904), 17, 23.

11. Jack N. Rakove, *Original Meanings: Politics and Ideas in the Making of the Constitution* (New York: Vintage Books, 1996), 32.

12. Max Farrand, *The Framing of the Constitution of the United States* (New Haven: Yale University Press, 1967), 119.

13. Farrand, *The Framing of the Constitution of the United States*, 119-21, 156-57; Rakove, *Original Meanings*, 173-77.

14. David M. O'Brien, *Storm Center: The Supreme Court in American Politics,* 7th ed. (New York: W.W. Norton, 2005), 106.

15. *Marbury v. Madison,* 5 U.S. 137 (1803).

16. Akhil Reed Amar, "*Marbury,* Section 13, and the Original Jurisdiction of the Supreme Court," *University of Chicago Law Review* (Spring, 1989), 443-98.

17. Felix Frankfurter and James M. Landis, *The Business of the Supreme Court: A Study in the Federal Judicial System* (New York: Macmillian Company, 1928), 60, 64. President Lincoln's quote is found in Russell R. Wheeler and Cynthia Harrison, *Creating the Federal Judicial System,* 2nd ed. (Washington, D.C.: Federal Judicial Center, 1994), 12.

18. As quoted in Frankfurter and Landis, *The Business of the Supreme Court*, 259 n. 13.

19. Richard A. Posner, *The Federal Courts: Challenge and Reform* (Cambridge: Harvard University Press, 1996), 87-123.

20. *Michigan v. Long,* 463 U.S. 1032 (1983).

21. Tarr, *Understanding State Constitutions*, 161-70; James N.G. Cauthen, "Expanding Rights Under State Constitutions: A Quantitative Appraisal," *Albany Law Review* 63 (2000), 1183-202. See generally Barry Latzer, "The Hidden Conservatism of the State Court "Revolution," *Judicature* 74 (1991), 190; William J. Brennan, Jr., "State Constitutions and the Protection of Individual Rights," *Harvard Law Review* 90 (1977), 489.

22. Ralph N. Kleps, "Reorganization and Simplification of Court Structure," in *The Improvement in the Administration of Justice,* 6th ed. Edited by Fannie J. Klein (Chicago: American Bar Association, 1981), 18, 21.

23. Larry Berkson and Susan Carbon, *Court Unification: History, Politics and Implementation* (Washington, D.C.: National Institute of Law Enforcement and Criminal Justice, Law Enforcement Assistance Administration, U.S. Dept. of Justice, 1978), 87.

24. Kenneth G. Pankey, Jr., Anne E. Skove, with Jennifer R. Sheldon, *Charting a Course to Strategic Thought and Action: Developing Strategic Planning Capacities in State Courts* (Williamsburg: National Center for State Courts, 2002), 26-27, available from www.ncsconline.org (retrieved October 20, 2005).

25. National Center for State Courts, *State Court Caseload Statistics, 2004: Supplement to Examining the Work of State Courts* (Williamsburg: National Center for State Courts, 2005), 8-59.

26. National Center for State Courts, *Examining the Work of State Courts, 2004: A National Perspective from the Court Statistics Project* (Williamsburg: National Center for State Courts, 2005), 14. The number of limited and general jurisdiction courts is discussed in National Center for State Courts. *Examining the Work of State Courts, 2003: A National Perspective from the Court Statistics Project* (Williamsburg: National Center for State Courts, 2004), 11.

27. National Center for State Courts, *Examining the Work of State Courts,* 2004.

28. National Center for State Courts, *State Court Caseload Statistics, 2004*, 7-59 (listing types of general jurisdiction courts across states). See also National Center for State Courts, *Examining the Work of State Courts,* 2003, 11.

29. National Center for State Courts, *Examining the Work of State Courts,* 2004, 14.

30. National Center for State Courts, *Examining the Work of State Courts,* 2004, 15.

31. National Center for State Courts, *Examining the Work of State Courts,* 2004, 64.

32. National Center for State Courts, "A Taxonomy of Appellate Court Organization," in *Caseload Highlights: Examining the Work of State Courts* (Vol. 3, No. 1 July 1997), available at http://ncsconline.org (retrieved January 31, 2004).

33. Harry P. Stumpf and John H. Culver, *The Politics of State Courts* (New York: Longman, 1991), 149. See also National Center for State Courts, *Examining the Work of State Courts,* 2004, 64.

34. National Center for State Courts. *Examining the Work of State Courts, 2002: A National Perspective from the Courts Statistics Project* (Williamsburg: National Center for State Courts, 2003), 74 (reporting on caseload data for 2001).

35. National Center for State Courts, *Examining the Work of State Courts,* 2004, 68.

36. National Center for State Courts, *Examining the Work of State Courts,* 2004, 66.

37. Paul R. Brace and Melinda Gann Hall, "Is Judicial Federalism Essential to Democracy? State Courts in the Federal System," in *The Judicial Branch*, edited by Kermit L. Hall and Kevin T. McGuire (New York: Oxford University Press, 2005), 186-89.

38. National Center for State Courts, *Examining the Work of State Courts, 2004*, 68. See also Brace and Hall, "Is Judicial Federalism Essential to Democracy?", 191.

39. Administrative Office of U.S. Courts, *Table C-2: U.S. District Courts-Civil Cases Commenced, by Basis of Jurisdiction and Nature of Suit, During 12-Month Period Ending March 31, 2005*, available from www.uscourts.gov (retrieved April 16, 2006). The number of district courts and authorized judgeships was obtained from Administrative Office of U.S. Courts, "Authorized Judgeships," available from www.uscourts.gov/history/contents.html (retrieved April 16, 2006).

40. Judicial workload statistics for the federal courts are found in Table 1.1 (Appeals Filed By Type) and Table 4.1 (Combined Civil and Criminal Cases), from the Administrative Office of U.S. Courts, "Judicial Facts and Figures," available from www.uscourts.gov (retrived April 16, 2006). The data for the U.S. Supreme Court was taken from the Final Statistical Worksheet 2004–2005 Term, the Public Information Office of the Supreme Court of the United States (on file with author).

41. Administrative Office of U.S. Courts, *Federal Judicial Caseload Statistics* (March 31, 2005) (Tables C-4 and D-4), available from www.uscourts.gov/ (retrieved April 16, 2006).

42. *Northern Pipeline Construction Company v. Marathon Pipe Line Company*, 458 U.S. 50 (1982).

43. David, S. Kennedy, and R. Spencer Clift III, "An Historical Analysis of Insolvency Laws and their Impact on the Role, Power, and Jurisdiction of Today's United States Bankruptcy Court and its Judicial Officers," *Journal of Bankruptcy Law and Practice* 9 (January/February 2000), 165–200.

44. See CCH, "CCH Bankruptcy Reform Act Briefing: Bankruptcy Abuse Prevention and Consumer Protection Act of 2005" (updated April 21, 2005), available from www.cch.com/bankruptcy/Bankruptcy_04-21.pdf (retrieved December 2, 2005). See also Administrative Office of the U.S. Courts, "New Law Creates Rush to File in Federal Court," *The Third Branch* 11 (November, 2005), 1.

45. James Risen and Eric Lichtblau, "Bush Said to Have Secretly Lifted Some Spying Limits After 9/11," *Chicago Tribune* (December 16, 2005), C30.

46. Judicial Conference of the United States, *Long Range Plan for the Federal Courts* (December, 1995), 43, n. 6; R. Polk Wagner and Lee Petherbridge, "Is the Federal Circuit Succeeding? An Empirical Assessment of Judicial Performance," *University of Pennsylvania Law Review* 152 (2004), 1105–80.

47. See Christopher P. Banks, "Protecting (or Destroying) Freedom through Law: The USA PATRIOT Act's Constitutional Implications," in *American National Security and Civil Liberties in an Era of Terrorism*, edited by David B. Cohen and John W. Wells (New York: Palgrave Macmillan, 2004). The USA Patriot Act is the acronym for "Uniting and Strengthening America By Providing Appropriate

Tools Required to Intercept and Obstruct Terrorism," P.L. 107-56, 115 Stat. 272 (2001). See generally U.S. Court of Appeals for the Federal Circuit Web site, available from www.fedcir.gov/; U.S. Court of Appeals for the Armed Forces Web site, available from www.uscfc.uscourts.gov/index.html; U.S. Court of Appeals for the Armed Services, available from www.armfor.uscourts.gov/; U.S. Tax Court Web site, available from www.ustaxcourt.gov/; information about the Foreign Intelligence Surveillance Court of Review was gathered from the Federal Judicial Center Web site, available from www.fjc.gov/, Foreign Intelligence Surveillance Act ,92 Stat. 1783, (1978) and the USA PATRIOT Act, 115 Stat. 272 (2001).

48. J. Woodford Howard, Jr., *Courts of Appeals in the Federal Judicial System: A Study of the Second, Fifth, and District of Columbia Circuits* (Princeton: Princeton University Press, 1981), 8. See generally Donald R. Songer, Reginald S. Sheehan, Susan B. Haire, *Continuity and Change on the United States Courts of Appeals* (Ann Arbor: University of Michigan Press, 2000); David E. Klein, *Making Law in the United States Courts of Appeals* (Cambridge: Cambridge University Press, 2002).

49. Posner, *The Federal Courts*, 160-63.

50. Tony Mauro, "Judicial Conference Supports Citing Unpublished Opinions," *Legal Times* (September 21, 2005).

51. Administrative Office U.S. Courts, "Judicial Facts and Figures" (Table 1.1), available from www.uscourts.gov (retrieved October 25, 2005).

52. Christopher P. Banks, "The Politics of *En Banc* Review in the 'Mini-Supreme Court,'" *Journal of Law and Politics* (Spring 1997), 377-414; Stephen L. Wasby, "How Do Courts of Appeals *En Banc* Decisions Fare in the U.S. Supreme Court?" *Judicature* (January/February 2002), 182-89.

53. O'Brien, *Storm Center*, 218.

54. See Barbara A. Perry, *The Priestly Tribe: The Supreme Court's Image in the American Mind* (Westport: Praeger Publishers, 1999), 25-45.

55. H.W. Perry, Jr., *Deciding to Decide: Agenda Setting in the United States Supreme Court* (Cambridge: Harvard University Press, 1991).

56. David M. O'Brien, "A Diminished Plenary Docket: A Legacy of the Rehnquist Court," *Judicature* (November/December, 2005), 134-37, 183.

57. William H. Rehnquist, *The Supreme Court: How It Was, How It Is* (New York: William Morrow and Company, Inc. 1987), 253.

58. O'Brien, *Storm Center*, 195.

59. Rehnquist, *The Supreme Court*, 276.

60. Owen M. Fiss, "The Bureaucratization of the Judiciary," *Yale Law Journal* 92 (1983), 1442; Wade H. McCree, Jr., "Bureaucratic Justice: An Early Warning," *University of Pennsylvania Law Review* 129 (1981), 777.

61. Robert W. Tobin, *Creating the Judicial Branch: The Unfinished Reform* (Williamsburg National Center for State Courts, 1999), 51-115; Peter Graham Fish, *The Politics of Federal Judicial Administration* (Princeton: Princeton University Press, 1973), 19-24.

62. Larry C. Berkson, "A Brief History of Court Reform," in *Managing the State Courts: Text and Readings,* edited by Larry C. Berkson, Steven, W. Hays, and Susan J. Carbon (St. Paul: West Publishing Co., 1977), 7–8.
63. Tobin, *Creating the Judicial Branch,* 105–06.
64. Fish, *The Politics of Federal Judicial Administration,* 32–33, 61–62, 125–45, 387; Russell Wheeler, "The Administration of the Federal Courts: Understanding the Entities and Interrelationships That Make Federal Courts Work," in *The Improvement of the Administration of Justice,* 7th ed. (Chicago: Judicial Division, American Bar Association, 2001), 54–57; Judicial Conference of the United States. *Long Range Plan for the Federal Courts* (December, 1995), 74 n. 1, available from www.uscourts.gov/lrp/ (retrieved March 1, 2004).
65. Russell Wheeler, "The Administration of the Federal Courts: Understanding the Entities and Interrelationships that Make Federal Courts Work," in *The Improvement of the Administration of Justice,* 7th ed., 60–63.
66. *Bush v. Gore,* 531 U.S. 98 (2000).
67. The different types of political actions that potentially threaten judicial independence are surveyed in American Bar Association, *An Independent Judiciary: Report of the Commission on Separation of Powers and Judicial Independence* (Chicago: American Bar Association, 1997).
68. "State to Appeal Judge Pay Ruling," *Chicago Tribune* (December 3, 2003), available from www.chicagotribune.com (retrieved February 23, 2004). See also James W. Douglas and Roger E. Hartley, "The Politics of Court Budgeting in the States: Is Judicial Independence Threatened by the Budgetary Process?" *Public Administration Review* 63 (July/August 2003), 441–54, and James W. Douglas and Roger E. Hartley, "State Court Strategies and Politics During the Appropriations Process," *Public Budgeting and Finance* 21 (2001), 35–57.
69. Ohio Courts Futures Commission, *A Changing Landscape: Ohio Courts Futures Commission Report* (May 2000), available from www.sconet.state.oh.us/publications/futures/ (retrieved March 1, 2004).
70. Kenneth G., Jr., Pankey, Anne E. Skove, and Jennifer R. Sheldon, *Charting a Course Through Strategic Thought and Action: Developing Strategic Planning Capacities in State Courts* (Williamsburg: National Center for State Courts), available from www.ncsconline.org/ (retrieved January 28, 2004), xi–xii, 25–27.
71. See generally Judicial Conference of the United States, *Long Range Plan for the Federal Courts* (December, 1995), available from www.uscourts.gov/lrp/ (retrieved March 1, 2004).
72. See Frank M. Coffin and Robert A. Katzmann, "Toward Optimal Judicial Workways," in *Workways of Governance: Monitoring of Government's Health* (Washington, D.C.: Governance Institute, Brookings Institution Press, 2003); Daniel J. Meador, "A Perspective on Change in the Litigation System," *Alabama Law Review* 49 (1997), 8–10. The Civil Justice Reform Act is technically called the Judicial Improvements Act of 1990, Pub. L. No. 101-650, 28 U.S.C. 471–82 (1994).

CHAPTER FOUR

Judicial Recruitment, Retention, and Removal

Justice Sandra Day O'Connor's announcement of her plans to retire and Chief Justice William H. Rehnquist's death in 2005 gave President George W. Bush the rare opportunity to fill two vacancies and shape the Court for the next generation. President Bush's first pick, Judge John G. Roberts, Jr., was originally slated to fill Justice O'Connor's seat. But, after the chief justice's death, the president quickly nominated him to become chief justice and assume the position of his mentor, for whom Roberts once clerked. By virtually unanimous consensus, the fifty-year-old Roberts was exceptionally well qualified as a Harvard law graduate, a D.C. Circuit appellate judge, and frequent litigator before the high court. Despite criticism that Roberts revealed little at his confirmation hearings about how he would rule on hot-button issues such as abortion, federalism, and religious freedom, he was confirmed by a large margin in the Senate, seventy-eight to twenty-two.[1]

President Bush's second choice, sixty-year-old White House legal counsel Harriet Miers, did not fare as well. Named to fill Justice O'Connor's seat, Miers was immediately attacked by Bush's right-wing constituents, who charged that Miers was not a proven conservative, lacked judicial experience, and, as a long-time friend of the president, a crony. Leading conservative thinkers, including columnist George Will and former circuit judge Robert Bork, denounced her nomination. Arlen Specter (R-Pa.), the chairman of the Senate Judiciary Committee, went so far as to say that Miers needed "a crash course on constitutional law."[2] The weight of the infighting between conservative factions within the Republican Party took its toll. In late October 2005, Miers withdrew her nomination.

President Bush's third pick, federal appeals court Judge Samuel A. Alito, Jr., was nominated shortly thereafter. Even though most court watchers believed Judge Alito was more conservative than Justice O'Connor, the confirmation hearings produced relatively little drama. Despite allegations that Judge Alito was not forthcoming about stating his views on abortion and that his membership in a conservative group called the Concerned Alumni of Princeton implied he was hostile to recognizing women and minority rights, liberal Democrats and organized interests could not unite effectively to defeat the nomination. As a result, Democrats and liberal critics failed in portraying Alito as an extremist judge, and the effort by Massachusetts Senators John Kerry and Ted Kennedy to prevent an up or down vote through a filibuster failed when nineteen Democrats voted with all of the Republicans in the Senate to end the filibuster debate. In late January, 2006, by a 58:42 vote that was mostly along party lines, the Senate confirmed Judge Alito as the 110th Justice of the Supreme Court.[3]

As the Roberts, Miers, and Alito nominations demonstrate, the controversies surrounding the president's choices register how the federal judicial selection process has become highly politicized. Perhaps even more so, that trend is apparent in state judicial selection processes. Accordingly, this chapter explores the politics of judicial selection by examining (1) the different methods of judicial selection in the states; (2) the appointment politics of filling vacancies on the federal bench; and, (3) whether the American judiciary is moving toward a "career judiciary" by examining the issues of judicial retirement, discipline, and removal.

STATE JUDICIAL SELECTION

The debate over how to select judges originated during the American Revolution. In the colonies, royal judges were appointed by the crown and perceived to be corrupt and tyrannical. The Declaration of Independence thus identified the royal administration of justice as one of several grievances against the king, stating he "has made Judges dependent on his Will alone, for the tenure of their offices, and the amount and payment of their salaries." The objection to royal judges created the need to separate the judiciary from the executive and legislative branches. Still, judicial independence—the principle requiring the insulation of courts from the ordinary political processes in order to render impartial justice—had to be counter-balanced with judicial accountability.

In historical perspective, most state judges were appointed either by the legislature or the governor. Judges were given some measure of independence through the imposition of "good behavior" tenure requirements and fixed or "adequate" salary provisions. But judges were also constrained by impeachment and removal for misconduct or abuse of power.[4]

However, a majority of states changed their judicial selection processes during the era of Jacksonian democracy—the populist reform movement beginning in the 1830s. By the Civil War, most states held judicial elections, but the change from an appointive to elective systems was soon overwhelmed by problem of cronyism and the growing impact of political parties. The problems of bias and corruption were made worse because judges campaigned to get elected, which created an appearance of impropriety.

Consequently, the shift in the midnineteenth century to partisan elections led to a movement to take the politics out of judicial selection through the adoption of nonpartisan ballots—ballots omitting the partisan affiliation of judicial candidates.[5] Another reform was the adoption of "merit" plans—hybrid judicial selection methods using nomination commissions (composed of citizens, lawyers, and sometimes judges), gubernatorial appointment, and retention elections.

The prototype of state "merit judicial selection" systems was formulated by Albert M. Kales, a founder of the American Judicature Society (AJS), in 1914. The Kales plan featured the appointment of lower court judges by state court chief judges who made their selections from a preapproved list of candidates compiled by a judicial council. After appointment, judges retained their seats only if they received a majority vote in an unopposed, nonpartisan election. The plan's design was later modified in 1926 by political scientist Harold Laski. Under Laski's version, a multimember advisory board, picked by judges, prepared a slate of candidates for selection by the governor and subject to senate confirmation.[6]

In 1934, California became the first state to adopt a version of the merit plan. But judges were appointed by the governor from a list of candidates proposed by a commission, consisting of the chief justice, the presiding judge of a district court of appeal, and the attorney general. Shortly thereafter, the American Bar Association (ABA) endorsed a slightly different merit plan that was adopted by Missouri in 1940. Under the so-called Missouri merit plan, a multimember nomination commission (consisting of citizens and attorneys) propose a list of three candidates whose choice is then ratified or rejected in an unopposed, nonpartisan retention election held in the next general election. For appellate judges, a favorable vote guarantees a twelve-year term, whereas other judges are elected for shorter terms. If a judge is voted out of office, the commission compiles another three-person list from which the governor fills the vacancy.[7]

The Missouri plan has been adopted in fourteen states. If hybrid (mixed judicial selection methods) systems are considered, merit plans are now widely used: twenty-five states use some type of merit selection in picking judges. Still, twenty-one states use either partisan or nonpartisan elections. Of the states with judicial elections, thirteen hold non-partisan elections for some for all of their judges, making it the dominant method.

In sum, more than two-thirds of the states use either merit or elective systems. Of the two methods, judicial elections are most predominant, but merit plans are responsible for staffing some or all of the courts in more states. Accordingly, though the merit plan may have lost some of its appeal as the preferred reform method to take the politics out of judicial selection, as some have suggested,[8] it remains still widely used.

A minority of the states retain judicial appointments by the governor or legislature. Moreover, some states, such as New Hampshire, incorporate elective aspects: Judicial candidates are nominated by the governor, but the choices are ratified by a five-person executive council, whose membership is chosen by partisan election every two years. Eleven states are "hybrid" states that use different methods to staff the bench at different levels of the judiciary. In Arizona and Indiana, for example, trial court judges are selected through a combination of a merit plan and elective methods; but, appellate judges are exclusively chosen on the basis of merit. With the exception of California, states using hybrid methods follow a similar pattern of selection but give their citizens a chance to vote on the appointment of trial judges.

The diversity of state judicial selection processes underscores the controversy over the best method to balance judicial independence with political accountability. Furthermore, politics cannot be entirely removed from the judicial selection process. Some states, such as Ohio and Michigan, elect candidates from nonpartisan ballots but nonetheless use a partisan nominating process (see Table 4.1). Several studies also demonstrate that political influences—including pressures exerted by political parties, community groups, and the politics of bar associations—affect the composition and deliberations of judicial nominating commissions.[9] In Florida, a hybrid state using a merit system for appellate court judges, the judicial staffing process is more akin to a political appointment system because the governor has

TABLE 4.1   Judical Selection Methods in the States

Method	General Operation	Number	Percentage	Key States
Merit	Governor appoints from list by nomination commission	14	27%	Alaska, Colorado, Connecticut, Delaware, Dist. Columbia,[a] Hawaii, Iowa, Massachusetts, Nebraska, New Mexico,[b] Rhode Island, Utah, Vermont, Wyoming
Elective		**21**	**41%**	
• Partisan	Party affiliation on ballot	6	12%	Alabama, Illinois, Louisiana, Pennsylvania, Texas, W. Virginia
• Nonpartisan	No party affiliation on ballot	13	25%	Arkansas, Georgia, Idaho, Kentucky, Minnesota, Mississippi, Montana, Nevada, N. Carolina, N. Dakota, Oregon, Washington, Wisconsin
• Partisan and Nonpartisan	Party affiliation and no party affiliation	2	4%	Michigan (NPE in TC and ICA; PE in CLR); Ohio (PE in TC, ICA, and CLR)[c]
Appointment		**5**	**10%**	
• By governor	Without nomination commission	3	6%	Maine, New Jersey, New Hampshire
• By legislature	Without nomination commission	2	4%	Virginia, S. Carolina[d]

(continued)

TABLE 4.1 (Continued)

Method	General Operation	Number	Percentage	Key States
Hybrid Methods		**11**	**22%**	
MS and Elective (NPE, PE or MS) in TC; MS in IAC and CLR		5	10%	Arizona, Indiana, Kansas, Maryland, Missouri
NPE in TC; GA in IAC and CLR		1	2%	California
NPE in TC, MS in IAC and/or CLR		3	6%	S. Dakota (MS in CLR only); Florida and Oklahoma (MS in IAC and CLR)
PE in TC, MS in IAC and CLR		2	4%	New York, Tennessee

Note. = Fifty-one percentages may not equal 100 percent as a result of rounding error. Unless a hybrid state, the method identified is used across all trial, intermediate appellate, and/or courts of last resort. MS = merit; NPE = nonpartisan elective; PE = partisan elective; GA = gubernatorial appointment; LA = legislative appointment; TC = trial court; IAC = intermediate appellate court; CLR = court of last resort.
[a]In the District of Columbia, the president instead of a governor appoints from a nomination list.
[b]In New Mexico, initial selection is by gubernatorial appointment, with the help of a nominating commission. The newly appointed judge then must compete in a partisan election in the next election cycle, and the winner completes the remainder of the term, and then retained through regular retention elections. [c]In Ohio, candidates identified on general ballot without party affiliation, but are nominated in partisan primaries; in Michigan, candidates for court of last resort identified on general ballot without party affiliation, but are nominated in political party conventions. [d]In South Carolina, there is a ten-member judicial merit selection commission that screens candidates and reports to the legislature, which then makes a selection.

Source: "Judicial Selection in the States: Appellate and General Jurisdiction Courts," from American Judicature Society, "AJS Judicial Selection Methods," available from www.ajs.org/js/materials.htm (retrieved October 10, 2005).

a predominant role in selecting members of the judicial nomination commission. Before 2000, the Florida governor could fill vacancies from a list compiled by a nine-member commission composed of six persons selected by the governor and bar, and those six chose three other members of the public. Since 2000, the governor names all nine members, with four drawn from lists nominated by the bar.[10]

Because most state judges face the voters in some type of election, judicial recruitment and retention has become increasingly politicized, especially for supreme court seats. Judicial races are getting "nastier, nosier, and costlier,"[11] a trend that has grown since the 1980s. Special interests and political parties have increasingly become involved in judicial races, typically pitting trial lawyers against the insurance industry and the business community. In 2004, judicial candidates raised a total of over $46.8 million dollars in state supreme court elections, and at least ten of those vying for seats had election war chests of over 1 million dollars. The most money was spent in so-called battleground states, such as Alabama, Michigan, Illinois and Ohio, which featured hotly contested issues regarding tort reform, crime control, and family values. In these states and a growing number of others, contested supreme court elections have been characterized by an influx of negative television advertisements sponsored by the trial bar, business interests, and organized groups. In West Virginia, an incumbent justice lost his seat in 2004 after one group, "And for the Sake of the Kids," ran an ad accusing the justice of releasing a known sex-offender to work as a janitor in a high school. In the same year, trial lawyers and a labor group, the "Justice for All Political Action Committee," broadcast an ad accusing a Republican judicial candidate of being too lenient on criminals because he gave probation to kidnappers who "tortured and nearly beat a ninty-two-year-old grandmother to death." Similarly, in an Ohio 2000 election, one ad sponsored by a conservative Chamber of Commerce group asked if Democratic incumbent Justice Alice Robie Resnick was "for sale" because she took $750,000 in campaign contributions from personal injury lawyers.[12]

In short, state judicial elections, which ensure judicial accountability, foster political attacks that may mislead voters about the merits of a judge and, therefore, may actually diminish judicial independence. In addition, the problem is compounded by a combination of two other interrelated factors: low voter information and high retention rates of judges. Each tends to prevent voters from making meaningful choices about judicial candidates because they lack the interest in or information about judicial performance on the bench. As one study of 3,912 retention elections in ten states between 1964 and 1994 found, most judges are retained in office, except in the rare instance when a portion of the electorate targets a judge for defeat. Indeed, only fifty judges, or 1.3 percent, were defeated; whereas, on average, about seventy-five percent won retention elections during that thirty year period. Furthermore, the average rate of "voter rolloff"—that portion of voters who vote for the lead partisan office on the ballot, but omit voting for the judicial retention candidates—was 34.5 percent. In other words, a significant portion of voters do not bother to cast a vote for judges, even though they do so for other nonjudicial candidates. Accordingly, in the "typical retention election there is little voter differentiation among the judges and they are all routinely returned to the bench for another term."[13] Although it is unclear what prompts voters to target and remove a single judge from the bench, many studies demonstrate that the electorate is constrained from voting wisely because voters are typically uninformed about the identity of the judges, their judicial performance, or even the nature of the retention election process itself.[14]

The politicization of judicial campaigns also presents special ethical problems for judges. Although they are bound by ethical rules to remain impartial and independent from the political influence, they are nonetheless forced to engage in campaigns increasingly infused with negative advertising and which often require large sums of money to run. Until the Supreme Court's decision in

Republican Party of Minnesota v. White (2002),[15] judges on the campaign trail could not announce their views on disputed political or legal issues on the grounds that doing so would compromise their judicial impartiality, as well as the judicial canons of ethics. But, *White* held that judicial candidates who wish to express their political viewpoints in judicial elections deserve First Amendment protection. (See the Controversies over Courts box in this chapter for further discussion). In response, the federal and state judiciaries, along with the American Bar Association and many state bar associations, have wrestled with *White's* implications and whether it is permissible for judges to engage aggressive political campaigning.

Controversies over Courts

Are State Judicial Campaigns and Elections Too Partisan?

More than eighty-five percent of state judges face elections, far more than the number of elected state legislators and executive officials. Over the last decade judicial elections have become increasingly contentious and campaign costs have escalated.[a] As a result, a growing controversy involves whether state judicial campaigns and elections are too partisan and should be regulated or abandoned.

Some states have adopted provisions similar to the ABA's code of judicial conduct that bar judicial candidates from saying anything about their views on legal and political issues. In 1986, California amended its constitution to forbid political parties from endorsing judicial candidates. But, federal courts declared the restriction unconstitutional. The prevailing view appeared, as Justice Thurgood Marshall put it, that "the prospect that voters might be persuaded by party endorsements is not a *corruption* of the democratic political process; it *is* the democratic political process."[b] Nonetheless, in 2000 a "chief justices summit" was convened by the chief justices of the seventeen most populous states with judicial elections and recommended reforms, including public financing of and other campaign restrictions on judicial elections.

The Michigan Supreme Court went even further in prohibiting judicial candidates from soliciting campaign contributions, declaring their party affiliation, and even voicing their positions on controversial issues or criticizing past judicial decisions. Strong sanctions were also imposed; judicial candidates who as sitting judges violate the ban were subject to discipline, civil penalties, and removal from office. But, in *Republican Party of Minnesota v. White* (2002),[c] the Supreme Court of the United States struck down the limitation judicial candidates' announcing their positions on controversial legal and political issues as a violation of the First Amendment.

In *Republican Party of Minnesota v. White*, however, the justices split five to four. Writing for the majority, Justice Antonin Scalia, joined by Chief Justice William H. Rehnquist, and Justices Anthony Kennedy, Sandra Day O'Connor, and Clarence Thomas, took the position that the restriction violated the First Amendment because "it prohibits speech on the basis of its content and burdens a category of speech that is at the core of First Amendment freedoms—speech about candidates for public office." By contrast, writing for the dissenters, Justice Ruth Bader Ginsburg, joined by Justices John Paul Stevens, David Souter, and Stephen Breyer defended the power of states to regulate judicial campaigns and elections. Notably, as the excerpts below indicate, the majority and the dissenters advance competing conceptions of the role of judges and how partisan judicial campaigns and elections should be.

JUDGES ARE POLITICAL ACTORS: JUSTICE SCALIA'S VIEW[d]

We think it plain that the announce clause is not narrowly tailored to serve impartiality (or the appearance of impartiality). . . . Indeed, the clause is barely tailored to serve that interest at all, inasmuch as it does not restrict speech for or against particular parties, but rather speech for or against particular issues. To be sure, when a case arises that turns on a legal issue on which the judge (as a candidate) had taken a particular stand, the party taking the opposite stand is likely to lose. But not because of any bias against that party, or favoritism toward the other party. Any party taking that position is just as likely to lose. The judge is applying the law (as he sees it) evenhandedly.

It is perhaps possible to use the term *impartiality* in the judicial context (though this is certainly not a common usage) to mean lack of preconception in favor of or against a particular legal view. This sort of impartiality would be concerned, not with guaranteeing litigants equal application of the law, but rather with guaranteeing them an equal chance to persuade the court on the legal points in their case. Impartiality in this sense may well be an interest served by the announce clause, but it is not a compelling state interest, as strict scrutiny requires. A judge's lack of predisposition regarding the relevant legal issues in a case has never been thought a necessary component of equal justice, and with good reason. For one thing, it is virtually impossible to find a judge who does not have preconceptions about the law. . . .

A third possible meaning of impartiality (again not a common one) might be described as open-mindedness. This quality in a judge demands, not that he have no preconceptions on legal issues, but that he be willing to consider views that oppose his preconceptions, and remain open to persuasion, when the issues arise in a pending case. This sort of impartiality seeks to guarantee each litigant, not an equal chance to win the legal points in the case, but at least some chance of doing so. It may well be that impartiality in this sense, and the appearance of it, are desirable in the judiciary, but we need not pursue that inquiry, because we do not believe the Minnesota Supreme Court adopted the announce clause for that purpose.

The short of the matter is this: In Minnesota, a candidate for judicial office may not say "I think it is constitutional for the legislature to prohibit same-sex marriages." He may say the very same thing, however, up until the very day before he declares himself a candidate, and may say it repeatedly (until litigation is pending) after he is elected. As a means of pursuing the objective of open-mindedness that respondents now articulate, the announce clause is so woefully under-inclusive as to render belief in that purpose a challenge to the credulous. . . .

There is an obvious tension between the article of Minnesota's popularly approved Constitution which provides that judges shall be elected, and the Minnesota Supreme Court's announce clause which places most subjects of interest to the voters off limits. The disparity is perhaps unsurprising, since the ABA, which originated the announce clause, has long been an opponent of judicial elections. That opposition may be well taken (it certainly had the support of the founders of the federal government), but the First Amendment does not permit it to achieve its goal by leaving the principle of elections in place while preventing candidates from discussing what the elections are about.

JUDGES ARE NOT POLITICAL ACTORS: JUSTICE GINSBURG'S VIEW[e]

Whether state or federal, elected or appointed, judges perform a function fundamentally different from that of the people's elected representatives. . . . Unlike their counterparts in the political branches, judges are expected to refrain from catering to particular constituencies or committing themselves on controversial issues in advance of adversarial presentation. Their mission is to decide "individual cases and controversies" on individual records, neutrally applying legal principles, and, when necessary, "stand[ing] up to what is generally supreme in a democracy: the popular will." . . .

The speech restriction must fail, in the Court's view, because an electoral process is at stake; if Minnesota opts to elect its judges, the Court asserts, the State may not rein in what candidates may say. . . . I do not agree with this unilocular, "an election is an election," approach. Instead, I would differentiate elections for political offices, in which the First Amendment holds full sway, from elections designed to select those whose office it is to administer justice without respect to persons. Minnesota's choice to elect its judges, I am persuaded, does not preclude the State from installing an election process geared to the judicial office.

Legislative and executive officials serve in representative capacities. . . . Judges, however, are not political actors. They do not sit as representatives of particular persons, communities, or parties; they serve no faction or constituency. "[I]t is the business of judges to be indifferent to popularity." They must strive to do what is legally right, all the more so when the result is not the one "the home crowd" wants. Even when they develop common law or give concrete meaning to constitutional text, judges act only in the context of individual cases, the outcome of which cannot depend on the will of the public.

Thus, the rationale underlying unconstrained speech in elections for political office—that representative government depends on the public's ability to choose agents who will act at its behest—does not carry over to campaigns for the bench. As to persons aiming to occupy the seat of judgment, the Court's unrelenting reliance on decisions involving contests for legislative and executive posts is manifestly out of place. In view of the magisterial role judges must fill in a system of justice, a role that removes them from the partisan fray, States may limit judicial campaign speech by measures impermissible in elections for political office....

Notes

[a]See, Roy A. Schotland, "Financing Judicial Elections." In David B. Magleby, ed., *Financing the 2000 Elections* (Washington, D.C.: The Brookings Institution, 2002), 103; Anthony Champagne, "Political Parties and Judicial Elections," *Loyola of Los Angeles Law Review* 1411 (2001).

[b]*Renne v. Geary*, 501 U.S. 312 (1991).

[c]*Republican Party of Minnesota v. White*, 536 U.S. 765 (2002).

[d]Excerpted from ibid. (Scalia, J.), 768–88.

[e]Excerpted from ibid. (Ginsburg, J.), 803–21.

Some critics believe *White* "threatens to turn judges into a set of politicians in black robes."[16] However, its long-term impact remains uncertain because courts and bar associations have yet to determine its scope and applicability in future judicial elections. Some states, such as North Carolina, have amended their judicial conduct rules and made it easier for judicial candidates to engage in overt political activity, such as directly asking for campaign contributions without using a campaign committee, endorsing nonjudicial candidates, and announcing their party affiliation. Other states, however, like Missouri and Texas, have strengthened prohibitions on judicial candidates making campaign pledges, promises, or commitments.[17] In other words, although *White* invalidated Minnesota's "announce clause," the ruling has prompted additional litigation over whether judges may directly raise money during a campaign, negatively attack opponents, or make "pledges or promises" or "commitments."

As a result of *White*, the ABA formed a joint commission to reevaluate its guidelines so as to comport with the Court's decision, and state and federal courts have confronted difficult questions as to where to draw the line in permitting or rejecting certain types of political activity during judicial campaigns. Thus far, state and federal courts applying *White* have not been uniform in their responses, but most seem inclined to allow for greater political activity so long as judicial candidates do not make pledges, promises, or commitments to vote a particular way once on the bench.[18] Notably, some federal courts have interpreted *White* to permit judicial candidates to make direct appeals to voters and actively engage in fundraising during campaigns.

Because judicial elections increasingly bear on the characteristics of general political elections, the legal profession has proposed reforming the process of

Sidebar 4.1

Should Judges Make Direct Appeals to Voters During Judicial Campaigns?

In the aftermath of *Republican Party of Minnesota v. White* (2002),[a] federal and state courts have addressed the open constitutional question of whether judges may make personal appeals to voters and directly solicit campaign contributions. Two federal courts, the Eleventh Circuit and the Northern District of New York district court, have reaffirmed the majority's viewpoint in *White* that judges are not any different than ordinary politicians in judicial campaigns.

In *Weaver v. Bonner* (2002),[b] the Eleventh Circuit held that the judicial canons in Georgia prohibiting candidates from making misrepresentations or personally soliciting campaign funds during a judicial election were unconstitutional violations of free speech. George M. Weaver, a challenger for a seat on the Georgia Supreme Court in 1998, distributed brochures and aired television ads portraying his opponent as endorsing gay marriage, disagreeing with criminal laws punishing pedophiles and opposed to applying the death penalty. In holding that both canons chilled Weaver's speech, the court interpreted *White* to require that lower courts adjudicate the constitutionality of the restrictions on judicial campaigns by using the same standards applying to legislative and executive elections. Specifically, the court did not see any distinction between judicial or political elections in terms of constitutional analysis. Similarly, in striking down the ban on personal solicitation of campaign funds, the court observed that the state's interest in promoting judicial impartiality was contradicted by "[t]he fact that judicial candidates require financial support and public endorsements to run successful campaigns," which, in turn, "does not suggest that they will be partial if they are elected."

In *Spargo v. N.Y. State Commission on Judicial Conduct* (2003),[c] a district court extended *White's* rationale in striking down, as constitutionally vague under the First Amendment, New York's ethical prohibitions against judicial candidates engaging in political activities. In vying for a spot on the New York Appellate Court in 2000, Thomas J. Spargo was disciplined for misconduct for offering free cider, donuts, alcohol, and gasoline while campaigning. He was also sanctioned for participating in a "loud and obstructive demonstration" against the recount vote in Miami-Dade County Board of Elections during the disputed 2000 presidential election, as well as making payments to consultants who assisted in his campaign. On appeal, the Second Circuit reversed the lower court's ruling on procedural grounds, but it did not address the merits of Spargo's constitutional challenge. In June 2004, the U.S. Supreme Court denied a writ of *certiorari* to hear Spargo's appeal of the Second Circuit's ruling.

However, other federal and state courts have upheld the kinds of restrictions on political activity that were struck down in *Weaver* and *Spargo*. Moreover, North Carolina amended its judicial code to permit direct solicitation of campaign funds. Still, until the

Supreme Court again confronts these issues, it remains an open question whether other states will follow the approach adopted by North Carolina or the federal courts in the Eleventh and Second Circuit.

Notes

[a]*Republican Party of Minnesota v. White*, 536 U.S. 765 (2002).

[b]*Weaver v. Bonner*, 309 F.3d 1312 (11th Cir. 2002).

[c]*Spargo v. N.Y. State Commission on Judicial Conduct*, 244 F. Supp. 2d 72 (N.D.N.Y. 2003).

Further Readings

Michael R. Dimino, "Pay No Attention to That Man Behind the Robe: Judicial Elections, the First Amendment, and Judges as Politicians," *Yale Law & Policy Review* (Spring 2003), 301–82; American Bar Association, "ABA Joint Commission to Evaluate the Model Code of Judicial Conduct," available from www.abanet.org/judicialethics/about/background. html (retrieved July 21, 2004).

selecting state judges. An ABA report, "Justice in Jeopardy," argues that states should adopt merit-based appointive systems. In particular, (1) governors should make judicial appointments based on merit after a neutral and nonpartisan commission reviews the qualifications of a pool of candidates; (2) judicial appointees should serve at least for a fifteen-year term, or until a specified age, and then take retirement benefits at the end of service; (3) they should not be subject to retention elections; and, (4) judges in service should be subjected to regular judicial performance evaluations and disciplinary processes, including removal for misconduct.

For states that do not change their election formats, the ABA also recommends nonpartisan judicial elections and public financing of judicial campaigns or, alternatively, campaign contribution limits. Moreover, for those states using judicial elections, the ABA endorses the distribution of voter guides, based on judicial performance evaluations, in order to inform the electorate better about their voting choices. However, only a few states, notably North Carolina, Georgia, Illinois, and Wisconsin, have taken steps to institute public financing for judicial elections, and only on a voluntary basis.[19]

Finally, another reform proposal is for judges to serve single, nonrenewable terms, but for lengthier periods (typically fifteen years). That is the process used in European constitutional courts, such as those in France, Germany, Spain, and Italy. Moreover, the ABA proposal is similar to that advocated by the AJS, which has long advocated merit selection. The AJS, however, does not endorse limited judicial tenures and does not object to judicial elections.[20] Still, both the ABA and AJS embrace an appointive method of selecting judges similar to that used in appointing federal judges.

FEDERAL JUDICIAL SELECTION

This section first briefly examines the constitutional history underlying the president's power to select and the Senate's role in confirming the appointment of federal judges, as well as the role political ideology—as opposed to "merit"—plays in the selection process. Then, the specific steps and the roles of the main political actors in the process are considered, along with proposals for reform.

The Framers and Judicial Selection

The recruitment process for federal judges centers on Article II of the U.S. Constitution which declares that the president has the power "by and with the Advice and Consent of the Senate" to appoint "Judges of the supreme Court, and all other officers of the United States." Significantly, the president retains authority "to fill up all Vacancies that may happen during the Recess of the Senate, by granting Commissions which shall expire at the End of their Next Session." Although the process of selecting federal judges is explicitly a shared power, the full scope of the president's power in filling federal judgeships and making recess appointments remains unclear. Article II is vague because the framers were trying to accommodate the competing values of judicial independence and accountability.

Alexander Hamilton argued in *The Federalist Papers* that the president's "sole duty" was to nominate judges. The Senate, on the other hand, rendered "advice and consent" and would only "ratify or reject the choice" the president presumably makes on the basis of merit. In doing so the Senate would act, in Hamilton's words, as "an excellent check upon a spirit of favoritism in the President, and . . . to prevent the appointment of unfit characters from State prejudice, from family connection, from personal attachment, or from a view to popularity."[21] The framers' decision give the president authority to fill vacancies when the Senate is adjourned in recess—and, thus, to make temporary judicial appointments that lapse at the end of the next congressional session unless they receive Senate confirmation—is further evidence that judicial appointments were envisioned to be the product of negotiated compromises between the president and the Senate. Moreover, because Article III judges are granted basically life tenure, presidents have increasingly turned federal judgeships into a way to extend their political legacy beyond their White House tenure. The Senate, on the other hand, also realized how valuable lower federal court judgeships were as patronage tools to dispense political favors. Because the meaning of senatorial "advice and consent" has never been settled, the political self-interest of presidents and senators makes the federal judicial appointment process politically contentious.

Ideology or Merit?

Although all presidents seek qualified and meritorious judicial candidates who will withstand Senate scrutiny, a host of interrelated political factors drive the selection and confirmation processes. Before announcing their nominations, presidents generally base their selection decisions on ideological considerations that make the appointment politically expedient and necessary. The candidate's "merit" to hold the position is less crucial even though it is usually the baseline for the president's choice and Senate confirmation. As political scientist Henry J. Abraham suggests, nominees should demonstrate "objective merit": a proven judicial temperament; professional expertise and competence; personal and professional integrity; an able, agile and lucid mind; appropriate professional educational background or training; and the ability to communicate well, both orally and in writing. But Abraham also notes that Supreme Court appointments are often affected by the president's personal relationship to the candidate, the nominee's political compatibility with the president, and whether the president believes the selection brings a geographic, racial, gender-based, or religious balance to the Court.[22] In his study of circuit court appointments, political scientist J. Woodford Howard likewise found similar criteria. Personal competence, along with extensive political participation, personal ambition, and a "pinch of luck," all contribute to securing a federal judgeship.[23]

Although "objective merit" or "professional competence" are a part of the president's criteria, the terms are not entirely useful in accurately describing the process of federal judicial selection. For one thing, defining "merit" is notoriously difficult because "a credible case can be made for the competence of almost any nominee."[24] Further, emphasizing merit-based explanations obscures the reality that all appointments are inescapably political, and presidents generally try to "pack" the courts with their preferred nominees. As political scientists George L. Watson and John A. Stookey remind us, finding the most qualified candidate is "the motivation least likely to drive presidential considerations" in selecting judges.[25] Exceptionally qualified nominees, such as President Ronald Reagan's nomination of Robert Bork to the Supreme Court in 1987, are meritorious selections, but Bork was nonetheless rejected by the Senate as a politically unacceptable candidate who was deemed to be ideologically "out of the mainstream."

Accordingly, the recruitment of federal judges is more complex and is usually based on a combination of the following four broad considerations: (1) a candidate's professional competence; (2) whether the selection is a patronage-based and is used to reward those loyal to the party; (3) "representative" factors, such as religion, race, ethnicity, and gender or, alternatively, taking into account the nominee's home state or the geographical balance on a court; and (4) the nominee's ideological positions and general judicial philosophy. Using these factors, presidents assign different priorities to their judicial selections, depending upon the level of court in which the vacancy arises (Supreme Court, court of appeals, or district court) and, of course, the amount of political opposition they are likely to encounter in the Senate.[26] In applying these principles, federal judicial selection is, arguably, a function of three general types of presidential selection models: the *classic Democratic model*, a *bipartisan approach*, and a *Republican ideological judicial selection* model.

The classic Democratic model, represented by Presidents Franklin D. Roosevelt, Harry Truman, John F. Kennedy, and Lyndon B. Johnson, deemphasizes the pursuit of specific policy agendas and, instead, rewards personal friends and favored individuals with judgeships as political patronage appointments. Patronage, however, is sometimes considered in conjunction with a candidate's professional qualifications and symbolic representation. President Johnson's selection of the Court's first African American Justice Thurgood Marshall, falls into this category as would his choice of appointing to the Court a close friend, Jewish Justice Abe Fortas, to replace another Jewish Justice, Arthur J. Goldberg.[27]

The bipartisan approach, on the other hand, puts a premium on the nominee's professional competence while emphasizing, to some degree, patronage or symbolic representation characteristics like race or gender. Republican Presidents Dwight D. Eisenhower and Gerald R. Ford, along with Democratic presidents Jimmy Carter and Bill Clinton, appear to have adopted this model. With the exception of President Clinton, these presidents vested in their attorney generals the power to make judicial appointments and, generally, the selections were not based on stringent ideological considerations. Instead, for different reasons the choices made by these Presidents were framed by institutional constraints facing a Senate dominated by the opposition party that hampered their ability to make more controversial ideological selections.[28]

Unlike those models, Republican ideological judicial selection, associated with President Richard M. Nixon and refined by President Ronald Reagan, presumes that judgeships are symbolic instruments of presidential authority. For those presidents, the touchstone for selection is that nominees share the President's political preferences and policy agenda. As a result, whether the candidate was a loyal party foot soldier or even professionally qualified is less critical. By using a strict ideological screening process, for example, Nixon appointed judges that would ostensibly act with "judicial restraint" and advance his "law and order" policy agenda, a centerpiece of his 1968 presidential campaign. Similarly, Ronald Reagan's appointment of conservative lower court judges, the elevation of Justice Rehnquist to the chief justiceship, and the appointment of Justice Scalia are good illustrations of the type of politically conservative judge Reagan favored.[29] Likewise, President George W. Bush gave high priority to appointing lower court judges favoring a conservative ideology. The same was true in naming Judge John G. Roberts to fill the seat of Chief Justice Rehnquist and in appointing Judge Samuel Alito to fill Justice O'Connor's seat, despite countervailing pressures for him to appoint another woman or Hispanic.

The federal judicial selection process begins with the president's staff initiating a search for an acceptable judicial nominee through a preliminary screening process. Vetting the candidate helps to ensure that nominee will withstand Senate review, but it does not guarantee confirmation success. The subsequent confirmation process is no less fluid and dynamic. Any number of political factors—including presidential style and power, the political composition of the Senate, the presence of divided government (when the president and the Senate are from opposite political parties), the activity of organized interests as well as the media, public opinion, and the polarization of the electorate—can generate opposition and defeat a nominee's confirmation (see Figure 4.1).

The Nomination Process

Since the New Deal, the staffing of the federal bench has become increasingly controlled by the President's closest advisors within the White House and the Department of Justice. Lower court judicial selection has tended to be defined by the president's skill in negotiating with senators after they make their initial recommendations and are reviewed by the president's legal and policy staff. Although most presidents have taken a keen interest in personally making Supreme Court appointments, all routinely rely on subordinates who bear most of the responsibility for generating a list of names of acceptable candidates for lower court judgeships and Supreme Court justices. Much of this behind-the-scenes activity usually occurs either before or immediately after a vacancy arises on the bench.[30]

Though the procedure for compiling a list of federal court nominees varies from president to president, all modern presidencies from Jimmy Carter to George W. Bush have staffed the bench with different legal policy goals in mind (see Table 4.2). Each president puts his own imprint on the judicial selection process by setting priorities. The Carter and Reagan presidencies, however, remain especially significant, because each broke with established norms of judicial selection and influenced how their successors structured the task of seeking qualified nominees.

One of President Carter's policy objectives was to diversify the federal bench and make it more representative. After striking a deal with the powerful chair of the Senate Judiciary Committee, James Eastland (D-MS.), Carter issued an executive order establishing that federal appellate court judgeships were to be recommended by nominating, or "merit," commissions. Subsequently, Congress enacted the Omnibus Judgeship Act of 1978, creating 152 new judgeships. That legislation inspired a second executive order which encouraged senators to set up their own nominating commissions for district court vacancies. But, because of protracted resistance by some senators to Carter's initial circuit court plan, the president could only ask them to cooperate on a voluntary basis and in the end only about thirty senators did so.[31]

President Carter's initiatives were historic, but some had mixed success. Although he appointed an unprecedented number of women, African Americans, and other minorities, Carter alienated powerful senators who strongly opposed relinquishing their traditional patronage authority over lower court appointments. Moreover, the merit commissions, arguably, did little to depoliticize the selection process. Not only did Carter personally select who sat on the commissions, many of the nominees were asked questions about their views on divisive social issues, including affirmative action, women's rights, abortion, capital punishment, and desegregation through forced busing.[32] Those inquiries were an unparalleled attempt to vet judicial candidates on the basis of how they would

FIGURE 4.1 **The Nomination and Confirmation Process for Federal Judges.**

The Nomination Process

Initial Vetting of Potential Nominees
- White House Counsel, Staff, Advisors
- Department of Justice's Attorney General
- American Bar Association (at President's discretion)
- Federal Bureau of Investigation Security Check

Formal Nomination by President

Senatorial Courtesy/Blue Slip

The Confirmation Process

External Evaluation of Nominee's Merits
- American Bar Association Ratings
- Organized Interest Groups
- The Print, Radio, Television Media, and Internet

Senate Judiciary Hearing
- Nominee Testimony
- Statements by Interested Persons
- Senate Judiciary Committee Vote

Confirmation/Rejection Vote by Full Senate

Formal Appointment by President

TABLE 4.2 Federal Judicial Selection Methods During Modern Presidencies

Presidential Administration	Principal Actors	Selection Method Characteristics	Selection Method Impact
Carter (D) (1976–1980)	* President * DOJ Attorney General * U.S. Senators	* Federal judicial (merit) nominating commissions, circuit, and district courts * Minimal prenomination ABA consultation, but increased consultation with federal women lawyers and national bar association groups	* Increased ethnic, racial, and gender diversity in lower federal courts
Reagan (R) (1980–1988)	* President * President's Commission on Federal Judicial Selection, led by White House counsel * DOJ Attorney General * DOJ Office of Legal Policy, led by Assistant Attorney General	* Abolished nominating commissions * Formal centralization of selection power in White House counsel's office and less DOJ collaboration * Intensified screening of nominees by DOJ with personal interviews * Decreased ABA role in prenomination screening	* Appointed new chief justice and three Justices to Supreme Court * Increased scrutiny of circuit court nominees by ideological screening in prenomination phase * Continued conservative ideological transformation of Supreme Court and lower federal courts initiated by President Nixon
G. H. W. Bush (R) (1989–1992)	* President * President's Committee on Federal Judicial Selection, led by White House Counsel * DOJ Attorney General	* DOJ Office of Legal Policy dismantled * Continued centralization of selection power in White House Counsel's Office but more collaboration with DOJ in screening and personal interviewing * Return to ABA prenomination role in screening	* Appointed two Supreme Court Justices * Continued conservative ideological transformation of lower federal courts initiated by President Reagan, but more diversification of judiciary (especially women)

(continued)

TABLE 4.2 (Continued)

Presidential Administration	Principal Actors	Selection Method Characteristics	Selection Method Impact
Clinton (D) (1992–2000)	* President * Federal Judicial Selection Committee, led by White House Counsel * DOJ Office of Policy Development, led by Assistant Attorney General	* DOJ Office of Policy Development created * Continued centralization of selection power in White House, but more collaboration with DOJ in vetting nominees * Continued ABA prenomination screening	* Appointed two Supreme Court Justices * Moderate conservative staffing of lower federal courts * Increased ethnic, racial, gender diversity in lower federal courts
G. W. Bush (R) (2000–2008)	* President * Federal Judicial Selection Committee, led by White House Counsel * DOJ Office of Legal Policy, led by Assistant Attorney General	* Reinstated DOJ Office of Legal Policy, dismantled Office of Policy of Development * Centralization of Selection Power in White House, and less collaborative with groups * Abandoned ABA prenomination screening	* Return to conservative ideological transformation of federal courts initiated by George H. W. Bush and Reagan Administrations * Appointed new John G. Roberts as chief justice and one Associate Justice to Supreme Court

Note: DOJ—Department of Justice; ABA—American Bar Association; CJ—chief justice.

Source: Sheldon Goldman, Elliot Slotnick, Gerard Gryski, and Sara Schiavoni, "W. Bush's Judiciary: The First Term Record," *Judicature* (May/June 2005), 244–75; Sheldon Goldman, Elliot Slotnick, Gerard Gryski, Gary Zuk, and Sara Schiavoni, "W. Bush Remaking the Judiciary: Like Father Like Son?" *Judicature* (May/June 2003), 282–309; Sheldon Goldman. "Clinton's Judges: Summing Up the Legacy," *Judicature* (March/April 2001), 228–54; Sheldon Goldman, "Bush's Judicial Legacy: The Final Imprint," *Judicature* (April/May 1993), 282–97; Sheldon Goldman, "Reagan's Judicial Legacy: Completing the Puzzle and Summing Up," *Judicature* (April/May 1989), 318–30; Sheldon Goldman. "Carter's Judicial Appointments: A Lasting Legacy," *Judicature* (March 1981), 341–55.

decide controversial cases. But, ironically, they helped establish an institutional basis for the White House to screen nominees more rigorously, a practice followed by Republican Presidents Reagan, George H. W. Bush, and George W. Bush. Even though Carter and his Attorney General Griffin Bell did not make a candidate's ideology the sole criteria for selection, the reality was that most judgeships went to party faithful; for example, 94.1 percent of Carter's district court judges and 89.3 percent of circuit court judges were Democrats.[33] Yet, Republican presidents likewise tend to appoint their party faithful and rarely cross party lines.

"Most presidents name justices who, they think, will vote the way they would vote. That is what I would do were I president." Those words of liberal Justice William O. Douglas capture the thrust of President Reagan's approach to judicial recruitment. Like Carter, Reagan's approach to staffing the federal bench broke with convention, though in a different way. Reagan centralized the selection process in the White House by creating the President's Commission on Federal Judicial Selection, chaired by the White House counsel and staffed with various assistants to the President, including some from personnel, legislative affairs, and the attorney general's office. The commission worked in conjunction with the Justice Department's Office of Legal Policy to screen potential nominees. Some critics charged that the process imposed an "ideological litmus test," requiring not just loyalty to the Republican Party but a commitment to the conservative ideology of the "Reagan revolution." To an unprecedented degree, the Reagan White House and Justice Department sifted through the political and professional qualifications of candidates by inspecting their written record (past judicial opinions, academic writings, and written commentary) and conducting personal interviews to discover their ideological compatibility. In the process, the ABA's prenomination advisory role, which had been firmly entrenched since the Eisenhower presidency, was greatly reduced.[34]

Reagan's innovations in judicial selection paid big dividends in the modern politics of court packing. Reagan appointed a total of 290 district and 78 circuit court judges to the federal bench, for a total of 368 lower court judges. Reagan also elevated William H. Rehnquist to chief justice on the Supreme Court and he named Justices Antonin Scalia, Sandra Day O'Connor, and Anthony Kennedy. Significantly, not a single nominee from the opposition party was put on the circuit court in eight years, something no president (Republican or Democrat) had done since the administration of Warren G. Harding. Overall, the voting behavior of Reagan's appointments extended a conservative revolution started by President Nixon and subsequently reinvigorated by George W. Bush's judicial appointees.[35]

The changes made during the Carter and Reagan years set the basic framework for the judicial selection process for subsequent administrations. In particular, Presidents George H.W. Bush, Bill Clinton, and George W. Bush each anchored their selection processes in the White House and Department of Justice and used vetting processes spearheaded by a judicial selection committee. Although George H. W. Bush dismantled the DOJ's Office of Legal Policy, Presidents Clinton and George W. Bush revived its role in screening judicial nominees.

All three administrations relied upon recommendations made from a judicial selection committee to the president.

Although the degree to which the White House collaborates with the Department of Justice during screening varies, every president since Reagan has used both to oversee the vetting process. The vetting process includes inspecting a potential nominee's professional qualifications, financial status, physical condition, and judicial philosophy, along with investigating a candidate's past work experience and written record (academic writings, judicial opinions, or political commentary). It also necessitates the completion of lengthy questionnaires and biographical statements from the Department of Justice, the American Bar Association, the Federal Bureau of Investigation, and the Internal Revenue Service. Supreme Court nominees are personally interviewed by administration staff and taken around the Capitol for office "courtesy calls" to influential senators and representatives, but increasingly lower court nominees are also given special attention, usually through a personal or telephone interview with attorneys in the White House and Department of Justice. Typically staff from the Department of Justice will also seek input from a variety of legislative and executive branch personnel on the federal and state level, including members of Congress, state governors, and state or local bar associations—who might have a keen interest in judicial selection.[36]

THE ABA RATINGS   With the notable exception of George W. Bush's presidency, since 1956 all presidents have solicited an informal evaluation of potential nominees from the ABA, which played a role in "rating" the quality of judicial nominees since the administration of Dwight D. Eisenhower. In 2001, Bush stopped sending nominees' names to the ABA, arguing that the organization should not be given a special advising role and that it was too liberal. In practice, the diminished capacity of the ABA to affect the prenomination process has meant that it no longer has access to prenomination materials, a shift in procedure that nonetheless probably gives the organized bar more influence in the confirmation (as opposed to the nomination) process. The ABA, though, remains an active player in confirmation politics, principally because its evaluations are still used by Democrats on the Senate Judiciary Committee and, for them, receipt of the ratings is a prerequisite to beginning the confirmation process.[37]

The ABA's Standing Committee on Federal Judiciary has fifteen members appointed by the President of the ABA for staggered three-year terms and represents each of the thirteen judicial circuits with two from the Ninth Circuit and one member-at-large. It rates candidates as *well qualified*, *qualified*, and *not qualified* after examining their professional qualifications and written record. In addition, how much support each candidate receives from members on the committee is also disclosed as each rating carries a *substantial majority, majority*, or *minority* designation.[38] At a minimum, the ABA's assessment of judicial nominees offers the potential for an objective evaluation of a candidate's merits. But critics have maintained that the ABA rating system is sometimes politically biased and, accordingly, should not be a part of the judicial selection process.[39]

SENATORIAL COURTESY AND THE "BLUE SLIP"   Judicial nominees are also screened by the Senate's Judiciary Committee. The Judiciary Committee's investigation of candidates may greatly affect the success or failure of nominations. The views of senators from the nominee's home state are highly significant because of two closely guarded Senate traditions: *senatorial courtesy* and the *blue slip* procedure.

Traditionally, senatorial courtesy required the president to consult with senators from a nominee's home state prior to making a judicial nomination. Senatorial prescreening of judicial nominees dates back to George Washington's administration. Senators from a nominee's home state and the president's party can effectively derail a nomination by objecting to it. Historically, senatorial courtesy was usually invoked on the Senate floor by an objecting senator declaring that the nomination is "personally obnoxious."[40] But, in contemporary politics, senatorial courtesy extends to the period well before a Senate deliberation and vote. In explaining why some of President Clinton's judicial nominations were not confirmed, Orrin Hatch (R-Utah), who chaired the Judiciary Committee when Clinton was in office, said that "there was no way to confirm those nominations without completely ignoring the senatorial courtesy we afford to home state Senators in the nomination process."[41] The tradition of senatorial courtesy has less force in affecting circuit court vacancies because federal districts are confined to one state (instead of to several states as with circuit courts) and is more easily treated by senators as political patronage. But, increasingly, senators have tried to exert greater influence over the selection of circuit court judges and blocked some nominees.[42]

Although the blue slip procedure is a manifestation of senatorial courtesy, it remains a distinct tradition since the 1940s. After the president formally sends a nomination to the Senate, the chair of the Senate Judiciary Committee sends out a form (on blue paper) requesting the home-state senator's opinion about whether the nomination is approved or opposed. Once the blue slip is received, the home-state Senator has two choices: He or she may endorse the nomination by returning it with a favorable opinion or by blocking it by not returning it (amounting to a *pocket veto*). The propriety of the senator's decision, though, is often clouded by the uncertainty of whether home-state senators enjoy veto power if they are not from the president's party because the blue slip is sent without regard to a home-state senator's partisan affiliation.

As a result, from either side of the aisle, the blue slip can be used defensively or offensively to advance or hinder the president's attempt to pack the courts. If the senator and President are from the same party, the blue slip may be manipulated as a defensive tactic to advise the president in advance that a nomination is in trouble and that further consultations are needed. Or, as Senator Edward Kennedy of the Judiciary Committee did as chair in the 1970s, the blue slip may be used to prevent home-state senators in the opposing party from blocking the nomination. Accordingly, it matters a great deal how the chair of the Senate Judiciary Committee specifically chooses to exercise the power to invoke the blue slip process.

For example, when Congress created a number of new judgeships during the Carter Administration, the Committee's Chair, Senator Kennedy, altered tradition by announcing that withholding blue slips would not necessarily delay or defeat a nomination. That move eliminated any opposition to Carter's appointments and improved the odds of a favorable confirmation vote. Similarly, when the Republicans controlled the Senate during the Clinton Administration, Senator Orrin Hatch (R-Utah) let home-state Republicans use the blue slip to prevent or delay confirmation hearings on several nominations. Shortly thereafter, Chairman Hatch varied the blue slip procedure again, but this time in anticipation that Democratic home-state senators would use blue slips to block President George W. Bush's judicial appointments. Hatch changed the process to require that both home-state senators withhold blue slips before a nomination was terminated, which drew heavy criticism from opponents across the Senate aisle.[43]

By the same token, if the senator and president are from different parties the blue slip may be applied as an aggressive, offensive ploy by a senator from the opposing minority party who wishes to delay or defeat a nomination. Even the threat to use the blue slip may be an imposing weapon, as was evidenced by President George W. Bush's decision in 2001 to withdraw Christopher Cox's nomination to the Ninth Circuit after Senator Barbara Boxer (D-CA) declared she intended to invoke the blue slip practice. After Cox decided to withdraw, conservatives pejoratively described the blue slip as a "blackball" and a "burial shroud" for judicial nominees.[44]

Depending on how it is politicized by the chair of the Senate's Judiciary Committee, the blue slip process may either enhance or diminish the president's authority to make appointments. After the president formally announces the nomination and a blue slip is not used by a home-state senator, the Senate Judiciary Committee takes up the nomination before the full Senate gives its "consent."

The Confirmation Process

Historically, ninty-nine percent of presidential appointees, typically consisting of tens of thousands of military appointments, promotions, and civilian appointments, are perfunctorily confirmed by the Senate. Although executive nominations involving nonpolicymaking positions are afforded quick confirmation, the selection of Cabinet officials and other high-ranking policymaking executive officials usually receive closer scrutiny.[45] Similarly, appointments for federal court vacancies are usually routinely confirmed if a home-state senator does not object. In such cases a short hearing, sometimes lasting five minutes or less, is held by a subcommittee of the Senate Judiciary Committee. Barring any unexpected objections, the nomination is reported out of the committee and then moves to the full Senate for a final confirmation vote.

For the Supreme Court, and increasingly for circuit courts, the same general procedure applies, but the scrutiny accompanying the confirmation process is much more rigorous. Such scrutiny may be intensified when the political opposition objects to controversial selections by resorting to hardball tactics, such as delaying the nomination in committee (thus preventing a quick confirmation hearing) or by denying an up-or-down vote in the Senate by using *filibusters*—a senatorial procedure that prevents legislative action by continuously debating the issue on the Senate floor. In the aftermath of *Bush v. Gore*,[46] Senate Democrats filibustered ten Bush circuit court nominees to the point that the Republican leadership threatened to invoke the so-called nuclear option—a strategy to end filibusters by rewriting the Senate rules and closing the debate, thus permitting an up-or-down vote. The threat was accompanied by President Bush's decision to give two nominees who were targets of the filibuster, Charles Pickering and William Pryor, "recess" appointments. The Republican strategy worked. In May, 2005, the White House and the so-called Gang of fourteen senators—a bipartisan coalition responsible for allowing the filibusters to continue—reached an agreement: A list of filibuster targets would be confirmed without opposition, so long as the President agreed not to make any more recess appointments until the end of his term.[47]

Because appellate judges play important policymaking roles, the chances of Senate rejection are considerably higher than for other nominations. One study found that since 1789 nearly a quarter of Supreme Court nominations have not been confirmed.[48] Similarly, an examination of circuit and district court nominations between 1977 and 1998 reveals that one in five circuit court and one in seven district court nominations failed.[49] Though the reasons for nonconfirmation vary, they are typically predicated on one or more political factors: opposition to the president, to the nominees' views, or to the incumbent on the Court; the invocation of senatorial courtesy; and the nominee's questionable professional competence. Any or all of these reasons can work alone, or in conjunction with the others, to defeat a nomination.

Several historical episodes illustrate the Senate's capacity to derail judicial appointments. Nominations from lame-duck presidents—coming in their last year of office—have often created sufficient opposition and defeated confirmation. Ostensibly several of President John Tyler's candidates, along with President Lyndon Johnson's selection of Abe Fortas as chief justice, fall into this category. Senate opposition to the president's and the nominee's policy positions may also lead to defeat. For example, President George Washington's selection in 1795 of John Rutledge as Chief Justice, a nominee who denounced the Jay Treaty (an accord that had just been ratified by Federalists controlling the Senate); and President Reagan's nomination of Robert Bork in 1987 also produced senatorial opposition and thwarted confirmation. It is significant that the lack of clear, demonstrable judicial philosophy may cause a nomination to fail even if the nominee is from the majority party in the Senate, as illustrated by Harriet Miers' decision to withdraw in 2005. Specifically, the decision was prompted in large part due to mounting criticism from right-wing conservatives that Miers lacked sufficient ideological credentials to assume the pivotal role of replacing Justice O'Connor on the Court. A summary of unsuccessful Supreme Court nominations is presented in Table 4.3.

TABLE 4.3 Unsuccessful U.S. Supreme Court Nominations

Nominee	Year Nominated	Nominating President	Final Disposition	Reason(s) for Nonconfirmation
William Patterson	1793	Washington	Withdrawn (for technical reasons)	Opposition to nominee's views
John Rutledge	1795	Washington	Rejected (10–14)	Opposition to nominee's views
Alexander Wolcott	1811	Madison	Rejected (9–24)	Opposition to nominee's views; lack of professional qualifications
John J. Crittenden	1828	J. Q. Adams	Postponed (23–17)	Opposition to lame-duck president
Roger B. Taney	1835	Jackson	Postponed (24–21)	Opposition to nominee's views
John C. Spencer	1844	Tyler	Rejected (21–26)	Opposition to lame-duck president
Reuben H.Walworth	1844	Tyler	Tabled and withdrawn	Opposition to lame-duck president
Edward King	1844	Tyler	Tabled and withdrawn	Opposition to lame-duck president
John M. Read	1845	Tyler	No action	Opposition to lame-duck president
George W. Woodward	1845	Polk	Rejected (20–29)	Senator's blue slip; opposition to nominee's views
Edward A. Bradford	1852	Fillmore	Tabled, no action	Opposition to lame-duck president
George E. Badger	1853	Fillmore	Postponed (26–25), then withdrawn	Opposition to lame-duck president
William C. Micou	1853	Fillmore	No action	Opposition to lame-duck president
Jeremiah S. Black	1861	Buchanan	Rejected (25–26)	Opposition to lame-duck president
Henry Stanbery	1866	A. Johnson	No action	Opposition to lame-duck president
Ebenezer R. Hoar	1869	Grant	Rejected (24–33)	Opposition to nominee's views
George H. Williams	1873	Grant	Withdrawn	Lack of professional qualifications
Caleb Cushing	1874	Grant	Withdrawn	Lack of political reliability
Stanley Matthews	1881	Hayes	No action	Interest group opposition; opposition to nominee's views
William B. Hornblower	1893	Cleveland	No action, rejected (24–30)	Senator's blue slip

Nominee	Year	President	Outcome	Reason
Wheeler H. Peckham	1894	Cleveland	Rejected (32–41)	Senator's blue slip
Pierce Butler	1922	Harding	No action	Opposition to nominee's views
John J. Parker	1930	Hoover	Rejected (39–41)	Opposition to nominee's views; interest group opposition
John Marshall Harlan II	1954	Eisenhower	No action	Opposition to nominee's views
Abe Fortas	1968	L. Johnson	Withdrawn	Opposition to lame-duck president and nominee's views; interest group opposition; opposition to incumbent Court
Homer Thornberry	1968	L. Johnson	Withdrawn	Opposition to lame-duck president; interest group opposition
Clement F. Haynsworth, Jr.	1969	Nixon	Rejected (45–55)	Opposition to nominee's views; interest group opposition
G. Harrold Carswell	1970	Nixon	Rejected (45–51)	Opposition to nominee's views; lack of professional qualifications
Robert H. Bork	1987	Reagan	Rejected (42–58)	Opposition to nominee's views; interest group opposition; fear of altering ideological balance of Court
Douglas H. Ginsburg	1987	Reagan	Withdrawn	Admitted to past use of marijuana
Harriet Miers	2005	W. Bush	Withdrawn	Opposition to nominee's views; interest group opposition; allegations of cronyism; lack of professional qualifications

Note. Rutledge, Williams, Cushing, and Fortas (as Associate Justice) were nominated for Chief Justice. Taney was later renominated and confirmed as Chief Justice. Some justices were nominated multiple times but were never confirmed (Walworth [3], King [2], and Hornblower [2]), whereas others were renominated later and confirmed (Matthews, Butler, Harlan II).

Source: Henry B. Hogue, CRS Report for Congress: Supreme Court Nominations Not Confirmed, 1789–2002 (Order Code RL 31171, Updated July 9, 2003), Table 4, and ibid., 5–13; Henry J. Abraham, Justices, Presidents, and Senators: A History of the U.S. Supreme Court Appointments from Washington to Clinton (Lanham: Rowman & Littlefield Publishers, 1999), 18–19; Joyce A. Baugh, Supreme Court Justices in the Post-Bork Era: Confirmation Politics and Judicial Performance (New York: Peter Lang Publishing, 2002), 16–17; Jeffrey A. Segal, "Senate Confirmation of Supreme Court Justices: Partisan and Institutional Politics," Journal of Politics (November, 1987), 998–1015.

The success of federal judicial appointments also depends increasingly on whether the nominee is assessed favorably by organized interests and the media. Their involvement since the 1970s has caused the confirmation process to become more contentious and politicized. Before 1925, nominees for the Supreme Court were not asked to testify before the Senate Judiciary Committee, and the hearings were not televised until Sandra Day O'Connor's nomination in 1981. President George W. Bush's decision to withdraw his nomination of Harriet Miers illustrates the power organized interests have in defeating even the prospect of having a confirmation hearing in a controversial nomination; Miers voluntarily withdrew her name as a result of mounting pressure. Several conservative groups, including the Family Research Council and the Concerned Women for America, openly opposed the pick, and some did so the very day the president announced his choice. Furthermore, as shown by the bitter battle over the nomination of Bork and the persistent problem of filling judicial vacancies in the appellate courts expeditiously, the confirmation process has become more unstable when the government is divided and due to the impact that organized groups and the media have in targeting judicial nominees.[50]

THE POLITICS OF ORGANIZED INTERESTS AND PUBLIC ADVOCACY GROUPS In the summer of 1987, a few hours after President Reagan announced the nomination of Judge Bork to replace retiring Justice Lewis F. Powell, Massachusetts's Senator Edward Kennedy denounced the nominee on the Senate floor in his famous "Robert Bork's America" speech:

> Robert Bork's America is a land in which women would be forced into back-alley abortions, blacks would sit at segregated lunch counters, rogue police could break down citizens' doors in midnight raids, schoolchildren could not be taught evolution, writers and artists would be censored at the whim of the government, and the doors of the federal courts could be shut on the fingers of millions of citizens for whom the judiciary is often the only protector of the individual rights that are at the heart of our democracy.[51]

Despite Senator Kennedy's partisan hyperbole, Bork was a meritorious candidate who had strong legal credentials: He earned his law degree at the University of Chicago Law School; he was a Marine and a Yale University law professor; he served as U.S. Solicitor General and as acting U.S. Attorney General during the Nixon administration; and, for a short time he served on the Court of Appeals for the D.C. Circuit. Yet, he was also a well-known conservative and liberals criticized his advocacy of a jurisprudence of "original intent" and his opposition to unenumerated constitutional rights, such as the right to privacy.[52]

Bork's nomination and defeat left a lasting mark on the modern confirmation process. As an opponent of abortion rights and an advocate of "strict constructionism," Bork drew the ire of a multitude of liberal interest groups. Liberals were especially concerned about the role he would play on the Court because he was slated to replace Justice Lewis F. Powell, who had been a swing vote on abortion and civil rights issues. Over 150 interest groups mobilized for battle, with at least eighty-three liberal organizations opposed to the nomination.[53] Although historically it is not unusual for organized interests to fight or support a Supreme Court nomination, the Bork controversy was unprecedented, specifically in the extensive use of the media as well as the strategic utilization of tactics normally reserved for nonjudicial, grassroots political campaigns.

Notably, in order to win the votes of about twenty-five undecided senators, organized interests from both sides of the aisle mounted extensive letter-writing campaigns, and 250 op-ed articles (both supporting and opposing Bork's nomination) appeared in newspapers. The People for the American Way, a liberal interest group founded by Norman Lear of television fame, launched a $2 million media campaign featuring movie actors such as Gregory Peck (who portrayed Bork as supporting the disenfranchisement of African Americans). Conservative groups, such as the National Conservative Political Action Committee, did the same, spending over a $1 million in support of Bork. Other conservative groups, such as Free the Court, chartered an airplane to fly over the Iowa state fair with a banner trailing behind castigating "Bork Bashers" and "liberal lap-dogs," whereas another, the Concerned Women for America, initiated a sophisticated phone bank and letter writing campaign in order to influence the votes of senators in their districts.[54]

The mobilization of organized interests, both against and for Bork, resembled the kind of political activity that was previously confined to general political campaigns. Interest groups used a variety of tactics, including (1) testifying at congressional hearings; (2) direct lobbying of legislators and their staff; (3) fundraising or campaign contributions; (4) organizing grassroots support; (5) direct mail or letter-writing campaigns; (6) dissemination of key information (e.g., written opinions, law review articles, voting records) to educate the public about the nominee; (7) media advertisements; and, (8) demonstrations, marches, and protests. The tactics sometimes distorted Bork's position on key issues. Bork's personal recollection of the nomination recounted that Planned Parenthood, a pro-choice abortion group, sponsored a full-page newspaper ad crediting him with authoring *Moore v. City of East Cleveland* (1977),[55] a ruling affirming the power of a local zoning board to prevent a grandmother from living with her grandchildren—even though he was not on the Court and despite the fact that *Moore* was announced five years before he became a judge on the DC Circuit.[56]

As a result, critics have argued that the Bork controversy proves the Senate lost control over the confirmation process. Yet, for others, the emergence of interest group advocacy was a key factor in the confirmation process, a political phenomenon that political scientist Nancy Scherer argued increasingly affects Supreme Court and even lower court federal judgeships.[57] In the last twenty-five years, interest groups routinely target judicial nominees in an effort to persuade senators who, in turn, engage in strategic behavior that also mobilizes voters at the grassroots level. As law professor Michael Gerhardt observed, pro-choice interest groups played a key role in Bork's defeat by threatening to divert money away from senators of supporting Bork. Similarly, a few years later, civil rights and womens interest groups translated their opposition to Clarence Thomas's confirmation by voting to unseat incumbents John Seymour (R-CA) and Alan Dixon (D-IL) because they publicly discredited Anita Hill's allegations of sexual harassment and voted to confirm Thomas.[58]

Still, the politics of interest group advocacy was not the only factor in Bork's defeat: His judicial philosophy, along with his conduct during the unusually lengthy period between nomination and Senate vote, were also significant reasons to cause the Senate's rejection of the nomination by a 58:42 vote.

In the aftermath of Bork's defeat, the confirmation process has witnessed a dramatic proliferation of interest groups monitoring the judicial process from both ends of the political spectrum. Whereas for Justice William Brennan's 1957 confirmation hearing, there was no interest group representation, eighty-six witnesses aligned with organized interests participated in Bork's hearings. In the post-Bork era, ninety-six witnesses appeared in Justice Clarence Thomas hearings; thirty-nine in Justice David Souter's confirmation hearings; and twenty were a part of Justice Ruth Bader Ginsburg's hearings. Political scientists Gregory A. Calderia, Marie Hojnacki, and John R. Wright report a similar pattern: 145 active groups participated in the Bork hearings, and another eighty-one (Thomas), fifty-three (Souter), forty-one (Rehnquist), and thirty-nine (Kennedy) were involved in other Supreme Court confirmation hearings.[59] Today, some of the most influential conservative groups include the American Center for Law and Justice, the Center for Individual Freedom, the Washington Legal Foundation, the Free Congress Research and Education Foundation, the Heritage Foundation, and the Institute for Justice. Conversely, groups such as the Alliance for Justice, People for the American Way, the Leadership Conference on Civil Rights, and the NAACP Legal Defense and Educational Fund represent liberals.

Finally, a repercussion of the Bork battle is found in the lessons that interest groups learned in managing subsequent confirmation battles. Although liberal interest groups were instrumental in defeating Bork, their efforts were helped by the complacency of conservative groups, which in part grew accustomed to previous Republican successes, particularly in Reagan's first term. Since Bork's defeat, conservative groups have been significantly more active in countering the influence of liberal groups.[60] During George W. Bush's administration, for example, the ABA's influence as a prescreener of judicial nominations has been supplanted by the rise of the Federalist Society for Law and Public Policy Studies—a coalition of about 25,000 conservative and libertarian scholars, academics, jurists, and student members (with an estimated budget of $3 million) that now plays a vital behind-the-scenes role in the federal judicial selection process in the conservative Bush administration. The Federalist Society and other like-minded groups, in fact, have displayed their muscle in affecting the success of presidential judicial appointments by supporting John Roberts, which led to a smooth confirmation process, and objecting to Harriet Miers, which led to her withdrawal as a judicial candidate a week before the confirmation hearings were scheduled to begin.

Sidebar 4.2

The Federalist Society's Role in the Modern Confirmation Process

Once existing merely as a debating society in law schools at Harvard, the University of Chicago, and the University of Virginia, beginning in 1982 The Federalist Society for Law and Public Policy Studies grew into a multifaceted conservative organization with considerable influence. It now boasts over 25,000 members committed to "reform[ing] the current legal order," ostensibly by cultivating a "greater appreciation for the role of separation of powers, federalism, limited constitutional government, and the rule of law in protecting individual freedom and traditional values." In at least sixty cities, it is organized into three student, lawyer, and faculty divisions that affect over 145 ABA-accredited law schools. Its main headquarters is located in Washington, DC.

Since its inception, it has evolved into a "central nervous system for a network of conservative lawyers," which, in turn, strongly influences the selection of law clerks and federal judges, particularly during the administrations of Ronald Reagan, George H.W. Bush, and George W. Bush. Its members include former White House Counsel C. Boyden Gray; former Attorney General Edwin Meese; former DC Circuit Judge Robert Bork; Energy Secretary Spencer Abraham; former Interior Secretary Gale A. Norton; former Attorney General John Ashcroft; former Solicitor General Theodore Olsen; and several lawyers in the White House counsel's office.

Though the Federalist Society denies that it plays a direct role in confirmation politics, it concedes that it does "act as the network, forum, and information clearinghouse for its members," often espousing the values underlying a conservative agenda that, notably, includes filling the courts with opponents of judicial activism and proponents of judicial restraint. *The Washington Post*, also asserts that Society members are an integral part of George W. Bush's Federal Judicial Selection Committee. According to some estimates, it is responsible for generating at least one-third of the candidates seeking judicial office in the Bush Administration. As one prominent appeals judge mused, "a clerkship is a useful credential, and if I want to advance my philosophy I'd rather give it to someone who thinks like me" and, accordingly, the judge gives the nod to those affiliated with the Federalist Society.

In response to the success of the Federalist Society, liberal activists, under the leadership of Georgetown law professor Peter Rubin, created the Madison Society for Law and Policy at Georgetown University Law School in 1999, later renamed to the American Constitution Society. Although the influence of the American Constitution Society remains unclear, its presence, along with the continuing impact of the Federalist Society and other single and multiple policy issue groups monitoring judicial activity, underscores the growing role organized interests play in the confirmation process.

Source: "The Federalist Society for Law and Public Policy Studies," available from www.fed-soc.org/ (retrieved September 30, 2004); Terry Carter, "Conservatives Who Sought Refuge in the Federalist Society Gain Clout," *American Bar Association Journal.* (September, 2001), 46; Neil A. Lewis, "A Conservative Legal Group Thrives in Bush's Washington," *New York Times* (April 18, 2001), available from www.nytimes.com (retrieved April 24, 2001); Thomas B. Edsall, "Federalist Society Becomes a Force in Washington," *Washington Post* (April 18, 2001), A04.

SENATE CONFIRMATION HEARINGS   Ordinarily, the fate of judicial nominations rests with the Senate Judiciary Committee's decision to recommend confirmation. The Committee's recommendation is based on a written record of the nominee's background and professional qualifications, as compiled by the committee's staff, the ABA, interest groups, academics, and interested persons. At the hearing, the committee also considers the nominee's answers to questions about his or her views of the law. One measure of the contemporary importance of the public hearing is the increasing length of the hearing transcript. Between 1930 and 1949, the length of a transcript for Supreme Court justices' hearings averaged only forty-two pages. But, since 1970, the average has grown to 1,117 pages.[61]

Confirmation proceedings in controversial nominations are lengthy because the public hearing is the forum for attacking the ideological views and judicial philosophy of the candidate. When President Nixon nominated G. Harrold Carswell, several interest groups in a five-day hearing claimed Carswell was a racist on the basis of his remarks in a 1948 state legislative campaign. In 1987, Senator Edward Kennedy publicly chastised Judge Bork by playing an audiotape of disparaging remarks he made at a college seminar several years earlier. In an eleven-day confirmation hearing in 1991, Clarence Thomas was extensively questioned by senators about his views concerning abortion, natural law, and the judicial philosophy of original intent, and, finally, regarding his response to allegations against him made by law professor Anita Hill, who claimed that he sexually harassed her when she worked for him at the Equal Employment Opportunity Commission.[62] In Justice Thomas's confirmation hearing, the Senate hearing culminated with a visibly shaken Thomas angrily accusing the senators for conducting a hearing that was "a national disgrace" and nothing more than a "high-tech lynching for uppity blacks who in any way deign to think for themselves, to do for themselves."[63]

In the past, lower court nominations were reported out of committee in short order and delivered to the Senate floor for a vote. Delaying the vote, however, has become more the rule than the exception in recent administrations, especially during President George W. Bush's tenure (see Table 4.4). Even though it is very rare that a nomination is defeated in a Senate floor vote, the specter of divided government and the openness of the confirmation hearing have made the political struggle to confirm Supreme Court and circuit court nominees increasingly more intense and less certain. It is not surprising, therefore, that political scientist John Maltese observes that between 1969 to 2003, in periods of unified government (when the same party controls the White House or Senate), the rate of confirmation success for Supreme Court nominees is almost 90 percent, but when government power is divided between the White House and Congress the success rate drops to only fifty-five percent.[64]

The presence of divided government is only one factor among many others—including whether the confirmation takes place in a presidential election year, whether the appointment will tip the ideological balance of a court that is perceived to be important to a political party, and the partisan composition of the Senate Judiciary Committee—that contributes to politicizing the confirmation process and to significantly delaying final Senate action.[65] Yet, historically, the prospect of delay has not defined many Supreme Court appointments because most have been considered by the Senate relatively quickly, often within twenty-four days of the nomination. Some recent justices, however, have faced considerably longer confirmation periods: Justice O'Connor was approved within fifty

TABLE 4.4   The Duration of the Confirmation Process in Lower Federal Court Nominations

Court	Carter	Reagan	H. W. Bush	Clinton	G. W. Bush
District	52.7	39.7	61.5	76.4	96.3
Circuit	50.9	43.3	60.0	100.3	238.4
Total average days	51.8	41.5	60.8	88.4	153.8

Note. For Carter to Clinton data, the data record the number of days between nomination and confirmation, as corrected for Senate recess days. For G. W. Bush data, the data record the average number of days from time of nomination received by Senate Judiciary Committee to date of hearing from 2001–2002.

Source: For Carter to Clinton data: Wendy L. Martinek, Mark Kemper, and Steven R. Van Winkle, "To Advise and Consent: The Senate and Lower Federal Court Nominations, 1977–1998," *Journal of Politics* (May 2002), 337–61 (Table 2). For G. W. Bush data: Sheldon Goldman, "Assessing the Senate Judicial Confirmation Process: The Index of Obstruction and Delay," *Judicature* (March/April 2003), 251–57 (Tables 1 and 2).

days; Justices Anthony Kennedy and David Souter were confirmed within seventy-five days; but Justices William Rehnquist and Clarence Thomas, who were more controversial appointments, had to wait 100 and 125 days, respectively, to receive the Senate's consent.[66]

The trend toward delaying Senate action is even more apparent for court of appeals' judgeships. On average, between 1979 and 1994 it took seventy-one days to confirm a federal court judgeship and well over a year (457 days) before a vacancy was filled.[67] Moreover, at least two months elapsed before a confirming circuit court judge in George H. W. Bush's presidency and, during Clinton's tenure, nominations sat idle for 100 days. According to political scientist Sheldon Goldman, the trend underscores the politics of "obstruction and delay" that began in earnest with the 100th Congress (1987–1989) when President Reagan was confronted by a Democratic Senate.

Delays have progressed through the presidencies of Bill Clinton and George W. Bush. Senatorial obstruction (which Goldman defines as "Senate inaction on a nomination") and delay (i.e., when it takes 180 days or more to cast a confirmation vote after nomination) especially took its toll on Clinton's judicial nominees. Even though he managed to appoint 366 lower court judges to the bench, during the last six years of his presidency Clinton faced a Republican-controlled Senate and fourteen district court nominations lingered on for a year or more; sixty-four nominees were not processed through confirmation; and forty-eight had no hearing. Clinton's circuit court choices did not fare any better: Eight nominees waited a year or more until confirmation, whereas another thirty-six were not processed and twenty-eight received no hearings. Moreover, Clinton experienced the ignominious distinction of having Missouri Supreme Court Justice Ronnie White, a candidate for a district court vacancy in Missouri, defeated by a party-line Senate floor vote, even though the nomination was reported out of the Senate Judiciary Committee.[68]

What the Republican-controlled Senate did during the Clinton years was identical to how the Democratic-led Senate treated Reagan's and George H. W. Bush's judicial nominees. In the mid-1980s a Senate under the control of Democrats took an average of four months to confirm Reagan/H. Bush judicial nominees, and during the first term of George W. Bush there was similar obstruction and delay obstacles.[69] Still, even though the judicial confirmation process in first five years of George W. Bush's tenure was often contentious, and even though about a dozen court of appeals' nominees were held up by filibusters and two judicial candidates were given recess appointments, by the end of his first term in office the president had appointed 202 judges, about twenty-three percent of the entire federal judiciary.[70]

IS THE CONFIRMATION PROCESS "BROKEN"?   There is little doubt that the politicization of the federal judicial appointment process may threaten the legitimacy of courts and access to justice. Institutional trend(s), include (1) the expansion of the federal judiciary, (2) the prolonged delay in filling vacancies,

(3) the centralization of judicial selection power in the White House, (4) the activism of interest groups, (5) instantaneous media coverage, and (6) the polarization of party conflict in the Senate in sustained periods of divided government. These trends add to the perception that the confirmation process needs reform.

Calls for reform are necessarily political, as was evidenced by President George W. Bush's proposal to improve the appointing process by requiring that (1) judges announce their intention to retire one year before they actually leave the bench; (2) nominations be made within 180 days of learning of the vacancy; and, (3) the Senate vote on the nomination within 180 days after receiving it. Likewise, New York's Democratic Senator Charles Schumer proposed to use "citizen judicial nomination commissions" to preselect judicial appointees. Notably, Senator Schumer's proposal reversed his earlier advocacy that judicial nominees be confirmed on the basis of passing an "ideological litmus test" for confirmability.[71]

Although critics have accused President Bush and Senator Schumer of floating reform proposals driven by partisan politics, their proposals mirror recommendations by others. President Bush's proposals, for example, embraced reforms issued from the University of Virginia Miller Center for Public Affairs in 1996. Its bipartisan commission concluded that a number of steps could be taken to shorten the time it takes to fill vacancies on the lower court bench, including (1) encouraging Senators to identify and vet candidates before a vacancy occurs or within thirty days thereafter and then recommending at least two or more candidates no later than ninety days after a vacancy occurs; (2) suggesting that the White House and the Department of Justice complete their investigations of potential nominees within ninety days; (3) asking the Senate to forego confirmation hearings for noncontroversial nominees and to take action on all nominees within two months after receiving them. The Miller Center report also concluded that presidents should make recess appointments of district court nominees if their confirmations are delayed for more than ninety days.[72]

The Twentieth Century Fund Task Force on Judicial Selection anticipated Senator Schumer's proposal to use bipartisan nominating commissions to screen and recommend candidates for lower federal court judgeships.[73] Unlike Schumer, however, the Task Force did not believe that candidates should be questioned about their ideological views, but instead selected for their professional qualifications on the basis of their written records. For Supreme Court nominations, the Task Force went further in recommending that the Senate Judiciary Committee depoliticize confirmation hearings by abolishing the practice of having nominees appear before the committee.[74]

In addition to the foregoing reform proposals, political scientist Richard Davis took a rather unique approach by calling for reform that does not depoliticize the selection process, but that instead takes advantage of it by allowing for some type of direct participation by the electorate to confirm nominees. Observing that many states elect justices, Davis argued that judicial elections should be part of the federal selection process as well. One reform, for example, would require the public to elect justices in general elections held every two years. Candidates would be placed on the ballot after the president makes nominations from a slate of three candidates and, thereafter, the Senate would "advise" the public by making recommendations about the candidates after it conducts an investigation by holding hearings. Under the proposal, justices would serve staggered terms (so one, or perhaps two, justices would be seated in an election cycle) and no longer hold lifetime appointments. Davis made similar proposals, all on the basis of the assumption that the people must have a voice in ratifying the ideological choices the president and the Senate make in packing the federal courts.[75]

Still, the charge that the confirmation process is broken must be weighed against the fact that only six percent of the federal judiciary remained vacant by the end of the fifth year of George W. Bush's presidency and that he appointed a greater number of lower court judges than did Clinton during his first term.[76] Though most scholars agree that the appointment process must be depoliticized, many court watchers reaffirm the premise of the Twentieth Task Force's report, namely, that the federal judicial appointment process has "worked reasonably well" and does not need "major changes." Likewise, surveying federal judicial appointments over a fifty-six-year period from Roosevelt to Reagan, Sheldon Goldman concluded that

> [d]espite occasional dissatisfaction with how a particular nomination is handled, or charges that excessive partisanship or ideological litmus tests are being applied, our current judicial selection process, with the checks and balances envisioned by the framers (and even with some that were not, such as the role of the ABA), appears under most circumstances (with the possible exception of presidential election years) to be working reasonably well. There will always be tension between patronage, merit, and ideological considerations, and how that tension is resolved will differ from administration to administration. It will depend upon the point in political time in which an administration is functioning. It will depend upon the personalities and the nature of the interactions within and between the executive branch and the Senate.[77]

In sum, the judicial selection process is inherently political, and reforms are only required to correct some of the institutional norms and practices that periodically cause extreme conflict or that significantly impede the confirmation process.[78]

TOWARD A REPRESENTATIVE BENCH AND A CAREER JUDICIARY?

For most citizens, the power and prestige of a state or federal judgeship is enviable. As federal appellate Judge James Buckley observed, "The federal judiciary is recruited from a professional elite, it enjoys life tenure, and, at the appellate level at least, it is sheltered from the rough and tumble of everyday life."[79] Still, the members of state and federal courts routinely confront difficult political challenges that test the patience of even the most seasoned judge. The balance of this chapter presents a profile of the American judiciary and then considers, on the one hand, whether the United States is moving toward a *career judiciary*— a relatively homogeneous cadre of professional judges—and, on the other hand, the disincentives for judicial service and why some judges either opt to leave or are removed from the bench.

A Representative Bench?

It is surprising that demographic statistics—the racial, ethnic, religious and socioeconomic characteristics of the state and federal judiciaries—show that the makeup of state and federal courts is identical despite different selection methods. Though the composition of U.S. courts has become more diversified over the past half century, the state and federal benches remain relatively homogeneous and elitist. In general, state and federal judgeships are occupied by those who are nearing retirement age and who are white, male, and Protestant. A study of the demographic characteristics of state supreme court justices, for example, found that at the turn of the twenty-first century only twenty-six percent of justices were women, and only twelve percent were nonwhite. In addition, sixty-one percent were Protestant, whereas twenty-six percent and six percent, respectively, were Catholic and Jewish.[80]

The backgrounds of appointees from the Eisenhower to the G. W. Bush administrations underscore the lack of diversity in federal courts. Tables 4.5 and 4.6 show that since the 1950s lower federal court judges are usually about fifty years old at the time of appointment, and nearly nine out of ten judges are white. People of color represent less than twelve percent (eight percent African American and four percent Latino), even though African Americans and Latinos increasingly represent larger segments of the general population. Still, beginning with the Carter administration and extending through the first Bush, Clinton, and the second Bush presidencies, appointments of women have become more numerous—at least two of every ten judges have been women in the post-Reagan years. In contrast to the pre-Reagan administrations, both Bush presidencies appear to have had some success in placing more women on the bench, a trend that is likely to continue.[81]

Like state judges, federal judges are basically recruited from three religious groups and, on balance, represent the upper class. Sixty percent of judges are Protestants, whereas roughly twenty-five percent are Catholic and about ten percent are Jewish (see Tables 4.5 and 4.6). Notably, judicial appointments by Democratic Presidents Carter and Clinton broke with the trend by making significant inroads in diversifying the federal bench. During their tenures, African Americans, Hispanics, Catholics, and Jewish appointees assumed more of a presence in the lower federal courts.

TABLE 4.5 Demographic Characteristics of U.S. District Court Appointees

		Race/Ethnicity			Gender		Religion		
	Age	White	Black	Hispanic	Male	Female	Protestant	Catholic	Jewish
Eisenhower	52.3	100.0	—	—	100.0	—	73.0	19.0	6.4
Kennedy/Johnson	51.4	93.9	3.9	1.8	98.7	1.3	60.3	27.1	10.0
Nixon/Ford	49.1	93.9	3.9	1.3	99.1	0.9	67.5	16.4	7.8
Carter	49.6	78.7	13.9	6.9	85.6	14.4	52.5	27.7	11.4
Reagan	48.7	92.4	2.1	4.8	91.7	8.3	51.4	27.6	9.3
G. H. W. Bush	48.1	89.2	6.8	4.0	80.4	19.6	64.2	28.4	7.4
Clinton	49.5	75.1	17.4	5.9	71.5	28.5	NR	NR	NR
G. W. Bush	49.0	82.1	6.6	10.7	79.2	20.8	NR	NR	NR
Total Avg.	49.7	88.1	7.8	5.0	88.2	13.4	61.4	24.3	8.7

Note. Some percentages within a category do not equal 100 percent because of exclusions. NR = not reported data. Data only to the end of W. Bush's first term are reported. Except age, all figures are percentages and reflect only major categories.

Source: Data for the Eisenhower to Reagan Administrations: Sheldon Goldman, *Picking Federal Judges: Lower Court Selection from Roosevelt through Reagan* (New Haven: Yale University Press, 1997), Tables 9.1, 9.2. Excepting religious affiliation for Clinton and G. W. Bush appointees, data for the G. H. W. Bush to G. W. Bush Administrations: Sheldon Goldman, Elliot Slotnick, Gerard Gryski, and Sara Schiavoni, "W. Bush's Judiciary: The First Term R ecord," *Judicature* (May/June 2005), 269 (Table 2); Sheldon Goldman, Elliot Slotnick, Gerard Gryski, Gary Zuk, and Sara Schiavoni, "W. Bush Remaking the Judiciary: Like Father Like Son?" *Judicature* (May/June 2003), 282–309 (Table 2); Sheldon Goldman, "Clinton's Judges: Summing Up the Legacy," *Judicature* (March/April 2001), 228–54 (Table 3); Sheldon Goldman, "Bush's Judicial Legacy: The Final Imprint," *Judicature* (April/May 1993), 282–97 (Table 2).

TABLE 4.6 Demographic Characteristics of U.S. Court of Appeals' Appointees

	Age	Race/Ethnicity			Gender		Religion		
		White	Black	Hispanic	Male	Female	Protestant	Catholic	Jewish
Eisenhower	55.9	100.0	—	—	100.0	—	80.0	13.3	6.7
Kennedy/Johnson	52.7	95.1	4.9	—	98.4	1.6	63.9	24.6	11.5
Nixon/Ford	53.4	98.2	—	—	100.0	—	68.4	19.3	8.8
Carter	51.8	78.6	16.1	3.6	80.4	19.6	50.0	26.8	17.9
Reagan	50.0	97.4	1.3	1.3	94.9	5.1	50.0	29.5	14.1
G. H. W. Bush	48.7	89.2	5.4	5.4	81.1	18.9	59.4	24.3	16.3
Clinton	51.2	73.8	13.1	11.5	67.2	32.8	NR	NR	NR
G. W. Bush	50.5	79.4	11.8	8.8	79.4	20.6	NR	NR	NR
Total Avg.	51.7	88.9	8.7	6.1	87.6	16.4	61.9	22.9	12.5

Note. Some percentages within a category do not equal 100 percent because of exclusions. NR = not reported data. Data only to the end of W. Bush's first term are reported. Except for age, all figures are percentages and reflect only major categories.

Source: Data for the Eisenhower to Reagan Administrations: Sheldon Goldman, *Picking Federal Judges: Lower Court Selection from Roosevelt through Reagan* (New Haven: Yale University Press, 1997) (Tables 9.1, 9.2). Excepting religious affiliation for Clinton and W. Bush appointees, data for the G. H. W. Bush to G. W. Bush Administrations: Sheldon Goldman, Elliot Slotnick, Gerard Gryski, and Sara Schiavoni, "W. Bush's Judiciary: The First Term Record," *Judicature* (May/June 2005), 274 (Table 4); Sheldon Goldman, Elliot Slotnick, Gerard Gryski, Gary Zuk, and Sara Schiavoni, "W. Bush Remaking the Judiciary: Like Father Like Son?" *Judicature* (May/June 2003), 282–309 (Table 4); Sheldon Goldman, "Clinton's Judges: Summing Up the Legacy," *Judicature* (March/April 2001), 228–54 (Table 6); Sheldon Goldman, "Bush's Judicial Legacy: The Final Imprint," *Judicature* (April/May 1993), 282–97 (Table 4).

In addition, both state and federal judges are well compensated, although they probably would earn more money in the private sector (see Table 4.7). They also generally receive substantial fringe benefits, including reimbursed travel expenses, medical and retirement plans, death benefits, vacation and holiday pay, and sick leave. Moreover, federal appellate judges do not have to draw from their salaries to contribute to retirement funds while in active service and, upon retirement, retire with full pay under certain conditions.[82]

The lack of diversity also raises the basic issue of whether the salaries of judges, which are often not competitive with those from the private sector, provide a disincentive to service. The salary issue has constitutional dimensions. Congress's historical reluctance to pass legislation affording cost-of-living increases for federal judges has periodically resulted in litigation by judges on the ground that the failure to do so violates the constitutional requirement that Congress may not diminish judicial compensation.[83] Thus far, that litigation has not been successful.

Even though the connection between low compensation and early retirements is unclear, the trend to professionalize the bench is apparent. Since the 1950s, judges on state and federal courts have assumed their positions with extensive prior judicial service. Chris Bonneau's examination of the of state supreme court justice characteristics in 2000 found that seventy-two percent of appointees were former judges, a fourteen percent increase from those who were on the state bench in the 1960s. Similarly, Lee Epstein, Jack Knight, and Andrew D. Martin reported that sixteen percent of U.S. Supreme Court justices came from circuit courts before 1953 and, thereafter, the rate increased to forty-three percent.[84] Albert Yoon, in a study of federal district and circuit court judges, concluded that all presidents dating back to the Truman Administration frequently used the courts as an important source of talent and experience for new judicial appointments. Six of the last ten presidents, for example, had thirty percent or more of their district court selections take the judicial oath with prior courtroom service; and, fifty percent of circuit court judges had prior judicial employment and, accordingly, were picked in nine of the last ten presidencies.[85]

At least on the federal level, the recruitment of sitting judges has been accompanied by a trend toward appointing independently wealthy persons. Data collected by Sheldon Goldman, for example, indicate that the net assets of federal judges appointed during the Carter Administration averaged $884,605, whereas those named by Reagan ($1,167,464), George H.W. Bush ($1,384,522), and Clinton ($1,471,409) appointees were millionaires at the time of appointment. The net worth of district and circuit court judges selected by President George W. Bush has continued the pattern of selecting the financially elite: fifty-three percent of district court appointees had a net worth of over $1 million, and 12.4 percent were in the $500,000 to $999,999 range. About twenty-six percent of judges had an affluence level under $499,999, with most (19.6 percent) falling in the $200,000 to $499,999 range. The net worth of George W. Bush's circuit judge selections were roughly the

TABLE 4.7 Judicial Salaries of State and Federal Judges

| Position | State | | Federal | |
	Mean Salary	Salary Range	Position	Salary
Chief, Highest Court	$134,788	$97,000 – 198,567	Chief Justice, U.S. Supreme Court	$212,100
Associate Judge, Court of Last Resort	$130,328	$95,493 – 182,071	Associate Justice, U.S. Supreme Court	$203,000
Judge, Intermediate Appellate Court	$125,745	$101,612–170,694	Judge, U.S. Court of Appeals	$175,100
Judge, General Jurisdiction Court	$117,328	$88,164 – 163,850	Judge, U.S. District Court	$165,200
State Court Administrator	$116,347	$82,567 – 175,728	Judge, U.S. Claims Court	$162,000
			Judge, Court International Trade	$162,000
			Judge, U.S. Magistrate (FT)	$149,000
			Judge, U.S. Bankruptcy	$149,000
			Administrative Director, U.S. Courts	$162,000

Source: National Center for State Courts, "Survey of Judicial Salaries," (Vol. 30, No. 1, as of April 1, 2005), available from www.ncsconline.org (retrieved April 13, 2006); Administrative Office of U.S. Courts, "Judicial Salaries Since 1968," available from www.uscourts.gov (retrieved April 13, 2006). The salaries of the U.S. Supreme Court Chief Justice and Associate Justices, plus those for U.S. Court of Appeals and District Judges, are current as of April, 13, 2006; the rest of the federal judges and administrators are current as of January 1, 2005.

same, although the percentages of wealthier judges, especially in the $500,000 to $1 million range, was slightly higher.[86]

Some court watchers claim that there is growing evidence of a career judiciary in the sense that federal and state courts tend to draw judges with pre-existing professional qualifications.[87] Nonetheless, the state and federal courts are distinct and stand in sharp contrast to the kind of professionalized judiciaries found in Europe and elsewhere (see In Comparative Perspective: The Career Judiciary in Japan). Notwithstanding the comparative differences between the U.S. courts and other career judiciaries across the globe, the fact remains that the delivery of justice in the U.S. is increasingly committed to those who are professionally homogenous and financially affluent.

In Comparative Perspective

The Career Judiciary in Japan

The creation of Japan's postwar judicial system aimed to forge revolutionary change in the role of courts. Under the prewar Meiji Constitution, the courts and the *Diet* (legislature) exercised their powers in the name of the emperor. But, the 1947 Constitution provided for U.S.-style judicial review, with courts given the power to strike down laws that violate the Constitution, and established a parliamentary system with a separation of powers, unlike the system of parliamentary sovereignty in Great Britain. The Supreme Court acquired extensive authority over the training, nomination, assignment, promotion, and oversight of lower court judges and other judicial personnel through its supervision of the Legal Training and Research Institute (LTRI).

The Japanese judiciary is unitary, unlike systems of judicial federalism in Australia and elsewhere that have both a national judicial system and separate state judiciaries. There are basically three levels of courts. At the apex is the Supreme Court of Japan, composed of fifteen justices. It generally decides cases as petty benches composed of five justices each. Major cases and administrative matters are decided by the entire Court, which sits *en banc* as the Grand Bench. Below the Supreme Court are eight high courts, located in the major cities, as well as six branches in other cities. There are approximately 285 high-court judges, appointed by the prime minister and the Cabinet on the recommendation of the Supreme Court; they are subject to periodic reassignments and mandatory retirement at age sixty-five.

Appeals to high courts come from district courts and from family courts. District courts are the principal trial courts. There are fifty of them, located in all major cities, and another 203 branches in smaller towns. Except for minor cases, trials in district courts are presided over by three-judge panels. There are also fifty family courts and 203 branches located alongside the district courts. They have specialized jurisdiction over family and domestic matters and use conciliation procedures. Unlike other courts, they are staffed primarily by lay conciliators, appointed by the Supreme Court. Below these courts are 438 summary courts with 806 judges, who have jurisdiction over minor civil (less than U.S. $8,000) and criminal cases. These judgeships are filled by former clerks, prosecutors, and judges from within the career judiciary who have reached retirement age (at age sixty-five for judges and age sixty-three for prosecutors) but who may extend their careers serving as summary court judges until age seventy.

The Japanese judicial system employs more than 21,000 judges, clerks, secretaries, marshals, and other personnel. Central to the operation of the contemporary Japanese judiciary is its system of recruiting, training, appointing, and promoting an elite cadre of highly professional judges. With the exception of Supreme Court justices, the lower courts are staffed by career judges who must survive a series of professional hurdles, beginning with admission into a university. Unlike legal education in the United States, but like that in Great Britain, Germany, and France, undergraduates earn a BA in law. After graduation, most take bar-exam cram courses in preparation for the National Law Examination. That test, which may be taken numerous times, is rigorous. Out of the more than 20,000 students who annually take the test, only about 1,000 pass; prior to changes in the 1990s, only 500 were permitted to pass. Graduates of the leading law schools tend to be favored. However, a reform committee recommended the creation of American-style graduate-level law schools, and in 2004 several public and private universities opened these new law schools. After two to three years of study, students in these programs nevertheless still need to be admitted into the LTRI, as determined by the LTRI's capacity.

Only after passing the national examination, submitting a thesis, and passing a personal interview are students admitted into the LTRI. There, at the government's expense, they pursue a two-year course of study. It includes four, four-month internships—in an attorney's office, a prosecutor's office, a criminal court, and a civil court. After graduating, they may then apply to become assistant judges, although there are only as many positions as there are vacancies, about 100 per year. Some students are thus discouraged by faculty at the LTRI from applying for judgeships. Still others are deemed unsuited and denied appointments.

Judicial careers begin with a ten-year appointment as an assistant judge, another apprenticeship. But, actually, assistant judges function like full judges after five years. They may become associate judges on a three-judge district court or preside over a single-judge court. After a decade, they become full judges, subject to reappointment every ten years. During the course of their careers, they are reassigned many times and to several different courts, or to other positions within the judiciary, such as to the LTRI or as law clerks at the Supreme Court. A judge may move from a district court to being an acting high-court judge. After five more years, the judge may then become a regular high-court judge, sitting on the right side of a more senior presiding judge. Eventually, the judge may be elevated to the position of a presiding judge on a three-judge court. A very few are then given an opportunity to become chief judges on Japan's most prestigious high courts. Later, from that select group, who have reached their mid-sixties, a few are rewarded with an appointment to the Supreme Court.

Already selective, the Japanese judiciary becomes increasingly competitive the higher judges move up within the hierarchy. Over the years, many are encouraged to abandon their judicial careers and to move into private practice. Reassignment to less prestigious courts, salary rankings, and the remote, but real possibility of being denied reappointment are powerful incentives for achieving conformity. In addition, some judges are put on fast tracks, whereas most reach dead ends sooner or later.

Unlike lower court judges, not all members of the Supreme Court are career judges, however. The appointment process and tenure for Supreme Court justices is also somewhat different from that for lower court judges. The drafters of the Constitution and the Court Organization Law of 1947 modeled the appointment process for justices along the lines of the so-called Missouri Plan. The Missouri Plan was first adopted by that state in 1940; subsequently, almost half of the other states enacted some version of it. The basic elements of the plan are as follows: (1) a nonpartisan commission nominates three candidates for every vacancy, (2) from those three, the governor appoints one, and (3) the judge must then be approved by the voters at the next general election; if approved, the judge receives a twelve-year appointment.

Although modeled after the Missouri Plan, the constitutional and statutory provisions for the selection, appointment, and tenure of Japanese Supreme Court justices have been circumvented. The use of a nominating commission was short lived, for instance. In April 1947, an eleven-member Advisory Committee for Appointing Justices was appointed, and it nominated thirty candidates for justiceships and three for chief justice. Later that year, however, the Japan Socialist Party (JSP) won the general election and temporarily controlled the government for one year. A new fifteen-member nominating committee was created and recommended thirty candidates, from which the Cabinet named the first fifteen justices. A year later, however, the JSP was driven from office, with the Liberal Democracy Party winning control of the government for most of the last fifty years. And judicial nominating committees were never used again.

In practice, justices are appointed after Cabinet officials consult with the chief justice and the General Secretariat, as well as with bar associations and administrative heads when a practitioner, administrator, or a diplomat is to be appointed. As with the appointment of lower court judges, the chief justice largely determines the appointments of members of the Supreme Court, including his own successor. In other words, appointments are formally made by the prime minister and the Cabinet, but only on the recommendation of the chief justice. There is no "advice and consent" process, as with the U.S. Senate's confirmation of the president's nominees to federal courts. As a result, little media attention is paid to judicial appointments in Japan.

The appointment of justices is also conditioned by the stipulation in Article 31(1) of the Court Organization Law that they "shall be among persons of broad vision and extensive knowledge of law, who are not less than forty years of age." Moreover, a convention was established, in the words of Chief Justice Hattori, that "Supreme Court justices are appointed in roughly equal numbers from among three broad groups: (1) inferior court judges; (2) practicing lawyers; and (3) public prosecutors, law professors, or other persons of broad knowledge and experience."[a] Furthermore, it became the rule instead for there to be six career judges, four lawyers, two former bureaucrats, two prosecutors, and one law professor on the Supreme Court.

No less significantly, like the Missouri Plan, the Constitution of Japan provides for a system of judicial retention elections, or *popular review*, as it is known. After their appointment, according to Article 79(2), members of the Court "shall be reviewed by the people at the first general election of the members of the House of Representatives following their appointment." Thereafter, justices face retention elections after each ten years of service. Under the system, voters place an "X" in a box next to the name of a justice they think should be dismissed; otherwise, the ballot is counted as a vote for retention. Yet, an end run around the system has been made by the practice of appointing older and older justices who must retire at age seventy. In other words, justices are simply not on the bench long enough to face retention elections. In addition, the average age of appointees has incrementally inched up from an average age of 61.2 in the 1950s, to 62.9 in the 1960s, 63.7 in the 1970s, sixty-four in the 1980s, and sixty-five in the 1990s.

In sum, the appointment of judges in Japan is largely determined by the recruitment, training, and promotion of career judges admitted into the LTRI and overseen by the chief justice. Most judges begin their careers in their mid-twenties and serve until age sixty-five, though some may extend their careers until age seventy by serving on the Supreme Court or a summary court. Throughout their careers they have periodically spiraling assignments in various courts within the overarching judicial hierarchy. Their careers are throughout governed by senior judges and the central personnel bureaucracy of LTRI. These two features—spiraling career paths within a judicial hierarchy that is closely overseen and controlled by a judicial bureaucracy—set the Japanese judiciary apart from not only other judicial selection systems within Asia, but also from those in Western Europe and North America. Not even Germany's judicial system, which Japan's judicial system most closely resembles, shares both of these features. From beginning to end, judicial careers are determined by senior judges and judicial peers, not political branches or agencies outside the courts. As a result, the Japanese judiciary maintains its institutional independence and integrity, though at the price of conformity and the sacrifice of individual judicial independence on the bench.

Notes

[a] Yakaaki Hattori, "The Role of the Supreme Court of Japan in the Field of Judicial Administration," *Washington Law Review* (1984), 72.

Source: David M. O'Brien, *To Dream of Dreams: Religious Freedom and Constitutional Politics in Postwar Japan* (Honolulu: University of Hawaii Press, 1996); Hiroshi Itoh, *The Japanese Supreme Court* (New York: Markus Wiener, 1989); and J. Mark Ramseyer and Eric B. Rasmusen, *Measuring Judicial Independence: The Political Economy of Judging in Japan* (Chicago: University of Chicago Press, 2003).

Leaving the Bench

"Fortunately most of the judiciary is honest," Judge Jerome Frank once remarked, but added "a very few scamps manage to get on the bench, and the best way to avoid unfairness to the vast majority of judges is to oust the few rascals."[88] Judges, of course, voluntarily leave the bench because of ill health, advancing age (retirement), or personal reasons. But, as Judge Frank suggested, on occasion there is a need to force a judge off the bench because of misconduct, incompetence, intemperance, neglect, or disability. Judges may also be targeted by opponents for making unpopular rulings and subsequently impeached.

Forcing otherwise qualified judges to step down raises separation of powers and broader constitutional concerns: How much power should legislatures have in policing the internal affairs of the judiciary? Or should court administrators, judges, and lawyers have the flexibility to discipline judges without external political interference? In short, the problem of judicial removal and discipline arises from the inherent tension between judicial independence and accountability and has been an ongoing political struggle. The balance of this chapter explores the methods used to persuade or force judges to leave the bench.

Historically, state constitutions or statutes have authorized the disciplining of state judges by the legislature through a variety of means, including *impeachment* (removal by trial by the upper house after lower house votes to impeach), *legislative resolution* (removal by concurrent vote of each legislative chamber), *legislative address* (by majority vote legislature directs the governor to remove a judge), and, since the first decades of the twentieth century, *legislative recall* (after petition for a special election to vote on removal).

Each method, however, has proven subject to political abuse or has been rarely used.[89] As a result, beginning in the 1940s, the task of disciplining judges incrementally shifted to state courts. In 1960, California established the prototype for judicial discipline and removal became a model for sanctioning judges in virtually all the other states. California's Commission on Judicial Qualifications, a multimember commission of judges, lawyers, and citizens, was empowered to investigate complaints about judicial performance and then, with or without a hearing, to make recommendations to the state's highest court about final disposition. Today, every state and the District of Columbia acts has some type of *judicial conduct organization*—referred to as commissions, councils, committees, courts, or boards—which are charged with the duty of investigating allegations of judicial misfeasance or disability.[90]

Judicial commission's membership is usually determined by state supreme courts, the state bar, or the governor; but their size and jurisdiction vary. Some commissions have the power to prosecute specific violations of the state's code of judicial conduct, in accordance with standards set by the ABA and local bar groups. Typically, once a written complaint is filed, the commission investigates the allegations—at first in confidence—and then, after concluding its inquiry, resolves the case through dismissal, informal private sanction, or formal referral to the state's highest court after conducting a public hearing on the charges. Although many commissions have authority to dispose of cases through private informal means, in nearly all the states a court renders a final judgment by reviewing the commission's findings. In general, the kind of informal or formal sanction levied, including removal, involuntary retirement, suspension without pay, the payment of a fine, public or private censure, public or private reprimand, professional counseling and education, admonishment, or advisory letters, often depends on the nature of the offense and whether there is a pattern of misconduct.[91]

Although the imposition of penalties is relatively infrequent, state judicial commissions have nonetheless disciplined judges, sometimes severely. Between 1990 and 2001, 110 state judges were removed from office for judicial misconduct; by contrast, during roughly the same period, 625 judges left office by retiring, suffering election defeats, resigning, or dying while complaints were pending against them. In 2001, slightly over 100 judges were publicly sanctioned (resulting in eight removals, six resignations, fourteen suspensions without pay, two suspensions from legal practice, and at least seventy-three public censures, admonishments, or warnings). Although approximately 100 judges per year are sanctioned for disciplinary reasons, the tendency to do so is offset by the fact that eighty percent or more of all complaints are usually dismissed, often on the grounds that the complainant was simply unhappy with a case's outcome.[92]

Federal judges may be removed by impeachment for taking bribes, engaging in treasonous activity, or committing "other high Crimes and Misdemeanors." Under Article I, Section 2 of the Constitution, the House of Representative has the authority to pass articles of impeachment. The Senate is vested with power to try impeachment cases. Historically, impeaching federal judges has been problematic for the same reasons that the procedure proved unwieldy in the states. Impeachment may be politically abused and awkward because the Senate must convene specially to adjudicate the case. In addition, not all instances of judicial misfeasance rise to the level of impeachable offenses, and the Constitution is silent about the removal of inept, intemperate, or disabled judges. The success of removing federal judges by impeachment has also been minimal: Only fourteen federal judges have been impeached, and of those only seven were convicted.[93]

Consequently, since the first half of the twentieth century, Congress and the federal courts have moved toward adopting the same type of commission format for disciplining judges that became prevalent in the states. However, the federal procedure is distinct because public citizens and attorneys do not play a role in sitting on the committee that is empowered by Congress to discipline judges.

Under the Administrative Office Act of 1939, and then through the Judicial Code in 1948, circuit court councils (staffed by appellate judges from all circuits) were given responsibility to set ethical standards and, in limited circumstances, discipline judges by certifying cases of physical or mental disability. The constitutionality of the authority of circuit courts to sanction federal judges, however, remained unclear. Hence, Congress, after debating the various reform options in the 1960s and 1970s, enacted the Judicial Councils Reform and Judicial Conduct and Disability Act of 1980. That legislation, as amended by the Judicial Improvements Act of 2002, remains the principal means for disciplining federal judges, except Supreme Court justices in nonimpeachment cases.[94]

Under the Judicial Conduct and Disability Act, a complaint must be filed with a federal court of appeals asserting that a judge has become disabled or "prejudicial to the effective and expeditious administration of the business of the courts." After reviewing the charges, the chief judge of the circuit may dismiss the complaint on procedural grounds or upon finding that corrective action has already been undertaken; or, alternatively, a special committee of district and circuit court judges might be created to investigate further and make a written recommendation to the circuit council about what action should be taken. After conducting its own review, the circuit council may disregard or adopt the recommendation and, if necessary, may levy sanctions against the judge. Penalties include certifying that there is a disability, requesting voluntary retirement, or otherwise reprimanding the judge, either publicly or privately. Notably, the council does not have the power to compel removal but instead refers such cases to the House of Representatives for impeachment proceedings.

As in the state courts, the process of disciplining federal judges has had relatively little impact in removing judges. Between 1999 and 2003, 3,733 complaints were filed against the 1,726 federal judges, which is an average of 747 per year. Of those complaints, the majority alleged "abuse of judicial power" or "prejudice or bias"; other, less prevalent rationales for investigating judicial conduct include having a mental or physical disability, exhibiting improper demeanor, taking bribes or engaging in corrupt behavior, incompetence or neglect, and deciding cases when there was a conflict of interest. Furthermore, sixty-seven percent of complaints were dismissed, and the balance were rejected or withdrawn as either frivolous, improperly filed under the statute, or moot. Of the final action taken by judicial councils, less than one percent provoked any kind of disciplinary sanction: Only four judges, for instance, were censured publicly, and only one was privately censured.[95]

In sum, federal and state court judges are likely to stay on the bench, and they are infrequently disciplined or removed.

SELECTED READINGS

Abraham, Henry J. *Justices, Presidents, and Senators: A History of the U.S. Supreme Court Appointments from Washington to Clinton.* Lanham: Rowman & Littlefield Publishers, Inc. 1999.

Atkinson, David. *Leaving the Bench: Supreme Court Justices at the End* Lawrence: University Press of Kansas, 1999.

Bushnell, Eleanore. *Crimes, Follies, and Misfortunes: The Federal Impeachment Trials.* Urbana: University of Illinois Press, 1992.

Comiskey, Michael. *Seeking Justice: The Judging of Supreme Court Nominees.* Lawrence: University Press of Kansas, 2004.

Davis, Richard. *Electing Justice: Fixing the Supreme Court Nomination Process.* New York: Oxford University Press, 2005.

Epstein, Lee, and Jeffrey Segal. *Advice and Consent: The Politics of Judicial Appointments.* New York: Oxford University Press, 2005.

Gerhardt, Michael J. *The Federal Appointments Process: A Constitutional and Historical Analysis.* Durham: Duke University Press, 2003.

Goldman, Sheldon. *Picking Federal Judges: Lower Court Selection from Roosevelt Through Reagan.* New Haven: Yale University Press, 1997.

Malleson, Kate, and Peter Russell, eds. *Appointing Judges in an Age of Judicial Power.* Toronto: University of Toronto Press, 2006.

Maltese, John Anthony. *The Selling of Supreme Court Nominees.* Baltimore: John Hopkins University Press, 1995.

Massaro, John. *Supremely Political: The Role of Ideology and Presidential Management in Unsuccessful Supreme Court Nominations.* Albany: State University of New York Press, 1989.

O'Brien, David M. *Judicial Roulette: Report of the Twentieth-Century Fund Task Force on Judicial Selection.* New York: Priority Press, 1988.

Sheldon, Charles H., and Linda S. Maule. *Choosing Justice: The Recruitment of State and Federal Judges.* Pullman: Washington State University Press, 1997.

Volcansek, Mary L. *Judicial Impeachment: None Called for Justice.* Urbana: University of Illinois Press, 1992.

Watson, George L., and John A. Stookey. *Shaping America: The Politics of Supreme Court Appointments.* New York: Longman, 1995.

Yalof, David Alistair. *Pursuit of Justices: Presidential Politics and the Selection of Supreme Court Nominees.* Chicago: University of Chicago Press, 1999.

NOTES

1. Maura Reynolds, "Roberts is Sworn in as Chief Justice," *Los Angeles Times* (September 30, 2005), available from www.latimes.com (retrieved September 30, 2005).

2. David Stout, "Withdrawal is Greeted with a Mix of Regret and Relief," *New York Times* (October 27, 2005), available from www.nytimes.com (retrieved October 27, 2005).

3. Lois Romano and Juliet Eilperin, "Republicans were Masters in the Race to Paint Alito," *Washington Post* (February 2, 2006), A1.

4. Charles H. Sheldon and Linda S. Maule, *Choosing Justice: The Recruitment of State and Federal Judges* (Pullman: Washington State University Press, 1997), 2–3.

5. Larry C. Berkson, "Judicial Selection in the United States: A Special Report," in *Judicial Politics: Readings from Judicature*, edited by Elliot E. Slotnick (Chicago: American Judicature Society 1999), 45.

6. Evan Haynes, *The Selection and Tenure of Judges* (Newark: The National Conference of Judicial Councils, 1944), 235–36.

7. Lee Epstein, Jack Knight, and Olga Shvetsova, "Selecting Selection Systems," in *Judicial Independence at the Crossroads: An Interdisciplinary Approach,* edited by Stephen B. Burbank and Barry Friedman (Thousand Oaks: Sage Publications, 2002), 199–200; Joel F. Knutson, "Judicial Selection in the States: Historical Context and Ongoing Debates," in *The Improvement of the Administration of Justice,* 7th ed. (Chicago: Judicial Division, American Bar Association, 2002), 200–02.

8. Knutson, "Judicial Selection in the States: Historical Context and Ongoing Debates," in *The Improvement of the Administration of Justice,* 7th ed., 205; G. Alan Tarr, "Selection of State Appellate Judges: Reform Proposals, Rethinking the Selection of State Supreme Court Justices," *Williamette Law Review* (Fall, 2003), 1445–46.

9. Richard A. Watson and Rondal G. Downing, *The Politics of Bench and Bar: Judicial Selection Under the Missouri Non-Partisan Court Plan* (New York: Wiley, 1969); Beth M. Henschen, Robert Moog, and Steven Davis, "Judicial Nominating Commissioners: A National Profile," *Judicature* (April/May 1990), 328–34; Charles H. Sheldon, "The Role of State Bar Associations in Judicial Selection," *Judicature* (May/June 1994), 300–05.

10. Gary Blankenship, "Partisan Attacks Threaten Judicial Independence," available from www.flabar.org (retrieved July 15, 2004).

11. Roy Schotland, "Comment," *Law and Contemporary Problems* (Summer, 1998), 150.

12. Deborah Goldberg, Sarah Samis, Edwin Bender, and Rachel Weiss, *The New Politics of Judicial Elections 2004* (New York: Brennan Center for Justice, New York University Law School, 2005); Deborah Goldberg, Craig Holman,

and Samantha Sanchez, *The New Politics of Judicial Elections* (New York: Brennan Center for Justice, New York University Law School, 2002).

13. Larry Aspin, William K. Hall, Jean Bax, and Celeste Montoya, "Thirty Years of Judicial Retention Elections: An Update," *The Social Science Journal* 37 (2000), 12.

14. See, e.g., Lawrence Baum and Marie Hojnacki, "Choosing Judicial Candidates: How Voters Explain Their Decisions," *Judicature* (April/May 1992), 300-09.

15. *Republican Party of Minnesota v. White*, 536 U.S. 765 (2002).

16. Stephen Lubet, "Black Robe Politics," *The American Lawyer* (July, 2003).

17. Julie Schuering Schuetz, "Judicial Campaign Speech Restrictions in Light of Republican Party of Minnesota v. White," *Northern Illinois University Law Review* (Spring, 2004), 340-41. See also North Carolina Administrative Office of the Courts, "North Carolina Rules: Judicial Code of Conduct," available from www.aoc.state.nc.us/www/public/html/rulesjud.htm (retrieved July 21, 2004).

18. See, e.g., *In re Matter Concerning a Judge (Kinsey)*, 842 So.2d 877 (Fla. 2003) (disciplining judge for making improper campaign statements).

19. David Brody, "The Relationship Between Judicial Performance Evaluations and Judicial Elections," *Judicature* (January/February 2004), 168-77. See generally American Bar Association, Standing Committee on Judicial Independence, *Report of the Commission on Public Financing of Judicial Campaigns* (February 2002), available from www.abanet.org/judind/jud_campaign.html (retrieved August 24, 2004).

20. American Judicature Society, "Model Merit Selection Plan," available from www.ajs.org/selection/sel_stateselect.asp (retrieved July 21, 2004); see also *Justice in Jeopardy: Report of the American Bar Association Commission on the 21st Century*, available from www.abanet.org/media/nov03/111803.html (retrieved July 8, 2004): 70, 74-86.

21. Alexander Hamilton, "Federalist No. 76," *The Federalist Papers*, edited by Clinton Rossiter (New York: Mentor, 1961), 457.

22. Henry J. Abraham. "A Bench Happily Filled: Some Historical Reflections on the Supreme Court Selection Process," *Judicature* (February, 1983), 282-95.

23. J. Woodford Howard, Jr., *Courts of Appeals in the Federal Judicial System: A Study of the Second, Fifth, and D.C. Circuit Courts of Appeals* (Princeton: Princeton University Press, 1981), 90.

24. Michael J. Gerhardt, *The Federal Appointments Process: A Constitutional and Historical Analysis* (Durham: Duke University Press, 2003), 190.

25. George L. Watson and John A. Stookey, *Shaping America: The Politics of Supreme Court Appointments* (New York: Longman, 1995), 64.

26. David M. O'Brien, "Federal Judgeships in Retrospect," in *The Reagan Presidency: Pragmatic Conservatism and Its Legacies*, edited by W. Elliot Brownlee and Hugh Davis Graham (Lawrence: University Press of Kansas, 2003), 329.

27. Ibid., 329.

28. Ibid., 329-30.

29. Ibid., 330.

30. David Alistair Yalof, *Pursuit of Justices: Presidential Politics and the Selection of Supreme Court Nominees* (Chicago: University of Chicago Press, 1999), 12–18.

31. David M. O'Brien, *Judicial Roulette: Report of the Twentieth Century Fund Task Force on Judicial Selection* (New York: Priority Press, 1988), 58–60.

32. O'Brien, *Judicial Roulette*, 59 n. 38.

33. Sheldon Goldman, "Carter's Judicial Appointments: A Lasting Legacy," *Judicature* (March, 1981), 344–55 (Tables 2 and 3).

34. Sheldon Goldman, "Reagan's Judicial Legacy: Completing the Puzzle and Summing Up," *Judicature* (April/May 1989), 319–20. Justice Douglas is quoted in Graeme Browning, "Reagan Molds the Federal Court in His Own Image," *American Bar Association Journal* (August, 1985), 60.

35. Jon Gottschall, "Reagan's Appointments to the U.S. Courts of Appeals: The Continuation of a Judicial Revolution," *Judicature* (June/July 1986), 48–54.

36. Sheldon Goldman, Elliot Slotnick, Gerard Gryski, Gary Zuk, and Sara Schiavoni, "W. Bush Remaking the Judiciary: Like Father Like Son?" *Judicature* (May/June 2003), 285.

37. Sheldon Goldman, Elliot Slotnick, Gerard Gryski, and Sara Schiavoni, "W. Bush's Judiciary: The First Term Record," *Judicature* (May/June 2005), 244, 254–55.

38. American Bar Association, Standing Committee on Federal Judiciary, "ABA Standing Committee on Federal Judiciary," available from www.abanet.org/scfedjud/ (retrieved October 30, 2005).

39. For a sample of this criticism, see Paul D. Kamenar, "The Role of the American Bar Association in the Judicial Selection Process," in *Judicial Selection: Merit, Ideology, and Politics* (Washington: D.C., National Center of the Public Interest, 1990), 93–101.

40. The history of senatorial courtesy is discussed in Gerhardt, *The Federal Appointments Process*, 143–44; see also John Anthony Maltese, *The Selling of Supreme Court Nominees* (Baltimore: John Hopkins University Press, 1995), 121.

41. Senator Hatch is quoted in Betsy Palmer, "Evolution of the Senate's Role in the Nomination and Confirmation Process: A Brief History" *Report for Congress,* Order Code RL31948 (Updated March 29, 2005) (Washington, D.C.: Congressional Research Service, 2003), 8.

42. Brannon P. Denning, "The Judicial Confirmation Process and the Blue Slip," *Judicature* (March/April 2002), 218–26.

43. Denning, "The Judicial Confirmation Process and the Blue Slip," 218, 221, see also Joseph A. Pike and John Anthony Maltese, *The Politics of the Presidency,* 6th ed. (Washington, D.C.: CQ Press, 2004), 264–65.

44. Denning, "The Judicial Confirmation Process and the Blue Slip," 219.

45. Elizabeth Rybicki, *CRS Report for Congress: Senate Consideration of Presidential Nominations: Committee and Floor Procedure*, Order Code RL 31980, (Updated July 1, 2003), 1–2.

46. 531 U.S. 98 (2000).

47. Sheldon Goldman, Elliot Slotnick, Gerard Gryski, and Sara Schiavoni, "W. Bush's Judiciary: The First Term Record," *Judicature* (May/June 2005), 244-75.
48. Henry B. Hougue. *CRS Report for Congress: Supreme Court Nominations Not Confirmed, 1789-2002*, Order Code RL 31171, (Updated July 9, 2003), 2-13.
49. Wendy L. Martinek, Mark Kemper, and Steven R. Van Winkle, "To Advise and Consent: The Senate and Lower Federal Court Nominations, 1977-1998" *Journal of Politics* (May, 2002), 337-61.
50. Robert A. Kagan, *Adversarial Legalism: The American Way of Law* (Cambridge: Harvard University Press, 2001), 50.
51. As quoted in John Massaro, *Supremely Political: The Role of Ideology and Presidential Management in Unsuccessful Supreme Court Nominations* (Albany: State University of New York Press, 1989), 165.
52. For a description of Bork's judicial philosophy, see generally, Robert H. Bork, *The Tempting of America: The Political Seduction of the Law* (New York: The Free Press, 1987), 143-60.
53. Joyce A. Baugh, *Supreme Court Justices in the Post-Bork Era: Confirmation Politics and Judicial Performance* (New York: Peter Lang Publishing, 2002), 10; O'Brien, *Judicial Roulette*, 100.
54. William G. Myers, III, "The Role of Special Interest Groups in the Supreme Court Nomination of Robert Bork," *Hastings Law Quarterly* 17 (1990), 411, 414; Bork, *The Tempting of America*, 288.
55. *Moore v. City of East Cleveland*, 431 U.S. 494 (1977).
56. Bork, *The Tempting of America*, 289; An analysis of interest group pressure tactics is found in Gregory A. Calderia, Marie Hojnacki, and John R. Wright. "The Lobbying Activities of Organized Interests in Federal Judicial Nominations," *Journal of Politics* (February, 2000), 51-69.
57. Nancy Scherer, "The Judicial Confirmation Process: Mobilizing Elites, Mobilizing Masses," *Judicature* (March/April 2003), 240-50.
58. Gerhardt, *The Federal Appointments Process*, 222-23. For a critical view of interest group advocacy, see Gregory A. Calderia, "Commentary on Senate Confirmation of Supreme Court Justices: The Roles of Organized and Unorganized Interests," *Kentucky Law Journal* 77 (1988), 531.
59. Calderia, Hojnacki, and Wright, "The Lobbying Activities of Organized Interests in Federal Judicial Nominations," 58 (Table 2); see also Gerhardt, *The Federal Appointments Process*, 219, 230.
60. The impact of organized interests is analyzed in Caldeira and Wright, "Lobbying for Justice: Organized Interests, Supreme Court Nominations, and the United States Senate," *American Journal of Political Science* 42 (1998), 499-523; Jeffrey A. Segal, Charles M. Cameron, and Albert D. Cover, "A Spatial Model of Roll Call Voting: Senators, Constituents, Presidents, and Interest Groups in Supreme Court Nominations," *American Journal of Political Science* 36 (1992), 96-121.
61. Michael Comiskey, *Seeking Justice: The Judging of Supreme Court Nominees* (Lawrence: University Press of Kansas, 2004), 12-13.
62. Ibid., 12-13.

63. Richard L. Berke, "Thomas Accuser Tells Hearing of Obscene Talk and Advances; Judge Complains of 'Lynching.'" *New York Times* (October 12, 1991), 1; see also Comiskey, *Seeking Justice*, 12.

64. John Anthony Maltese, "The Impact of *Bush v. Gore* and Election 2000 on the Judicial Selection Process," in *The Final Arbiter: The Consequences of Bush v. Gore for Law and Politics*, edited by Christopher P. Banks, David B. Cohen, and John C. Green (Albany: SUNY Press, 2005), 229–30.

65. See, e.g., Charles R. Shipan and Megan L. Shannon, "Delaying Justice(s): A Duration Analysis of Supreme Court Nominations," *American Journal of Political Science* (October, 2003); 654–68; Sarah A. Binder and Forrest Maltzman, "Senatorial Delay in Confirming Federal Judges, 1947–1998," *American Journal of Political Science* 46 (January, 2001), 190–99; Wendy L. Martinek, Mark Kemper, and Steven R. Van Winkle, "To Advise and Consent: The Senate and Lower Federal Court Nominations, 1977–1998," *Journal of Politics* (May, 2002), 337–61.

66. Shipan and Shannon, "Delaying Justice(s)," 665.

67. Miller Center Commission on the Selection of Federal Judges, *Improving the Process of Appointing Federal Judges: A Report of the Miller Center Commission on the Selection of Federal Judges* (Appendix B), (Charlottesville: Miller Center of Public Affairs, University of Virginia, 1996).

68. Goldman, Slotnick, Gryski, Zuk, and Schiavoni, "W. Bush Remaking the Judiciary," 293.

69. Sarah Binder, "The Senate as a Black Hole," *The Brookings Review* available from www.brook.edu/press/review/spring2001/binder.htm (retrieved September 10, 2004).

70. Goldman, Slotnick, Gryski, and Schiavoni, "W. Bush's Judiciary," 269, 274; U.S. Department of Justice, Office of Legal Policy "Judicial Nominations," www.usdoj.gov/olp/judicialnominations.htm (retrieved October 30, 2005).

71. The details of President Bush and Schumer's proposals are outlined in "5/6/03 Letter from Counsel to the President Alberto R. Gonzales to Senator Schumer Regarding the Judicial Confirmation Process," available from www.usdoj.gov/olp/judicialnominations.htm (retrieved September 14, 2004); and Charles E. Schumer, "Judging By Ideology," *New York Times* (June 26, 2001), A19.

72. Miller Center Commission on the Selection of Federal Judges, *Improving the Process of Appointing Federal Judges*, 6–10.

73. O'Brien, in "Report of the Task Force," *Judicial Roulette*.

74. Ibid., 5, 10–11.

75. Richard Davis, *Electing Justice: Fixing the Supreme Court Nomination Process* (New York: Oxford University Press, 2005), 170–72.

76. U.S. Department of Justice, Office of Legal Policy, "Judicial Nominations: 109th Congress" (updated through September 16, 2005), available from www.usdoj.gov/olp/judicialnominations.htm (retrieved October 30, 2005).

77. Sheldon Goldman, *Picking Federal Judges: Lower Court Selection from Roosevelt through Reagan* (New Haven: Yale University Press, 1997), 362–63; O'Brien, "Report of the Task Force," *Judicial Roulette*.

78. Comiskey, *Seeking Justice*, 81, 134; Gerhardt, *The Federal Appointments Process*, 287; O'Brien, "Report of the Task Force," *Judicial Roulette*.
79. As quoted in Michael J. Frank, "Judge Not, Lest Yee Be Judged Not Worthy of a Pay Raise," *Marquette Law Review* (Fall, 2003), 81.
80. Chris W. Bonneau, "The Composition of State Supreme Courts 2000," *Judicature* (July/August 2001), 26–31 (Table 1); see also, John B. Wefing, "State Supreme Court Justices: Who Are They?" *New England Law Review* (Fall, 1997), 47–100.
81. See, e.g., American Bar Association Commission on Women in the Profession, "Current Glance of Women in the Law," available from www.abanet.org/women/articles.html (retrieved September 25, 2004) (noting as of 2000 women comprise 29.7 percent of all lawyers and, as of 2001, forty-eight percent of law students are women).
82. Albert Yoon, "Love's Labor's Lost? Judicial Tenure Among Federal Court Judges: 1945–2000," *California Law Review* (2003), 1055, 1056 n. 86; see also Goldman, Slotnick, Gryski, and Schiavoni, "W. Bush's Judiciary," 269, 274 (Tables 2 and 4) (reporting net worth of judges).
83. See, e.g., *Atkins v. United States*, 556 F.2d 1028 (Ct. Cl. 1977); *Williams v. United States*, 48 F. Supp. 2d 53 (D.D.C. 1999), *aff'd and rev'd*, 240 F.3d 1019 (D.C. Cir. 2001), petition for *cert.* denied, 535 U.S. 911 (2002).
84. Lee Epstein, Jack Knight, and Andrew D. Martin, "The Norm of Prior Judicial Experience and Its Consequences for Career Diversity on the U.S. Supreme Court," *California Law Review* (July, 2003), 912; see also Bonneau, "The Composition of State Supreme Courts 2000" (Table 1).
85. Yoon, "Love's Labor's Lost?," 1029–60.
86. Goldman, Slotnick, Gryski, and Schiavoni, "W. Bush's Judiciary," 269, 274 (Tables 2, 4); Goldman's data for non-G. W. Bush Administrations is reported by Yoon, "Love's Labor's Lost?," 1055 (Table 5).
87. Epstein, Knight, and Martin, "The Norm of Prior Judicial Experience and Its Consequences for Career Diversity on the U.S. Supreme Court," 903–65; see also Goldman, Slotnick, Gryski, and Schiavoni, "W. Bush's Judiciary," 275.
88. Jerome Frank, *Courts on Trial: Myth and Reality in American Justice* (Princeton: Princeton University Press, 1949), 241.
89. Berkson, "Judicial Selection, Compensation, Discipline and Mandatory Retirement," in *The Improvement of the Administration of Justice*, 72–73.
90. Cynthia Gray, *A Study of State Judicial Discipline Sanctions* (Chicago: American Judicature Society, 2002), 3, 5.
91. Cynthia Gray, "How Judicial Conduct Commissions Work," in *The Improvement of the Administration of Justice*, 7th ed., edited by Gordon M. Griller and E. Keith Stott, Jr. (Chicago: Lawyers Conference, Judicial Division, American Bar Association, 2002), 215–24.
92. Gray, *A Study of State Judicial Discipline Sanctions*, 3, 6–7.
93. Eleanore Bushnell, *Crimes, Follies, and Misfortunes: The Federal Impeachment Trials* (Urbana: University of Illinois Press, 1992); Mary L. Volcansek,

Judicial Impeachment: None Called for Justice (Urbana: University of Illinois Press, 1992).

94. 28 U.S.C. §§ 351–64, as amended by The Judicial Improvements Act of 2002, 28 U.S.C. §§ 11041, et seq. A significant challenge to circuit court council disciplinary authority is found in *Chandler v. Judicial Council of Tenth Circuit*, 398 U.S. 74 (1970).

95. Administrative Office of U.S. Courts, "Report of Complaints Filed and Action Taken Under Authority of 28 U.S.C. 351–364" (Tables S–22, S–23), available from www.uscourts.gov (retrieved September 30, 2004).

CHAPTER FIVE

The Practice of Law

As Alexis de Tocqueville observed in the 1830s, lawyers possess a "specialized knowledge of the law" that enables them to "fill most public functions" in society.[1] Not much has changed, though de Tocqueville probably underestimated the prominent role lawyers play in private and public affairs. They shape public policy and distribute private economic resources by advising their clients and pursuing their interests. In short, lawyers perform a variety of critical functions. Most important, they are the "primary gatekeepers to the administration of justice" and have a critical role in providing access to courts.[2] In this chapter, we examine the practice of law, the growth and changing nature of the legal profession, and the opportunities and limits of the profession in providing access to justice.

THE RISE OF THE AMERICAN LEGAL PROFESSION

Traditionally, the public image of lawyers has been dim because they are viewed as mercenaries who needlessly stir up litigation. In colonial times, a North Carolina vigilante group, "The Regulators," characterized lawyers as "cursed Hungry Caterpillars [who charged] fees that eat out the very bowels of [the] Commonwealth."[3] Colonial laws tried to curb the number and influence of lawyers by limiting their ability to make money and preventing them from assuming public leadership positions. In 1641, it was illegal for Massachusetts lawyers to charge a fee for their services, and they were barred from holding a seat in the legislature. In 1657, Virginia lawyers paid heavy fines if they appeared in court on behalf of clients. These restrictions were not only disincentives to practice law, they were also created a prejudice against lawyers that has endured.[4]

Because law schools as we know them did not yet exist, the primary methods of colonial legal training involved self-study or apprenticeships. Apprenticeships were supposed to give students theoretical and practical experience by reading books in the law library, watching other attorneys in court, and performing menial tasks, such as copying pleadings, drafting wills, and drawing up contracts. Still, the value of an apprenticeship was questionable because most of the work was drudgery and there was often little time to read law books. In other words, colonial lawyers "mastered the law not because of their legal apprenticeship, but in spite of it."[5]

Despite their shortcomings, apprenticeships were an important part of early attempts to institutionalize legal education. Another was the movement toward university instruction, first at the College of William and Mary in 1779 and then elsewhere. The first private law school opened under the direction of Judge Tapping Reeve in 1784 in Litchfield, Connecticut. Unlike William and Mary's approach, which taught principles of law through a formal interdisciplinary curriculum, Litchfield's pedagogy provided students with legal training from the practitioners' perspective. The issue of whether lawyers are best trained through formal academic study or by practical experience was partially resolved with Harvard University's decision to open a law school in 1826. Harvard reduced the practitioner's perspective to insignificance and began the process of transforming law schools into the institutional basis for a legal education.[6]

The growth of the modern legal education, however, was slowed by Jacksonian democracy in the 1830s, a populist social reform movement that helped cause the legal profession to become more accountable to the people. First, many state legislatures changed their methods of judicial selection by replacing the appointment of judges with popular elections. Second, common law was assailed by attempts to replace it with the adoption of written codes. Third, the spirit of equality underlying the Jacksonian era mandated that legal practice remain open to all, and bar admission standards were relaxed or abolished.[7]

Diversifying the practice of law also created more opportunities to enter the profession. Anyone possessing minimum age and "good moral" requirements could be licensed. Lax standards also encouraged students to go to law schools because several states allowed direct bar admission (without taking an exam) upon law school graduation. Using the so-called diploma privilege, about 2,400 persons entered the legal profession between 1860 and 1875 in fifteen states. Some states even had "twenty dollar" lawyers, who simply paid twenty dollars to become licensed. Moreover, apprenticeships could not compete with law schools in raising the professional standards. Consequently, although Jacksonian democracy encouraged greater access to the legal profession, it also created a corresponding movement for professional self-regulation by the organized bar.[8]

The post-Civil War and Reconstruction period expanded the scope of the national economy and sharply increased the demand for law education.[9] Local bar associations, first established in New York City, Cleveland, Chicago, St. Louis, and Boston, worked with the American Bar Association (ABA) to restrict entry into the profession. The bar argued that stricter standards were necessary to ensure the quality of the legal profession. Moreover, the law school curriculum was idiosyncratic and varied from school to school. Accordingly, bar associations and a new private accreditation organization, the American Association of Law Schools

(AALS; founded in 1900), lobbied state legislatures to restrict law school entry and bar admissions. Tightening standards enabled ABA-approved law schools to become the exclusive path to the practice of law and impose self-regulation.[10]

The accreditation standards initiatives of the ABA, the AALS, and local bar associations eventually created national standards for bar examinations. The push toward professional self-regulation allowed new requirements to be instituted, including ending the diploma privilege, imposing the requirement of college study as a precondition for law school admission, requiring compulsory attendance in law schools for three years, and making graduation from a law school a prerequisite for taking compulsory bar examinations.[11]

The rise of the legal profession was also greatly affected by two closely related developments: the institutionalization of the *casebook method* and the establishment of the so-called Wall Street law firm. The casebook method was introduced in 1870 by Christopher Columbus Langdell, the dean of Harvard University's law school. In contrast to a lecture style of instruction, students learned law by studying appellate judicial opinions, reprinted in casebooks. For Langdell, "law, considered as a science, consists of certain principles or doctrines, [and] a mastery of these ... is what constitutes a true lawyer ... and [the] ... best, if not the only way of mastering the doctrine effectually is by studying the cases in which it is embodied." Studying case law as a science facilitated logical reasoning or, in popular terms, "thinking like a lawyer." Casebooks isolated key legal principles, and professors asked students to determine whether judges properly adhered to precedent (past decisions). In time, Langdell's "case method" became associated with the "Socratic method" of modern classroom instruction.[12]

The casebook method became widely adopted as an effective tool to increase class size and to keep law schools profitable with higher enrollments. Its popularity made apprenticeships virtually irrelevant, and it facilitated the rise of the Wall Street law firm by encouraging law firms to hire young associates directly from law school, without prior legal experience. The Wall Street law firm emerged in the 1890s as an innovation of a Columbia University law school graduate and New York City attorney, Paul D. Cravath. Sometimes called a "factory system of law," Cravath structured the law office as a bureaucratically efficient and profitable entity, with a filing system, typewriters, stenographers, and typists. Cravath recruited new, aggressive associates from elite law schools. As a result, the Cravath law firm produced "anonymous organization men, steadfastly loyal to the firm that had hired them fresh out of law school, [and] moving only if the firm informed them it could not advance them to partnership."[13]

The Cravath system caught on quickly and several large firms appeared in major metropolitan areas, especially New York, Chicago, Boston, and Cleveland. The institutionalization of the corporate law firm brought with it legal specialization and commercialization, and both remain today. Though rhetorical skill in a courtroom was valued, it was no longer perceived to be the ticket to professional success. Instead, professional advancement was conditioned on generating a profitable client base, a precursor for the modern professional norm of "billable hours" which is the method by which lawyers earn fees on the basis of the time spent performing legal work and the measure for professional advancement. If an associate met the firm's expectations, promotion to partner was likely and an attorney could then share in the firm's profits.

The socialization of the contemporary lawyer remains a byproduct of the historical changes made to accreditation standards, the structure of legal education, and law firm organization after 1870. Once admission standards were tightened and nationally applied, learning the trade by apprenticeship yielded to learning the skills of a professional lawyer in a classroom with a casebook. With the rise of the large law firm, the traditional conception of the generalist lawyer gradually yielded to the pragmatic reality that attorneys were specialists, cultivating the business of legal practice and reaping its financial awards. Significantly, the new emphasis on corporate practice brought with it an increasing stratification within the legal profession, separating the elite performers from the "also-rans."

CONTEMPORARY LEGAL EDUCATION AND BAR ADMISSION

Since the 1960s, the number of attorneys has doubled. Presently, there are 229 law schools in the United States, 189 with ABA accreditation and forty nonaccredited institutions. Although at least fifty new ABA-approved law schools have opened since 1964, the popularity of the Internet has facilitated the appearance of nearly twenty new, but non-ABA approved, online law schools (see Table 5.1).

The number of Law School Admission Test (LSAT) administrations, along with first-year enrollments and new bar admissions, grew apace and has not substantially abated since the 1980s. Today, the legal profession is a $182 billion industry, with over 180,000 legal establishments; 169,000 law offices; and over 1.4 million lawyers, judges, and legal support staff. As a result, between 1947 and 2002, the ratio of population to lawyers has shrunk from 790:1 to about 283:1, arguably transforming the United States into a nation of lawyers.[14]

Unlike many other legal systems in the world, eligibility to practice law in the United States typically begins with admission into law school after graduating from an undergraduate university or college with a baccalaureate degree. In many common law and civil law countries, applicants receive legal training in their undergraduate schooling. For U.S. students, the chances of admission are strengthened if the undergraduate record shows a high grade point average (GPA) in a major area of study. In addition, applicants must take the standardized LSAT. The LSAT has five parts, plus a short writing sample section, which tests reading comprehension, analytical reasoning, and logical reasoning.

Although law schools usually consider a range of factors in reviewing applications, including letters of recommendations, work experience, personal maturity, and extracurricular activities, the GPA and the LSAT score are the most critical elements for admission. Another key factor, though, is cost. Typically, students

TABLE 5.1   Demand for Legal Education, 1964–2005

Academic Year	Total LSAT Administrations	ABA-Approved Law Schools	J.D. Enrollments	Admissions to Bar
1964–1965	39,406	135	51,079	12,023
1970–1971	107,479	146	78,018	17,922
1974–1975	133,546	157	105,708	30,707
1980–1981	108,022	171	119,501	41,997
1984–1985	95,563	174	119,847	42,630
1990–1991	152,685	175	127,261	43,286
1994–1995	128,553	177	128,989	57,875
2000–2001	109,030	186	132,885	51,773
2004–2005	145,258	188	140,376	NA

Note. LSAT = Law School Admission Test; J.D. = Juris Doctorate; NA = not available.

Source: American Bar Association, "Legal Education and Bar Admission Statistics, 1963–2005," available from www.abanet.org/legaled/statistics/le_bastats.html (retrieved December 8, 2005).

spend several hundred, and sometimes thousands, of dollars in paying the fees for applications to several schools, registering to take the LSAT, and ensuring that the Law School Data Assembly Service distributes transcripts and letters of recommendation to targeted schools. Given the significance of scoring well on the LSAT, many applicants also opt to take expensive LSAT-preparation classes (typically costing $1,000 or more), a fee that substantially raises the cost of applying to law school.

Entry into legal practice also necessitates paying for law school, a disincentive for some applicants, but also a burden to those who graduate. Between 1992 and 2002, the cost of living in the United States has risen twenty-eight percent, but the cost of law school tuition has jumped 134 percent in public law schools. One study has reported that although the median salary for private practitioners is $90,000, public interest attorneys typically make only $36,000. Even more significantly, the median law school tuition is $24,920 in private schools, $18,131 for nonresident students in public schools, and $9,252 for resident students in public schools. That study also found that eighty-seven percent of law students take out loans to finance their education. Law school graduates may have an average of $80,000 in student loan debt as they enter the workforce and, on average, pay $1,000 per month during a ten-year repayment period. As law professor Mary Ann Glendon quipped, the specter of paying off student loans means: "The gilded cage has a trapdoor."[15]

Law students are trained through a combination of the Socratic casebook method, lectures, legal clinics, moot courts, legal research and writing exercises. Although there are opportunities to gain practical law office or trial court experience, the thrust of legal training remains learning legal doctrine through casebook analysis. There is little emphasis on interdisciplinary training, so most law students are not exposed to the relationship that law has to political science, sociology, psychology, anthropology, and related liberal arts. In the first year, law students are taught both private law subjects, including torts, contracts, civil procedure, property, and public law courses in constitutional law and criminal law. The second and third years are usually reserved for elective subjects, including professional responsibility, tax, wills and trusts, business corporations, commercial transactions, family law, debtor/creditor relations, insurance, trial and appellate practice. By and large, students are graded by essay examinations (based on hypothetical fact patterns and emphasizing the skill of legal "issue" spotting) and are taught by professors who hold a Juris Doctorate (the three-year law degree) and other credentials, such as law review membership and, perhaps, a judicial clerkship. Some law professors have an additional master's degree in law (L.L.M.) or, less often, a Doctor of Science in Law (S.J.D.) or a Ph.D. in a related field, but many simply hold a J.D. and have little formal teaching experience beyond their nonacademic professional activities.

The preoccupation with doctrinal legal instruction in contemporary legal education underscores that it is "still almost entirely about law and . . . only incidentally and superficially about lawyering."[16] Moreover, with few exceptions, students are taught by law professors who are hired through a narrow path of achievement that only a relatively few transverse. Through a socialization process akin to a type of academic inbreeding, law teachers are assimilated into a professoriate that share identical academic and professional credentials: a law degree, law review experience, legal practice (usually with a prestigious law firm) or government service experience and, sometimes, a judicial clerkship. A study of 872 professorships (about fifteen percent of the profession) found that only about a handful of elite schools, Harvard, Yale, Columbia, Chicago, Michigan, and NYU, are responsible for producing almost one-third of the nation's law professors. Also, sixty percent of the professorate came from top-twenty schools. Significantly, law professors are truly "gatekeepers and molders" of the legal profession.[17]

Bar admissions are similarly restrictive and typically predicated on completing a variety of requirements that limit the number of practicing lawyers. With the exception of a handful of states allowing admission by apprenticeship or diploma privilege, applicants must pass a national standardized Multiple Bar Examination (MBE) test, offered semiannually by the National Conference of Bar Examiners (NCBE), (established in 1931). The MBE consists of multiple choice questions typically covering most first-year law school subjects. Most applicants also must pass an essay portion of the bar, usually covering subjects that test substantive and procedural competence to practice law in a particular state.

In response to the criticism that law schools do not teach enough practical skills, about one-half the states condition bar admission on passing a national clinical skills test, the Multistate Performance Test, or MPT. The MPT requires applicants to handle hypothetical cases or client files by evaluating pertinent pleadings, drafting briefs, or constructing questions for a mock client interview or mock trial deposition. In addition to meeting residency and character fitness requirements, nearly all states require applicants to pass a national ethics examination, the Multistate Professional Responsibility Examination (MPRE). The MPRE is a standardized test offered by the NCBE measuring competence with the Canons of Professional Ethics and the Rules of Professional Responsibility, model sets of ethical guidelines governing attorney behavior in legal practice.

Despite these institutional and financial barriers, several tens of thousands of lawyers are admitted into practice each year. Since the 1980s, the total number of bar admissions have steadily climbed, and generally the annual national pass rate has remained between sixty and seventy percent. In 2004, 77,246 took bar examinations, with sixty-four percent passing.[18] In addition, more women, and to a lesser degree minorities, have entered the profession. In 1947, only three percent of women pursued a J.D., and, before 1972, women represented less than ten percent of the profession. By 1980, the number rose to thirty-four percent and, by 2000, increased to forty-eight percent. In contrast, minority enrollments have not increased as quickly; in 2003 minorities constituted twenty-one percent of total J.D. enrollments.[19]

Despite the substantial gains made by women and minorities in entering the profession, social norms substantially prevent employment equality (see Table 5.2). Women, for example, generally earn less than men, and fewer succeed in getting promoted to high-status positions, such as becoming a partner in a law firm. As law professor Deborah Rhode describes it,

> Women and men of color are still overrepresented at the bottom of the academic pecking orders and underrepresented in the upper ranks of tenured faculty and senior administrative positions. Only twenty percent of full professors and ten percent of law school deans are female, and only ten percent of those in either position are faculty of color.[20]

TABLE 5.2   Legal Profession Occupations by Gender and Position

Legal Occupation	Male		Female		Total	
	N	**Percent**	*N*	**Percent**	*N*	**Percent**
Lawyers	616,159	43.6%	245,878	17.4%	862,037	61.0%
Judges, magistrates, and other judicial workers	36,223	2.5%	21,568	1.5%	57,791	4.0%
Legal support workers	94,788	6.7%	398,121	28.1%	492,909	34.8%
Total	747,170	52.8%	665,567	47%	1,412,737	99.8%

Source: U.S. Census Bureau, "PCT86. Sex By Occupation For The Employed Civilian Population sixteen Years And Over (Census 2000 Summary File 4)," available from www.factfinder.census.gov/ (retrieved October 16, 2004).

THE BUSINESS OF LEGAL PRACTICE

The organization of legal practice has also undergone a significant transformation since the 1960s. The traditional career choice of a solo practitioner has yielded to the pressure of securing stable and cost-effective employment in a law firm. This change has encouraged attorneys, trained as "generalists," to develop specialties in the business of legal practice, often acquired during their first job after law school. Moreover, the law school from which a graduate is hired usually affects a lawyer's career path, reputation, and success. Within private practice, graduates from more prestigious law schools are likely to wind up in large law firms, whereas students from less renowned institutions tend to be employed in midsize to small law firms. Once employed, lawyers are prone to making lateral career changes by taking the skills learned in one job and applying them to another. Government lawyers thus may become criminal defense attorneys in private practice or, similarly, a law firm associate's experience might be later channeled into corporate work or even into a judgeship. Notably, attorneys in civil law countries do not have nearly as much lateral mobility because their training as civil bureaucrats locks them into certain positions, often for life.[21]

Lawyers are principally problem solvers, but they also routinely engage in negotiations, perform research, and conduct factual investigations. As counselors, they dispense advice to clients by explaining to them the strengths and weaknesses of adopting different courses of action. But, contrary to popular opinion, relatively few lawyers regularly appear in court. Most attorneys are behind-the-scenes technicians serving a range of clientele spanning private practice, government, and corporate industry. A small percentage of lawyers take public interest jobs or become law teachers.

The exponential growth and diversity of the legal profession, along with the increasing complexity of the law, has produced some discernible employment trends. The most important is that the private practice of law remains the bedrock of the legal profession. Still, since the 1960s, lawyers have gone increasingly into government service. Another trend is that many attorneys look for more lucrative employment in larger law firms, causing the percentage of solo practitioners to diminish.[22] These historical indicators roughly correspond to the distribution of jobs in the contemporary legal market. As of 2005, fifty-six percent of law school graduates found work in private law firms, whereas twenty-three percent were employed in government (eleven percent as attorneys, eleven percent as judicial clerks, and one percent in military service) and twelve percent engaged in corporate practice. Only seven percent of lawyers settled for public interest law practice (five percent) or legal academic careers (two percent).[23]

Private Practice

Attorneys in private practice work in law firms of different sizes and less frequently in solo practice. Most solo practitioners and small firms, especially in rural areas, represent individual clients, often by defending them in criminal court or in civil cases involving domestic relations or personal injury claims, landlord and tenant matters, real estate transactions, drafting wills and trusts, or setting up estate plans. As such they are the last vestiges of a dying breed, namely, the general practitioner. In contrast, attorneys working in larger law firms tend to serve business clientele, representing large corporations and small businesses in tax, securities, acquisitions, franchise, antitrust, and commercial transactions. A majority of the practitioners in large law firms have moved toward specialization instead of clinging to general practices.[24]

The clientele of different sized law firms underscores that most of the legal profession is highly stratified. The profession's stratification causes it to be separated into what some scholars refer to as two "hemispheres." On the one hand, lawyer elites practice law by catering to the affluent or to political elites (large organizations, corporations, labor unions, and government). On the other hand, nonelites take care of lesser business interests and all others, including the politically and economically disadvantaged.[25]

Contemporary law firm practice remains patterned after the Cravath bureaucratic model. But many of the organizational norms have changed with the increasingly entrepreneurial legal marketplace. At midtwentieth century, there were only a handful of large firms (consisting of fifty or more lawyers), and many medium- to large-sized law firms were relatively homogenous. Associates and managing partners were devoted to the firm as well. Consequently, most partners and many associates stayed with the same firm for years, and there was little lateral movement within the profession to competitor firms. As Joseph Hinsey, a former partner for twenty years at New York City's White & Case, remarked, "[m]oving from Firm A to Firm B, and taking a client group, was basically unheard of, at least in New York."[26]

The introduction of the billable hour in the late 1950s was an early sign that traditional legal practice was destined to become more dynamic and entrepreneurial. As law became more voluminous and complex, lawyers found creative ways to market their increasingly specialized skills, especially after the Supreme Court struck down restrictions on legal advertising in the 1970s.[27] In response to competitive pressures, large law firms adopted many of the business practices of their corporate clientele. Corporate clients became more selective in hiring law firms, and a simultaneous shift toward using cheaper, in-house counsel after the 1970s. That, in turn, was followed by an aggressive, "eat what you kill" revenue-producing system of legal practice.[28]

Loyalty to the firm gave way to longer partnership tracks and a growing tendency for employees and partners to make lateral moves within the profession. These trends were reinforced by the introduction of "up-or-out" promotion policies for associates—the up-or-out policy enabled associates to advance to partner only if they developed a productive client base that made them indispensable. Similarly, two-tiered partnerships for senior management—compensation systems preventing partners from being relegated into permanent, fixed salaried positions if they were able to prove that an equitable share of the firm's profits was warranted, as based on the partners' ability to bring large volumes of business into the firm—became yardsticks for measuring a partner's professional worth.[29]

Unlike the lifetime security that once defined large law firm practice, a "new disloyalty" is a characteristic of contemporary law practice. As political scientist Herbert Kritzer concluded, "corporate legal practice has become a world of change and turmoil," with firms regularly losing partners, dissolving, or merging.[30] In 2003, only about one-third of associates in their sixth year at a law firm worked at the firms they were hired from after law school, and less than one-half found employment in another law firm. Partners at big firms no longer rest on their past accomplishments or reputations. Likewise, associates are forced to generate anywhere between 1,800 to 2,300 billable hours per year to advance to partnerships. For many lawyers, billing 2,100 hours per year at "treadmill" law firms is like "drinking water from a fire hose" because sixty-five to seventy hours a week is spent in the office.[31]

In addition, there have been two other interrelated developments: (1) the growing tendency of corporate law firms to use part-time help, like contract lawyers or nonlawyer staff, such as paralegals; (2) and an explosion of large law firms that are as complex as the corporate giants they service. By the 1990s, there were close to 300 large firms with fifty lawyers, plus nearly 250 other firms with over 100 or more attorneys. By 2001, the average size of the *American Lawyer* top 100 law firms was 621 lawyers, and many competed to recruit associates by paying $125,000 or more as starting salaries.[32] Today, the legal landscape is infused with multiple one-stop, full-service global *megafirms*, headed by CEO's and supported by legions of professional and preprofessional personnel. Megafirms have numerous branch offices domestically and abroad and also boast several corporate legal departments, thousands of attorneys and staff, and separate recruiting and marketing departments. Some even have full-time lobbyists who do not even engage in the practice of law; and several have become even more entrepreneurial by diversifying their practices into peripheral activities, such as rendering financial advice, developing real estate and tourism interests, engaging in management consultation, and providing technological services.[33]

Chicago's Baker & McKenzie, for example, is one of the nation's largest global megafirms. It generates over $1.2 billion in annual fee revenues from about seventy locations in over thirty countries, while staffing over 1,100 partners and 3,300 attorneys. The firm maintains a press office and separate marketing and recruitment departments. Also, its principal legal activities are just as impressive but are heavily corporate-laden with specialties ranging from antitrust to litigation practice, with nine different legal departments staffed by hundreds of attorneys.[34]

See Table 5.3 which shows some top megafirms in the United States.

TABLE 5.3   Top Megafirms in the United States

Law Firm and Locations	Selected Legal Departments and Areas of Practice	Total Number of Attorneys	Total Number of Partners/ Associates	Starting Salaries of Associates
Baker & McKenzie (Chicago) ■ www.bakernet.com/	■ Antitrust & Trade ■ Banking & Finance ■ Corporate ■ Insurance ■ Intellectual Property ■ International/ Commercial ■ IT/Communications	3,309	1,136/2,173	$97,000– $125,000
DLA Piper, Rudnick, Gray, and Cary (Chicago) ■ www.dlapiper.com/	■ Commercial ■ Corporate & Finance ■ Human Resources ■ Legislative & Regulatory ■ Litigation ■ Real Estate ■ Technology, Media & Communications	3,159	1,134/1,917	$95,000– $125,000
Jones Day (Washington) ■ www.jonesday.com/	■ Business Practice ■ Litigation ■ Government Regulation ■ Tax ■ Health Care ■ Life Sciences ■ Technology	2,297	646/1,455	$110,000– $125,000
White & Case (New York) ■ www.whitecase.com/	■ Banking & Corporate ■ Energy ■ Insurance ■ Intellectual Property ■ International Trade ■ Litigation ■ Telecommunications	1,983	385/1,139	$125,000
Latham & Watkins (New York) ■ www.lw.com/	■ Corporate ■ Environment ■ Finance ■ Tax ■ Litigation	1,840	527/1,234	$125,000

Note. Only top five megafirms for 2004 listed.

Source: "The NLJ 250", *The National Law Journal* (November 14, 2005), S16.

Government Attorneys

Unlike private practitioners, government attorneys are civil servants, a role Justice Stephen Breyer once described as performing public service as "citizen-statesmen." In lamenting the decreasing percentage of law graduates interested in public service, Justice Breyer observed that though government jobs do not pay as well as the private sector, they nonetheless provide professional experience that may be used to obtain higher paying jobs, either in business or in private law practice. The path for his own success, he recounted, was first paved as a staff member of the Senate Subcommittee on Administrative Practices and Procedures. As Justice Breyer pointed out, many law graduates of his generation also began careers in government service directly after graduation or after judicial clerkships. What is most significant, he concluded is that the professional satisfaction derived as a public servant with direct responsibility for making policy decisions in regulation, substantially outweighed the benefits of earning higher salaries.[35]

Some lawyers find jobs in the judiciary, and it is not unusual for them to opt for careers as prosecutors, public defenders, law clerks, or central staff attorneys. Others choose a military career as judge advocates. Yet a large proportion of attorneys in federal or state governments work in the executive branch and generally assume policymaking positions. On the federal level, almost 30,000 attorneys work in cabinet-level agencies and independent agencies. Whereas fifty-two percent are employed in the departments of Treasury, Defense, and Homeland Security, a large majority (thirty-two percent) work in Justice.[36] Many Justice Department attorneys work for the U.S. Attorney General, which is the chief law enforcement officer for the United States. But many others find positions in the Office of Solicitor General, which represents the government in litigation before the Supreme Court; the Office of Legal Policy, which assists the president in making judicial selections; or the Federal Bureau of Investigation, an agency in charge of domestic law enforcement. Within Congress, it is common for lawyers to serve as counsel for congressional committees in the House and Senate.

Regardless of their role, working as a civil servant is usually a stepping stone for other legal career paths that might be more prestigious or profitable. As law professor Thomas O. McGarity explains,

> [G]overnment attorneys must live with the reality of very limited resources and maximize the attendant benefits. On the one hand, the offices will not be as large, the secretaries will not be as adept, the computers will not work as well, and the pay will not be as high as in private law firms. On the other hand, the fact of limited resources means that young government lawyers are given far more responsibility than their counterparts in private law firms, and they have a correspondingly greater opportunity to gain valuable professional experience at an early stage of their careers.[37]

Corporate Legal Practice

A significant proportion of lawyers work in the private corporate sector. Major Fortune 500 corporations, including General Motors, General Electric, Procter & Gamble, and Microsoft, staff their own legal departments. Corporations cut costs associated with outside legal counsel by employing their own lawyers to manage routine corporate affairs. Yet, even corporations with their own legal departments are likely to farm out specialized matters or those that involve major litigation. According to one survey, about forty percent of a corporation's average legal budget (of $1.2 million, in 2001) was spent on outside fees.[38]

There are an estimated 65,000 in-house counsel working in more than 21,000 for-profit and not-for-profit business organizations in the United States. The demand for in-house counsel has created new opportunities for attorneys to cross over from government positions into private industry. Furthermore, women and minorities have gained a significant foothold in the corporate legal marketplace. One study of the corporate legal profession found that slightly over thirty percent of in-house counsel are women.[39]

Although working as corporate counsel is less stressful than working in private practice, the tasks remain inherently transactional and may not be as fulfilling as working in other positions that cultivate prestige and political power. Still, working in-house is attractive because the positions generally pay well. The retention rate is high, and there is growing evidence that senior-level partners in law firms continuously compete for open vacancies in corporate legal departments.[40]

Public Interest Lawyers and Legal Academia

A small percentage of attorneys choose to be policy advocates for a variety of private concerns and public-interest law firms. Those contemplating a career in public interest law, however, are discouraged from doing so because of low salaries and high student loan debt. Between 1992 and 2002, public interest salaries have slightly increased from $26,000 to $36,000, but wages at law firms grew from $47,500 to $90,000. By some estimates, sixty-six percent of law graduates decide to avoid public service. In response, a growing number of law schools offer loan-forgiveness programs, sometimes referred to as *Loan Income Protection Plans*, to entice their graduates to enter public service careers. In 2000, only about forty-seven schools offered such assistance, but only a few years later the number increased to eighty. The type of plan varies with the school. At Harvard, 100 percent of student loans are eliminated for graduates making less than $37,000, whereas at Rutgers fifty percent forgiveness is given to those making less than $45,000.[41]

Likewise, only a small percentage of law graduates become law professors. There is approximately 9,700 law faculty in ABA-approved law schools. However, the growing disparity between salaries in the private sector and in law schools is a disincentive to becoming a law professor. As legal scholar Richard Abel points out, many law professors describe themselves as teachers instead of scholars and devote much of their time to classroom activities instead of to publishing articles and books. Yet, many law professors enjoy their autonomy and job security, and those benefits offset the lower incomes.[42]

ACCESS TO LAWYERS AND EQUAL JUSTICE

"Our system of justice is adversarial," Justice Harry Blackmun once said, "and depends for its legitimacy on the fair and adequate representation of all parties at all levels of the judicial process."[43] Justice Blackmun's noble vision of equal justice, however, has never been fully realized. Historically, common law rules allowed lawyers to represent misdemeanor offenders, but they were barred from defending clients charged with felonies. Although most U.S. states and the federal government broke from that practice and allowed for representation in a broader range of criminal prosecutions, it was also widely understood that the right to an attorney generally extends only to those who could afford it then. As a result, the right to an attorney only applied in practice to a narrow class of criminal defendants and not in civil cases. Though the Supreme Court started to loosen the restrictions on the right of legal representation in the early twentieth century, for some critics today it remains a "shameful irony that the country with the world's most lawyers has one of the least adequate systems for legal assistance."[44]

The Right to Counsel in Criminal Cases

The Sixth Amendment of the U.S. Constitution provides that "[i]n all criminal prosecutions, the accused shall . . . have the assistance of counsel for his defense." It was not until 1932 that the Supreme Court took the initial step of requiring the appointment of counsel for indigent defendants in death penalty cases. In *Powell v. Alabama* (1932), an all-white jury in Scottsboro, Alabama convicted several young black men without the assistance of counsel of raping a white woman, an offense carrying the death penalty. In reversing the convictions and ordering a new trial, Justice George Sutherland held that the Fourteenth Amendment's due process clause required the appointment of counsel in order to preserve the defendants' right to a fair trial. Still, the court's holding was narrowly tailored to the facts of the case. As Justice Sutherland explained,

> All that it is necessary now to decide, as we do decide, is that in a capital case, where the defendant is unable to employ counsel, and is incapable adequately of making his own defense because of ignorance, feeble mindedness, illiteracy, or the like, it is the duty of the court, whether requested or not, to assign counsel for him as a necessary requisite of due process of law.[45]

Accordingly, *Powell* did not establish a precedent obliging state courts to appoint counsel for indigent defendants in all cases.

Powell's rationale nonetheless signaled that the court might expand the scope of the right if fundamental due process values were at stake. In *Johnson v. Zerbst* (1938),[46] the court declared a right to appointed counsel for indigent defendants in federal criminal cases. But, in *Betts v. Brady* (1942),[47] the court retreated and ruled that in state courts counsel was only mandated in capital or in those cases presenting "special circumstances." *Betts* prompted a sharp attack from dissenting Justice Hugo Black, who argued that depriving counsel for the poor "defeat[s] the promise of our democratic society [of] providing equal justice under the law" and threatened "innocent men [with] increased dangers of conviction merely because of their poverty."

The fuzzy line the court drew in these cases remained until the landmark decision in *Gideon v. Wainwright* (1963).[48] In *Gideon*, the court reversed Clarence Gideon's state felony conviction for breaking into a pool hall. At trial, Gideon asked for, but was denied, legal representation because he could not afford to hire a lawyer in his defense. In rejecting his request, the trial judge ruled that state law prohibited the appointment of counsel except in capital cases. From his prison cell, however, Gideon asserted his position by filing a handwritten, *in forma pauperis* ("in the form of a pauper") petition to the Supreme Court alleging that his Sixth Amendment right was violated. The court agreed. Writing for a unanimous court, Justice Black overruled *Betts v. Brady* and its so-called special circumstances rule, observing that "any person haled into court, who is too poor to hire a lawyer, cannot be assured a fair trial unless counsel is provided for him." He concluded that "government hires lawyers to prosecute, and defendants who have the money hire lawyers to defend are the strongest indications of the widespread belief that lawyers in criminal courts are necessities, not luxuries." Notably, *Gideon* ratified what a majority of states were doing in providing counsel to indigents accused of committing felonies. Still, *Gideon* forced the states to recognize that the Fourteenth Amendment's due process clause established a constitutional obligation to furnish indigents with appointed counsel in felony cases.

Subsequent cases expanded *Gideon* to guarantee indigent defendants the right to appointed counsel on their first appeal of a conviction; a similar right has been applied to juvenile defendants and in cases involving misdemeanor and suspended sentence prosecutions carrying sentences of imprisonment.[49] Although the conservative Burger and Rehnquist courts substantially cut back on the scope of the right to appointed counsel in a variety of post-*Gideon* cases,[50] the ruling in *Gideon* has not been disturbed and it established a judicially created policy of affording indigents court-appointed lawyers.

In general, federal and state governments use a variety of programs and funding systems to provide indigent defense services. Public defender programs, assigned counsel appointments, or competitive private contracts are the most common. *Public defender programs* either employ full-time, salaried government employees to deliver legal aid to criminal defendants or, instead, work through public or private nonprofit organizations. *Assigned counsel systems* let judges appoint members of the local private bar association on an ad hoc basis. Jurisdictions using *competitive private contracts* let individual practitioners, bar associations, law firms, and nonprofit organizations provide legal services under contracts secured by competitive bidding. The need for indigent defender services is great. One study found that an estimated sixty-six percent of federal felony defendants and eighty-two percent of felony in large state courts were represented by public defenders or assigned counsel.[51]

The Criminal Justice Act of 1964 controls legal services for indigents in federal courts. Counsel are assigned from panels of attorneys chosen from a list of private lawyers on an ad hoc basis, federal defender organizations (staffed with salaried government employees and led by a public defender selected by the court of appeals) or community defender organizations (state incorporated, nonprofit legal services). State governments usually use defender services. Public defender and assigned counsel systems are most frequently used, but problems of adequate funding, high caseloads, and limited judicial resources have compelled states to resort to contractual systems that are more cost efficient. Under contract systems, court-appointed lawyers represent indigent clients for fixed fees, flat fees, or hourly fees with compensation caps and many times with no prescribed case limit.[52]

Although federal and state governments spend an estimated $3.3 billion annually on providing legal services to the poor, critics lament that crushing caseloads, insufficient staffing, inadequate budgetary funding, mismanagement, and attorney incompetence or indifference (caused by low compensation) combine to favor the rich and disproportionately discriminate against those who cannot afford private counsel.[53]

Sidebar 5.1

The Poor State of Indigent Defense Systems in the States

In *Argersinger v. Hamlin* (1972),[a] which extended the right to court-appointed counsel to misdemeanor offenses carrying a six-month sentence of imprisonment, Justice Lewis Powell warned that "[n]o one can foresee the consequences of such a drastic enlargement of the constitutional right to free counsel" by expanding the right too far. And, he concluded that it "could have a seriously adverse impact upon the day-to-day functioning of the criminal justice system."[b] In response, Justice William O. Douglas countered that "the Nation's legal resources are sufficient to implement the rule we announce today," arguing that the number of existing lawyers and new members of the bar vastly exceeded the volume of indigent defendants requiring appointed counsel.[c]

Nonetheless, as Justice Powell predicted, Court decisions extending the right to appointed counsel to juveniles as well as for cases involving misdemeanors offenses and suspended sentences, have severely strained the ability of state governments to supply court-appointed counsel for criminal defendants. The problem is aggravated by the reluctance of law schools to train students to become attorneys for indigents; budgetary constraints; and state legislation such as "three strikes and you're out" laws, which incarcerate convicted defendants for longer time periods through the use of determinate, mandatory sentencing.[d]

Critics charge that the legal profession and state governments do a poor job in providing indigent defender services. Although about half the states rely upon state-wide funding for indigent defense systems, the balance use county-level or local funding. But neither method has been immune from constitutional attack in state courts and, increasingly, state governments are being haled into court. Such lawsuits claim that the lack of funding causes excessive pretrial detentions, deficient attorney consultations, and general neglect by attorneys. In the past decade, multiple lawsuits have been filed in Washington, Mississippi, Louisiana, Montana, Nevada, Pennsylvania, and Minnesota by attorneys complaining about low compensation rates and high caseloads.[e]

In response, many states are enacting reimbursement or "co-pay" laws that make indigents financially responsible for the cost of providing legal representation in criminal cases.[f] Predictably, these laws are increasingly challenged in court as equal protection violations that discriminate against indigents and impede their access to courts. Although state supreme courts are divided on the issue, they have uniformly applied U.S. Supreme Court holdings that recovering costs from indigent defenders is constitutional so long as not to result in a "manifest hardship."[g]

Notes

[a]*Argersinger v. Hamlin,* 407 U.S. 25 (1972).

[b]Ibid., 52 (Powell, J., concurring in result).

[c]Ibid., 37 n. 7 (Douglas, J., Opinion for the Court).

[d]See James Q. Whitman, *Harsh Justice: Criminal Punishment and the Widening Divide Between America and Europe* (New York: Oxford University Press, 2003), 49–62

[e]Leonard Post, "Lack of Lawyers for the Poor Fuels Suits in Six States," *The Recorder* (November 2, 2004), 2; The Spangenberg Group, *Contracting for Indigent Defense Services,* available from www.bjs.org (retrieved November 25, 2004).

[f]See generally National Association of Criminal Defense Lawyers, "Indigent Defense," available from www.criminaljustice.org (retrieved November 27, 2004) (listing updates of lawsuits and events in states relating to indigent defense).

[g]*James v. Strange,* 407 U.S. 128 (1972); *Fuller v. Oregon,* 417 U.S. 40 (1974). See, e.g., *State v. White,* 2004 Ohio 5989 (November 24, 2004) (upholding Ohio's court costs' recoupment law); *State v. Tennin,* 674 N.W.2d 403 (Minn. 2004) (striking down Minnesota's co-pay statute).

The inability to come up with a workable system tends to inhibit court access for indigents and diminishes the quality of legal services. Representation of indigents is thus likely to be different than that for clients with privately retained attorneys. Those differences result in more plea bargains, less attorney contact, a diminished number of trials, and more guilty pleas (see Table 5.4). And as the next section illustrates, the same kind of problems also affect the delivery of legal aid to indigents in civil cases.

TABLE 5.4   Salient Differences in Legal Representation in Indigent Criminal Cases

Institutional and Legal Representation Characteristics	State Defendants		Federal Defendants	
	Public Defender	Private Counsel	Public Defender	Private Counsel
Total Number of Inmates	765,763	236,550	53,215	32,032
Contact with Counsel				
Within twenty-four hrs of arrest	8.8%	26.3%	17.6%	38.2%
Within week of arrest	27.7	33.9	36.1	36.3
More than week before trial	32.8	29.6	33.1	18.4
Within week of trial	12.6	4.8	6.6	4.3
At trial	13.6	3.5	4.9	1.7
Did not talk with counsel	4.5	1.9	1.6	1.2
Number of Times Talked with counsel				
0–1	29.2	11.6	12.1	8.0
2–5	57.9	51.3	65.4	46.7
Six or more times	12.9	37.2	22.5	45.3
Case Disposition				
Not guilty plea	24.3	31.4	25.4	31.7
Bench trial	7.7	9.0	4.5	5.2
Jury trial	16.6	22.4	20.9	26.5
Guilty or no contest plea with plea bargain	50.6	47.2	50.5	48.4
Guilty or no contest plea without plea bargain	25.1	21.4	24.0	19.9

Source: Data collected as of 1997; some data and categories are not reported; percentages do not necessarily equal 100 percent. Caroline Wolf Harlow, *Defense Counsel in Criminal Cases* (Bureau of Justice Statistics Special Report, November 2000, NCJ 179023), Table 17, available from www.bjs.org (retrieved November 25, 2004).

Legal Representation in Civil Litigation

Roughly less than one percent of spending on legal services is devoted to civil legal aid. Consequently, a majority of legal needs of civil indigents remains unmet. In a speech delivered to the National Legal Center for the Public Interest, Justice Stephen Breyer estimated that eighty percent of low-income clients actually receive civil aid but, paradoxically, the government only spends about two dollars per person, a figure far less than in comparable Western democracies. Another study reported that although the legal profession generates approximately $100 billion annually, less than $1 billion goes to low-income citizens, which, in turn, roughly translates into about one lawyer for every 9,000 low-income citizens.[54]

Unlike criminal prosecutions, receiving legal aid or counsel is not a constitutional right in civil cases. Although *Boddie v. Connecticut* (1971)[55] held that indigents have a right of due process to maintain divorce proceedings in state courts if they could not pay the filing fee, the ruling was limited to overturning Connecticut's monopoly over the right of marriage. Thus, a broad right of access for all civil cases was not established. Subsequent cases held that it was constitutional to prevent litigants from filing for bankruptcies when they could not afford to pay filing fees.[56] Impoverished claimants in civil actions aimed at terminating parental rights were also denied a right to court-appointed counsel in *Lassiter v. Department of Social Services* (1981). But, in *M. L. B. v. S. L. J.* (1996), a narrow exception was created permitting litigants to receive a free transcript of court proceedings terminating parental rights for the purpose of filing an appeal.[57]

Consequently, in most civil cases clients must pay lawyers a fee plus expenses. The burden of attorney fees is eased in certain cases, however. In personal injury lawsuits, clients may hire lawyers by signing *contingency fee contracts*—agreements stipulating that legal fees are only paid as a percentage of the total amount of monetary damages recovered. Although clients remain responsible for litigation expenses, contingency fees facilitate access to attorneys because clients do not have to pay legal fees unless there is a successful conclusion. Alternatively, prepaid legal services may be available as part of an employee's insurance benefits. By paying premiums to a group insurance plan, employees can get legal advice, but such plans are not widespread, largely because of resistance from the organized bar.[58]

Government Subsidized Legal Aid

Legal assistance for low-income civil litigants remains available through federal and state government subsidies. As an outgrowth of President Lyndon B. Johnson's Great Society Program and War on Poverty, in 1964 Congress created the federally funded Legal Services Program (LSP). Launched as an ambitious program of law reform designed to fight poverty by asserting federal control over local legal aid efforts, the LSP immediately encountered political opposition. As a result, in 1974 the LSP was removed from the executive branch and replaced by the Legal Services Corporation (LSC), an independent nonprofit corporation managed by a board appointed by the president with the Senate's approval.[59]

In the 1980s, the Reagan administration was adverse to the LSC and tried unsuccessfully to end the program. It succeeded, though, in severely cutting the LSC's funding and enacting a number of restrictions on the types of cases handled. By 1996, LSC's funding was cut by one-third and LSC-funded organizations in the states were barred from participating in school desegregation cases, labor boycotts, class actions, and, among other controversial areas, cases involving abortion.

Congress banned LSC recipients from spending nonfederal funds for these activities. In *Legal Services Corporation v. Veazquez* (2001),[60] however, the Supreme Court ruled that the First Amendment prevents Congress from enacting legislation that cut funds to legal aid organizations seeking to represent indigent clients challenging welfare laws on the basis that it prevented attorneys from making legal arguments, thereby chilling the free speech rights of their clients.

Pro Se Representation

An old adage is that a person who represents himself has a fool for a client. Nonetheless, one of the most important trends in civil justice is the increasing number of citizens representing themselves. According to the president of the California Bar Association, one or both parties do not have counsel in at least eighty to 90 percent of all family law cases. Since the 1990s, other bar associations have chronicled a similar sharp upturn in self-representation in landlord–tenant disputes, bankruptcies, small claims actions, and other miscellaneous civil actions. One scholar found that *pro se representation* accounts for about twenty-five percent of all new civil cases filings in the United States.[61]

A number of interrelated factors have led to more pro se litigants, including the lack of affordable legal counsel, the increased demand for legal aid by moderate- to low-income litigants, and the proliferation of "do it yourself" legal aids, as facilitated by the Internet. Even though *Faretta v. California* (1972)[62] held that the Sixth Amendment contains a right of self-representation, the organized bar has traditionally resisted assisting pro se litigants. The bar has defended its position by claiming that it is trying to protect the consumer from fraud and incompetent practitioners. But cynics counter that the legal profession is simply trying to preserve its monopoly over the practice of law. The judiciary, moreover, has contributed to the perception that it is unwilling to help pro se litigants by adapting "no legal advice" policies on the ground that they might be sued or accused of showing favoritism toward the unrepresented. As a result, courts have been slow in upgrading their facilities and training their staff to assist pro se litigants.[63]

The upsurge in self-representation has nevertheless forced the organized bar and courts to reexamine some policies. In the past decade, the American Judicature Society and the ABA launched extensive public relations campaigns and Web sites to educate the bar and to help pro se litigants. A few states—California, Colorado, Florida, Maine, Washington, and Wyoming—have formally revised rules to permit "unbundling," a form of quasi-legal representation letting lawyers contract with clients to perform specific legal tasks without taking the whole case for a reduced fee. Such services might include appearing in court on a limited basis, rendering legal advice over the telephone or over the Internet, engaging in negotiations, or assisting in document preparation. At least eleven other states are considering taking the same approach.[64]

Pro Bono Legal Services

An alternative type of legal representation includes the volunteer efforts of the organized bar and individual attorneys. Whereas performing legal work *pro bono publico* ("in the public good") has long been considered a public responsibility of the legal profession, court watchers and scholars agree that relying upon the cooperation of private lawyers to deliver free legal services is impractical.[65] Moreover, most rules of professional ethics state that attorneys need only set an aspirational goal of completing fifty hours of pro bono work annually, but they do not require or penalize lawyers and law firms from not doing so.

Because none of the states impose mandatory rules requiring pro bono activity, and less than a handful have established pro bono requirements, such as obligating lawyers to disclose how many hours they contributed to volunteer work or compelling indigent representation, critics report that the legal profession averages less than thirty minutes of pro bono work per week. Only a third of the nation's largest law firms donate contributions for pro bono work equal to three to five percent of their gross revenues—a goal set by the ABA's public campaign, the "Pro Bono Challenge." Only eighteen of the country's top 100 most successful firms meet the ABA's standard of fifty hours of annual pro bono work. As one law professor concluded, "[t]he central dilemma of pro bono remains: [A] system that depends on private lawyers is ultimately beholden to their interests."[66]

SELECTED READINGS

Abel, Richard L. *American Lawyers.* New York: Oxford University Press, 1989.

Auerbach, Jerold S. *Unequal Justice: Lawyers and Social Change in Modern America.* New York: Oxford University Press, 1976.

Clayton, Cornell W., ed. *Government Lawyers: The Federal Legal Bureaucracy and Presidential Politics.* Lawrence: University Press of Kansas, 1995.

Epp, Charles R. *The Rights Revolution: Lawyers, Activists, and Supreme Courts in Comparative Perspective.* Chicago: University of Chicago Press, 1998.

Epstein, Lee. *Conservatives in Courts.* Knoxville: University of Tennessee Press, 1984.

Galanter, Marc, and Thomas Palay. *Tournament of Lawyers: The Transformation of the Big Law Firm.* Chicago: University of Chicago Press, 1991.

Heinz, John P., Robert L. Nelson, Rebecca L. Sandefur, and Edward O. Laumann. *Urban Lawyers: The New Social Structure of the Bar.* Chicago: University of Chicago Press, 2005.

Kritzer, Herbert M., and Susan B. Silbey, eds. *In Litigation: Do the Haves Still Come Out Ahead.* Stanford: Stanford University Press, 2003.

Lawrence, Susan E. *The Poor in Court: The Legal Services Program and Supreme Court Decision Making.* Princeton: Princeton University Press, 1990.

Mather, Lynn, Craig A. McEwen, and Richard J. Maiman. *Divorce Lawyers at Work: Varieties of Professionalism in Practice.* New York: Oxford University Press, 2001.

McGuire, Kevin T. *The Supreme Court Bar: Legal Elites in the Washington Community.* Charlottesville: University Press of Virginia, 1993.
Zemans, Frances Kahn, and Victor G. Rosenblum. *The Making of a Public Profession.* Chicago: American Bar Foundation, 1981.

NOTES

1. Alexis de Tocqueville, *Democracy in America*, translated by George Lawrence, edited by J. P. Mayer (New York: Harper & Row, 1988), 264, 268–69.
2. Frances Kahn Zemans and Victor G. Rosenblum, *The Making of a Public Profession* (Chicago: American Bar Foundation, 1981), 2.
3. Lawrence M. Friedman, *A History of American Law*, 2nd ed. (New York: Simon & Schuster, 1985), 96.
4. For a description of some of the colonial restrictions placed on lawyers, see Charles Warren, *A History of the American Bar* (New York: Howard Fertig, 1966), 8.
5. Charles R. McKirdy, "The Lawyer as Apprentice: Legal Education in Eighteen Century Massachusetts," *Journal of Legal Education* 28 (1976), 134–35.
6. Zemans and Rosenblum, *The Making of a Public Profession*, 5–6; Robert Stevens, "Two Cheers for 1870: The American Law School," in *Law in American History*, edited by Donald Fleming and Bernard Bailyn (Boston: Little, Brown, and Company, 1971), 413–16.
7. Kermit L. Hall, *The Magic Mirror: Law in American History* (New York: Oxford University Press, 1989), 126–27; Robert Stevens, *Law School: Legal Education in America from the 1850s to the 1980s* (Chapel Hill: University of North Carolina Press, 1983), 5–9.
8. Stevens, "Two Cheers for 1870," 417.
9. Stevens, *Law School*, 22.
10. Richard L. Abel, *American Lawyers* (New York: Oxford University Press, 1989), 41–73.
11. Stevens, *Law School*, 94–95, 105 n. 23.
12. Stevens, "Two Cheers for 1870," 435–36. See also Anthony Chase, "The Birth of the Modern Law School," *American Journal of Legal History* 23 (1979), 329–39, 337.
13. Wayne K. Hobson, "Symbol of the New Profession: Emergence of the Large Law Firm, 1870–1915," in *The New High Priests: Lawyers in Post-Civil War America*, edited by Gerard W. Gawalt (Westport: Greenwood Press, 1984), 19–20.
14. U.S. Census Bureau, *Legal Services: 2002* (2002 Economic Census: Professional, Scientific, and Technical Services), Table 1, available from www.census.gov (retrieved October 19, 2004). See also American Bar Association, Section of Legal Education and Admissions to the Bar, *Legal Education and Professional Development-An Educational Continuum. Report of the Task Force on Law*

Schools and the Profession: Narrowing the Gap (July 1992), (Chicago: American Bar Association), 13, 15 (The "MacCrate Report"). See also Katherine S. Mangan, "Justice Ginsburg Raises Questions About Internet-Only Law School," *The Chronicle of Higher Education* (September 13, 1999), available from www.chronicle.com (retrieved November 4, 2004).

15. Mary Ann Glendon, *A Nation Under Lawyers: How the Crisis in the Legal Profession is Transforming American Society* (Cambridge: Harvard University Press, 1996), 90. See also ABA Commission on Loan Repayment and Forgiveness, *Law Student Debt as a Barrier to Public Service: The Final Report of ABA Commission on Loan Repayment and Forgiveness ABA Commission on Loan Repayment and Forgiveness* (Chicago: American Bar Association 2003), available from www.abanet.org (retrieved October 19, 2004), 10–11.

16. As quoted by UCLA law professor Gerald Lopez, in Deborah L. Rhode, *In the Interests of Justice: Reforming the Legal Profession* (New York: Oxford University Press, 2000), 198.

17. Robert J. Borthwick and Jordan R. Schau, "Gatekeepers of the Profession: An Empirical Analysis of the Nation's Law Professors," *University of Michigan Journal of Law Reform* 25 (Fall, 2001), 191–92.

18. The National Conference of Bar Examiners, "Bar Admission Statistics," available from www.ncbex.org/stats.htm (retrieved December 8, 2005), excluding 1988 and 1989, since aggregate pass rates were not compiled.

19. American Bar Association, "Enrollment Statistics 1947–2004 (Percentage of Women)," available from www.abanet.org/legaled/statistics/femstats.html (retrieved December 8, 2005); American Bar Association, "J.D. Degrees 1984–2004 (Total/Women/Minorities)," available from www.abanet.org/legaled/statistics/jd.html (retrieved December 8, 2005).

20. Deborah L. Rhode, *In the Interests of Justice: Reforming the Legal Profession* (New York: Oxford University Press, 2000), 192. See also Wynn R. Huang, "Gender Differences in the Earnings of Lawyers," *Columbia Journal of Law and Society Problems* 30 (1997), 267. See generally American Bar Association. "Enrollment Statistics 1947–2002 (Percentage of Women)," available from www.abanet.org/legaled/statistics/femstats.html (retrieved October 21, 2004).

21. Abel, *American Lawyers*, 175–76. See also *MacCrate Report,* 226.

22. Lynn Mather, Craig A. McEwen, and Richard J. Maiman, *Divorce Lawyers at Work: Varieties of Professionalism in Practice* (New York: Oxford University Press, 2001), 184–85.

23. Law School Admission Council and the American Bar Association, *ABA-LSAC Official Guide to ABA-Approved Law Schools: 2007 Edition* (Newtown: Law School Admission Council, 2006), 37.

24. Herbert M. Kritzer, "The Professions Are Dead, Long Live the Professions: Legal Practice in a Postprofessional World," *Law and Society Review* 33 (1998), 735.

25. John P. Heinz and Edward O. Laumann, *Chicago Lawyers: The Social Structure of the Bar*, rev. ed. (Evanston: Northwestern University Press, 1994), 127-28. The nature of solo law practice is analyzed in Carroll Seron, *The Business of Practicing Law: The Work Lives of Solo and Small-Firm Attorneys* (Philadelphia: Temple University Press, 1996).

26. Martha Neil, "Brave, New World of Partnership," *American Bar Association Journal* (January, 2004), 56.

27. *Bates v. State Bar of Arizona*, 433 U.S. 350 (1977) (striking down legal advertising restrictions).

28. Glendon, *A Nation Under Lawyers*, 24 ("eat what you kill" business orientation). See also *Goldfarb v. Virginia State Bar Association*, 421 U.S. 773 (1975) (striking down minimum fee schedules).

29. Marc Galanter and Thomas Palay, *Tournament of Lawyers: The Transformation of the Big Law Firm* (Chicago: University of Chicago Press, 1991), 28 ("up-or-out" policy); Martha Neil, "Brave, New World of Partnership," *American Bar Association Journal* (January, 2004), 30 (two-tiered partnerships).

30. Kritzer, "The Professions Are Dead, Long Live the Professions," 731-32.

31. As quoted by a lawyer referred to in Stephen Breyer, "The Legal Profession and Public Service" (lecture given in New York, September 12, 2000), available from www.supremecourtus.gov/publicinfo/speeches/speeches.html (retrieved November 12, 2004), 2. See also Stephanie B. Goldberg, "Then and Now: 75 Years of Change" *American Bar Association Journal* (January, 1990), 56; Marie Beaudette, "Associates Leave Firms in Droves," *National Law Journal* (October 26, 2003), 8.

32. Scott L. Cummings, "The Politics of Pro Bono" *University of California Law Review* (October 2004), 1, 36-37 (discussing growth of large corporate law firms).

33. Stephanie B. Goldberg, "Then and Now: 75 Years of Change," *American Bar Association Journal* (January, 1990), 56 (analyzing the emergence of the megafirm).

34. The firm history, along with the firm's "facts and figures" and different areas of legal practice, are found in Baker and McKenzie's Web site, www.bakernet.com/BakerNet/default.htm (retrieved April 19, 2006).

35. Breyer, "The Legal Profession and Public Service," 9. See also Hope Viner Samborn, "Government Agents: Some Find Perks of Public Sector Work Beat the Potential of Private Practice," *American Bar Association Journal* (December, 2002), 64.

36. United States Office of Personnel Management, "Federal Employment Statistics," available from www.opm.gov/feddata/ (retrieved November 16, 2004) (various tables in 0905 General Attorney category, as of June 2004). For some of the roles government attorneys play, see John C. Yoo, "Lawyers in Congress," *Law and Contemporary Problems* (Spring 1988), 1-19.

37. Thomas O. McGarity, "The Role of Government Attorneys in Regulatory Agency Rulemaking," *Law and Contemporary Problems* (Winter 1988), 32.

38. Susan Hackett, "Inside Out: An Examination of Demographic Trends in the In-House Profession," *Arizona Law Review* (Fall / Winter 2002), 613. See also Abel, *American Lawyers*, 168–72.

39. American Corporate Counsel's Association, "American Corporate Counsel's Association Census of U.S. In-House Counsel (Executive Summary, December 2001)," available from www.acca.com/Surveys/census01 (retrieved November 13, 2004). See also Hackett "Inside Out," 610; Abel, *American Lawyers*, 171.

40. Abel, *American Lawyers*, 171.

41. Tresa Baldas, "Paying the Way: Loan Programs Booming for Grads in Public Service Jobs," *National Law Journal* (July 5, 2004), 1.

42. Abel, *American Lawyers*, 174. Demographic statistics about the composition and total number of law faculty is found in Association of American Law Schools, *Statistical Report on Law School Faculty and Candidates for Law Faculty Positions 2002-03*, available from www.aals.org/statistics/2002-03/2002-03statistics.pdf (retrieved November 18, 2004) (Table 2C, Year 2002–03).

43. *McFarland v. Scott*, 512 U.S. 1256 (1994) (Blackmun, J., dissenting).

44. Deborah L. Rhode, *Access to Justice* (New York: Oxford University Press, 2004), 3. See also David Cole, *No Equal Justice: Race and Class in the American Criminal Justice System* (New York: The New Press, 1999), 65–66.

45. *Powell v. Alabama*, 287 U.S. 45 (1932), 71.

46. *Johnson v. Zerbst*, 304 U.S. 458 (1938).

47. *Betts v. Brady*, 316 U.S. 455 (1942).

48. *Gideon v. Wainwright*, 372 U.S. 355 (1963).

49. *Argersinger v. Hamlin*, 407 U.S. 25 (1972) (misdemeanors); *Alabama v. Shelton*, 535 U.S. 654 (2002) (suspended sentences); *In re Gault*, 387 U.S. 1 (1967) (juveniles); and *Douglas v. California*, 372 U.S. 353 (1963) (first, mandatory appeals).

50. See, e.g. *Scott v. Illinois*, 440 U.S. 367 (1979); *Ross v. Moffitt*, 417 U.S. 600 (1974); *Pennsylvania v. Finley*, 481 U.S. 551 (1987). See also David M. O'Brien, *Constitutional Law and Politics: Civil Rights and Liberties*, 6th ed., Vol. 2 (New York: W. W. Norton, 2005), 1093–95.

51. Caroline Wolf Harlow, *Defense Counsel in Criminal Cases* (Bureau of Justice Statistics Special Report, November 2000, NCJ 179023), available from www.bjs.org (retrieved November 25, 2004).

52. The Spangenberg Group for the Bureau of Justice Assistance, Office of Justice Programs, *Contracting for Indigent Defense Services: A Special Report* (April 2000, NCJ 181160), available from www.bjs.org (retrieved November 25, 2004).

53. See, e.g., Rhode, *Access to Justice*, 11–13. See also The Spangenberg Group, *Contracting for Indigent Defense Services*, available from www.bjs.org (retrieved November 25, 2004); U.S. Department of Justice, Office of Justice Programs, *Indigent Defense Services in Large Counties, 1999 (November 2000, NCJ 184932)*, available from www.bjs.org (retrieved November 25, 2004).

54. David Luban, "Taking Out the Adversary: The Assault on Progressive Public Interest Lawyers," *California Law Review* (January 2003), 209, 211.

55. *Boddie v. Connecticut*, 401 U.S. 371 (1971).

56. *United States v. Kras*, 409 U.S. 434 (1973).

57. *M. L. B. v. S. L. J.*, 519 U.S. 102 (1996); *Lassiter v. Department of Social Services*, 452 U.S. 18 (1981).

58. See Jerold S. Auerbach, *Unequal Justice: Lawyers and Social Change in Modern America* (New York: Oxford University Press, 1976), 285-88.

59. Susan E. Lawrence, *The Poor in Court: The Legal Services Program and Supreme Court Decision Making* (Princeton: Princeton University Press, 1990), 25-36.

60. *Legal Services Corporation v. Velazquez*, 351 U.S. 533 (2001).

61. Rhode, *Access to Justice*, 82.

62. *Faretta v. California*, 422 U.S. 806 (1972).

63. Paula L. Hannaford-Agor, "Helping the Pro Se Litigant: A Changing Landscape," *Court Review* (Winter, 2003), 8-16; Rhode, *Access to Justice*, 82-83.

64. Mark Hansen, "Helping Self Helpers: ABA Web Site Offers Information on Limited Representation of Clients," *American Bar Association Journal* (September, 2004), 72.

65. See, e.g., Ruth Bader Ginsburg, "In Pursuit of the Public Good: Lawyers Who Care" (Speech Delivered on April 9, 2001, University of District of Columbia), available from www.supremecourtus.gov/publicinfo/speeches/speeches.html (retrieved November 28, 2004); Margaret Graham Tebo, "Lag in Legal Services: Conference Speakers Make the Case for More Pro Bono Efforts by Lawyers," *American Bar Association Journal* (July, 2002), 67; Rhode, *Access to Justice*, 145-84.

66. Cummings, "The Politics of Pro Bono," 147. The specific calculations of pro bono contribution by the legal profession and top law firms are found in Deborah L. Rhode and Geoffry C. Hazard, Jr., *Professional Responsibility and Regulation* (New York: Foundation Press, 2002), 162-63.

CHAPTER 6

Access to Courts

"I am an atheist," Dr. Michael Newdow asserted during oral argument before the Supreme Court, "[a]nd every school morning, my child is asked to stand up, face that flag, put her hand on her heart and say that her father is wrong." Millions of public school children say the Pledge of Allegiance every day, but the practice was offensive to Newdow because he thought the words "under God" in the pledge violated the First Amendment's *establishment clause*, the provision erecting a wall of separation between religion and state. The Court of Appeals for the Ninth Circuit agreed, and Newdow defended his parental right to assert that he was entitled to control his daughter's religious upbringing before the nation's highest court. As he put it, "I have the right to see that my daughter is not indoctrinated."[1]

But, Newdow's right to bring the lawsuit on his daughter's behalf was challenged by his ex-wife, Sandra Banning. Banning was a born-again Christian who supported the pledge and had sole legal custody of her daughter. She was also unaware that a lawsuit had been filed until after the Ninth Circuit issued its ruling. In *Elk Grove Unified School District v. Newdow* (2004),[2] the Supreme Court dismissed the lawsuit, ruling Newdow did not have legal standing to bring the suit because he was not his daughter's legal custodian. By denying his right to sue, the Court avoided answering the more contentious First Amendment claim. For some court watchers, the outcome was ironic because shutting the courthouse door meant that "the justices found it easier to separate parent and child than to separate church and state."[3]

Elk Grove illustrates that judicial policymaking is often formulated in the preliminary stages of lawsuits when determining a litigant's right to bring a lawsuit.[4] By requiring litigants to overcome threshold barriers for access to courts, such as the law of standing and other jurisdictional doctrines, courts create opportunities to avoid, delay, or resolve contentious issues of public policy.

Although courts are passive institutions that respond to claims for legal relief, they nonetheless retain the power to determine whether litigants have properly invoked their jurisdiction. The scope of that authority is addressed in the first part of this chapter. Then, the different methods by which organized interests and public advocacy groups strategically access the courts and influence public policy is discussed.

Courts are not self-starters, so litigants must invoke the jurisdiction of a court before they may request relief. In general, the U.S. Constitution and state constitutions, federal or state statutes, and rules of courts are the principal sources of formal legal authority vesting courts with jurisdiction. After reviewing some of the formal barriers to judicial access, the informal constraints are considered, along with the various discretionary methods used to grant or deny litigants access.

FORMAL BARRIERS

Under Article III of the U.S. Constitution, federal courts may decide select "cases or controversies." As explained by Chief Justice Charles Evan Hughes, a court's jurisdiction extends to controversies that are "definite and concrete, touching the legal relations of parties having adverse legal interests." Moreover, the controversy admits of "specific relief through a decree of a conclusive character, as distinguished from an opinion advising what the law would be upon a hypothetical state of facts."[5]

Article III prohibits courts from entertaining so-called friendly lawsuits—those that do not raise adverse interests. Nor may courts give advisory opinions about hypothetical cases. For example, the Supreme Court in 1793 rejected Secretary of State Thomas Jefferson's request to advise President George Washington on how to interpret international law. Though many state courts follow the model suggested by Article III, there are exceptions. In 1993, for instance, the Alabama supreme court issued an advisory opinion informing the legislature of its duty to comply with a court order finding that the method of funding state public schools violated the state constitution's guarantee of a "liberal" education. At least eight states permit their courts to advise the governor or legislature on questions of policy, and several state courts have pressed to assume jurisdiction over political disputes and legal matters that ordinarily are nonjusticiable in the federal courts.[6]

Both federal and state courts use procedural rules to manage their dockets and to instruct litigants regarding how to file legal claims. Under the 1789 Judiciary Act, federal courts followed the rules of state judiciaries, but as the federal system grew, Congress authorized federal courts to develop their own procedural rules and practices. With the passage of the Rules Enabling Act in 1934, Congress gave the Supreme Court the power to create its own rules on the basis of recommendations made by the Judicial Conference of the United States. As a result, the Court enacted the 1938 Federal Rules of Civil Procedure (FRCP), the body of rules that now governs federal judicial procedure.[7]

The FRCP quickly became the model for most states as well. The model rules require pretrial meetings between judges and lawyers, a practice that helps settle cases without trials. In 1946, the Court created the Federal Rules of Criminal Procedure, and in the 1970s the Federal Rules format was adopted for administrative actions as well as for evidentiary hearings.

The proliferation of judicial rule making has been both a boon and a bane, however. Though the goal of greater uniformity has been arguably achieved, the simplicity of procedure has been undermined by the balkanization of federal and state practices, because each judicial district promulgates its own set of rules. Congress also complicated the development of uniform rules by amending the federal rules, often without consulting the U.S. Judicial Conference or the Supreme Court.[8]

The political struggle over the development of rules of procedure has also had contradictory effects. On the one hand, the open and deliberative process of rule creation contributed to a rulemaking process that is democratic and accountable to the public. On the other hand, the openness underlying the process has resulted in state and federal judiciaries promulgating their own sets of procedural rules that independently define, control, and manage relevant practice, procedure, and evidentiary standards. The collaborative, but disjointed rule-making process thus exacts a cost on litigants seeking to gain access because the delivery of legal services is increasingly parochial and centered on discrete rules that make the judicial process complicated, time-consuming, and expensive.[9]

Sidebar 6.1

The *Ashwander* Rules of Constitutional Avoidance

In *Ashwander v. Tennessee Valley Authority* (1936),[a] Justice Louis Brandeis outlined some of the principles the Supreme Court developed to avoid answering constitutional questions. The principles of avoidance are important for understanding the ways the Court uses its discretion to forestall deciding difficult constitutional or policy issues that may bring the judiciary into conflict with Congress or the president. Justice Brandeis explained it as follows:

> The Court developed, for its own governance in the cases confessedly within its jurisdiction, a series of rules under which it has avoided passing upon a large part of all the constitutional questions pressed upon it for decision. They are:
>
> 1. The Court will not pass upon the constitutionality of legislation in a friendly, nonadversary, proceeding, declining because to decide such questions "is legitimate only in the last resort, and as a necessity in the determination of real, earnest and vital controversy between individuals. It never was the thought that, by means of a friendly suit, a party beaten in the legislature could transfer to the courts an inquiry as to the constitutionality of the legislative act."

2. The Court will not "anticipate a question of constitutional law in advance of the necessity of deciding it." . . . "It is not the habit of the Court to decide questions of a constitutional nature unless absolutely necessary to a decision of the case."

3. The Court will not "formulate a rule of constitutional law broader than is required by the precise facts to which it is to be applied."

4. The Court will not pass upon a constitutional question although properly presented by the record, if there is also present some other ground upon which the case may be disposed of. This rule has found most varied application. Thus, if a case can be decided on either of two grounds, one involving a constitutional question, the other a question of statutory construction or general law, the Court will decide only the latter . . . Appeals from the highest court of a state challenging its decision of a question under the Federal Constitution are frequently dismissed because the judgment can be sustained on an independent state ground.

5. The Court will not pass upon the validity of a statute upon complaint of one who fails to show that he is injured by its operation . . . Among the many applications of this rule, none is more striking than the denial of the right of challenge to one who lacks a personal or property right. Thus, the challenge by a public official interested only in the performance of his official duty will not be entertained.

6. The Court will not pass upon the constitutionality of a statute at the instance of one who has availed himself of its benefits.

7. When the validity of an act of the Congress is drawn in question, and even if a serious doubt of constitutionality is raised, it is a cardinal principle that this Court will first ascertain whether a construction of the statute is fairly possible by which the question may be avoided.

Note

[a]*Ashwander v. Tennessee Valley Authority*, 297 U.S. 288 (1936) (Brandeis, J., concurring).

DISCRETIONARY BARRIERS

Case and controversy limitations on judicial power are present in several discretionary doctrines that make a case *justiciable*. The concept of *justiciability* is a form of judicial self-governance that allows courts to exercise restraint and deny access to cases not deemed "fit" for resolution. If a case is justiciable, the litigant has properly invoked the court's jurisdiction. Political scientists have dubbed this "access to judicial policymaking"—that is, the initial decisions granting litigant access allows courts to make final decisions on the merits of cases and controversies.[10] In addition to ruling that a case lacks adverse parties or definitive issues, courts routinely determine whether lawsuits are "ripe," "moot," or otherwise improperly raise a "political question." These doctrines are commonly called "the law of standing."

The Law of Standing

Although the *law of standing* has been called one of "the most amorphous concepts in the entire domain of public law,"[11] it simply means that a party must have a personal stake in the outcome of a case. In theory, the doctrine of standing turns upon resolving questions of a litigant's status and not whether the underlying claim is meritorious. Thus, who is seeking relief is more important than what is being sought.

The amorphous character of the law of standing is demonstrated by the conflicting approaches courts have taken in opening or closing the courthouse door to certain classes of litigants. In *Frothingham v. Mellon* (1923),[12] for example, the Supreme Court signaled it would not entertain lawsuits by taxpayers seeking to challenge the constitutionality of federal laws unless they could prove they suffered a "direct injury." But, in *Flast v. Cohen* (1968),[13] the Court rejected *Frothingham* and granted taxpayer standing to prevent the federal government from giving religious schools a subsidy for instructional materials and textbooks. Although the impact of the ruling was limited to the facts of the case, *Flast* liberalized taxpayers' standing by granting them access to courts if they could satisfy a two-prong test: First, litigants must demonstrate a logical connection between their status as taxpayers and the challenged legislation, and, second, there must be a link between their status and the "precise nature of the constitutional infringement alleged." These principles made it easier for taxpayers in establishment clause cases to bring lawsuits in federal courts and expanded the role of courts in determining public policy.

Furthermore, in the 1970s Congress passed legislation encouraging special interest groups and other third parties to sue if they were "adversely affected or aggrieved" by regulatory action that allegedly violated federal environmental, health, and safety laws. Thereafter, the Supreme Court granted standing in some cases but increasingly denied it in others, as the Court's membership became more conservative during the Burger (1969–1986) and Rehnquist (1986–2005) eras. Whereas, *United States v. Students Challenging Regulatory Agency Procedure* (1973)[14] allowed environmental groups to bring suit attacking a freight tax that impeded recycling efforts and contributed to pollution, standing was denied in *Lujan v. Defenders of Wildlife* (1992).[15] There, the Court held that a pro-wildlife organization did not suffer any "imminent injury in fact" resulting from a change in federal policy applying the Endangered Species Act to federally funded projects abroad. Unlike *Flast*, however, *Lujan* involved a challenge to an agency decision and did not concern a taxpayer lawsuit.

Still, *Friends of the Earth, Inc. v. Laidlaw Environmental Services, Inc.* (2000)[16] considerably relaxed the barriers to granting standing to an environmental group, Friends of the Earth and Citizens Local Environmental Action Network, against a corporation that owned a wastewater treatment plant that was polluting the North Tyger River in Roebuck, South Carolina. In dismissing the argument that the group lacked standing because there was no proof that the environment was harmed by the toxic discharges, Justice Ruth Bader Ginsburg's opinion for the

Court countered that there was ample proof showing that several members of the group were specifically injured because their recreational, economic, and aesthetic interests in using the river were diminished. In addition, the Court made clear that citizens have standing to seek civil penalties against polluters that continue to violate the law, even though the fines are paid to the government.

Mootness and Ripeness

Marco DeFunis, Jr., a white student, applied to law school at the University of Washington but he was denied admission, allegedly because of his race. DeFunis believed that less qualified, minority applicants were accepted under the school's affirmative action program. After filing suit, the state trial court agreed, but on appeal the state supreme court reversed. However, that decision was stayed while DeFunis's appeal was pending before the U.S. Supreme Court. By the time the Supreme Court was ready to hear the case, DeFunis was in his last year of law school. Accordingly, in *DeFunis v. Odegaard* (1974),[17] the Court dismissed the lawsuit on the ground it was *moot*—that is, the controversy had ceased to be "definite and concrete" and "no longer touch[ed] the legal relations of parties having adverse legal interests." Four dissenters, however, thought the "reverse affirmative action" claim was capable of repetition and had to be resolved by the Court. But a bare majority disagreed, and the controversy disappeared and the Court avoided addressing it in that case.

DeFunis illustrates that a live controversy can lose its adverseness upon a change in facts or law after a lawsuit is filed. But mootness may also be found if a case is brought too late or there is nothing left for the court to decide because the legal issue is already settled. Alternatively, a lawsuit may also become nonjusticiable on the grounds of *ripeness* if it is brought too early, either because the anticipated legal injury has not yet occurred or because the litigant has not yet exhausted all other available legal appeals. In *Renne v. Geary* (1991),[18] for example, a challenge to a state constitutional provision banning political endorsements during elections was held not ripe because the complaining parties failed to allege that a political party had not actually endorsed a candidate in a voting pamphlet and compromised their First Amendment rights. Absent such an allegation, the case did not present a live controversy for the Court to decide.

Notably, the doctrines of mootness and ripeness may be manipulated, either to avoid deciding contentious social issues of public policy, or, conversely, to confront them. Although *DeFunis* declined to review the merits underlying reverse-affirmative action claims, four years later, in *Regents of the University of California v. Bakke* (1978),[19] the Court did so and upheld such programs so long as they do not impose a quota system. Likewise, in *Roe v. Wade* (1973),[20] the landmark abortion decision, the Court decided the case even though Jane Roe had delivered a baby by the time the Court handed down its decision. Instead of mooting the case, the Court invoked the same exception that the dissenters in *DeFunis* had unsuccessfully tried, namely, by holding a woman may become pregnant again and the issues that were raised had to be judicially resolved because they were "capable of repetition, yet evading review."

The Political Question Doctrine

The origin of the political question doctrine is found *Marbury v. Madison* (1803).[21] In *Marbury,* Chief Justice Marshall said, "[t]he province of the court is, solely, to decide on the rights of individuals, not to inquire how the executive, or executive officers, perform duties in which they have discretion. Questions in their nature political, or which are, by the constitution and the laws, submitted to the executive, can never be made in this court." The doctrine limits judical authority by removing political disputes from the Court's jurisdiction. As an element of justiciability, it means that a court must decide whether judicial intervention is advisable in a dispute that should be decided by the other political branches, or for which there was no clear judicial remedy.

Before 1962, the Supreme Court generally refused to hear political questions. As Justice Felix Frankfurter stated in *Colegrove v. Green* (1946),[22] a political redistricting case, intervening in political disputes would require the judiciary to do "what is beyond its competence to grant." For Justice Frankfurter, proper respect for constitutional "duties in our governmental scheme [often] depend on the fidelity of the executive and legislative action and, ultimately, on the vigilance of the people in exercising their political rights." And, he warned, "[c]ourts ought not to enter this political thicket."

However, the Court abruptly reversed course in *Baker v. Carr* (1962),[23] another redistricting case. In a 6:2 ruling, Justice William J. Brennan held that the judiciary had the authority to address the constitutional issue of whether the malapportionment of state legislatures violated individuals' voting rights because they were not equally weighted. Since *Baker,* the Court has not hesitated to enter into the "political thicket" of superintending the electoral process in a wide range of cases implicating the basic principles of a representative democracy, including the regulation of political parties, campaign finance regulation, political patronage, voting, and redistricting.

In *Bush v. Gore* (2000), an election saga and legal contest that Justice Ginsburg later referred to as a "December storm over the U.S. Supreme Court,"[24] the Court bypassed the political question doctrine and decided in a 7:2 vote that the manual recount conducted in certain Florida voting districts violated the equal protection clause by not providing precise standards for determining a voter's intent in casting a ballot. Four justices—Stevens, Souter, Ginsburg, and Breyer—disagreed. Justice Stephen Breyer made the most forceful case for nonintervention, arguing that the Twelfth Amendment and the federal Electoral Count Act vested in Congress, not the Court, the power to decide the outcome of presidential elections. For Justice Breyer, the Court should have avoided the inherently political question and followed the advice of Justice Brandeis who once said that "[t]he most important thing we do is not doing."

These doctrines are critical gateways for litigants to gain access to courts. Even so, their scope and application remains contentious and subject to ongoing debate. For legal scholar Alexander Bickel, the doctrines are "passive virtues." In other words, the courts should exercise judicial restraint and not decide controversial cases in the absence of a clear "neutral" constitutional principle. By contrast, Gerald Gunther argued that the doctrines are "subtle vices." They allow courts to avoid responsibility to decide difficult cases and are an abuse of judicial discretion because the Court has the duty to uphold basic constitutional values.[25]

The differing viewpoints of Bickel and Gunther highlight the contrasting approaches taken by the Court in *Newdow* and *Bush v. Gore*.[26] Furthermore, these and other cases illustrate the central role lawyers play in crafting legal arguments that embrace or deny that courts have authority to rule on socially controversial areas of public policy.

Sidebar 6.2

"Public Interest" Lawsuits in the United States and Abroad

The Constitution's Article III "case or controversy" requirement ordinarily prevents federal courts from hearing cases that do not allege specific, concrete injuries to individuals but that instead involve generalized allegations of public harm, as in lawsuits brought by taxpayers, legislators, or citizens. *Raines v. Byrd* (1997),[a] for example, denied standing to members of Congress who voted against the federal Line Item Veto Act, giving the president authority to cancel certain spending and tax benefits measures after the president had signed them into law. The Court also observed, however, that there was "nothing irrational" about granting standing in such cases and that some European constitutional courts, such as in Italy, do so.[b]

Congress by legislation may authorize "citizen standing," which allows members of the public to bring lawsuits as so-called private attorney generals, in order to enforce certain environmental, consumer, or discrimination claims against specific agencies on behalf of the U.S. government. Many foreign countries, and some U.S. state governments, permit identical *public interest lawsuits*. In Canada, public interest standing is granted if (1) there is a "justiciable and serious issue" as to the challenged legislation's validity, (2) the litigant seeking standing is "directly affected" by the legislation or has a "genuine issue" in its validity, and (3) there is no other "reasonable and effective way" to bring the legislation's validity before a court.[c] In India, courts may recognize public interest petitioners filing lawsuits under Article 32 of the Constitution of India, but only if litigants are "bona fide" and have "sufficient interest" in "the enforcement of public interest or general interest in which the public or a class of the community have pecuniary interest or some interest by which their legal rights or liabilities are affected." Hence, one Indian court did not grant standing to a citizen seeking to challenge the execution of a prisoner on the grounds that a television news program reported that the state delayed too long in carrying out the sentence.[d]

In the United States, civil claims may be consolidated and brought by a class of aggrieved litigants through a *class action*, a lawsuit that is often commenced in the public interest of correcting abuse of the environment, consumer protection laws, and public safety. Congress enacted The Class Action Fairness Act of 2005, which put greater restrictions on some types of class actions by requiring that they are filed in federal courts. The new law reforms past practice by reducing the availability of class actions in state courts because those forums traditionally were perceived as more receptive to mass tort claims than were the federal courts, a problem that allegedly led to larger legal fees for attorneys filing frivolous claims. As a result, the law also increases judicial oversight over attorney's fees. Although the legislation may facilitate access to federal courts, critics argue that the restrictions are business-friendly and ultimately deprive injured individuals of opportunities to bring class action lawsuits in the public interest against wealthy corporations in a cost-effective manner.[e]

Notes

[a]*Raines v. Byrd*, 521 U.S. 811 (1997).

[b]Ibid., 828.

[c]See *Thorson v. Canada* (1975) 1 S.C.R. 138; *MacNeil v. Nova Scotia* (1975) 12 N.S.R. (2d) 85; *Borowski v. Canada* (1982) 1 W.W.R. 97. See also Lorne Sossin, *Boundaries of Judicial Review: The Law of Justiciability in Canada* (Scarborough, Ontario: Carswell, 1999), 203–04.

[d]See *Pandey v. State of West Bengal & ORS* (2003) 4 LRI 868.

[e]William Branigin, "Congress Changes Class Action Rules," *Washington Post* (February 17, 2005).

Controversies over Courts

Is the Federal Judiciary Too Small to Provide Equal Access to Justice?

A controversy facing the federal judiciary is whether the number of federal judgeships should be increased to keep pace with rising caseloads and to provide equal access to justice. The Committee on Long-Range Planning of the Judicial Conference of the United States is studying the increasing caseload of federal courts and projects continued growth in cases and a need for more judges.[a]

Year	District Court Caseloads	Judges	Circuit Court Caseloads	Judges
1950	91,005	224	2,830	65
1960	87,421	245	3,899	68
1970	125,423	401	11,662	97
1980	196,757	516	23,200	132
1990	264,409	575	40,898	156
2000	386,200	940	84,800	430
2010	642,500	1,510	171,600	840
2020	1,109,000	2,530	325,100	1,580

Despite the projected trends, the growing federal deficit does not bode well for dramatically increasing the number of judges, courthouses, and staff as occurred in the 1970s and 1980s. Moreover, federal judges themselves are sharply divided over the wisdom of increasing their numbers. Some maintain that the number of judgeships should be increased in order to ensure timely and equal access to justice. A backlog of cases, they insist, underscores the truth of the old adage "justice delayed is justice denied." But others counter that a larger federal judiciary would present numerous problems and make it even more difficult to recruit "the best and the brightest."

THE CASE FOR INCREASING THE SIZE OF THE FEDERAL JUDICIARY

U.S. Court of Appeals for the Ninth Circuit Judge Stephen Reinhardt has championed the cause for increasing the size of the federal bench in order to keep pace with caseloads and to ensure equal and timely access to justice. He contends that[b]

> [we] hear much about the problem of increasing delay in our federal courts. We hear complaints that litigants are frequently denied oral argument, that the size of briefs is being limited unreasonably, that written opinions are being replaced by inadequate informal memorandum dispositions. All these charges are true, all these complaints are justified, and all result from a single cause. We do not have enough federal judges to do all the work that is necessary to provide first-class justice to all.
>
> The solution is simple. There are only 170 federal appellate court judges in a country of [280] million people. Yet, except for the 100 odd cases a year the Supreme Court hears, courts of appeals are the courts of last resort in all federal cases. Why only 170 judges, sitting in panels of three—meaning only roughly fifty-five panels—to hear all the federal appeals affecting two to three hundred million people? No reason at all ...
>
> At the heart of the freeze movement is judicial elitism. It is the view that federal courts and federal judges are too important for routine matters that only affect ordinary persons. Conservative judges, such as former Judge Bork and his intellectual allies, have long urged that the federal court system be preserved as a small jewel, to

resolve major disputes with significant economic consequences. In short, the elitists think that the federal courts exist primarily in order to resolve cases involving large business interests—to decide "big buck" cases, cases that interest them....

The opponents of growth also argue that bureaucratization will result, and that the quality of federal judges will decrease. Both these arguments are demonstrably wrong. Bureaucracy occurs when there are too few judges, not too many. When there are too few judges for the number of cases, we lean too heavily on staff, enact procedures that result in the arbitrary classification of cases that receive second class treatment, and then dispose of them by shortcuts taken behind closed doors....

As to the quality of federal judges—we are simply deluding ourselves if we think that we are the brightest and the best. There are three, four, ten, or more lawyers out there, at least as well qualified as each judge who is appointed. Nor will the quality diminish because the selection process will become "routine." There is nothing routine about the judicial selection process. The struggles for appointments will be just as fierce, the examination of qualifications by opponents just as rigorous ...

Finally, let me add one word about cost. Doubling the size of the judiciary will cost a small amount of money. That is true. But the price is right. The annual cost of operating the federal court system is less than the cost of building one space shuttle, only slightly more than one stealth bomber. We receive less than three-tenths of one percent of the federal budget. Doubling our size would be a drop in the bucket. And the benefits to our criminal and civil justice system would be enormous ...

THE CASE AGAINST INCREASING THE SIZE OF THE FEDERAL BENCH

In contrast, U.S. Court of Appeals Judge J. Harvie Wilkinson III, among others, has emphasized the problems created for the judiciary by increasing the number of federal judgeships:[c]

Growth in the number of federal judges is a powerful invitation to Congress to assign more and more of the nation's judicial business to the federal courts.... The more judges there are, the more jurisdiction will be assigned them and the more federal rulings will be handed down. The sphere of federal law will gradually but inevitably expand at the expense of the law of the states....

The phenomenon of growth, however, promises not only to alter the federal-state balance. It threatens to change the character of the federal judiciary itself. Some years ago, Justice Felix Frankfurter predicted that "a steady increase in judges ... is bound to depreciate the quality of the federal judiciary and thereby adversely to affect the whole system." ...

[T]he concern over the quality reflects the public interest in attracting the best people possible to perform an important public service. Quality is critical in federal judicial appointments for several reasons. Predictable quality obviously promotes respect for the federal judicial process itself. It would seem beyond dispute that the complexities of federal tax, labor, and securities law, to take but a few examples, should be addressed by persons who clarify rather than confuse the scope and meaning of the governing legal principles in those areas. A federal judiciary number in the thousands would undoubtedly have its share of clarifiers. Regrettably, however, an institution of that size would have its complement of confusers too . . .

The problem of personnel growth poses special difficulties for the courts of appeals. The appellate courts were designed as deliberative bodies, and their functions include not only the resolution of cases but also the exposition of legal precedent. . . . Collegiality may be the first casualty of expansion on the Federal Appellate Courts. I recognize that to speak of collegiality may have a quaint and antique ring. Collegiality is one of those soft, intangible words which may ring hollow upon the congressional ear. Judges, however, have a deep conviction that a collegial court does a better job . . .

Growth undermines and destabilizes the law of the circuit in several important ways. Simply as a matter of basic mathematics, the addition of each new judge creates many new possible panel combinations. . . .

As the number of judges rolls ever upward, the law of the circuit will become more nebulous and less distinct. Indeed, it is likely that the law of circuit will be replaced by the law of the panel. Judicial decisions may come to be viewed as resolving only that day's dispute. Litigation will become more a game of chance and less a process with predictable outcomes. . . .

Notes

[a]Committee on Long-Range Planning, Judicial Conference of the United States, *Proposed Long-Range Plan for the Federal Courts* (Washington, D.C.: Judicial Conference of the United States, 1995), 14–15.

[b]Stephen Reinhardt, "Whose Judiciary Is It Anyway?" 27 *Loyola of Los Angeles Law Review* 1 (1993).

[c] J. Harvie Wilkinson, III, "The Drawbacks of Growth in the Federal Judiciary," 43 *Emory Law Journal* 1147 (1994), 1165, 1167–69, 1173–77.

Further Readings

See Richard A. Posner, *The Federal Courts: Crisis and Reform,* 2nd ed. (Cambridge: Harvard University Press, 1996); Jon O. Newman, "1,000 Judges—The Limit for an Effective Federal Judiciary," *Judicature* 76 (1993), 187; J. Harvie Wilkinson, III, "The Drawbacks of Growth in the Federal Judiciary," *Emory Law Review* 43 (1994), 1147.

ORGANIZED INTERESTS AND STRATEGIC LITIGATION

"We can now look forward to at least another term," complained Justice Scalia, "with carts full of mail from the public, and streets full of demonstrators, urging us—their unelected and life-tenured judges who have been awarded those extraordinary, undemocratic characteristics precisely in order that we might follow the law despite the popular will—to follow the popular will." Justice Scalia's disappointment, expressed in a concurring opinion in *Webster v. Reproductive*

Health Services (1989), was over the Court's failure to overturn *Roe v. Wade* (1973). Because *Webster* generated an unprecedented amount of attention from organized interests and public advocacy groups from both sides of the political spectrum—78 amicus, or "friend of the court" briefs were filed, and over 400 different interest groups co-sponsored the abortion litigation—many believed that the Court might use *Webster* to reverse *Roe*. But it did not happen.[27]

Justice Scalia's comment and the wide attention given *Webster* by interest groups illustrate the critical role interest group litigation plays in shaping judicial policy. The organizations mobilized in *Webster* correctly perceived that the recently appointed Justice Anthony Kennedy, who replaced Justice Lewis Powell's "swing vote," split the Court into two equal factions on the abortion issue and that Justice O'Connor would have the critical vote in determining *Roe's* survival. As a result, organized interests on both sides vigorously competed for Justice O'Connor's vote by making a variety of strategic legal arguments in their briefs concerning the scope of the right to privacy, medical science, states' rights, and judicial power. Because Justice O'Connor cast a moderate vote in choosing to uphold Missouri's abortion restrictions but also supporting *Roe* as precedent, "both [pro-choice and pro-life supporters] made inroads with the Court."[28] Not only did they shape the Court's decision with the information they supplied, but the interest groups also accomplished many of their policy goals as nonparty participants in the case, and they enhanced their own legitimacy and expertise as litigants in the judicial process.

Just as Justice Scalia predicted, the abortion controversy did not die down after *Webster*. Organized interest groups continue to play a vital role in influencing court decisions in that area as well as many others. According to one report, during the Court's 2003 term the Justices read a record number (107) of interest group *amicus curiae* briefs in the University of Michigan affirmative action cases, *Grutter v. Bollinger* (2003) and *Gratz v. Bollinger* (2003).[29] That organized groups have become a pervasive part of appellate litigation in controversial cases is a rough measure of their significance in law and courts. Accordingly, the rest of this chapter examines the different methods by which organized interest groups attempt to influence judicial policymaking.

Interest Group Politics and Litigation Strategies

The significance of interest group politics is widely acknowledged in political science, and scholars have demonstrated that all levels of government are susceptible to group pressure. Organized interests broadly consist of institutional or membership-based entities, such as nonprofit corporations, private foundations, think tanks, public advocacy groups, trade associations, or public interest law firms. They exert pressure by lobbying legislators with letter-writing campaigns; organizing public demonstrations at executive agencies, courts, or assembly buildings; donating money for political campaigns; mobilizing grassroots support, arranging public appearances, and testifying at public hearings. The Internet has become a powerful tool for organized interests as well.[30]

Interest groups may influence judicial appointments and elections as well as organize public protests to send political messages to the judiciary. But the most common method of pressure is litigation, designed either to affect judicial policymaking or to advance general organizational goals.

Interest groups seeking economic, social, or political change generally adopt two basic litigation strategies: (1) as litigants they may file a lawsuit or, alternatively, act as litigant sponsors in "test" cases filed by other parties; or (2) they may participate in cases by submitting *amicus curiae* briefs. Apart from direct involvement as litigants, groups sponsor litigation by supplying legal talent and paying litigation expenses. The classic example is *Brown v. Board of Education* (1954), the landmark ruling ending racial discrimination in public schools. In *Brown*, the NAACP Legal Defense Fund was successful in overturning the "separate but equal" doctrine by sponsoring five "test" cases in the South, Midwest, and District of Columbia against school districts that denied black school children full and equal access to public educational facilities. Although sponsorship has the advantage of allowing the group to control litigation strategy, it also is highly expensive and, in contrast to the *Brown* litigation, can result in devastating losses if the opposing party wins. In other words, judicial support for group policy goals is conditional and not always achievable. As Susan Lawrence's study of the Legal Services Program's sponsorship of litigation demonstrated, the victories at the high court that expanded the rights of civil indigents were often offset by the defeats in cases which restricted the rights of the poor for decades afterwards.[31]

Filing *amicus curiae* briefs is less costly for interest groups, but they lose the advantage of controlling the litigation and making tactical decisions. Court rules generally permit organized groups to file *amicus* briefs if they have the consent of the parties or the leave of court. Yet, certain government entities, such as the U.S. Solicitor General or a state's attorney general, may be exempted from having to ask permission. In addition, though organizations may be permitted to file briefs, they are rarely allowed to participate in oral arguments. Under the Supreme Court's rules, counsel filing *amicus* briefs must also disclose who provided financial support in writing the brief and whether an attorney representing a party to the case assisted in the brief's preparation or submission.[32]

In spite of the procedural hurdles *amici* must overcome in filing briefs, courts generally allow greater *amici* participation. *Amici* filings in state supreme courts and in the Supreme Court have sharply increased in the past sixty years.[33] Appellate courts do not significantly restrict *amici* filings because the briefs provide more input about legal doctrine or extralegal sources (such as social science studies, public opinion polls, or foreign law precedent) that might otherwise be ambiguous or omitted.

Moreover, courts increasingly cite extralegal sources found in *amici* briefs in their rulings. In *Grutter v. Bollinger* (2003), Justice O'Connor's opinion for the Court referred to a variety of studies, reports, and data from a number of *amici* showing that student body diversity was critical to achieving learning outcomes, and that information supported upholding the constitutionality of University of Michigan's law school affirmative action program.[34]

In Comparative Perspective

Comparative Constitutional Law and Capital Punishment

Comparative constitutional law commands greater attention as a result of supranational courts, like the European Court of Justice and other transnational courts (further discussed in the In Comparative Perspective boxes in chapters 8 and 10), as well as national high courts, citing the decisions of other courts in their rulings. There are a number of reasons for that development. Following the collapse of the former Soviet Union, constitutional courts in Central and Eastern Europe turned to comparative constitutional law analysis when construing their new constitutions. High courts in Canada, Germany, and Japan also have frequently looked to the decisions of the U.S. Supreme Court when interpreting similar provisions in their post-World War II constitutions and bills of rights. The South African Constitution and Bill of Rights specifically requires its judiciary to consider foreign and international law. In addition, bar associations along with business and human rights organizations have promoted the development of international standards, and comparative constitutional analysis became easier with Internet access to high court decisions from around the world.[a]

An illustrative development is the reliance on comparative constitutional law in striking down capital punishment laws.[b] Within the U.S. Supreme Court, the justices sharply disagree over the use of comparative constitutional analysis. As a result, some foreign jurists have been highly critical of the U.S. Supreme Court for not paying more attention to comparative and international law, particularly with respect to human rights.[c] Yet, increasingly, attorneys and interest groups in their briefs cite foreign legal services and judicial decisions in support of their arguments.

When holding that the execution of mentally retarded criminals violates the Eighth Amendment in *Atkins v. Virginia* (2002),[d] Justice Stevens noted in a footnote that "within the world community, the imposition of the death penalty for crimes committed by mentally retarded offenders is overwhelmingly disapproved." But, that reference invited a sharp rebuke from Chief Justice Rehnquist and Justice Scalia; they maintain that "the viewpoints of other countries simply are not relevant to interpreting constitutional standards."

In fact, the decades-old debate over the abolition of the death penalty in the United States was sparked by Justice Arthur J. Goldberg's 1963 opinion dissenting from the denial of *certiorari* in *Rudolph v. Alabama*.[e] There, Justice Goldberg cited international developments and documents in urging lawyers to challenge the constitutionality of imposing capital punishment for rape as disproportionate and cruel and unusual punishment. More generally, the Court has at times taken judicial notice or in *dicta* taken note of comparative and international trends and legal developments in its opinions.[f]

A widely cited example of comparative constitutional analysis is the South African Constitutional Court's ruling striking down capital punishment as a violation of "human dignity" and the South African Constitution's guarantee of "the right to life."[g] Chief Justice Arthur Chaskalson emphasized the importance of taking into account international and comparative legal developments in order to "provide a framework within which [the South African Constitution's guarantee of a fundamental right to life] can be evaluated and understood." He then surveyed the U.S. Supreme Court's decisions but only to conclude that its approach to capital punishment presented "difficulties that have been experienced in following this path . . . [and] persuade me that we should not follow this routine." However, he also focused on Justice William J. Brennan's concurrence in *Furman v. Georgia*[h] and dissent in *Gregg v. Georgia*,[i] along with rulings going back to *Trop v. Dulles*,[j] for the proposition that "the concept of human dignity is at the core of the prohibition of 'cruel and unusual punishment' by the Eighth and Fourteenth Amendment."

From that Chief Justice Chaskalson buttressed his analysis that capital punishment violates human dignity by turning to Canadian and German high court rulings on the death penalty. He analyzed as well a ruling of the European Court of Human Rights that held that a fugitive in the United Kingdom should be extradited to Germany, which was his homeland and in which the death penalty had been abolished, rather than to the United States where the crime was committed and for which a death sentence could be imposed. The European Court of Human Rights concluded that extradition to the United States would violate the European Convention on Human Rights.[k] This latter decision underscored, in Chief Justice Chaskalson words, that "A holding by us that the death penalty for murder is unconstitutional does not involve a choice between freedom and death; it involves a choice between death . . . and the severe penalty of life imprisonment."

From these sources, the Chief Justice Chaskalson concluded that the South African Constitution embraced the concept of "human dignity" and on that basis invalidated South Africa's laws for imposing capital punishment, and he explained that

> [u]nder our constitutional order the right to human dignity is specifically guaranteed. It can only be limited by legislation which passes the strongest test of being "necessary." The weight given to human dignity by Justice Brennan is wholly consistent with the values of our Constitution and the new order established by it. It is also consistent with the approach to extreme punishments followed by courts in other countries . . .
>
> Taking these factors into account . . . and giving the words of Section 11(2) the broader meaning to which they are entitled at this stage of the enquiry, rather than a narrow meaning, I am satisfied that in the context of our Constitution the death penalty is indeed a cruel, inhuman and degrading punishment. . . .

Subsequently, constitutional courts in Albania,[l] Lithuania,[m] and the Urkraine[n] invalidated capital punishment, as did the Hungarian Constitutional Court earlier.[o] They based their decisions on, among other legal developments, a 1983 protocol abolishing capital punishment adopted by Western Europe countries. More recently, the Eastern

Caribbean Court of Appeal, the appellate court for the Organization of Eastern Caribbean States, struck down laws mandatory death penalty laws for certain crimes in St. Vincent and the Grenadines.[p] Likewise, in 2002 the Organization of American State's Inter-American Court on Human Rights invalidated mandatory death sentences in Trinidad and Tobago.[q]

Notes

[a]See, e.g., Sujit Choudhry, "Globalization in Search of Justification: Towards a Theory of Comparative Constitutional Interpretation," *Indiana Law Review* 74 (1999), 819; and Bruce Ackerman, "The Rise of World Constitutionalism," *Virginia Law Review* 83 (1997), 771.

[b]For further discussion, see Paolo G. Carozza, "'My Friend Is a Stranger': The Death Penalty and Global Ius Commune of Human Rights," *Texas Law Review* 81 (2003), 1031.

[c]See, e.g., the Honorable Claire L'Heureux-Dube, Justice of the Supreme Court of Canada, "The Importance of Dialogue: Globalization and the International Impact of the Rehnquist Court," *Tulsa Law Journal* 34 (1998), 15.

[d]*Atkins v. Virginia*, 536 U.S. 304 (2002).

[e]*Rudolph v. Alabama*, 375 U.S. 889 (1963).

[f]For a discussion of the U.S. Supreme Court's uses of comparative constitutionalism, see David Fontana, "Refined Comparativism in Constitutional Law," *UCLA Law Review* 49 (2001), 539.

[g]*The State v. T. Makwanyane and M. Mchunu,* 1995 (3)SA 391 (Const. Ct.).

[h]*Furman v. Georgia,* 408 U.S. 238 (1972).

[i]*Gregg v. Georgia*, 428 U.S. 153 (1976).

[j]*Trop v. Dulles*, 356 U.S. 86 (1958).

[k]*Soering v. United Kingdom*, 11 Eur. Ct. H.R. 439 (ser. A) (1989).

[l]*Fletorja Zyrtare*, 33, 1301 (Dec. 12, 1999), translated in the Venice Commission's CODIECES data base No. ALB-1999-3-008, available from www.codices.coe.int

[m]*Valstybes Zinios,* 109-3004 (Dec. 11, 1998), translated and available from www.lrkt.lt/1998/n8a1209a.htm

[n]*Ophitsiynyi Visnyk Ukrayiny* [The Official Bulletin of Ukraine], No. 11-rp99 4/2000 (Dec. 29, 1999).

[o]*Alkotmanybirosag,* Dec. No. 23/1990 (X. 31) AB (Oct. 24, 1990), translated in 1 *East European Case Reporter of Constitutional Law* 177 (1994).

[p]*Spence v. Queen,* Criminal Appeal No. 20 of 1998 and No. 14 of 1997 (April 2, 2001), available from www.ecsupremecourts.org.lc/index.htm

[q]*Hilaire v. Trinidad & Tobago*, Inter-Am. Ct. H.R. (ser. C) No. 94 (June 21, 2002), available from www.corteidh.or.cr/index-ingles.html

While *Gratz* and *Grutter* may suggest that lawyers and interest groups have tremendous clout as agents of legal policy change, the issue of whether *amici* brief filings actually explain judicial behavior is subject to considerable scholarly debate.[35] What seems clear is that certain *amici* participants, such as the U.S.

Solicitor General, enjoy more access and success because they are "repeat players." Established in the Department of Justice in 1870, the *solicitor general* is institutionally recognized by the Supreme Court as the sole legal representative of the U.S. in litigation. Consequently, the solicitor general has many advantages over "single shotters"—individual litigants or minorities who litigate infrequently, and often with scant resources or expertise. Because the solicitor general argues all of the federal government's cases before the Supreme Court, it is not surprising that the justices rely on the office's institutional expertise and, accordingly, are predisposed to grant *certiorari* in cases in which the government participates. For the same reasons, studies have shown that the solicitor general is more successful on the merits than are other organized litigants in cases argued before the Supreme Court, especially in cases when the Court's ideological membership matches the solicitor general's policy arguments.[36]

Nonetheless, it remains unclear whether comparable organized litigants with equal experience and resources win as often as the solicitor general does in Supreme Court litigation. The issues of court access and litigant success may call for a more complex and subtle explanation. Melinda Hall and Paul Brace's study of State Supreme Courts' agenda-setting and judicial behavior found that multifaceted institutional factors—including the supply of lawyers in states, whether state judiciaries had enough professional resources (financial and administrative staff) to manage their courts, and the type of judicial selection system used in states—significantly affected whether the "have nots" in civil litigation involving *amicus* participation were given access to courts and whether they won or not. A variety of institutional features and other contextual factors in the legal environment, in other words, explained who got access to courts and why they won or lost.[37] Similarly, Charles Epp and Thomas Burke found that the underlying institutional resources of the legal system—including lawyers, organized interests, money, and formal legal doctrines that encourage litigation—provide the necessary ingredients for mobilizing litigants and producing policy change in discrete areas of the law.[38]

In sum, the trend of having more *amicus* involvement in high-profile appellate litigation is consistent with the general thrust of studies that suggest that access and policy success for litigants is largely a function of whether sufficient institutional resources exist to accommodate their organizational goals and policy objectives.

SELECTED READINGS

Bickel, Alexander M. "Foreword: The Passive Virtues," *Harvard Law Review* 75 (1961), 40–79.

Gunther, Gerald. "The Subtle Vices of the 'Passive Virtues'—A Comment on Principle and Expediency in Judicial Review," *Columbia Law Review* 64 (January 1964), 1–25.

Kloppenberg, Lisa A. *Playing It Safe: How the Supreme Court Sidesteps Hard Cases and Stunts the Development of Law* (New York: New York University Press, 2001).

Strum, Philippa. *The Supreme Court and "Political Questions"* (Tuscaloosa: University of Alabama Press, 1974).

NOTES

1. Tony Mauro, "Against All Odds: Michael Newdow Takes the Pledge Personally," *The Recorder* (November 10, 2003), 1, Newdow's remarks at oral argument before the Supreme Court are found in David G. Savage, "Justices Debate 'God' in Pledge," *Los Angeles Times* (March 25, 2004), A12.
2. *Elk Grove Unified School District v. Newdow*, 542 U.S. 1 (2004).
3. Ellen Goodman, "One Child Indivisible," *The Washington Post* (June 19, 2004), 23.
4. Helen Hershkoff, "State Courts and the 'Passive Virtues': Rethinking the Judicial Function" *Harvard Law Review* 114 (May, 2001), 1833–1941.
5. *Aetna Life Insurance Company v. Haworth*, 330 U.S. 227 (1937), 240–41.
6. Hershkoff, "State Courts and the 'Passive Virtues,'" 1836 n. 17 and ibid., 1845–46.
7. Judith Resnik, *Processes of the Law: Understanding Courts and Their Alternatives* (New York: Foundation Press, 2004), 131–40.
8. Resnick, *Processes of the Law,* 132–37. See also Judicial Conference of the United States, *Long Range Plan for the Federal Courts* (December, 1995), available from www.uscourts.gov/lrp/ (retrieved March 1, 2004), 58–59.
9. Jack B. Weinstein, "Rule-making by the Courts," in *The Improvement in the Administration of Justice,* 6th ed., edited by Fannie J. Klein (Chicago: American Bar Association, 1981), 127–35.
10. Harold J. Spaeth and Stuart H. Teger, "Activism and Restraint: A Cloak for the Justices' Policy Preferences," in *U.S. Supreme Court Behavior Studies,* edited by Harold J. Spaeth and Saul Brenner (New York: Garland Publishing, 1990), 240.
11. *Flast v. Cohen*, 392 U.S. 83 (1962), 99 (quoting Professor Paul A. Freund).
12. *Frothingham v. Mellon*, 262 U.S. 447 (1923).
13. *Flast v. Cohen,* 392 U.S. 83 (1968).
14. *U.S. v. Students Challenging Regulatory Agency Procedure,* 412 U.S. 669 (1973).
15. *Lujan v. Defenders of Wildlife*, 504 U.S. 555 (1992).
16. *Friends of the Earth, Inc. v. Laidlaw Environmental Services, Inc.*, 528 U.S. 167 (2000).
17. *DeFunis v. Odegaard*, 416 U.S. 312 (1974), quoting *Aetna Life Ins. Co. v. Haworth,* 300 U.S. 227, 240–41 (1937).
18. *Renne v. Geary,* 498 U.S. 890 (1991).
19. *Regents of the University of California v. Bakke*, 438 U.S. 265 (1978).

20. *Roe v. Wade,* 410 U.S. 113 (1973).

21. *Marbury v. Madison,* 5 U.S. (1 Cranch) 137 (1803), 170.

22. *Colegrove v. Green,* 328 U.S. 549 (1946).

23. *Baker v. Carr,* 396 U.S. 186 (1962).

24. Christopher P. Banks, "A December Storm over the U.S. Supreme Court," in *Superintending Democracy: The Courts and the Political Process,* edited by Christopher P. Banks and John C. Green (Akron: University of Akron Press, 2001), 238.

25. Gerald Gunther, "The Subtle Vices of the 'Passive Virtues'—A Comment on Principle and Expediency in Judicial Review," *Columbia Law Review* 64 (January 1964), 1–25. But see Alexander M. Bickel, "Foreword: The Passive Virtues," *Harvard Law Review* 75 (1961), 40–79.

26. See Lisa A. Kloppenberg, *Playing it Safe: How the Supreme Court Sidesteps Hard Cases and Stunts the Development of Law* (New York: New York University Press, 2001).

27. *Webster v. Reproductive Health Services,* 492 U.S. 490 (1989). See also *Roe v. Wade,* 410 U.S. 113 (1973). The extensive role public interest groups played in *Webster* is analyzed in Susan Behuniak-Long, "Friendly Fire: *Amici Curiae* and Webster v. Reproductive Health Services," *Judicature* (February/March 1991), 261–70.

28. Behuniak-Long, "Friendly Fire," 270.

29. Tony Mauro, "Court Affirms Continued Need for Preferences," *New York Law Journal* (June 24, 2003), 1. See also *Lawrence v. Texas,* 539 U.S. 558 (2003). The University of Michigan affirmative action cases are *Grutter v. Bollinger,* 539 U.S. 306 (2003), upholding the law school's program; *Gratz v. Bollinger,* 539 U.S. 244 (2003), striking down the undergraduate program.

30. Clyde Brown and Herbert Waltzer, "Virtual Sources: Organized Interests and Democratization by the Web," *The Social Science Journal* 41 (2004), 543–58.

31. Susan E. Lawrence, *The Poor in Court: The Legal Services Program and Supreme Court Decision Making* (Princeton: Princeton University Press, 1990), 123–47.

32. Rule 37, Rules of the Supreme Court of the United States (Effective May 1, 2003), available from www.supremecourtus.gov/ (retrieved December 4, 2004).

33. Lee Epstein, "Exploring the Participation of Organized Interests in State Court Litigation," *Political Research Quarterly* 47 (1994), 335–52; Joseph D. Kearney and Thomas W. Merrill, "The Influence of Amicus Curiae Briefs on the Supreme Court," *University of Pennsylvania Law Review* (January, 2000), 743–855.

34. See *Grutter v. Bollinger,* 539 U.S. 306 (2003).

35. See, e.g. David M. O'Brien, *Storm Center: The Supreme Court in American Politics,* 7th ed. (New York: W.W. Norton, 2005), 226. See also Kevin T. McGuire, "Repeat Players in the Supreme Court: The Role of Experienced Lawyers in Litigation Success," *Journal of Politics* 57 (1995): 187–96.

36. See, e.g., Barbara L. Graham, "Explaining Supreme Court Policymaking in Civil Rights: The Influence of the Solicitor General, 1953–2002," *The Policy Studies Journal* 31 (2003), 253–71.
37. Paul Brace and Melinda Gann Hall, "'Haves' Versus 'Have Nots' in State Supreme Courts: Allocating Docket Space and Wins in Power Asymmetric Cases," *Law & Society Review* 35 (2001), 393–417.
38. Charles R. Epp, *The Rights Revolution: Lawyers, Activists, and Supreme Courts in Comparative Perspective* (Chicago: University of Chicago Press, 1998); Thomas F. Burke, *Lawyers, Lawsuits, and Legal Rights: The Battle Over Litigation in American Society* (Berkeley: University of California Press, 2002).

CHAPTER SEVEN

The Adversarial Process and Criminal Procedure

"This case is about the death of Joe Elton Nixon and whether it should occur within the next few years by electrocution or maybe its natural expiration after a lifetime of confinement." Thus began assistant public defender Michael Corin during the sentencing phase of a murder trial, arguing that Nixon should not be executed for the brutal killing of Jeanne Bickner. The tactical decision to plead for his client's life was risky because Corin conceded Nixon's guilt at the conviction phase of trial. But, because the jury was sure to conclude that Nixon committed murder, Corin reasoned that his client's best shot at avoiding the death penalty was to argue that he was mentally ill at the time of the crime. Yet, the strategy did not work and the jury sentenced Nixon to death.

On appeal with new counsel, however, Nixon sought a reversal, claiming the public defender's decision to admit guilt was done without his consent and violated his Sixth Amendment right to "effective" counsel. Even though the Florida supreme court agreed, the Supreme Court in *Florida v. Nixon* (2004) reversed and reinstated the death sentence.[1] Writing for a unanimous Court, Justice Ginsburg held that defense counsel's trial strategy was reasonable. Nixon was uncooperative and refused to object or to consent to what Cronin planned to do. On the basis of those facts, Nixon's public defender did not have to subject the prosecution's case to full and "meaningful adversarial testing."

Adversarial justice assumes that the facts underlying crimes and private disputes are discovered by advocates locked in trials supervised by impartial judges. In *Nixon*, the Court ratified the public defender's decision because it met the minimum standard of legal advocacy. Still, Cronin's strategy came perilously close to violating a constitutional norm requiring the ultimate question of guilt or innocence to be put to a jury by counsel. As one judge put it: "a criminal trial is not a game in which the participants are expected to enter the ring with a near match in skills, neither is it a sacrifice of unarmed prisoners to gladiators."[2] In other words, gladiator attorneys must fight for their client's interests in open court.

Adversarial litigation tends to blur truth and fiction. High-profile criminal prosecutions, such as O. J. Simpson's double murder trial and Michael Jackson's child molestation case, are ridiculed by late night comics because they suggest that verdicts result from high-priced "dream team" lawyers. Paradoxically, the success of television dramas like *Law & Order* and *The Practice* portray the legal system in flattering terms but incorrectly suggest that the bulk of lawsuits wind up in a courtroom. Such a picture of the U.S. legal system is contrary to the reality of the vast majority of lawsuits that are decided by negotiated settlements.

This chapter explores the myths and realities of the adversarial trial process by, first, outlining the purposes and characteristics of trials. It then analyzes the criminal justice system in terms of the role of prosecutorial discretion, the practice of plea bargaining, the role the jury plays in criminal trials, and the politics of posttrial sentencing.

THE ADVERSARY PROCESS

The purpose of litigation is to punish antisocial behavior in criminal prosecutions and, in civil cases, to resolve private disputes. In criminal prosecutions, offenders are sanctioned with fines, imprisonment, an array of intermediate sanctions (home confinement, community service, intensive-supervision probation), and sometimes the death penalty. Civil lawsuits are commenced either to stop or to rectify private behavior that causes harm, usually by compelling legally responsible parties to pay financial damages. In a sense, a civil litigant is made "whole" by receiving an award of monetary damages instead of being punished by a loss of liberty, which might happen to a criminal defendant who is found guilty.

Criminal and civil litigation have distinct purposes, but they are not mutually exclusive. Although criminal defendants are subject to governmental prosecution, injured litigants may also sue for civil damages in a separate lawsuit. A drunk driver, for example, may be criminally prosecuted but may also face civil liability if he or she has caused serious personal injuries in an automobile accident.

Both criminal and civil litigation share the same adversarial premise: The underlying facts are determined by public trials and the deliberation of citizen juries (and sometimes judges alone). Judges and juries are vested with primary responsibility for deciding the guilt of offenders in criminal law and for settling private disputes in civil litigation. Lawyers have substantial discretion to engage in "fact finding" before trial and, ultimately, they present the facts they discover to the jury in the form of evidence that is introduced during various stages of trial (Figure 7.1). Consequently, the pursuit of truth by adversaries is not only unpredictable but is also highly contentious.[3] A critical issue is whether adversarial justice works to hide the truth instead of revealing it.

FIGURE 7.1   The Stages of Trial and the Presentation of Evidence.

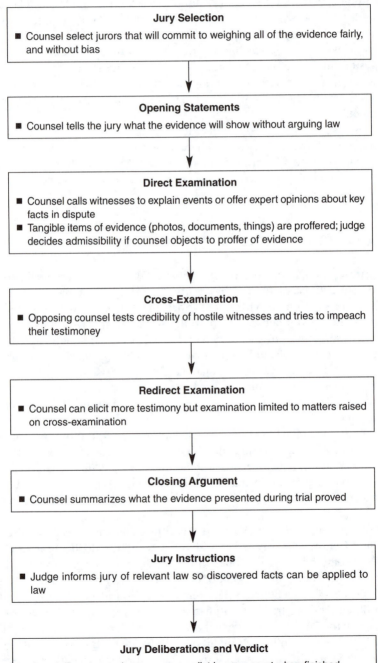

Jury Selection
- Counsel select jurors that will commit to weighing all of the evidence fairly, and without bias

Opening Statements
- Counsel tells the jury what the evidence will show without arguing law

Direct Examination
- Counsel calls witnesses to explain events or offer expert opinions about key facts in dispute
- Tangible items of evidence (photos, documents, things) are proffered; judge decides admissibility if counsel objects to proffer of evidence

Cross-Examination
- Opposing counsel tests credibility of hostile witnesses and tries to impeach their testimoney

Redirect Examination
- Counsel can elicit more testimony but examination limited to matters raised on cross-examination

Closing Argument
- Counsel summarizes what the evidence presented during trial proved

Jury Instructions
- Judge informs jury of relevant law so discovered facts can be applied to law

Jury Deliberations and Verdict
- Jury deliberates and announces verdict in open court when finished

Trials: Truth or "Fight" Theory?

Social scientists and legal scholars have long denounced the adversarial system. Former Judge Jerome Frank's famous "fight" theory of adversary process remains a seminal critique. According to Judge Frank, adversary trials are similar to "private out-of-court brawls." Because "the lawyer aims at victory, at winning in the fight, not at aiding the court to discover the facts," the truth often remains a mystery and becomes distorted when partisan attorneys coach witnesses or fail to disclose incriminating evidence. The adversary system encourages a hypothetical "litigious man" to use attorneys as surrogates in a fight for their self-interest. That behavior, argued Frank, makes the trial process unfair for a variety of reasons, including (1) the truth is often overlooked because judges have limited roles and are inhibited from taking proactive steps to find it; (2) crucial evidence is lost because of the incompetence of attorneys or because clients cannot afford to hire qualified counsel and other investigative staff or expert witnesses during trial preparation; and, (3) government institutions, including courts, do not have an affirmative duty to seek out the truth and accordingly rely too much on prosecutors and private attorneys to uncover relevant evidence.[4]

Defenders of the adversarial system respond that the clash of opposing interests is the best procedural method for uncovering the truth because partisan advocates are duty bound to protect their clients' interests. Without legal representation, critical facts surrounding crimes or disputes could remain undiscovered, whereas the government would operate unjustly against the innocent or the ignorant. Persons may be wrongfully convicted or suffer substantial financial losses without the aggressive efforts of attorneys. Partisan advocacy also protects significant constitutional values, such as the basic right to be heard in public forums and the right of criminal defendants to confront their accusers.[5]

Still, contemporary scholars extend their critiques by comparing the weaknesses of adversary systems with the strengths of inquisitorial legal systems found in Western European democracies, such as Germany and France (see Table 7.1). Political scientist Robert Kagan observed that inquisitorial regimes are reasonable alternatives to adversarial justice. In Germany, for example, criminal trials are tightly supervised by a panel of judges who do not use complex pretrial procedures or juries to determine a defendant's guilt. Instead, an extensive record of pretrial evidence is compiled by prosecutors, investigating judges, and the police, and defendants are given full access to it well in advance of trial. *Plea bargains*, or agreements between prosecutors and defendants that avoid trials by allowing the accused to plead guilty in exchange for more a lenient sentence, are constructed under strict guidelines. Plea bargaining translates into fewer trials. If there is one, they tend to be short and closely managed by judges who are actively questioning witnesses, including the defendant (who typically testifies first, without counsel). Moreover, because identical procedures are in place in inquisitorial systems for civil litigation, Kagan concludes that there is more streamlined adjudication in Germany and elsewhere in noncriminal cases.[6]

TABLE 7.1 Trial Court Characteristics in Adversary and Inquisitorial Legal Systems

Legal System Characteristics	Adversary Legal System	Inquisitorial Legal System
Type of Law	■ Common law ■ Judge-made law	■ Civil law ■ Code-based law
Judiciary	■ Non-professional; non-bureaucratic ■ No specially-trained judges ■ Judges enter career as "amateurs," often from private practice ■ Judges are independent and not directly supervised during career ■ More political, less objective in decision-making	■ Professional; bureaucratic ■ Specially-trained "career" judges ■ Judges enter career as civil servants, within bureaucracy ■ Judges are supervised by senior judges during career ■ More objective, less political in decision-making
Legal Profession	■ Not separated from judiciary ■ Individual attorneys have substantial discretion in controlling litigation ■ Individual attorneys are zealous advocates for clients' interest	■ Autonomous from judiciary ■ Individual attorneys have less discretion in controlling litigation ■ Individual attorneys are not zealous advocates for clients' interest
Trial Processes	■ Single judge in charge of case and attorneys find facts through pre-trial discovery processes and manage litigation up to trial ■ Trial record is built at trial, in single event, and judge does not find facts in pretrial investigations ■ Judges are neutral arbiters and less collaborative in trying to resolve disputes ■ Generalist courts are common ■ Lay juries often participate in final outcome ■ Costs of litigation mostly assumed by litigants	■ Several judges determines facts, manage litigation, and collaborate in decision; in significant cases, sit in panels ■ Trial record are built over time through series of judge-led investigations ■ Judges are pro-active problem solvers in collaborative effort to resolve disputes ■ Specialized courts are common ■ Lay juries rarely participate in final outcome ■ Costs of litigation mostly assumed by government

Source: Charles H. Koch, Jr, "Globalization, Courts, and Judicial Power: The Advantages of Civil Law Judicial Design as the Model for Emerging Legal Systems," *Indiana Journal of Global Legal Studies* (Winter, 2004), 139–60.

Despite criticisms, the inherent differences between legal systems in the United States and Europe make it doubtful that inquisitorial efficiency would completely mitigate or replace adversarial process in the United States. The structure, operation, and norms of adversary justice are "deeply rooted in the American system of government and in American political culture."[7] That is not to say, however, that certain features of inquisitorial justice are completely absent in the United States. The growing acceptance of therapeutic jurisprudence in state trial courts (discussed in chapter 2), along with the managerial role judges play in a civil cases and increasingly "alternative dispute resolution" procedures (discussed later in chapter 8), are significant trends that decrease partisan conflict.

Police and prosecutors know that evidence used against a criminal defendant must withstand judicial scrutiny. Law enforcement officers routinely consider the best means to elicit damaging evidence in accordance with controlling legal precedents. The landmark case of *Miranda v. Arizona* (1966) held that police must give suspects advance warnings of their constitutional rights, including the right to counsel, whenever they are placed in custodial interrogation. In *Miranda*, Chief Justice Earl Warren explained that police use "psychological stratagems"[8] to extract information from suspects during custodial interrogation. Before *Miranda*, many midtwentieth century police training manuals emphasized that suspects were more likely to confess under the pressure of being isolated in a room in the station house, away from familiar surroundings and the support of friends and family. One technique "instruct[ed] the police to display an air of confidence in the suspect's guilt and from outward appearance to maintain only an interest in confirming certain details because "[t]he guilt of the subject is to be posited as a fact." This "put the subject in a psychological state where his story is but an elaboration of what the police purport to know already—that he is guilty." Another tactic was the "friendly–unfriendly," or the "Mutt and Jeff act," an interrogation that is close to the "good cop, bad cop" routine popularized on television shows. According to the chief justice, these practices encouraged the "police [to] persuade, trick, or cajole [suspects] out of exercising [their] constitutional rights."[9]

Despite *Miranda*, the police in some states were taught to conduct "two-stage interrogations," a practice designed to circumvent the *Miranda* warnings. During a two-stage interrogation, a "question first" and "*Mirandize* later" strategy is followed. Once a suspect makes a confession (but without being *Mirandized*), the police were told to give the *Miranda* warnings but then ask for a waiver. If the suspect waived their *Miranda* rights, the police then used any subsequent incriminating statements against the accused in court. Such two-stage style of interrogation was finally declared unconstitutional in *Missouri v. Seibert* (2004).[10]

In *Seibert*, police used a two-stage interrogation to get a second degree murder conviction of a mother who helped cause the death of a mentally ill teenager that was asleep in the family's trailer home. A closely divided Supreme Court held that the question first style of interrogation violated the Fifth Amendment's prohibition against self-incrimination. Thus, the mother's confession and her subsequent conviction were both thrown out of court. In barring that evidence, Justice

David Souter reaffirmed the values of deterring police misconduct under *Miranda* and its corollary, the "exclusionary rule"—the rule that excludes damaging evidence from trial if police conduct in securing it is unconstitutional.[11]

The constitutional dynamics and practical application of the *Miranda* and *Seibert* rulings register what criminologist Herbert L. Packer described as the adversarial clash between the "crime control" and "due process" models of criminal procedure. The models "represent an attempt to abstract two separate value systems that compete for priority in the operation of the criminal justice system." On the one hand, the crime control model favors the swift prosecution and suppression of crimes with "assembly-line" efficiency, particularly during the early stages of apprehension, investigation, and pretrial prosecution. Given the institutional constraints of the criminal justice system (high demand and limited resources), expedient resolution of criminal cases is both necessary and, in most cases, accurately separates the guilty from the innocent. In effect, the model is equivalent to a screening process that most often results in conviction of those who are probably guilty.[12] The evidence generated from the two stage interrogation in *Seibert*, for example, was instrumental in securing the swift prosecution of a criminal defendant that was in all likelihood guilty.

Yet, the exclusion of evidence also illustrates that the *crime control model* has little tolerance for recognizing the values underlying the due process model, which in *Seibert* prevented the prosecution from making the conviction stick on appeal. The *due process model* operates like "an obstacle course" and slows down the efficacy of criminal prosecutions. More specifically, it assumes that police investigations and criminal prosecutions are fraught with error and, hence, incapable of always correctly predicting guilt. Thus, in an effort to prevent mistakes from happening, the due process model insists that the factual questions underlying guilt and innocence be tested through formal adversary processes, a rights-based approach that considerably impedes the speedy dispatch of criminal prosecutions through judicial interventions. The *Miranda* rule is but one example of the kind of due process guarantee that is available to criminal suspects.

By interposing a procedural objection to the admission of evidence at trial, the defense counsel in *Seibert* thwarted the conviction of his client. In other cases, a court may decide that the prosecution's evidence must be admitted because it is necessary to protect the public order by repressing crime. The political dynamics of the crime control and due process models thus underscore that the clash of opposing interests are typically framed by competing notions of adversarial justice and rival political ideologies. They are further illustrated by examining the method by which suspects are prosecuted.

Table 7.2 denotes constitutional protections in criminal cases.

Sanctions for breaking the law originate from criminal law. Criminal law defines culpability by defining the intent (*mens rea*, or "guilty mind") and conduct (*actus reus*, or "criminal act") of offenders. In addition, the law's substantive content is carried out by criminal procedure or by the rules which substantive rights are enforced.

TABLE 7.2 Constitutional Protections in Criminal Cases

Source in Bill of Rights	Scope of Constitutional Right
Fourth Amendment	■ Prohibition of "Unreasonable" Searches and Seizures ■ Requirement of Warrant based on "Probable Cause"
Fifth Amendment	■ Grand Jury Indictment in Capital Cases ■ Prohibition of "Double Jeopardy" attaching in "same offenses" ■ Testimonial Privilege against Self-Incrimination ■ Right to Due Process (Notice and Opportunity to be Heard)
Sixth Amendment	■ Right to Speedy and Public Trial ■ Right to Impartial Jury ■ Right to be Informed of Charges ■ Right to Confront Accusers ■ Right to Compulsory Process to Secure Witnesses ■ Right to "Assistance" of Counsel
Eighth Amendment	■ Prohibition against "Excessive" Bails or Fines ■ Prohibition against "Cruel and Unusual" Punishments
Fourteenth Amendment	■ Prohibition against deprivation of "privileges or immunities" of U.S. citizens ■ Right to "Equal Protection" of the Laws ■ Right to "Due Process" (Notice and Opportunity to be Heard)

Criminal trials are designed to establish guilt or innocence, thereby striking a proper balance between preserving public safety and safeguarding individual rights. In criminal cases, the government must prove its accusations "beyond a reasonable doubt," a rigorous standard of proof emphasizing the constitutional presumption of innocence. As Judge Benjamin Cardozo once said: "The prisoner is to go free because the constable has blundered." In other words, as Justice William Brennan reminded us, the *reasonable doubt standard* is "a prime instrument for reducing the risk of convictions resting on factual error" because it "provides concrete substance for the presumption of innocence."[13] Because of these principles, the government has the burden to rebut the presumption of innocence with reliable facts showing the accused committed a crime beyond a reasonable doubt.

Criminal trials begin after the investigation and arrest of defendants accused of committing misdemeanors or felonies. Misdemeanors such as petty larceny, drunk driving, or disorderly conduct are acts punished by minor fines, incarceration for up to one year, or both. Felonies, such as manslaughter or rape are punished by higher fines, incarceration of one year or more, or both. Certain offenses, such as premeditated murder or the killing of a police officer during the commission of a felony, may carry the capital penalty. In comparable Western democracies, such as France or Germany, the death penalty is outlawed. In contrast, in the United States only twelve states, plus the District of Columbia, do not have the death penalty.[14]

Although the police have the responsibility for investigating and arresting criminal suspects, several participants in the judicial process exercise considerable discretion in determining the fate of the accused. Initially, federal U.S. Attorneys or state chief prosecutors decide whether to charge suspects with a crime. If a suspect is charged, the prosecutor ascertains whether a conviction is best secured by a plea bargain or by trial. If the case is taken to trial, the jury decides the defendant's guilt or innocence (if a judge does not do so in a bench trial). In the absence of an acquittal, a judge then sentences defendants in accordance with the law.

The prosecutor, the jury, and the judge wield enormous influence. The different roles they play are best explained by exploring the critical stages of the trial process, including (1) the discretion prosecutors have in charging defendants from the time of arrest to formal arraignment; (2) the influence prosecutors have in striking plea bargains; (3) the democratic role citizens play as jurors in criminal trials; and (4) the underlying politics of posttrial sentencing process.

Figure 7.2 maps out the criminal trial and appeal process.

PROSECUTORIAL DISCRETION: FROM ARREST TO TRIAL

Since the 1960s, the U.S. political system has grown more conservative and has encouraged legislation controlling crime and sharply limiting the rights of criminal defendants. In Congress, anticrime legislation, including measures authorizing preventive detention (allowing judges to deny bail to dangerous criminals), the death penalty, harsher penalties under mandatory sentencing, and fixed sentencing guidelines, were enacted in an effort to prevent judges from showing leniency to offenders. Although the "get tough" approach has limited judicial discretion and restricted individual rights, the police and prosecutors retain virtually unfettered discretion. It is not an exaggeration to say, as former Attorney General Robert Jackson once did, that prosecutors retain "more control over life, liberty, and reputation than any other person in America."[15]

Whereas U.S. Attorneys are appointed by the president and confirmed by the Senate, in all but four states (Alaska, Connecticut, District of Columbia, and New Jersey), state prosecutors are elected to office. Although federal and state prosecutors are distinct law enforcement officials, both represent the government, the community at large, and victims of crime. Although federal prosecutors occasionally litigate civil cases, the nation's ninety-three U.S. Attorneys primarily investigate and enforce violations of federal criminal law. Federal prosecutions are brought annually against approximately 81,000 defendants, resulting in roughly 70,000 in convictions (a ninety-two percent conviction rate). Notably, eighty-two percent of those convicted are sent to prison.[16] About 2,300 state prosecutors' offices, employing over 79,000 attorneys, investigators, victim advocates, and support staff, handle nearly 1.1 million felony prosecutions. As a result, state

FIGURE 7.2 The Criminal Trial and Appeal Process.

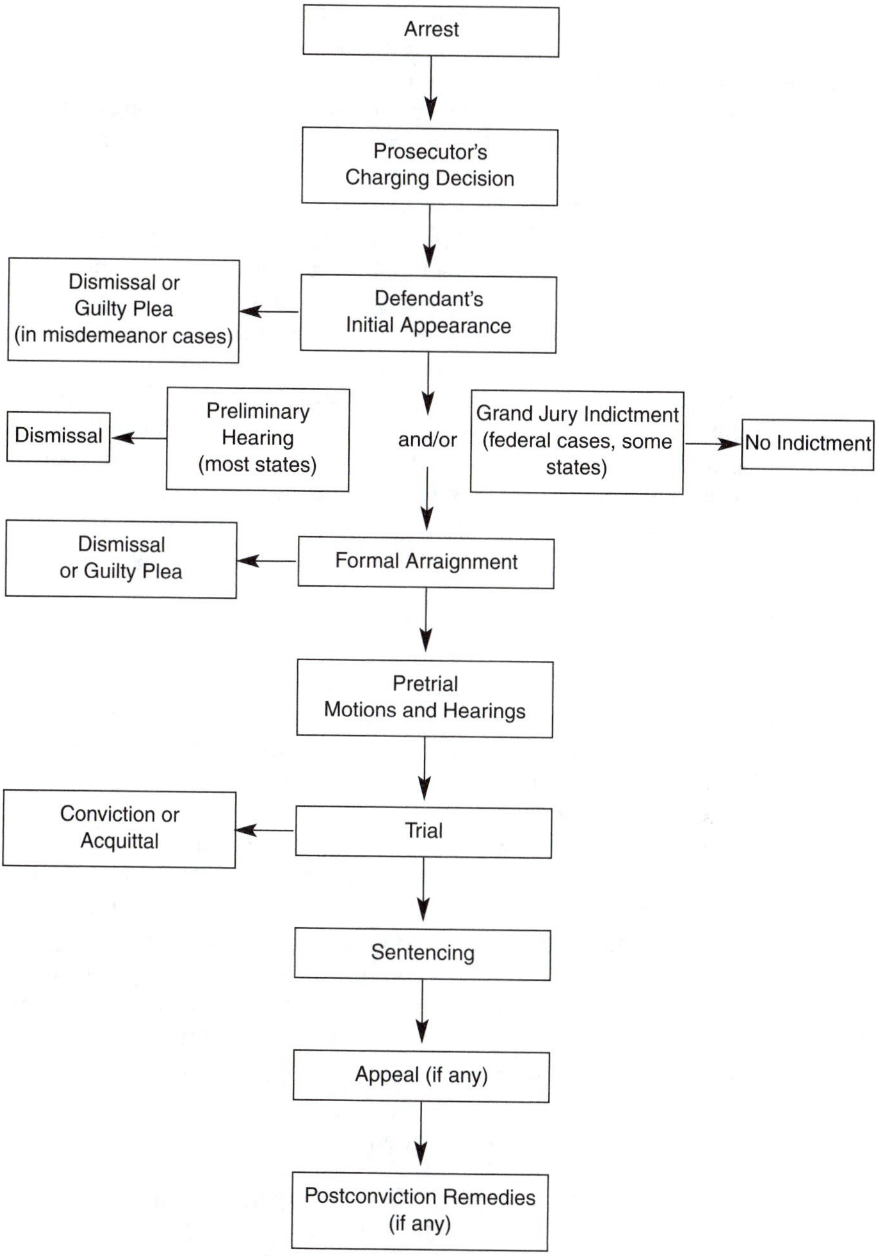

courts adjudicate about ninty-four percent of all felony crimes. Few state prosecutions actually go to trial: 95 percent of state felony convictions result from guilty pleas, with sixty-nine percent leading to incarceration in state prisons or local jails; of the remaining, thirty-one percent receive probation.[17]

Federal and state prosecutors have discretion in (1) conducting criminal investigations; (2) initiating and executing arrest or search warrants; (3) subpoenaing witnesses and compelling testimony at preliminary proceedings and trial; (4) convening grand juries and secure indictments in serious cases; (5) formally charging criminal defendants at arraignment and placing them on trial; (6) negotiating and obtaining plea bargain agreements in lieu of trial; (7) supporting or contesting post-conviction sentencing dispositions, including issuing recommendations about enhancing penalties, the length of incarceration, whether to seek the death penalty, and (in the states) structuring the terms of probation and the conditions for parole; and (8) making appellate litigation decisions. Defense counsel, and juries, prosecutors truly are at the forefront of determining whether an individual's liberty is won or lost and, in some cases, whether offenders live or die.[18] The influence of prosecutorial discretion comes into play at several preliminary stages of the adversarial process, specifically (1) the defendant's initial appearance, (2) the preliminary hearing or grand jury indictment stage, and (3) formal arraignment.

Initial Appearance

Once a complaint is filed with the prosecutor, the defendant is brought into court to answer criminal charges at an initial appearance hearing. Defendants briefly appear before a judge, ordinarily within forty-eight hours of arrest and are informed of their rights and the charges they face.[19] Defendants accused of misdemeanor crimes often plead guilty at this stage and are sentenced immediately. In felony cases, counsel might be appointed for those who qualify for legal assistance. A bail bond might also be set, if the judge releases the defendant into the community pending trial. Although the defendant's right to bail derives from the Eighth Amendment, and necessarily limits the prosecutor's power to detain indefinitely the accused, judges routinely set bail or deny it on recommendations of prosecutors. Once bail is set, a monetary bond is posted, typically with the aid of a professional bondsmen, in order to secure the defendant's presence at trial. If there is a failure to appear at trial, the full amount is forfeited and an arrest warrant is issued.

Preliminary Hearings and Grand Jury Indictments

After the initial appearance, the prosecutor formally charges the accused with a crime, either by "information" or "grand jury indictment." In jurisdictions where preliminary hearings are used, an "information form," stating the charges and evidence against the defendant, is filed by the prosecutor. In grand jury jurisdictions, the grand jury approves the prosecutor's initial charging decision through an indictment. A few jurisdictions use both types of methods.

A preliminary hearing is held to determine whether there is probable cause to charge the accused with criminal violations shortly after arrest. The hearing resembles a "minitrial" in that witnesses may be compelled to testify and an official transcript is created. Ordinarily, only the prosecution presents its evidence because it has the legal burden of proving probable cause. The defendant is not similarly obligated and, hence, the preliminary hearing favors the defense because it gives counsel the strategic advantage of hearing the prosecution's theory of the case.

In some states, and in federal prosecutions (as required by the Fifth Amendment), grand juries are used to secure either a felony indictment, often called a *true bill*, or to ignore prosecution, often called a *no bill*, against an accused. In a few states grand juries are only used to determine probable cause in death penalty or life imprisonment cases, and in other states they are used for all crimes.[20]

Historically, the grand jury's purpose was to prevent arbitrary charging decisions. Under the prosecutor's direction, grand juries have the power to subpoena witnesses, provide immunity for key witnesses, compel the production of evidence and, if probable cause exists, indict the accused. The size of grand juries varies widely in the states, with panels typically ranging from five to twenty-three. In federal prosecutions, between sixteen and twenty-three citizens are impaneled. They review the prosecutor's evidence in a secret, nonadversarial proceeding. Defendants do not have the right to be represented by counsel, witnesses are not cross-examined, and the prosecution's evidence generally is not rebutted; unless they are called as a witness, defendants do not even have the right to testify in their own defense.[21] Consequently, an old saw in the legal profession is that prosecutors can usually get a grand jury to indict a ham sandwich if they so desired—a joke that speaks volumes about the prosecutor's sway over grand juries.

Still, the very existence of preliminary hearings and grand jury proceedings ensures that prosecutorial discretion is not completely unfettered. With preliminary hearings, judges initially assess the reasonableness of believing that a defendant is guilty of committing a crime; whereas, in grand jury jurisdictions, citizens make a similar evaluation. Even so, the prosecutor's decisions and recommendations about how to proceed against the defendant carries great weight, particularly in determining whether to continue the prosecution or to end it by plea bargain or dismissal (*nolle prosequi*, "the decision to stop prosecution").

Formal Arraignment

After a preliminary hearing or a grand jury proceeding, defendants are formally charged and arraigned. Arraignment signals that the prosecution intends to pursue a case to trial, and defendants are formally charged and asked to enter a plea. If a defendant pleads guilty, the decision usually is at the advice of counsel. Defendants may make two types of guilty pleas: a guilty plea and a plea of *nolo contendere* (a "no contest" plea, admitting only that the government probably has enough evidence to convict). Both pleas accept criminal culpability, but *nolo* pleas cannot be used in a subsequent civil lawsuit.

In most states and federal prosecutions, defendants may also make an insanity plea as a defense (which means they must prove insanity instead of requiring the prosecution to establish sanity). Insanity pleas absolve mentally ill defendants of criminal responsibility and usually result in commitments to a mental institution. Not surprisingly, high-profile insanity cases, such as those involving Lee Boyd Malvo, the "Beltway sniper" who terrorized Maryland, Virginia, and Washington, D.C. residents for three weeks, have made the insanity defense extremely unpopular. Legislative reforms generally make it more difficult for defendants to use mental illness as an excuse.[22]

As a result of such reforms, insanity pleas are available on a limited basis and defendants usually have the burden of proving that mental illness ought to be a mitigating factor during sentencing. Although some states prohibit the use of the defense, jurisdictions that do use it allow defendants to claim insanity under four basic standards. Under the *M'Naughten rule*, in force in about half of the states and in federal prosecutions, an accused is not criminally responsible if a "defect of reason from [a] disease of the mind" prevents the defendant from distinguishing right from wrong. Under the *substantial capacity standard*, which is in place in about twenty-two states, defendants are not criminally liable if they lack "substantial capacity" to appreciate the wrongfulness of their illegal conduct. A third option, used in only a handful of states, is the *irresistible impulse rule*, declaring that an uncontrollable urge prevented the accused from controlling actions that were known to be wrong. A fourth standard, used in some states, permits defendants to plead *diminished capacity*, or "guilty but mentally ill," a finding that does not absolve guilt but permits the judge or jury to sentence the defendant less harshly. Finally, Idaho, Kansas, Montana, and Utah have abolished the use of the insanity defense.[23]

If a defendant pleads not guilty, then a trial date is set and opposing counsels continue to engage in discovery of information through an exchange of pretrial motions. In the vast majority of cases, however, defendants choose to "cop" a plea as a result of a plea bargain agreement between the prosecution and defense.

Plea Bargaining

Although the adversarial model presumes that the truth underlying a defendant's guilt or innocence emerges after a jury trial, in reality the vast majority of defendants strike plea bargains. Typically, less than five percent of all state and federal criminal cases actually go to trial. In some cases, involving murder or rape, defendants tend to opt for a trial more frequently because they have little to lose in pushing the case to trial. In most others, a negotiated guilty plea is the better option because it provides leniency and allows prosecutors to secure convictions expeditiously. Although not unproblematic, because defendants waive their constitutional rights to a trial, the *mutuality of advantage* of plea bargaining was upheld in *Brady v. United States* (1972).[24]

TABLE 7.3   Criminal Convictions Resulting from Trials and Pleas in State Felony Cases

Type of Offense	Bench Trial	Jury Trial	Guilty Plea
Violent offenses			
Murder	5%	27%	68%
Sexual assault	2	8	90
Rape	4	12	84
Other sexual assault	1	5	94
Robbery	3	6	91
Aggravated assault	4	4	92
Miscellaneous violent	4	4	92
All violent cases	3%	7%	90%
Property offenses			
Burglary	2%	2%	96%
Larceny	3	1	96
Motor vehicle theft	1	2	97
Fraud	2	1	97
All property offenses	3%	1%	96%
Drug offenses			
Possession	1%	1%	98%
Trafficking	3	5	92
All drug offenses	2%	2%	96%
Weapons offenses	4%	3%	93%
Miscellaneous nonviolent offenses	2%	1%	97%

Source: Derived from Matthew R. Durose and Patrick A. Langan, *Felony Sentences in State Courts, 2002*, available from www.ojp.usdoj.gov/bjs/abstract/fssc02.htm (retrieved February 26, 2005).

Table 7.3 denotes criminal convictions resulting from trials and pleas in state felony cases.

Plea bargaining remains controversial because the deals struck result from a variety of institutional, political, and legal considerations that have little to do with discovering guilt or innocence. Judges and prosecutors, confronting heavy caseloads and limited resources, use plea bargains to reduce their dockets. For defendants, a more lenient sentence under a plea bargain is attractive as well. In sum, the respective interests of the judge, prosecution, and defense counsel combine to promote negotiated pleas.[25]

There are other criticisms of plea bargaining as well, including that negotiated pleas are coerced and originate in secrecy. During the negotiation process, defendants are compelled to relinquish their due process rights and forfeit any chance to challenge the prosecutor's charges. The guarantees that are sacrificed are not insignificant: They include the Fifth Amendment right against self-incrimination and, under the Sixth Amendment, the rights to have a public jury trial and to confront accusers. In addition, the constitutional presumption that a defendant is innocent until proven guilty is forfeited. As legal historian George Fischer put it: "In place of a noble clash for truth, plea bargaining gives us a skulking truce. Opposing lawyers shrink from battle, and the jury's empty box signals the [criminal justice] system's disappointment."[26]

Such criticisms underscore that prosecutors have the upper hand in negotiating pleas. Using their discretion, prosecutors may opt for *charge plea bargains,* agreements allowing defendants to plead guilty to charges that are less serious. Likewise, prosecutors may *sentence plea bargain* and procure guilty pleas upon the condition that prosecutors will recommend a lenient sentence.[27] Or, in determinate sentencing jurisdictions, prosecutors may *fact plea bargain* and obtain convictions on the basis of agreements to accept those facts that statutorily define fixed punishments under sentencing guidelines. In sum, plea bargaining remains controversial because it vests in prosecutors virtually unbridled discretion to obtain convictions and determine punishments, with little oversight from courts.[28]

Sidebar 7.1

Plea Bargaining Practices in the United States and Continental Europe

Plea bargaining practices in the United States differ considerably from those in Germany, Italy, and France. Once known as the "land without plea bargaining," beginning in the 1970s Germany began to develop bargains (*Absprachen*) in a response to heavy caseloads and longer trials in criminal, environmental, and drug cases. As in the United States, the bargains for leniency were negotiated before or during trial; but defendants could only "confess" to crimes which, unlike guilty pleas, only shorten the trial but do not determine guilt or innocence. Also, unlike in the United States, the German defense counsel has access to the "written dossier" containing the complete pretrial investigation. As a result, the prosecution and defense are on more of an equal footing during plea negotiations. Another difference is that a German judge is an active participant in plea negotiations, whereas in the United States the primary plea negotiators are the prosecution and defense counsel.

Italian plea bargaining (*patteggiamento*) is close to that in the United States since the adoption of a new criminal code in 1989. The prosecution and defense counsel may now conduct their own pretrial investigations. Under *patteggiamento*, the prosecution and defense may request *sentence bargains* that reduce a sentence by up to one-third in minor cases if the sentence does not exceed five years imprisonment. Still, unlike in the United States, the charges cannot be dropped. Because the agreement is not considered a guilty plea, the Italian judge retains the power to enforce the sentence bargain if there are insufficient grounds for acquittal, and if the charge and sentence are proportional to the crime. Also, if the prosecutor rejects the bargain, at the trial's end the defendant may ask the judge to impose the one-third reduction after examining why the prosecutor refused to accept the bargain.

French plea bargaining (*composition*) was introduced in 1999. At the beginning of formal proceedings, the prosecutor may offer to divert the case from the standard criminal trial process in exchange for an admission of guilt and an agreement to perform certain conditions, such as paying a fine or doing community service. Applying composition does not establish guilt and, if the defendant fulfills the conditions, the case is dismissed. In addition, the defendant can only accept what the prosecution demands and doing so is considered to be more an official act of case diversion by the prosecutor. Composition is not intended to punish French offenders in the same way that guilty pleas do in the United States.

Source: Maximo Langer, "From Legal Transplants to Legal Translations: The Globalization of Plea Bargaining and the Americanization Thesis in Criminal Procedure," *Harvard International Law Journal* (Winter 2004), 1-64.

THE JURY'S ROLE

In the event a plea cannot be negotiated before trial, the prosecution and defense must prepare their evidence by filing pretrial motions, such as a motion to dismiss or to suppress evidence. In criminal litigation, the prosecution is not under any constitutional obligation to share all that it learns during its investigation. Hence the defendant's right to collect critical facts (such as witness statements and forensic lab results) is usually determined by how discovery rules are applied, which vary around the country. Although some prosecutors favor a policy of liberal discovery as a plea bargaining strategy, others may not, and what is shared between opposing counsel ultimately may be adjudicated in pretrial motion hearings. In any event, the limited scope of criminal discovery tends to work in favor of the prosecution because it initially controls much of the information that can either be withheld or disclosed.

The Democratic Politics of Citizen Juries

The procedural difficulties encountered in contemporary trials may have been behind Justice Douglas's insight that "[m]uch of the Bill of Rights is designed to redress the advantage that inheres in a government prosecution."[29] Historically, a potent counterweight to the prosecutor's authority is the defendant's right to have a trial by an impartial jury drawn from the place where the crime occurred. Rooted in Article III, Section 2, as well as in the Sixth Amendment for criminal cases and the Seventh Amendment for civil cases (if a dispute exceeds more than twenty dollars), the jury trial is both an expression of democratic participation and a bulwark against oppressive government. Originally conceived as a right attaching to federal criminal prosecutions, the right to a jury trial was extended to the states in *Duncan v. Louisiana* (1969).[30]

In Comparative Perspective

Jury Systems Around the World

Jury trials around the world all trace their roots to the common law jury system that evolved in England over 800 years ago. With the expansion of the British Empire, jury trials were exported to the colonies in North America, the Caribbean, Africa, and parts of Asia. In the nineteenth century, elements of the common law jury were also adopted in France, parts of Germany, Spain, and some other European countries, along with Russia, as well in Central and South America.

The origins of the jury system in England stem from the Norman Conquest in 1066. The Normans had a practice of putting a group of individuals under oath (and thus the term *juror*) to tell the truth. Initially, contrary to what became the modern practice, jurors were chosen because of their knowledge of the case or the parties involved. They were eventually allowed to question witnesses, in contrast to the passivity of most contemporary juries, and served as adjudicators of both civil and criminal disputes. Only later did the principle of impartiality emerge, and by 1367 unanimous verdicts were required. Subsequently, jury trials were the only form of trials used by English common law courts. That lasted until the midnineteenth century when they were reserved for only the most serious crimes, but they continued to predominate in civil cases until the early twentieth century.

With British colonization, the English common law jury was introduced elsewhere, though often taking slightly different forms. Nowhere did the jury system become as entrenched as, perhaps, in the United States. Colonial experience with the British government and judiciary led to the enshrinement of the right to a common law jury trial in the constitutions of the original thirteen states and in the Sixth and Seventh Amendments of the U.S. Constitution's Bill of Rights. Juries were deemed an important political institution and a check on governmental power. Although until the twentieth century, juries in the United States generally excluded women and racial minorities, they were far more democratic in their representation and symbolism than they were in England.

Indeed, in the 1830s Alexis de Tocqueville emphasized that in the United States the jury is "pre-eminently a political [and democratic] institution," in sharp contrast with aristocratic juries in England.[a]

In England and in Wales, as in the United States, juries became more representative in the twentieth century. The Juries Act of 1974 required juries to be selected randomly from all registered voters, though exempted are members of Parliament, doctors, clergy, and anyone employed in the Administration of Justice or the armed forces. Ironically, given its origins, the English jury was also transformed in other ways that rendered it an even less important institution. The Criminal Justice Act of 1967 did away with unanimous verdicts and authorized convictions on the basis of a majority vote of ten of the twelve jurors, even for serious crimes. Furthermore, the incremental reclassification of crimes by Parliament during the last century has resulted in giving less than two percent of all criminal cases jury trials. The vast majority of criminal cases are now tried by magistrates' courts, which are composed of three lay magistrates. Likewise, because of the cost of jury trials, legislation gave judges the power to refuse jury trials in civil cases, and today less than one percent of all civil cases in England are tried before juries. The Supreme Court Act of 1981 preserves a qualified right to a jury trial in only four kinds of civil cases: libel and slander, fraud, malicious prosecution, and false imprisonment.

Whereas in England the use of juries has long been in decline, in Canada juries in serious criminal cases remain generally used, though in a system that mixes elements of the English and the U.S. jury systems. A right to a jury trial is constitutionally guaranteed in the 1982 Charter of Rights and Freedoms. That constitutional guarantee, though, is qualified by the criminal code, which is based on the Criminal Code of 1892. Basically, in Canada there are three types of criminal offenses: (1) *indictable* offenses are the most serious crimes, like murder and treason, and are tried before a judge and jury; (2) *summary conviction* offenses are less serious, carrying a maximum sentence of two years in jail or a fine of less than $5,000, and are tried before a judge alone; and (3) *hybrid* offenses may be treated either as an indictable or a summary conviction offense, and hence may or may not entail a jury trial. In the latter instance, the public prosecutor decides how to charge hybrid offenses such as serious fraud, conspiracy, and drug offenses and therefore effectively decides whether the accused is accorded a jury trial.

Like the traditional common law jury, Canadian juries are composed of twelve members and must render unanimous verdicts; sentencing, however, remains the responsibility of judges, not the jury. Because Canada has two official languages, English and French, the accused has the right to be tried by a judge and a jury who speak his or her native language. Juries were once composed almost exclusively of white males but are now selected randomly from the electoral rolls in provinces and local communities. As in England, however, juries in civil cases have virtually disappeared. They remain permitted, but not widely used, in Alberta, British Columbia, Ontario, and Saskatchewan, whereas they are expressly prohibited in Quebec and in the Federal Court of Canada.

Juries in criminal cases took a different historical twist in Australia because four of its six states (New South Wales, Queensland, Tasmania, and Victoria), originated as penal colonies. Initially, juries were composed of six military officers and later free settlers who had migrated from Britain; convicts and former convicts were excluded. But, because former convicts who stayed and settled Australia eventually outnumbered the free settlers, a major controversy arose over the rights of citizenship and focused on those who could serve on juries. By the 1830s, it became settled in a few (and by the end of the nineteenth century in all) colonies for former convicts—so-called emancipists—to serve on juries. When the six colonies federated to become the Commonwealth of Australia in 1901, the new states retained their powers over criminal law, including the jury trial process. Today, the overwhelming number of criminal cases are still brought under common law or state statutes. Notably, the Australian Constitution, which contains no bill of rights, does provide (in Section 80) for a jury trial for any crimes against the commonwealth.

The general availability of jury trials in Australia depends on whether the offense in an indictable one subject to a jury trial, or a summary (nonindictable) offense tried by a magistrate. Only the former require jury trials, although in four states (New South Wales, South Australia, Western Australia, and the Australian Capital Territory) the accused charged with an indictable offense may elect to be tried by a judge alone.

The introduction of juries varied considerably elsewhere, depending on indigenous culture. In Sierra Leone, England's oldest African colony, juries were used in both civil and criminal cases. But, they were not deemed to guarantee fair trials because jurors confronted considerable local community pressures and tribal rivalries. Within a couple of generations, juries in civil cases were abandoned and a two-thirds majority for conviction was adopted for criminal trials, except in capital cases which continued to require unanimous verdicts. A modified jury trial was implemented in Gambia in 1845, whereas the Gold Coast (Ghana) authorized the attorney general to order a trial by judge with lay persons, if eligible English-speaking jurors could be found, and to permit nonunanimous verdicts. Juries—typically composed of nine white males—were introduced in South Africa in 1828, but its usage gradually declined and was abolished in 1969. In other African countries, such as Kenya, Zimbabwe, and Tanzania, it was not until the twentieth century that jury systems, which were composed of white European male jurors, were established, though often only for white defendants.

In nineteenth century Western Europe, the Napoleonic Criminal Code of 1808 first introduced elements of the jury system into the French inquisitorial system with trials combining judges and lay jurors. Subsequently, Austria, parts of Germany, Belgium, Greece, Hungary, Portugal, and Spain, adopted various elements of the jury system. The Portuguese jury, for instance, consisted of six members and permitted nonunanimous verdicts, though they were subject to annulment by the trial judge.

As a result of Portuguese and Spanish colonialization, the jury system was also introduced in the nineteenth century in South American countries, including Brazil (1822), Uruguay (1830), Argentina (1853), Chile (1872), Ecuador (1890), and Venezuela (1898).

In sum, the "traditional common law jury," composed of twelve members who rendered unanimous verdicts, was neither uniform nor standard throughout the countries in which it was imported or adopted. Juries varied and continue to vary in terms of their size, permissible verdicts, and representation, among other features. Moreover, by the latter half of the twentieth century, the use of juries, particularly in civil cases but also in criminal trials, declined or was abandoned in many parts of the world, even in England and Wales. That is because juries have been increasingly criticized as too costly, incompetent in dealing with complex litigation, and subject to bias as a result of pre-emptory challenges and the influence of media coverage of trials. Consequently, jury trials in civil cases have largely been discontinued, except for in Canada and the United States. Jury trials in criminal cases have also been systematically cut back or abandoned in many countries. Nevertheless, although generally diminished in their usage, they survive in Australia, Canada, England and Wales, Ireland, New Zealand, the United States, and some forty-six other countries, including parts of the Mediterranean (Gibraltar and Malta), Africa (Ghana and Malawi), Asia (Hong Kong and Sri Lanka), the South Pacific (Tonga and The Marshall Islands), South America (Brazil and Guyana), and the islands of the British and Irish Caribbean (Barbados, Jamaica, and Montserrat). Variations of the jury system also remain in use in Austria, Belgium, Denmark, and, Norway; and, notably, in the 1990s Russia and Spain reintroduced juries in criminal cases.

Notes

[a]Alexis de Tocqueville, translated by Phillips Bradley, *Democracy in America* (New York: Knopf, 1945), 318.

Sources: Leonard W. Levy, *The Palladium of Justice: Origins of Trial by Jury* (Chicago: Ivan R. Dee, 1999); Neal Vidmar, ed., *World Jury Systems* (New York: Oxford University Press, 2000).

The democratic role juries play is significant because they represent the community and have the flexibility to acquit, convict, or force a mistrial. Still, the jury's role remains influenced by several different types factors: what kinds of criminal cases juries are permitted to adjudicate; whether it is possible to select an impartial jury that fairly represents the community and is free from bias; whether twelve-person juries or smaller sized juries are constitutionally appropriate; whether jury verdicts must be unanimous; and, whether the jury has the authority to nullify the law and acquit defendants in morally complex cases. Moreover, the jury's role as a passive player in the adversarial process has been increasingly called into question because some claim it impedes the discovery of facts.

In terms of the types of criminal cases juries may hear, the Supreme Court has established that the accused can only elect to have a jury trial in serious, "nonpetty" criminal cases—cases in which defendants face possible imprisonment of six months or more.[31] Yet, *Lewis v. United States* (1996)[32] held that a jury trial is not required if the defendant might actually be imprisoned for more than six months or when a multicount indictment charges the defendant with several petty offenses that each carry less than six months prison time. In addition, in federal courts the right to a jury is not required for contempt proceedings, petitions involving writs of *habeas corpus*, some civil and administrative proceedings involving disbarment of attorneys and immigrant deportations, and military court martials.[33]

Controversies over Courts

What is the Role of Courts in Times of Crisis and Wartime?

In the aftermath of the September 11, 2001 terrorist attacks on the World Trade Center and the Pentagon, President George W. Bush declared war on international terrorism. President Bush's decision to authorize the National Security Agency to conduct domestic wiretaps of American citizens without using the special legislatively created Foreign Intelligence Surveillance Court,[a] and some of his orders for holding and trying "enemy combatants,"[b] have reignited the controversy over the role of courts in times of national crisis. That controversy arises from the dilemma of preserving liberty and the rule of law along with ensuring national security. The self-preservation of the country, some politicians, judges, and scholars argue, may require extraordinary measures that are beyond the purview of courts or that at least require highly deferential judicial review. The Constitution and the rule of law, others argue, require the judiciary to assert its power in order to preserve due process and the equal protection of the law in times of crisis, no less than is done in peacetime. Still others contend that the balance between liberty and security must be drawn pragmatically, depending on the particular circumstances, and not dogmatically.

COURTS IN TIMES OF CRISIS IN HISTORICAL PERSPECTIVE

The controversy was given, perhaps, its classical formulation by President Abraham Lincoln. At the outset of the Civil War, he took extraordinary measures—calling up state militias, spending unappropriated funds, and blockading Southern ports—without constitutional or congressional authorization. Lincoln later defended his actions as essential to saving the Union, and thereby, paradoxically, as preserving the Constitution. In his words:

> I [understood] my oath to preserve the constitution to the best of my ability, imposed upon me the duty of preserving, by every indispensable means, that government— that nation—of which that constitution was the organic law. Was it possible to lose the nation, and yet preserve the constitution? . . . I felt that measures, otherwise unconstitutional might become lawful, by becoming indispensable to the preservation of the constitution, through the preservation of the nation."[c]

In *The Prize Cases*,[d] the Supreme Court upheld Lincoln's declaring the Southern states in rebellion and ordering blockades of their ports after the outbreak of the Civil

War. When the constitutionality of those orders was challenged, the Court affirmed the president's power. However, four justices dissented; Justice Samuel Nelson, along with Chief Justice Roger B. Taney and Justices John Catron and Nathan Clifford, denounced Lincoln's actions for waging "a personal war against those in rebellion." They compared Lincoln with the King of Great Britain at the time of the American Revolution and underscored that, unlike King George the III, under the Constitution the president is bound by the rule of law, including judicially enforced civil rights and liberties.

Subsequently, after the conclusion of the Civil War, in *Ex parte Milligan*[e] the Court declared unconstitutional Lincoln's orders suspending the writ of *habeas corpus* and for trying all persons suspected of disloyalty by military commissions. Somewhere between 20,000 and 30,000 people were arrested and detained by the military, without charges, on the suspicion of disloyalty. Many were never tried and those that were went before military tribunals, rather than civilian courts. Writing for the Court in *Milligan*, Justice David Davis, a Lincoln appointee, spoke eloquently of "the birthright of every American citizen when charged with crime, to be tried and punished according to law." Adherence to the rule of law was paramount, Justice Davis declared that "[t]he Constitution of the United States is a law for rulers and people, equally in war and in peace, and covers with the shield of its protection all classes of men, at all times, and under all circumstances."

In the view of some at the time (and some today) the ruling in *Milligan* was mistaken. Federal Judge Richard A. Posner, for one, writing in the aftermath of 9/11 pressed the point: "Lincoln's unconstitutional acts during the Civil War show that even legality must sometimes be sacrificed for other values. We are a nation under law, but first we are a nation."[f]

During World War II, the Court also approved President Franklin D. Roosevelt's order to use military tribunals to try German saboteurs, one of whom was a naturalized U.S. citizen. The "Nazi Saboteurs" were captured in the United States and charged with planning to sabotage bridges and utility plants. In *Ex parte Quirin*,[g] the Court unanimously ruled that the president has the "power . . . to carry into effect . . . all laws defining and punishing offenses against the law of nations, including those which pertain to the conduct of war." Writing for the Court, Chief Justice Harlan Fiske Stone underscored that the power to wage war includes the authority "to seize and subject to disciplinary measures those enemies who in their attempt to thwart or impede our military effort have violated the law of war." Nor did the chief justice distinguish between U.S. citizens and noncitizens; both were wartime belligerents and were to be treated as such. As Chief Justice Stone put it, "citizenship in the United States of an enemy belligerent does not relieve him from the consequences of a belligerency which is unlawful."

Nonetheless, the Court later reaffirmed the distinction between citizens and noncitizens with respect to access to U.S. courts. In *Johnson v. Eisentrager*,[h] the Court held that federal courts had no jurisdiction over *habeas corpus* petitions filed by German nationals who were captured and held in China by U.S. military forces at the end of World War II. (On this basis the Bush administration initially rebuffed challenges to holding indefinitely captured Taliban and al Qaeda fighters in Guantanamo Bay, Cuba).

Following World War II, the Court also stepped back to reaffirm the rights of citizenship in ruling that citizens may not be subject to court-martial or denied the guarantees in the Bill of Rights. The "cases of the murdering wives," as Justice Felix Frankfurter referred to them, *Reid v. Covert*[i] and *Kinsella v. Krueger*,[j] involved women who allegedly killed their husbands while stationed abroad in the military. They challenged the constitutionality of a treaty that subjected civilians living abroad with military personnel to court martial under the Uniform Code of Military Justice, which does not extend the same guarantees as the Bill of Rights. Chief Justice Earl Warren initially assigned the opinions, but Justice Stanley Reed changed his vote. The balance on the Court shifted and a bare majority voted to permit the court martial of civilians. The very next year, though, Justice Sherman Minton retired and Justice William J. Brennan, Jr. took his seat on the bench. When the justices reconsidered the matter in *Reid v. Covert*,[k] they reversed their earlier decision and ruled that the guarantees of the Bill of Rights may not be abrogated by treaties.

HOW DEFERENTIAL SHOULD THE COURTS BE IN THE "WAR AGAINST TERRORISM"?

The controversy over the role of courts in crisis times and the dilemma of preserving civil liberties loomed large since 9/11. The Bush administration and Congress took decisive action to deal with the terrorist threat with several legislative and executive enactments. The Authorization for Use of Military Force Joint Resolution (AUMF), passed by Congress a few days after the attacks, broadly authorized the president "to use all necessary and appropriate force" against nations, organizations, or persons that took part in the 9/11 plot. Less than six weeks after 9/11, on October 26, 2001, President Bush signed into law the sweeping and controversial (though passed by Congress without public hearings or extended debate) 342-page USA PATRIOT Act of 2001 or, more precisely, United and Strengthening America by Providing Appropriate Tools Required to Intercept and Obstruct Terrorism Act.[l] In November, 2001, President Bush also issued an order, as commander-in-chief of the armed forces, authorizing the indefinite detention of captured foreign terrorists and directing their trial by special secret military tribunals, without the possibility of appeal. His order invited controversy because the detainees are not treated as prisoners of war according to international law. Under the Third Geneva Convention of 1949, prisoners of war are entitled to an independent and impartial trial, the assistance of counsel, and the right of appeal.[m]

Because of their impact on personal freedoms, sixteen parts of the USA PATRIOT Act—those sections governing enhanced foreign intelligence and law enforcement surveillance powers, such as so-called sneak and peak searches, roving wiretaps, and the seizure of stored electronic communications—were set to expire by the end of 2005. But after extended debate, Congress reauthorized the law with the USA PATRIOT Improvement and Reauthorization Act of 2005, signed by President Bush on March 2, 2006.[n] Among other things, the new law reauthorized all expiring provisions of the USA PATRIOT Act, increased congressional and judicial oversight of Foreign Intelligence Surveillance Act (FISA) wiretap procedures, tightened port security, and intensified criminal restrictions on the illicit production of methamphetamine.

Still, the debate about the constitutionality of USA PATRIOT Act or of the exercise of President Bush's inherent wartime authority remains intense. Among the most controversial provisions of the USA PATRIOT Act is Section 412, authorizing the detention of suspected terrorists and supporters of terrorists. The provision authorizes the attorney general to detain alien terrorist suspects for up to seven days, if there are reasonable grounds to believe that they pose a threat to national security or are deportable on grounds of terrorism, espionage, sabotage, or sedition. Within the seven days, the attorney general must either initiate removal or criminal proceedings or release the alien. If the alien is held, the determination must be reexamined every six months to confirm that the alien's release would threaten national security.[o]

Especially controversial is the treatment of U.S. citizens allegedly linked to al Qaeda or other terrorist groups. In light of *Ex parte Quirin* and *Reid v. Covert*, John Walker Lindh, the young American captured fighting with the Taliban in Afghanistan, was accorded counsel and tried in court, though his case was eventually resolved by a plea bargain and he is currently serving a twenty-year prison term. Thus far, less than a handful of citizens have been declared *enemy combatants,* though several others have been detained as "material witnesses." Initially, the Department of Justice (DoJ) took the position that courts had no jurisdiction to review the basis for detaining citizens as enemy combatants. In other words, the administration initially appeared to completely deny judicial review of the matter.

The so-called dirty bomber, Jose Padilla or Abdullah al-Muhajir, as he become known after his conversion to Islam, was an American citizen detained after deplaning from a flight from Zurich, Switzerland, in Chicago's O'Hare airport. He was initially held as a material witness for allegedly meeting with al Qaeda officials in Pakistan and conspiring to detonate a radioactive bomb in the United States. Padilla was later moved to New York and taken into military custody. He was then designated an enemy combatant and moved to a Navy brig in Charleston, South Carolina.

As an enemy combatant, Padilla was held without specific charges, access to a lawyer, and other guarantees of due process. As with other post-9/11 detainees, lawyers challenged the administration's practice and denial of judicial review. In light of *Quirin*, few questioned the government's authority to hold him. Instead, at contention was the DoJ's position denying Padilla access to a lawyer and the opportunity to contest the basis for his detention in a court of law. Indeed, the Bush administration's position that enemy combatants may be denied the due process otherwise accorded citizens has its defenders. Like the administration, they draw on *Quirin* and more recent rulings by the late Chief Justice William H. Rehnquist as well as on his extrajudicial historical analysis of civil liberties in wartime.[p] Writing for the Court in *United States v. Salerno,*[q] for instance, Chief Justice Rehnquist held that the pretrial detention for more than two years, without bail, of an accused organized crime leader was "regulatory, not penal," and thus not a violation of due process. In his words: "We have repeatedly held that the government's regulatory interest in community safety can, in appropriate circumstances, outweigh an individual's liberty interest." In *dictum* referring to times of "war or insurrection," the chief justice added that "the government may detain individuals whom the government believes to be dangerous." War critics, and those supportive of detainee rights, counter that there is a strong presumption against military detention of American citizens absent explicit congressional authorization under the Non-Detention Act, penal legislation enacted by Congress in 1948.[r]

In December 2002, the federal district court held that Padilla had a right to consult with an attorney and to offer evidence contesting the government's allegations about his association with al Qaeda and that he poses a continuing danger to national security.[s] Thereafter, in an action challenging his military detention in a naval brig in South Carolina, the Supreme Court dismissed Padilla's *habeas corpus* petition on procedural grounds because it was improperly filed in the federal district court in the Southern District of New York.[t]

On remand, in a second *habeas* petition filed in South Carolina, a district court ruled in Padilla's favor, but that decision was reversed by the Fourth Circuit Appeals Court, holding that Congress's Joint Resolution (AUMF) gave President Bush constitutional authority to detain militarily a suspected terrorist as an enemy combatant.[u] After filing an appeal to the Supreme Court, however, the government switched tactics and removed Padilla from military custody, opting instead to file criminal charges against him. In light of the government's decision to indict Padilla, in *Padilla v. Hanft* (2006)[v] the Supreme Court declined to hear the appeal (but over the dissents of Justices Ginsburg, Souter, and Breyer), in part because resolving the constitutional issue of wrongful detention in a military brig was a "hypothetical" claim because he was removed from military custody. In practical terms, in avoiding the constitutional question the Supreme Court left the Fourth Circuit ruling intact and, perhaps, implied that a president in wartime enjoys broad authority to detain an American citizen captured on American soil.[w]

Furthermore, the Supreme Court has answered the closely related issue of whether the president may detain a U.S. citizen captured on foreign soil in the military campaign to dislodge the Taliban in Afghanistan shortly after 9/11. Like Padilla, President Bush labeled Yaser Esam Hamdi as an enemy combatant shortly after he was captured abroad. Hamdi was a nominal or a virtual U.S. citizen. He was born in Baton Rouge, Louisiana, but moved as a young child to his parents' homeland in Saudi Arabia, where he was raised. He eventually went to Afghanistan, where he was captured fighting alongside the Taliban by the Northern Alliance forces and turned over to the U.S. military. Hamdi was initially taken to Guantanamo Bay. But, once his U.S. citizenship was discovered, he was designated an enemy combatant and moved to a brig in Norfolk, Virginia.

Hamdi first challenged his detention, interrogation, and denial of legal representation as a violation of his citizenship rights in the federal trial court. Before the government could respond, a federal district court Judge Robert G. Doumar appointed a public defender and ordered the government to allow Hamdi to consult with the attorney. On appeal, the Fourth Circuit Court of Appeals reversed and also rejected the position that "with no meaningful judicial review, any American citizen alleged to be an enemy combatant could be detained indefinitely without charges or counsel on the government's say-so." Instead, the court sanctioned a limited, deferential judicial review of Hamdi's status and remanded the case to the district court.

Following the remand, District Court Judge Robert Doumar expressed concerns about Hamdi's rights as a citizen, questioned the government's basic contentions about its war effort, and directed the government to file a response to Hamdi's petition for a writ of *habeas corpus*. The government in turn filed a motion to dismiss and a response, including a two-page, nine-paragraph affidavit from Special Advisor to the Under Secretary of Defense for Policy Michael Mobbs detailing only the most rudimentary facts of Hamdi's capture and detention.

Judge Doumar was not satisfied and picked the Mobbs declaration apart "piece by piece." Ultimately, he held that the affidavit fell short of supporting Hamdi's detention. Judge Doumar ordered the government to turn over, among other things, copies of Hamdi's statements to interrogators and any notes taken of their interrogations of him. When the government then challenged the production of those materials, Judge Doumar certified for the Fourth Circuit's review the following question: "Whether the Mobbs Declaration, standing alone, is sufficient as a matter of law to allow a meaningful judicial review of Yaser Esam Hamdi's classification as an enemy combatant?"

Back in the Fourth Circuit, Chief Judge J. Harvie Wilkinson relied on *Quirin* in reaffirming the appellate court's earlier ruling in Hamdi's case that courts should show "great deference to the political branches when called upon to decide cases implicating sensitive matters of foreign policy, national security, or military affairs."[x] Chief Judge Wilkinson concluded that Hamdi could not challenge the Mobbs declaration and that the declaration was a sufficient basis to justify his incarceration as an enemy combatant.

Although reaffirming the judiciary's deference to the president in times of crisis and war, Chief Judge Wilkinson drew the line at the complete exclusion or abdication of the judiciary's role in exercising judicial review. On appeal, in *Hamdi v. Rumsfeld* (2004),[y] a bare majority of the Supreme Court held that the president has the power to detain U.S. citizens as enemy combatants, but in a six-to-three vote the Court ruled that they have a right to consult an attorney and to contest the basis for their detention before an independent tribunal. Notably, in reaffirming a strong judicial role in the war on terror the Court stated that due process requires U.S. citizens the right to challenge their detention before a "neutral decision-maker" and that the "state of war is not a blank check for the President when it comes to the rights of the Nation's citizens."[z]

In a significant companion case, *Rasul v. Bush* (2004),[aa] the Court also rejected the Bush Administration's position that federal courts lack jurisdiction over foreign nationals held in Guantanamo Bay, Cuba (GITMO) and affirmed their right to seek judicial review of the basis for their detention. In the aftermath of *Rasul*, the Pentagon created "Combatant Status Review Tribunals" (CSRTs) as an administrative procedure to hear claims by detainees contesting their status as enemy combatants. After *Rasul*, and although the CSRTs have adjudicated the status of some 500 GITMO detainees, federal courts continue to grapple with dozens of detainee lawsuits seeking to enforce constitutional rights and ascertain the scope of protections afforded prisoners of war under the Geneva

Convention precepts. In 2006, in *Hamdan v. Rumsfeld* (2006)[bb] the Supreme Court granted *certiorari* to review the D.C. Circuit's ruling that the president had the constitutional authority to use military tribunals and that the petitioner, Osama bin Ladin's personal driver, could not challenge his detention at GITMO under Geneva Convention rules.

The fate of other detainees and the power of courts to resolve enemy combatant status cases was affected by Congress's enactment of the Detainee Treatment Act of 2005, a law ostensibly passed to impose a ban on the use of torture on detainees during interrogation.[cc] Yet the legislation also severely restricted access to federal courts in Guantanamo Bay detainee cases and, in effect, overruled *Rasul*. It eliminated from courts the jurisdiction to hear *habeas corpus* petitions brought against the United States by detainees until after the question of their enemy combatant status had been determined by military commissions—although detainees still retained the right to appeal those findings in the D.C. Circuit Court of Appeals, *if* the court elected to hear the appeal. Because the Bush Administration raised the claim that the courts are deprived of power to hear detainee challenges under the Detainee Treatment Act in *Hamdan*, the Supreme Court had to decide that jurisdictional question as well.[dd]

In a historic ruling in *Hamdan v. Rumsfeld* (2006)[ee] the Court rebuffed the Bush administration's position that it could try enemy combatants by military commissions, rather than in civil courts or in courts martial, without congressional authorization and according to provisions of the Geneva Conventions. The Court also held that Congress had to authorize the procedures for trials by military commissions, as well as rejected the administration's contention that the Detainee Treatment Act of 2005 deprived the Court of jurisdiction over pending cases brought by enemy combatants like Hamdan.

Notes

[a] James Risen and Eric Lichtblau, "Bush Said to Have Secretly Lifted Some Spying Limits After 9/11," *Chicago Tribune* (December 16, 2005), C30.

[b] See, e.g. "Detention, Treatment, and Trial of Certain Non-Citizens in the War Against Terrorism," 66 *Federal Register* 57833 (November 13, 2001).

[c] John Nicolay and John Hays, eds., *The Complete Works of Abraham Lincoln*, Vol. 10 (New York: Francis D. Tandy, 1894), 65–68.

[d] *The Prize Cases*, 67 U.S. 935 (1863). See also David Cole, *Enemy Aliens* (New York: New Press, 2003).

[e] *Ex parte Milligan*, 71 U.S. 2 (1866).

[f] Richard A. Posner, "Security Versus Civil Liberties," *The Atlantic Monthly* (December 2001), 46–48.

[g] *Ex parte Quirin*, 317 U.S. 1 (1942). For a concise examination of the case and the Court's decision, see David J. Danelski, "The Saboteur's Case," *1996 Journal of Supreme Court History* (1996), 61–82; and Louis Fisher, *Nazi Saboteurs on Trial* (Lawrence: University of Kansas Press, 2003).

[h] *Johnson v. Eisentrager*, 339 U.S. 763 (1950).

[i] *Reid v. Covert*, 351 U.S. 487 (1956).

[j] *Kinsella v. Krueger*, 351 U.S. 470 (1956).

[k] *Reid v. Covert*, 354 U.S. 1 (1957).

[l] "Uniting and Strengthening America by Providing Appropriate Tools Required to Intercept and Obstruct Terrorism (USA PATRIOT Act), P.L. 107-56, 115 Stat. 272 (2001).

[m] See Geneva Convention Relative to the Treatment of Prisoners of War, Art. 5, 6 U.S.T. 3316, 75 U.N.T.S. 135. See also "Detention, Treatment, and Trial of Certain Non-Citizens in the War Against Terrorism," *Federal Register* 57833 (November 13, 2001).

[n] USA PATRIOT Improvement and Reauthorization Act of 2005, P.L. 109-177 (2006). See also Brian T. Yeh and Charles Doyle, *USA PATRIOT Improvement and Reauthorization Act: A Legal Analysis*, CRS Report 33332 (Washington, D.C.: Congressional Research Service, American Law Division, 24 March 2006).

[o] For the text and other important information on the USA PATRIOT Act go to www. personalinfomediary.com/USAPATRIOTAct_Text.htm. See also Charles Doyle, *The USA PATRIOT Act: A Legal Analysis: A Legal Analysis*, CRS Report RL31377 (Washington, D.C.: Congressional Research Service, American Law Division, 15 April 2002).

[p] See William H. Rehnquist, *All the Laws but One: Civil Liberties in Wartime* (New York: Knopf, 1998).

[q] *United States v. Salerno*, 481 U.S. 739 (1987).

[r] 18 U.S.C. Section 4001, P.L. 92-128 (1948).

[s] *Padilla v. Bush*, 233 F.Supp.2d 564 (S.D. N.Y. 2002).

[t] *Rumsfeld v. Padilla*, 542 U.S. 426 (2004).

[u] *Padilla v. Hanft*, 423 F.3d 386 (2005).

[v] *Padilla v. Hanft*, 2006 U.S. Lexis 2705 (April 3, 2006), (J. Kennedy, concurrence); but see ibid. (J. Ginsburg, dissenting).

[w] Charles Lane, "Justices Won't Review Padilla Case," *Washington Post* (April 4, 2006), A06.

[x] *Hamdi v. Rumsfeld*, 316 F.3d 450 (4th Cir. 2003), quoting *Hamdi II*, 296 F.3d at 281.

[y] *Hamdi v. Rumsfeld*, 542 U.S. 507 (2004).

[z] *Hamdi v. Rumsfeld*, 542 U.S. at 536.

[aa] *Rasul v. Bush*, 542 U.S. 466 (2004).

[bb] *Hamdan v. Rumsfeld*, 126 S. Ct. 622 (2006) (order granting *certiorari*). See also *Hamdan v. Rumsfeld*, 415 F.3d 33 (D.C. Cir. 2005).

[cc] Section 1005 of the Department of Defense Appropriations Act of 2006, Pub. L. No. 109-148 (2005).

[dd] Charles Lane, "Case Tests Power of Judiciary, President," *Washington Post* (March 29, 2006), A06.

[ee] *Hamdan v. Rumsfeld*, 126 S. Ct. 2749 (2006).

The difficulties of selecting an impartial jury, representing a cross-section of the community, invites the criticism that defendants are deprived of not only their Sixth Amendment rights but also of their rights to equal protection under the Fourteenth Amendment. Under these provisions, defendants may allege that the jury selection process is fraught with unfair racial, gender, and economic bias.[34]

In most jurisdictions, members of the jury panel are drawn from voting registration lists. But many persons do not register to vote and those who do tend to be more affluent, educated, and older.[35]

The problems of generating a representative jury pool are compounded by the strategic decisions of lawyers to pick a jury to their liking. A jury must be selected by the litigants through a *voir dire* selection process. Jurors are questioned and may be excused from serving if the lawyers exercise either a challenge for cause or a peremptory challenge (limited in number, but based on any grounds). Challenge for causes are unlimited in number and based on responses from prospective jurors, suggesting they cannot fairly weigh the evidence.

The Supreme Court has prohibited the discriminatory use of peremptory challenges if such challenges are based on race, gender, and (implicitly) ethnic origin.[36] But the prosecutor's choices are evaluated on "facially neutral" grounds; that is, defendants must prove the prosecutor was acting with "purposeful discrimination" in excluding certain classes of persons from the jury panel once the trial court initially accepts the prosecutor's race-neutral explanations. Some critics argue that the standard ironically facilitates discrimination by encouraging courts to accept *any* rationale for exclusion that the prosecutor can create on a pretext, or "after the fact," if it appears to be "neutral."[37] Notably, prosecutors are given the same right to challenge the defendant's peremptory strikes on discriminatory grounds as well. Although in some high-profile racially charged cases, defendant will be inhibited from selecting a jury stocked with a specific racial, gender, or ethnic bias, it is more difficult to prevent minority defendants from getting juries with more diversity.[38]

Court rulings reducing jury size and permitting nonunanimous verdicts also invite criticism. Traditionally, the size of the common-law jury was twelve and jury verdicts in criminal trials were required to be unanimous. In the 1960s, however, several states and the federal courts began to push for jury reform in an attempt to save costs and promote efficiency. *Williams v. Florida* (1970)[39] held that states could provide for six-person juries in felony cases. Subsequently, *Johnson v. Louisiana* (1972) and *Apodaco v. Oregon* (1972),[40] adopted a similar rationale by holding that unanimous and non-unanimous verdicts were "functionally equivalent," thereby approving nonunanimous, supermajority verdicts in criminal cases. But in *Ballew v. Georgia* (1978) and *Burch v. Louisiana* (1979),[41] the Court retreated and declared that five-person criminal juries were unconstitutional (in *Ballew*) and that six-member jury criminal verdicts had to be unanimous (in *Burch*).

Notably, *Ballew* recognized that a jury with less than six members "promotes inaccurate and possibly biased decisionmaking, . . . causes untoward differences in verdicts, and . . . prevents juries from truly representing their communities."[42] Perhaps for this reason the federal government still requires that twelve-person juries to deliver unanimous whereas, most states require them only for felonies. Still, approximately thirty states permit smaller juries and, less frequently, nonunanimous verdicts for misdemeanor prosecutions.

Jury reforms have produced significant changes in federal and state civil cases as well. Nearly forty state jurisdictions authorize some combination of nonunanimous verdicts, or juries consisting of between six and nine persons, in trials taking place in some or all of its courts. In federal courts, the six-person juries and unanimous verdicts remain the norm.[43]

Once the jury is impaneled, the evidence is heard at trial. The jury's most important task, namely to weigh the defendant's guilt or innocence, transpires only after it first learns from the judge what law to apply. Once opposing counsel finish closing arguments, the jury reaches a verdict after the judge instructs the jury about controlling law. If there is a reasonable doubt, the jury will acquit; if not, the jury will convict.

Sidebar 7.2

Jury Nullification and Hung Juries

Although the Sixth and Seventh Amendments of the U.S. Constitution guarantee citizens the right to a jury in criminal and civil actions, juries do not have a right to "nullify," or independently disregard, what the law commands in reaching verdicts. That principle was reaffirmed in *Sparf & Hansen v. United States* (1895), holding that the jury's proper role is to apply the law (as determined by the judge) to the facts they find after hearing the evidence at trial.[a]

Juries nonetheless engage in nullification. A jury may acquit because it perceives the law to be unjust. This might happen in an assisted suicide prosecution involving a senior citizen who intentionally killed their terminally ill partner. Alternatively, a jury may exonerate a defendant if the law is valid but views its application as unfair. In addition, a jury may disregard the law if the legal officials enforcing it engaged in prosecutorial or illegal police misconduct.

A study by the National Center for State Courts explored an analogous problem of jury behavior by identifying the frequency and causes of deadlocked juries in criminal and civil cases.[b] The study found that 2.5 percent of federal criminal trials result in hung juries, whereas in state prosecutions the average rate was 6.2 percent. The study also compared verdict cases (336) to hung jury cases (forty-six) and found that the average hung jury rate was 12.8 percent. The reasons juries could not render a verdict varied, but three patterns emerged. Hung juries are likely due to (1) the poor quality of the evidence, (2) difficult and contentious deliberations, and (3) jurors who perceive the law to be unfair.

Notes

[a] *Sparf & Hansen v. United States*, 151 U.S. 51 (1895).

[b] Paula L. Hannaford-Agor, Valerie P. Hans, Nicole L. Mott, and G. Thomas Munsterman, "Are Hung Juries a Problem?" (NCSC, September 30, 2002), available from www.ncsonline. org/WC/Publications/Res_Juires_HungJuriesPub.pdf (retrieved November 17, 2003).

Finally, the question of whether juries are neutral fact finders has ignited calls for reform in the states. In 2001, the National Center for State Courts launched a jury reform study, and at least thirty states commenced similar investigations. Test pilot programs, for example, have implemented a number of innovations, including (1) permitting jurors to take notes during trials; (2) allowing jurors to ask witnesses questions during trial; (3) giving jurors "preinstructions," or giving them a brief overview of the case before jury selection begins; (4) requiring "plain English" jury instructions; (5) facilitating posttrial meetings between the judge, jurors, lawyers, and other relevant courtroom actors; and, (6) increasing jury size in complex cases. Several states, including Ohio, Massachusetts, and Arizona, are exploring similar reforms, and New York enacted changes in the areas of expanding the master voting list, increasing juror pay, and publishing a handbook of jurors' rights and responsibilities.[44]

Typically the work of juries is attacked in high-profile cases that result in verdicts that appear to be miscarriages of justice. The Innocence Project, an investigation of wrongful convictions in death penalty cases launched by law professors Barry C. Scheck and Peter J. Neufeld in 1992, has documented numerous problems with juries convicting innocent defendants on the basis of faulty police investigations, false confessions, lawyer incompetence, mistaken identifications, and prosecutorial misconduct; it has also led to the exoneration of over 150 defendants.[45]

The advances in DNA technology and forensic science that have been popularized with televisions dramas such as *CSI* and *Crossing Jordan* have magnified not only the importance of getting the result right in criminal cases but also the consequences when the jury makes a serious mistake. That was the impetus for Illinois Governor George Ryan in 2000 to announce a moratorium in death penalty cases and, similarly, the drive in at least twelve states to form *innocence commissions*—public committees or investigations to assess whether their criminal justice procedures are operating fairly and not wrongfully convicting defendants, especially in capital cases.[46]

THE POLITICS OF THE POSTTRIAL SENTENCING PROCESS

Even though the jury's verdict ends a trial, a defendant's conviction begins the sentencing and punishment process. Persons convicted of crimes are sentenced in accordance with one or more of the following purposes of punishment: retribution, deterrence, incapacitation, and rehabilitation. *Retribution* is designed to exact revenge, to give offenders their "just desserts." *Deterrence* serves the population at large, whereas specific deterrence targets discrete offenders. *Incapacitation* seeks to protect society by removing offenders from the community and placing them in prisons. *Rehabilitation* attempts to treat offenders and subsequently reintroduce them into society. Rehabilitation involves some type of counseling or vocational treatment. In contrast to other sentencing philosophies, rehabilitation does not necessarily punish all offenders who commit the same crime equally, a criticism that crime control advocates say diminishes its legitimacy as a penal policy.[47]

Sentencing policies incorporate some or all of these philosophies and have evolved with the growth of the modern prison system. In the colonial era, communities used retribution and deterrence to maintain social control. Public shaming was a popular punishment, which included flogging, physical mutilation, and spending time in the stocks.[48]

Prison overcrowding, though, gave rise to the practice of using indeterminate sentencing—sentences imposed by judges after considering a broad range of minimum and maximum punishments to sanction offenders, especially after 1870. Incarceration and the imposition of fines became predominant sanctions. Although determinate sentencing practices were in use, rehabilitation and indeterminate sentencing were the basis of national penal policy for much of the nineteenth and twentieth centuries.[49]

Beginning in the mid-1970s, however, rehabilitation gave way to determinate sentencing practices that returned to emphasizing a combination of retribution, deterrence, and incapacitation philosophies. Such practices included mandatory minimum sentencing, "truth in sentencing," sentencing guidelines, and intermediate sanctions (see Table 7.4). The thrust of determinate sentencing is to punish offenders with fixed sentences that reduce the discretionary power of judicial and parole officers to deviate from the prescribed range of punishment. The shift in sentencing policy from indeterminate to determinate practices registers the ideological struggle between the different values underlying the crime control and due process models.

The Growth of Determinate Structured Sentencing

"[B]oth before and since the American colonies became a nation," Justice Black wrote in *Williams v. New York* (1949), "courts in this country and in England practiced a policy under which a sentencing judge could exercise a wide discretion in the sources and types of evidence used to assist him in determining the kind and extent of punishment to be imposed within limits fixed by law." *Williams* held that a New York state trial judge acted appropriately in using information from a probation department's presentence report when sentencing a convicted murderer to death, instead of following the jury's recommendation of life imprisonment. The scope of the trial court's discretion under indeterminate sentencing, Justice Black acknowledged, is vast and the "practice of probation" confirmed that "[r]eformation and rehabilitation of offenders have become important goals of criminal jurisprudence." Hence the trial court could rely upon witness's statements in the presentence report describing the defendant as a "menace to society" and having "a morbid sexuality" and therefore conclude that he should be executed. The defendant's due process rights were not violated because a judge could legally "consider information about the convicted person's past life,

TABLE 7.4   Sentencing Typologies and Practices

Sentencing Type/Practice	Main Characteristics
Indeterminate Sentencing	■ Judge imposes sentence within range of minimum and maximum penalties set by legislature, but parole boards determine actual length of time served ■ Prevalent as a sentencing policy up until the 1970s, but its use has been substantially diminished in the federal government and several states ■ Many states use hybrid indeterminate/determinate sentencing practices
Determinate Sentencing	■ Fixed prison terms imposed set by legislature that may be reduced by good-time or earned-time credits ■ Typically sets a release date, with no independent review by parole board, but post-incarceration supervision possible as part of the sentence ■ Increasingly prevalent in the federal government and the majority of states since the 1980s
Truth in Sentencing	■ Requires offenders to serve a substantial portion of their prison sentence (typically between 50 percent to 85 percent, or 100 percent of the minimum, depending upon class and degree of offense) ■ Parole eligibility and good-time credits are restricted or eliminated ■ First introduced in the states in the mid-1980s and prevalent in most jurisdictions
Mandatory Minimum Sentencing	■ Requires offenders, especially violent criminals, to serve minimum sentence before becoming eligible for parole ■ Typically target habitual offenders and often to violent, drug, sex offense, weapons, and driving under the influence of alcohol crimes ■ First introduced in the 1980s and prevalent in all states and District of Columbia
Sentencing Guidelines	■ Requires judges to impose sentences in accordance with fixed penalties often promulgated by sentencing commissions ■ Guidelines determine the sentence by taking into account the offender's criminal history and the severity of the crime

Sentencing Type/Practice	Main Characteristics
	▪ Judicial discretion in imposing sentences is restricted, and "upward" or "downward" departures from the guidelines are disfavored ▪ Parole restricted or eliminated ▪ Adopted by the federal government in 1984 through the Sentencing Reform Act of 1984; since then, about half the states have adopted or are seriously considering adopting some form of sentencing guidelines system to replace or supplement existing sentencing structures
Presumptive Sentencing Guidelines	▪ Sentencing guidelines are considered presumptively correct and judges cannot depart from them absent legally permissible reasons that are explained on the record ▪ Guidelines may require appellate review of departures by trial judge ▪ Prior to *Blakely v. Washington*, 542 U.S. 296 (2004), ten states using guidelines followed this approach (Indiana, Kansas, Michigan Minnesota, North Carolina, New Jersey, Ohio, Oregon, Tennessee, Washington)
Voluntary Sentencing Guidelines	▪ Sentencing guidelines are advisory (recommendations) only and judges have discretion can depart from the guidelines ▪ Prior to *Blakely v. Washington*, 542 U.S. 296 (2004), twelve states, plus the District of Columbia, using guidelines followed this approach (Arkansas, Delaware, Louisiana, Maryland, Montana, Pennsylvania, Rhode Island, South Carolina, Utah, Vermont, Virginia, Wisconsin)
Intermediate Sanctions	▪ Non-custodial sanctions, used to supplement guidelines sentencing ▪ Examples include home confinement, community service, residential treatment (health, drug illness), victim restitution, and intensive-supervision probation (day reporting) ▪ Used in only a few states, and minimally in federal government

Source: Anne Skove, "*Blakely v. Washington:* Implications for State Courts" (National Center for State Courts, July 16, 2004), available from www.ncsconline.org/WC/Publications/KIS_SentenBlakely.pdf (retrieved March 25, 2005); U.S. Department of Justice, Bureau of Justice Assistance, *1996 National Survey of State Sentencing Structures* (Monograph, NCJ 169270, September 1998), available from www.ncjrs.org/pdffiles/169270.pdf (retrieved March 25, 2005); Richard S. Frase, "Is Guided Discretion Sufficient? Overview of State Sentencing Guidelines," *Saint Louis Law Journal* 44 (Spring 2000), 425–46.

health, habits, conduct, and mental and moral propensities ... even though [it was] obtained outside the courtroom from persons whom a defendant has not been permitted to confront or cross-examine."[50]

It is surprising that Justice Black's defense of indeterminate sentencing was subsequently attacked by the political left and right. States and the federal government experimented with "structured" sentencing regimes. Early reformers, such as Andrew Von Hirsch and Alan Dershowitz, argued in favor of *presumptive sentences*—punishments that presumptively fix the sentence term by using ranges that base punishment on the seriousness of the offense and the offender's prior criminal history. These reform ideas were applied in few states with the adoption in the late 1970s of voluntary sentencing guidelines that typically used fixed sentences and abolished parole; but early release was also allowed by the accumulation of good time credits.[51]

In the 1980s, growing political dissatisfaction with indeterminate sentencing practices produced even more reforms. Over the following two decades, the federal government and all states established mandatory minimum sentences and, to a lesser degree, *truth in sentencing* laws (requiring certain offenders to serve most of their sentences) and *two and three strikes laws* (providing for life imprisonment after a second or third conviction). At the same time, some states started using presumptive sentencing guidelines, a reform that was later adopted by the federal government in chapter II of the Comprehensive Crime Control Act of 1984, otherwise known as the Sentencing Reform Act of 1984.[52]

The 1984 Sentencing Reform Act established an independent sentencing commission. The U.S. Sentencing Commission creates presumptive federal sentencing guidelines; advises Congress on sentencing policy; generates federal sentencing statistics; and provides education, training, and research material for judicial staff on how to implement the guidelines. As promulgated by the commission, the federal guidelines construct the penalty ranges in grid boxes that take into account the offense's severity and the defendant's criminal history. They discourage judges from making individualized assessments about the offender's personal circumstances. Instead, with the assistance of a presentence report prepared by probation officers, judges mechanically ascertain whether certain sentencing factors, as established by the commission, are factually present or absent in every case. The final sentence is arrived at by using mathematical equations that add or subtract points within fixed guideline ranges. Furthermore, judges generally must impose guideline-specified sentences unless, in atypical cases, an upward or downward departure is warranted on the basis of the presence of a narrowly defined set of aggravating or mitigating circumstances. If a judge departs from the guidelines, the reasons for it must be stated, and that decision is subject to appellate review. Finally, parole was abolished and the chances for early release were greatly diminished.[53]

The continuing viability of sentencing guidelines, however, was put into question in two Supreme Court's rulings. In *Blakely v. Washington* (2004),[54] the

Court invalidated Washington's Sentencing Reform Act because it allowed the trial judge to increase the length of a defendant's sentence on the basis of facts not admitted by the defendant or determined by the jury. In writing for a bare majority, Justice Scalia held that the Sixth Amendment right to a jury trial was violated when the trial judge found that the defendant acted with "deliberate cruelty" in kidnapping his wife, and thereupon increased the sentence by more than three years. He concluded that the Sixth Amendment safeguards the right of a jury to ascertain all essential facts that may be considered when sentencing a defendant.

Subsequently, *United States v. Booker* (2005)[55] struck down part of the U.S. Sentencing Guidelines and rendered them advisory. The Court, however, did not fashion a new Sixth Amendment rule that would require juries to discover all of the facts that might lead to an increased sentence. Instead, it held that the guidelines and their penalty ranges were "advisory." In other words, they were transformed into merely recommendations for the district judges in sentencing.

SELECTED READINGS

Abramson, Jeffrey. *We, The Jury: The Jury System and the Ideal of Democracy.* Cambridge: Harvard University Press, 2000.

Burns, Robert. *A Theory of the Trial.* Princeton: Princeton: Princeton University Press, 1999.

Damaska, Mirjan R. *The Faces of Justice and State Authority: A Comparative Approach to the Legal Process.* New Haven: Yale University Press, 1986.

Frankel, Marvin E. *Partisan Justice.* New York: Hill and Wang, 1980.

Frank, Jerome. *Courts on Trial: Myth and Reality in American Justice.* Princeton: Princeton University Press, 1949.

Fisher, George. *Plea Bargaining's Triumph: A History of Plea Bargaining in America.* Stanford: Stanford University Press, 2003.

Langbein, John H. *The Origins of Adversary Criminal Trial.* New York: Oxford University Press, 2003.

Nardulli, Peter F., James Eisenstein, and Roy B. Flemming. *The Tenor of Justice: Criminal Courts and the Guilty Plea Process.* Urbana: University of Illinois Press, 1988.

Packer, Herbert L. *The Limits of the Criminal Sanction.* Stanford: Stanford University Press, 1968.

Stith, Kate, and Jose A. Cabranes. *Fear of Judging: Sentencing Guidelines in the Federal Courts.* Chicago: University of Chicago Press, 1998.

Vogel, Mary E.. *Coercion to Compromise: Plea Bargaining, the Courts, and the Making of Political Authority.* New York: Oxford University Press, 2001.

Whitman, James Q. *Harsh Justice: Criminal Punishment and the Widening Divide between America and Europe.* New York: Oxford University Press, 2004.

NOTES

1. *Florida v. White*, 543 U.S. 175 (2004).
2. *U.S. v. Twomey*, 510 F.2d 634, 640 (7th Cir. 1975) (Wyzanski, J.).
3. Robert A. Kagan, *Adversarial Legalism: The American Way of Law* (Cambridge: Harvard University Press, 2001).
4. Judge Frank's analysis of his "fight" theory is found in chapter six of Jerome Frank, *Courts on Trial: Myth and Reality in American Justice* (Princeton: Princeton University Press, 1949), 80, 85.
5. See Gerald Walpin, "America's Adversarial and Jury Systems: More Likely to Do Justice," *Harvard Journal of Law and Public Policy* (Winter, 2003): 175-85.
6. Kagan, *Adversarial Legalism*, 4, 86-89, 104-25.
7. Ibid., 230.
8. *Miranda v. Arizona*, 384 U.S. 436 (1966), 449 n. 9.
9. Ibid., 455.
10. *Missouri v. Seibert*, 542 U.S. 600 (2004).
11. *Weeks v. U.S.*, 232 U.S. 383 (1914) (as applied to federal prosecutions) *Mapp v. Ohio*, 367 U.S. 643 (1961) (as applied to state prosecutions).
12. Herbert L. Packer, *The Limits of the Criminal Sanction* (Stanford: Stanford University Press, 1968), 153, 158-63.
13. *In re Winship*, 397 U.S. 358 (1970), 363. See also *People v. Defore*, 150 N.E. 585 (1926), 587.
14. Death Penalty Information Center, "State by State Information," available from www.deathpenaltyinfo.org/state/#dpstates (retrieved May 19, 2005). See generally, Thomas P. Bonczar and Tracy L. Snell, *Capital Punishment 2003*, available from www.ojp.usdoj.gov/bjs/pub/pdf/cp03.pdf (retrieved February 19, 2005); James Q. Whitman, *Harsh Justice: Criminal Punishment and the Widening Divide Between America and Europe* (New York: Oxford University Press, 2004).
15. Quoted in Kenneth Culp Davis, *Discretionary Justice: A Preliminary Inquiry* (Baton Rouge: Louisiana State University Press, 1969), 190. On the transition from a due process to a crime control model style of criminal justice, see Yue Ma, "Prosecutorial Discretion and Plea Bargaining in the United States, France, Germany and Italy: A Comparative Perspective," *International Criminal Justice Review* 12 (2002), 22, 23-24.
16. U.S. Department of Justice, Executive Office for United States Attorneys, *United States Attorneys' Annual Statistical Report, Fiscal Year 2003*, available from www.usdoj.gov/usao/reading_room/reports/asr2003/03_STAT_Report.pdf (retrieved February 19, 2005).
17. Matthew R. Durose and Patrick A. Langan, *Felony Sentences in State Courts, 2002*, available from www.ojp.usdoj.gov/bjs/abstract/fssc02.htm (retrieved February 19, 2005). See also Carol J. DeFrances, *Prosecutors in State Courts, 2001*, available from www.ojp.usdoj.gov/bjs/abstract/psc01.htm (retrieved February 19, 2005).

18. Sanford C. Gordon and Gregory A. Huber, "Citizen Oversight and the Electoral Incentives of Criminal Prosecutors," *American Journal of Political Science* (April, 2002), 334.

19. See *County of Riverside v. McLaughlin*, 500 U.S. 44 (1991); *Gerstein v. Pugh*, 420 U.S. 103 (1975).

20. See U.S. Department of Justice, Bureau of Justice Statistics, *State Court Organization, 1998* (Table 43, Grand Juries: Composition and Functions), 283–85, available from www.ojp.usdoj.gov/bjs/pub/pdf/sco9806.pdf (retrieved February 21, 2005).

21. For information about state and federal grand juries, see generally, "Federal Grand Jury," available from www.udayton.edu/~grandjur/ (retrieved February 20, 2005).

22. Associated Press, "Legal Experts Say Insanity Plea Unpopular with Jurors," *Akron Beacon Journal* (April 11, 2005), B4.

23. A summary of state laws governing insanity pleas is found in U.S. Department of Justice, Bureau of Justice Statistics, *State Court Organization 1998* (Table 38), available from www.ojp.usdoj.gov/bjs/pub/pdf/sco9805.pdf (retrieved March 3, 2005). See also Linda Greenhouse, "Supreme Court Considers Insanity Standard," *The New York Times* (April 19, 2006), available from www.nytimes.com (retrieved April 20, 2006).

24. *Brady v. United States*, 397 U.S. 742 (1972). See also U.S. Department of Justice, Bureau of Justice Statistics, *Federal Criminal Case Processing, 2002* (January, 2005), available from www.ojp.usdoj.gov/bjs/pub/pdf/fccp02.pdf (retrieved March 1, 2005) (reporting ninty-six percent of federal convictions in U.S. district court in 2002 were produced by guilty or no contest pleas).

25. See Peter F. Nardulli, James Eisenstein, and Roy B. Flemming, *The Tenor of Justice: Criminal Courts and the Guilty Plea Process* (Urbana: University of Illinois Press, 1988).

26. George Fisher. *Plea Bargaining's Triumph: A History of Plea Bargaining in America* (Stanford: Stanford University Press, 2003), 1.

27. Fisher, *Plea Bargaining's Triumph*, 12.

28. Fisher, *Plea Bargaining's Triumph*, 228. See also Peter Webster, in "Issues in Judicial Independence and Accountability [edited transcript of presentation at annual meeting of American Judicature Society on August 7, 2004]" *Judicature* (November/December 2004), 114, 116.

29. *Wardius v. Oregon*, 412 U.S. 470 (1973), 480 (Douglas, J., concurring).

30. *Duncan v. Louisiana*, 391 U.S. 145, 156 (1969) (White, J.).

31. *Baldwin v. New York*, 399 U.S. 66 (1970).

32. *Lewis v. United States*, 518 U.S. 322 (1995).

33. David M. O'Brien, *Constitutional Law and Politics (Volume Two): Civil Rights and Civil Liberties,* 6th ed. (New York: W. W. Norton & Co., 2005).

34. See, e.g., David Cole, *No Equal Justice: Race and Class in the American Criminal Justice System* (New York: New Press, 1999).

35. A summary of juror qualifications, source lists, and exemptions relating to juror service in the states is found in U.S. Department of Justice, Bureau of

Justice Statistics, *State Court Organization 1998* (Tables 39, 40), available from www.ojp.usdoj.gov/bjs/pub/pdf/sco98.pdf (retrieved March 7, 2005). See also Richard Seltzer, "The Vanishing Juror: Why Are There Not Enough Available Jurors?" The *Justice System Journal* 20 (1999): 203–18.

36. *Batson v. Kentucky*, 476 U.S. 79 (1986) (race); *J.E.B. v. Alabama*, 511 U.S. 127 (1997) (gender) *Hernandez v. New York*, 500 U.S 352 (1999) (ethnic origin).

37. See, e.g., William E. Martin and Peter N. Thompson, "Judicial Toleration of Racial Bias in the Minnesota Justice System," *Hamline Law Review* (Winter, 2002), 235, 263–69.

38. O'Brien, *Constitutional Law and Politics (Volume Two)*, 1100. See also *Georgia v. McCollum*, 505 U.S. 42 (1992).

39. *Williams v.* Florida, 399 U.S. 78 (1970).

40. *Johnson v. Louisiana*, 406 U.S. 356 (1972); *Apodaca v. Oregon*, 406 U.S. 404 (1972).

41. *Burch v. Louisiana*, 441 U.S. 130 (1979); *Ballew v. Georgia*, 435 U.S. 223 (1978).

42. *Ballew v. Georgia*, 435 U.S. 223, 239 (1978).

43. U.S. Department of Justice, Bureau of Justice Statistics, *State Court Organization 1998* (Table 42), available from www.ojp.usdoj.gov/bjs/pub/pdf/sco98.pdf (retrieved March 7, 2005). A survey of some of the criticisms regarding the trend reducing jury size and authorizing nonunanimous verdicts are found in Kim Taylor-Thompson, "Empty Votes in Jury Deliberations" *Harvard Law Review* (April, 2000), 1261–1320; Michael J. Saks, "The Smaller the Jury, the Greater the Unpredictability," *Judicature* (March/April 1996), 263–65.

44. James P. Levine and Steven Zeidman, "The Miracle of Jury Reform in New York," *Judicature* (January/February 2005), 178–84. See also Gregory E. Mize and Christopher J. Connelly, "Jury Trial Innovations: Charting a Rising Tide," *Court Review* (Spring, 2004), 4–10; Lynne Forster Lee and Irwin A. Horowitz, "The Effects of Jury-aid Innovations on Juror Performance in Complex Civil Trials," *Judicature* (January/February 2003), 184–90; "Michael Jackson, Silent Observer in Court Drama," *Political Gateway* (March 8, 2005), available from www.politicalgateway.com (retrieved March 8, 2005).

45. See Barry C. Sheck and Peter J. Neufeld, "Toward the Formation of 'Innocence Commissions in America,'" *Judicature* (September/October 2002), 98–105. The project's Web site, which details the causes and remedies relevant to wrongful convictions, is found at www.innocenceproject.org/ (retrieved on March 7, 2005).

46. Jon B. Gould, "A New Wave of Innocence Commissions," *Judicature* (November/December 2004), 126–31. See also The Governor's Commission on Capital Punishment, *Report of the Governor's Commission on Capital Punishment (April 2002, Recommendations Only)*, available from www.idoc.state.il.us/ccp/ccp/reports/commission_report/summary_recommendations.pdf (retrieved March 7, 2005).

47. On the collapse of the rehabilitative ideal, see Kate Stith and Jose A. Cabranes, *Fear of Judging: Sentencing Guidelines in the Federal Courts* (Chicago: University of Chicago Press, 1998), 29–37.
48. Samuel Walker, *Popular Justice: A History of American Criminal Justice* 2nd ed. (New York: Oxford University Press, 1998), 32–46.
49. Ibid., 80–81, 100–04, 119–20.
50. *Williams v. New York*, 337 U.S. 241, 245 (1949).
51. U.S. Department of Justice, Bureau of Justice Assistance, *National Assessment of Structured Sentencing* (Monograph, 1996), available from www.ncjrs.org/pdffiles/strsent.pdf (retrieved April 2, 2005), 6–17.
52. The Sentencing Reform Act of 1984, 18 U.S.C. Section 3551 et seq. See also U.S. Department of Justice, *National Assessment of Structured Sentencing*, 17, 20–21 (Table 3.1, Sentencing Practices in the United States, as of February 1994); U.S. Department of Justice, Bureau of Justice Assistance, *1996 National Survey of State Sentencing Structures* (Monograph, NCJ 169270, September 1998), available from www.ncjrs.org/pdffiles/169270.pdf (retrieved March 25, 2005).
53. See Stith and Cabranes, *Fear of Judging*, 82–85.
54. *Blakely v. Washington*, 542 U.S. 296 (2004). The Court based its holding on the principles first announced in *Apprendi v. New Jersey*, 530 U.S. 466 (2000).
55. *U.S. v. Booker*, 543 U.S. 220 (2005).

CHAPTER EIGHT

Civil Litigation

In its 2004 report on the most offensive "judicial hellholes,"[1] the American Tort Reform Association (ATRA) listed nine judicial districts as critical sources of *junk lawsuits*—lawsuits exhibiting systematic bias against small businesses in state civil litigation. At the top of the list was Madison County, Illinois, a district characterized as "lawyer heaven," a "jackpot jurisdiction," and a "hotbed of megabuck litigation," where courts often generate frivolous lawsuits and large multimillion dollar verdicts in favor of personal injury trial lawyers.

In his first campaign stop after his reelection, President George W. Bush touted the ATRA's report as proof that the judicial system and the trial bar were responsible for increasing insurance costs and forcing small-town doctors to leave their practices. Bush reiterated a stock message: The civil justice system was in need of reform. The solution, President Bush asserted, was to place legislative caps on jury awards for punitive and noneconomic damages (such as pain and suffering), enact asbestos litigation reform, and limit the number of *class action lawsuits* filed in state courts. At least one of those reforms, putting greater restrictions on class–action lawsuits, was signed into law in 2005.[2] Beneath the political rhetoric was the persistent and longstanding criticism that lawyers and judges routinely abuse the adversary legal system by manipulating its legal rules, and ultimately the truth, to their advantage.

The perception that the adversary system remains deeply flawed is not new, and is one that is shared by many American citizens. In a poll conducted by the American Bar Association (ABA), seventy-four percent of those surveyed were convinced that lawyers were more committed to winning their cases instead of guaranteeing that justice was served. Another seventy-three percent thought lawyers spend too much time trying to get criminal defendants released on legal technicalities, and sixty-nine percent believed lawyers were more interested in making money than in representing clients.[3]

This chapter investigates the nature of civil litigation, its political implications, and some of its special challenges, including the high cost of litigation and attorney's fees. The last section considers whether the civil trial process is in need of reform by discussing the growing influence of alternative methods of dispute resolution.

THE CIVIL TRIAL PROCESS

Civil actions involve claims arising from private disputes and conflicts over tort liability, such as paying compensation to an injured party as a result of negligence caused by defective products. But the civil process also resolves a variety of issues pertaining to divorce and child custody, the scope of juvenile rights, the regulation of business corporations, and the equitable distribution of estate property under a decedent's will. Unlike the criminal justice system, civil litigation cuts across subject matters that broadly affect a wide range of relationships. The range of civil litigation is demonstrated by its growing impact as a tool to impose economic liability against the firearms industry, street gangs, drug dealers, and even terrorists.[4] Still, civil litigation is different from criminal litigation because it ignores issues relating to a defendant's "criminal culpability" and carries only monetary penalties.

Civil litigation is often criticized as too expensive, elitist, capricious, and unjust. Fast food chains such as McDonald's have been sued and plaintiffs have recovered substantial widely publicized awards. Consequently, civil litigation is regularly attacked for producing too many frivolous lawsuits, court delays, and too many trials brought by "shyster" lawyer profiteers.[5] Although some of the criticisms are valid, many are not. Although it is true, for example, that civil filings have steadily increased since the 1960s, the trend has resulted from a "liability explosion" rather than a "litigation explosion." Thus the increase in filings is not necessarily clear proof that there has been a "litigation explosion." In fact, empirical studies strongly suggest otherwise.[6]

The political debate over tort reform, for instance, is but one manifestation of the confusion created by conflating litigation and liability trends. The distinction between the two becomes clearer upon learning that there have been several transformations in recent decades concerning the way in which civil disputes are processed. With few exceptions, the rate of civil trials has been in sharp decline since the 1980s because judges and attorneys use the pretrial hearings and procedural rules to resolve disputes by negotiated settlements. That in turn has led to a profound shift away from formal trials and has diminished the role juries play in civil disputes.[7] At the same time, the expense and delay has caused litigants to seek alternative methods of dispute resolution. In short, civil justice has become increasingly privatized.

These trends underscore two recurring themes: (1) whether litigants have sufficient access to civil justice is in accordance with the structure of legal compensation in civil cases, and (2) whether the truth underlying civil adversarial trials is impeded by changes that have been made to the rules of the civil discovery process in state or federal courts. Not surprisingly, the barriers to achieving access to the courts, and the related difficulties of ensuring expedient outcomes in the civil justice system, have led to reform movements, including the use of alternative methods for settling private disputes. Understanding these themes necessitates examining the nature of civil litigation and its political consequences.

The Nature of Civil Litigation

Over sixteen million civil cases are annually filed in the state courts, a figure that far exceeds the number commenced in the federal courts; the federal judiciary has slightly less than 300,000 civil filings annually.[8] Roughly one-quarter consist of domestic relations cases, typically involving marriage disputes. The balance is primarily made up of tort, contract, and real estate cases. A study examining civil suits in several states found that sixty-three percent were tort jury trials, nearly twice as many as all contract and real property trials combined. Of them, over one-half concerned motor vehicle accidents. Notably, the median jury award in contract cases exceeded the awards in tort cases, a finding that contradicts the popular image that tort cases are a boon for plaintiffs and their counsel (see Table 8.1). Despite the large number of civil filings in state courts, the National Center for State Courts reports that less than one percent of all civil suits go to jury trial.[9]

The decision to commence a civil action begins with an injury that is perceived to be a legitimate grievance (see Figure 8.1). Deciding to litigate is often a function of weighing a variety of factors that make the time, effort, and expense of a lawsuit worthwhile. Clearly, there are a number of disincentives to suing. Unlike in criminal trials, persons below the poverty line are not constitutionally entitled to legal representation, and a majority of civil litigants must be able to afford to pay a lawyer. In addition, with few exceptions, civil litigants cannot shift to the costs of incurring legal fees to the opposing party, so each side must pay their own counsel's fees. Although courts issuing final judgments will routinely award to the winning party "court costs," under the so-called American rule, the losing party does not have to pay the attorney's fees of opposing counsel. In most other countries, losers must bear some or all of the costs of litigation, including legal fees.[10]

Moreover, changes since the 1950s have passed most litigation costs onto the client instead of the attorney. Before World War II, professional norms encouraged lawyers to charge their clients by using fixed fee arrangements, agreements whereby clients paid a flat fee for services rendered, or contingency fees, a billing practice that ties fees to obtaining a successful outcome. Lawyers rarely kept track of their time and, in corporate practice regular clients were billed at year's end on the basis of what they thought their services were

TABLE 8.1 Number of Tort and Contract Trials and Median Jury Awards to Plaintiffs

	Percentage of Trials (per all tort or contract cases)	Percentage of Prevailing Plaintiffs	Median Jury Award (in dollars)
Tort Cases			
Motor vehicle	52.4%	62.0%	17,544
Premises liability	17.1	14.6	61,953
Medical malpractice	15.0	8.8	491,781
Intentional tort	4.5	4.4	48,997
Other product liability	1.6	1.4	405,483
Professional malpractice	1.2	.9	140,584
Slander/libel	1.1	.8	120,265
Animal attack	1.1	1.4	21,930
False arrest, imprisonment	.5	.4	94,546
Asbestos	.5	.6	1,649,597[a]
Conversion	.3	.2	23,871
Other tort	4.7	4.4	136,594
Total tort ($N = 5,659$ cases)	100.0%	100.0%	$32,406
Contract Cases			
Seller plaintiff	32.4%	21.2	64,974
Buyer plaintiff	22.0	27.9	64,792
Fraud	17.5	19.1	85,476
Rental/lease agreement	7.8	4.3	88,961
Other employment dispute	7.2	10.1	81,019
Employment discrimination	4.3	6.5	226,177
Tortious interference	3.3	4.5	112,336
Subrogation	1.8	2.9	7,864
Partnership dispute	1.1	1.4	139,968
Mortgage foreclosure	.6	—	—
Other contract	1.9	2.0	74,212
Total contract ($N = 2,471$)	100.0%	100.0%	$78,627

[a]The highest median award, but based on only fifteen prevailing plaintiffs; asbestos cases had the highest average number of plaintiffs per case, thus revealing that the awards were often divided among multiple plaintiffs.

Source: National Center for State Courts, *Caseload Highlights* ("An Empirical Overview of Civil Litigation"), Volume 11, No. 1 (February 2005), available from www.ncsconline.com (retrieved April 22, 2005). This study used data from 2001 and examined forty-six counties in the United States.

FIGURE 8.1 The Civil Trial and Appeal Process.

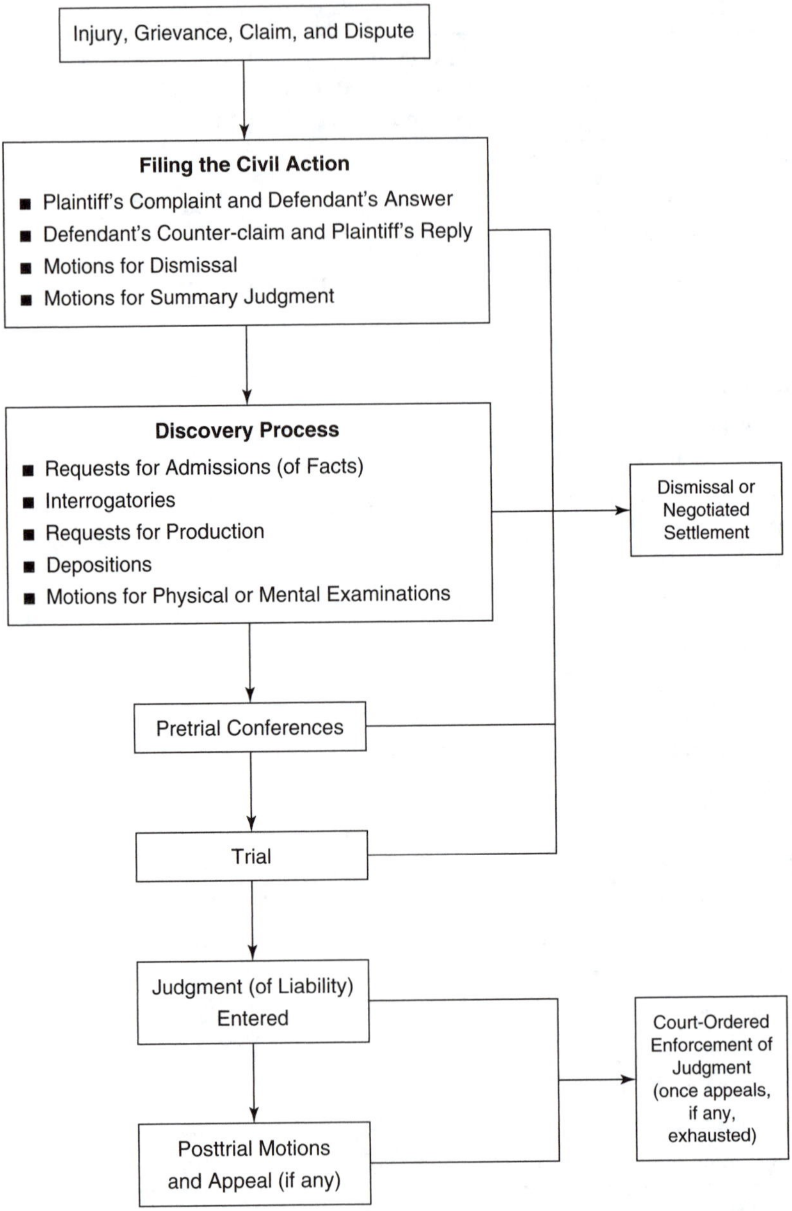

Injury, Grievance, Claim, and Dispute

Filing the Civil Action
- Plaintiff's Complaint and Defendant's Answer
- Defendant's Counter-claim and Plaintiff's Reply
- Motions for Dismissal
- Motions for Summary Judgment

Discovery Process
- Requests for Admissions (of Facts)
- Interrogatories
- Requests for Production
- Depositions
- Motions for Physical or Mental Examinations

Dismissal or Negotiated Settlement

Pretrial Conferences

Trial

Judgment (of Liability) Entered

Court-Ordered Enforcement of Judgment (once appeals, if any, exhausted)

Posttrial Motions and Appeal (if any)

worth. Thereafter, increased competition, the proliferation of lawyers, and the rise of the large law firm combined to cause attorneys to adopt the billable hour as the standard unit of compensation. Although contingency fees are still a part of legal billing practices in certain civil cases, hourly billing is the dominant form of compensation.[11]

However, the economics of legal practice dictates that contingency fee lawyers are "portfolio managers," weighing the risk of taking a case against the anticipated investment of return if liability is imposed. Herbert Kritzer explains,

> while virtually every contingency fee practitioner wants to find highly lucrative cases, such cases are relatively rare. Many cases presented to lawyers are not winnable, or they do not offer a prospect of even a moderately acceptable fee. The contingency fee practitioner seeks cases that offer a high probability of providing at least an acceptable return, hoping to find some fraction of cases that present the opportunity to generate a significant fee.[12]

The "portfolio of risks" is thus driven by economic self-interest, and a substantial number of prospective clients are turned away or referred to other lawyers. Even so, the issue remains hotly contested and the merits of contingency fees are usually defined in stark political terms: Plaintiff lawyers, representing the "victim" in personal injury cases, insist the contingency fee provides the "key to the courthouse," whereas defense lawyers aligned with business interests and the insurance industry declare it is a "key to enormous and untold riches" for unscrupulous plaintiffs' lawyers.[13]

In sum, as law professor Judith Resnik reported, in federal and state claims involving more than $1,000, only about eleven percent actually result in a lawsuit, and even fewer go to trial, mainly because it is cheaper to settle before trial.[14] These problems are inevitably connected to the larger difficulty of living up to the public perception that everyone is entitled to their fair day in court.

Civil Procedure

Adjudication of civil disputes begins with the payment of a fee and the filing of a *complaint*. The complaint identifies the relevant parties and establishes the factual and legal allegations underlying the conflict. In addition, the complaint describes what is sought in terms of *legal remedies*. Once the complaint is filed, the clerk of court issues a summons to the defendant to appear in court. The summons directs the defendant to respond, often within thirty days, and such responses are done in the form of an answer admitting or denying the plaintiff's allegations. If there is a legal basis to do so, defendants who are sued may file their own complaints by filing *counterclaims*, to which plaintiffs respond by filing a *reply*. Civil pleadings allow for frequent revision of complaints (and answers or replies) until the legal issues are no longer in dispute.

A significant method to aggregate civil claims is a class action lawsuit—a lawsuit that originally was designed to provide greater court access to plaintiffs sharing similar claims who might not otherwise sue because of the complexity of the suit or the high cost of doing so. Class actions, however, are politically controversial because they have resulted in mass tort actions and a variety of other civil claims seeking high damage awards (see Sidebar 8.1).

Sidebar 8.1

The Politics of Class Actions

In *Ortiz v. Fibreboard Corporation* (1999), a class action lawsuit that Justice David Souter referred to as part of the "elephantine mass of asbestos cases"[a] besieging the federal courts since the 1970s, the Supreme Court explained that the origin of class actions developed in part as an exception to the "necessary parties rule in equity." In 1966, Rule 23 of the Federal Rules of Civil Procedure was amended and liberalized class action practice by allowing persons with identical claims to aggregate their claims in federal court if class "certification" was granted. Since then, Rule 23 has remained the basis for analogous state laws authorizing class actions.

In the 1990s, the Republican-led Congress banned legal aid attorneys from instituting class actions and also outlawed class actions in state courts in securities fraud lawsuits.[b] In 2005, President George W. Bush signed into law The Class Action Fairness Act of 2005, legislation imposing further restrictions on filing aggregate claims. The new law advances corporate interests by limiting forum shopping in consumer fraud actions in state courts and, instead, channels those types of class actions into federal courts which, traditionally, are less prone to certifying aggregate claims. In addition, it restricts "coupon" settlements that might result in a windfall to plaintiff attorneys by increasing judicial oversight and imposing conditions on their use.[c]

Notes
[a] *Ortiz v. Fibreboard Corporation*, 527 U.S. 815 (1999) (Souter, J.) 821.
[b] Terry Carter, "Class Action Climax," *ABA Journal eReport* (February 18, 2005), 7; Judith Resnik, *Processes of the Law: Understanding Courts and Their Alternatives* (New York: Foundation Press, 2004), 30–31.
[c] Class Action Fairness Act of 2005, 109 P.L. 2 (February 18, 2005). See also John F. Harris and Jim VandeHei, "Senate Nears Revision of Class Actions," *Washington Post* (February 10, 2005), A4.

In addition, many jurisdictions permit either party to file a motion with the court asking it to dismiss the case. Another type of dismissal motion attacks the sufficiency of the complaint, arguing that it fails "to state a claim upon which relief can be granted."[15] Alternatively, federal courts permit either party to file a motion for *summary judgment*—a motion asserting that there is "no genuine issue as to any material fact and that the moving party is entitled to a judgment as a matter of law."[16] If granted, the court resolves the legal claims without further proceedings. Studies have demonstrated an inverse relationship between civil jury trial dispositions and summary judgment motions over time. This significant trend shows that there has been a sharp decline in jury trials while, simultaneously, there has been a conspicuous rise in summary judgment dispositions. In 1962, for example, 5.5 percent of all federal cases were decided by jury trial. But in 2002, that percentage had dropped to only 1.2 percent. At the same time, between 1975 and 2000, summary judgment adjudications rose from 3.7 percent to 7.7 percent, respectively. These figures suggest that procedural judgments "on the pleadings" are responsible for more case terminations instead of jury trials, thus perhaps marking a "new era in which dispositions by summary judgment are a magnitude several times greater than the number of trials."[17]

THE DISCOVERY PROCESS AND PRETRIAL SETTLEMENT CONFERENCES

The general burdens and costs of litigating civil claims are closely tied to the time and effort it takes for lawyers to gather key facts and evidence. As in the initial stages of litigation, discovering facts is accomplished by the operation of procedural rules that control all aspects of pretrial activity, including attempts to settle the case through pretrial conferences that are supervised by judges trying to clear the docket of cases scheduled for trial.

There are five basic types of discovery: requests for admissions, interrogatories, requests for production, depositions, and motions for physical or mental examinations. With the exception of depositions and motions for production, the party requesting the information can only seek the information from parties in the case. Furthermore, though most court rules allow a broad scope of discovery, the information sought generally must be relevant to the legal issues at hand and not "privileged" (e.g., the personal notes or the "work product" of opposing counsel, or the conversations between marital partners). Before 1990, the federal rules permitted discovery of "any matter, not privileged, which is relevant to the subject matter involved in the pending action."[18]

The judiciary, however, has realized that a broad right to discover key facts is not an unlimited one. Amendments to federal discovery practice, in 1993 and later in 2000, moved toward a system of mandatory disclosure for certain basic facts, such as revealing the names, addresses, and phone numbers of persons having discoverable information; disclosing the identity and location of all documents and tangible items; and supplying an initial computation of the type of damages claimed. Because they are mandatory, the scope of discovery has been narrowed. Instead of permitting broad inquiries into the relevant subject matter of the dispute, discovery requests are restricted to disclosing only facts "relevant to the claim or defense of any party." Only after good cause is demonstrated may a court order discovery for matters relevant to the subject matter of the case.[19] Though objections to discovery are still subject to court review, the federal rules restrict their frequency (and the potential for abuse) by giving more control over pretrial disclosure to judges possessing the power to enforce violations of discovery rules against attorneys.

State and federal litigants may still use generic discovery motions to uncover key facts and evidence. One way to establish facts or legal issues that may not actually be in dispute is by filing a request for admission to the opposing party.[20] The party receiving the request may answer it by the way in which a defendant responds to allegations in the complaint, by ignoring it (which "admits" the fact at issue), by admitting it, or by claiming insufficient knowledge.

Depositions are an expensive discovery technique that solicits the sworn testimony of a party or a third-party witness.[21] Still, it is a highly effective discovery method. Not only does it provide a first glimpse at how a witness and counsel may perform at trial, but it preserves the statements as evidence that can confirm what was said if a witness has died or who is otherwise unavailable at trial. Motions for physical or mental examinations, furthermore, are a significant discovery tool as well.[22]

Although there is no agreement on what effect the recent changes in federal discovery practice has had on state courts, several trends are apparent. State courts, once thought to be fairly consistent in following the model of the federal rules, are increasingly charting their own course in developing rules of civil discovery. Professor John Oakley's comprehensive analysis of the rules of state practice concludes that the trend toward conformity to the federal rules "reversed itself" after the 1990s and that the federal rules of civil procedure have "lost credibility as avatars of procedural reform."[23] Other studies have demonstrated that (1) many state rules now use different procedures for gathering information in different case types (e.g., professional malpractice versus domestic relations cases) as well as for different kinds of litigants (limiting discovery for prisoners); (2) many state courts do not go as far in requiring mandatory disclosure, but they do put more limitations on the amount of discovery the parties can undertake; and (3) unlike federal courts, many state courts do not use magistrates as much in handling pretrial discovery motions.[24]

Despite differences, both state and federal courts are more apt to manage the pretrial discovery and settlement process more proactively. Although it seems doubtful that state and federal courts will not adopt a uniform method of discovery practice in the near future, the movement toward increased judicial intervention at the pretrial stage is not only a significant sign that attorneys are not completely driving the discovery process but also that the task of judging is quickly moving away from the traditional adversarial model—and thus arguably becoming less like the kind of "sporting contests" that Judge Jerome Frank feared (see chapter 7).

Though, as Judge Frank believed, the high cost of litigation and the difficulties of obtaining legal representation probably continue to impede the pursuit of truth in the adversary system to some degree, contemporary jurists are no longer the passive spectators that he described before World War II. Unlike the judge in his day, today's judges are more aggressive in managing caseloads.

TRIAL, JUDGMENT, AND APPEAL Civil trials are conducted in the same way as criminal trials. Civil litigants enjoy the right to a jury trial if the amount in controversy is more than twenty dollars. However, despite their similarities, in two important respects civil trials differ from criminal proceedings.

The first relates to the burden of proof at trials. Unlike in criminal trials, civil claimants must prove their cases by a preponderance of the evidence instead of the beyond a reasonable doubt standard. Under the *preponderance standard*, the judge or jury weighs the facts and evidence in terms of whether the allegations are probably more true than not. Sometimes this is expressed in percentage terms: There must be at least a fifty-one percent certainty that the defendant committed the act or omission in question in order to be liable for its harmful consequences. In some cases a higher standard, a "clear and convincing evidence" level of proof, is used because the consequences of imposing liability are more serious, as in cases involving the termination of parental rights. Under that standard, the proof must show a greater certainty (beyond mere probability) that the allegations are true. Through the use of percentages, the clear and convincing standard might roughly require a seventy-five percent certainty that the facts happened as alleged. As one might expect, the standards of proof in civil and criminal trials reflect the different kinds of subject matter that characterize each type of legal proceeding.

The second is the type of relief available in civil cases. In most civil cases, courts award monetary damages. In general, damages consist of compensatory, punitive, or nominal awards. *Compensatory damages* attempt to put injured parties back into the positions they were before the harm occurred. By contrast, punitive damages are "smart money" because they are imposed to "hurt" defendants by punishing them for engaging in wanton, willful, or reckless behavior. *Punitive damages* are a deterrent against future violations of the law. *Nominal damages* symbolically deliver a positive outcome in cases involving no harm, and juries award a nominal sum.

The magnitude of some awards makes them constitutionally suspect, a problem that is underscored by research showing that well-intentioned juries simply cannot understand and apply the judge's instructions about what the law requires in making these awards. In a Florida class action against cigarette manufacturers, for example, the jury awarded $144 billion; whereas, in Alabama, a jury awarded $580 million in punitive damages despite allegations suggesting that the amount of compensatory damages did not equal more than $600.[25]

The Supreme Court has put more restrictive constitutional limits on punitive damage awards. In *BMW of North America, Inc. v. Gore* (1999), it reversed a jury award of over $4 million in a fraud case as a violation of due process, holding that it was excessive. The Court constructed a balancing test, weighing the interests of the government in punishing and deterring bad conduct as construed against the due process right to know in advance that engaging in prohibited acts will lead to severe, adverse economic liabilities. The Court ruled that the constitutionality of punitive damage awards must be based on (1) the degree of reprehensibility of the defendant's misconduct, (2) the disparity between the actual or potential harm suffered by the plaintiff and the punitive damages award, and (3) the difference between the punitive damages awarded by the jury and the civil penalties authorized or imposed in comparable cases. In *State Farm Mutual Automobile Insurance Co. v. Campbell* (2003), the Court likewise reversed a $25 million award of punitive damages in a bad-faith insurance contract case after holding that it too was excessive in accordance with the principles established in *Gore*.[26] As a result, *Gore* and *State Farm* indicate that punitive damage awards are permissible in civil cases but also that they must be reasonable and proportionate.

Finally, the next step in the civil justice system is to enforce the judgment against the defendant if there are no intervening posttrial motions that upset the verdict or if there is no appeal. Notably, the traditional form of pursuing remedies and enforcing civil judgments is buttressed by "alternative" methods of dispute resolution that are becoming a vital characteristic of the U.S. legal system.

ALTERNATIVE DISPUTE RESOLUTION

"We must move away from total reliance on the adversary contest for dispute resolution," declared Chief Justice Burger in his 1984 annual state of the judiciary address. "For some disputes," he acknowledged, "trials will be the only means, but for many claims, trials by the adversarial contest must in time go the way of the ancient trial by battle and blood. Our [adversarial] system," he concluded, "is too costly, too painful, too destructive, too inefficient, for a truly civilized people." Notably, the chief justice thought that judicial initiatives to change the federal rules of discovery were a step in the right direction. For Chief Justice Burger, they would help counter the perception that lawyers were "hired guns" instead of "healers," an image created by the high cost of litigation, burgeoning caseloads, and the eagerness of attorneys to advertise their services as if they were selling "mustard, cosmetics, laxatives, or used cars."[27]

Chief Justice Burger, however, failed to stress that alternative dispute resolution (ADR) movement had gained considerable traction in the 1980s. Prompted by his call to study the use of less costly and more efficient methods to resolve disputes at the Pound Conference on the Causes of Popular Dissatisfaction with the Administration of Justice in 1976, the academic and legal communities began to adopt a variety of nonadversarial alternatives to achieve civil justice. Chief Justice Burger's support for ADR was the backdrop for law professor Frank Sander's seminal lecture, delivered at the Pound Conference, suggesting that a "multi-door" courthouse be created, a reform that would allow clients to pick among a range of ADR options, including arbitration, mediation, and neutral third-party fact finding, to resolve conflicts. The heightened academic interest in ADR pushed the ABA and the nation's law schools to incorporate ADR into their agendas and graduate school curricula.[28]

Table 8.2 denotes alternative dispute resolution and settlement practices.

ADR has become an institutionalized element of the U.S. legal system. In the public sector, over 1,200 ADR programs have been established by or in conjunction with state courts as "court-connected" or closely related community initiatives that work with public officials. In Florida, over 16,000 individuals have been trained state mediators to assist in administering at least 100 different mediation programs.[29]

On the national level, Congress has supported the use of ADR in the federal courts by enacting the Civil Justice Reform Act of 1990 and the Alternative Dispute Resolution Act of 1998, which vest trial courts with the authority to create district-specific programs in civil cases. At least sixty-three districts allow mediation, whereas twenty-eight authorize some type of nonbinding arbitration, and another twenty-three use early neutral evaluation. As in the state courts, ADR's impact is considerable: In 2001, roughly 24,000 cases were processed by using ADR programs. Also, Justice Department lawyers processed nearly 3,000 cases with ADR methods in 2002. Similarly, ADR has gained a significant foothold in the private sector because there are a plethora of fee-based companies offering ADR services, and a growing number of corporations have turned to arbitration, mediation, and other in-house grievance procedures as preferred methods to deal with workplace conflict. Standardized provisions for binding arbitration (in lieu of pursuing court lawsuits) are now widely used in consumer goods, securities brokerage, construction, and employment contracts as well.[30]

Proponents of ADR observe that the methods are advantageous because (1) they give disputants more control over managing their personal conflict; (2) they protect individual privacy by using confidential sessions; and, (3) they reduce the time, cost, and delay associated with dispute adjudication.

On the other hand, opponents counter that (1) they are too cumbersome and slow; (2) they are prone to selecting third-party neutrals that are biased; and, (3) they remain unproven methods that do not considerably save time or cost in processing disputes. In criticizing summary trials, Judge Richard Posner adds another general objection. The benefits of privacy and confidentiality are outweighed by the cost of having the credibility of witnesses evaluated by the judge or jury in public proceedings that determine the facts underlying disputes.[31]

TABLE 8.2 Alternative Dispute Resolution and Settlement Practices

Method	Principal Elements
Arbitration	■ Quasi-formal adjudicatory process in which third-party neutral arbitrator evaluates competing positions and issues decision after adversary hearing conducted by attorneys representing each side under relaxed rules of evidence, with no witnesses; but documents can be submitted for arbitrator's review ■ Can be binding or nonbinding ■ Can be private or court-connected ■ Most often used in labor/management, construction contract, consumer protection, and medical malpractice disputes
Mediation	■ Flexible, informal nonbinding process in which third-party neutral mediator facilitates communication between parties in confidential session in order to reach voluntary settlement ■ Mediator ordinarily does not issue opinion or finding of facts ■ Can be private or court-connected ■ Has wide applicability in general civil cases, but popular in labor/management and family law cases
Early Neutral Evaluation	■ Informal, nonbinding process in which a third-party neutral, usually an experienced attorney with expertise in subject matter in dispute, evaluates each side's case in a confidential session with parties and counsel shortly after the lawsuit is filed and before discovery is completed ■ Designed to improve case planning and facilitate settlement prospects ■ Ordinarily court-connected ■ Has wide applicability in general civil cases
Summary Jury Trials	■ Nonbinding, informal adjudicatory process, supervised by judge or magistrate, using nonbinding abbreviated trials by mock jurors chosen from the jury pool ■ Evidence presented to jury by counsel in summary form and usually witnesses are not called ■ Jury evaluates competing positions and issues advisory decision that is used to facilitate settlement in trial-ready cases ■ Court-connected ■ Has wide applicability in general civil cases

Method	Principal Elements
Minitrials	■ Flexible, informal nonbinding process in which each side presents, in front of a third-party neutral, its case in abbreviated form to settlement-authorized representatives of disputing parties, with relaxed rules of evidence and no witnesses ■ Its primary use is to facilitate settlement between company's senior executives ■ Can be private or court-connected ■ Most often used in complex business litigation
Settlement Conferences	■ Judge or magistrate-hosted conference, held pursuant to court rules, between opposing counsel in order to explore settlement options ■ Court-connected ■ Has wide applicability in general civil cases
Online Dispute Resolution	■ Informal, flexible Internet-based online dispute resolution process, including arbitration, mediation, and other complaint-driven processes (e.g., escrow arrangements, complaint bulletin boards) ■ Ordinarily private, but method is still evolving and could expand to courts ■ Ordinarily used in business disputes between sellers and customers, or business-to-business disputes, relative to online transactions

Sources: Elizabeth Plapinger and Donna Stienstra, *ADR and Settlement in the Federal District Courts: A Sourcebook for Judges & Lawyers* (Washington, D.C.: Federal Judicial Center, 1996), 60–69; Henry H. Perritt, Jr., "Dispute Resolution in Cyberspace: Demand for New Forms of ADR," *Ohio State Journal on Dispute Resolution* 15 (2000), 675–703.

In all likelihood, the debate over whether ADR is better than traditional litigation will not lessen any time soon. The evidence is generally inconclusive. What is clear, however, is that ADR has found acceptance in the legal culture and remains a viable choice for litigants. Although published reports and research often divide on the question of whether ADR is actually less costly and time-intensive than adversary trials, it appears that disputants often receive significant personal satisfaction from ADR procedures. However, the greatest danger to ADR may not be that it works, but rather that such methods become more like the traditional adversary method they are replacing. As one court watcher put it: "As lawyers have colonized the ADR field, they have made its processes more comfortable for them [and arbitrations] look more and more like trials," replete with formal rules, extensive discovery, and a variety of scheduling and case backlog problems.[32] If that trend continues, the promise of ADR will eventually evaporate.

In Comparative Perspective

Transnational Courts—Quasi-Judicial Tribunals Under the North American Free Trade Agreement (NAFTA)

Even before the war against international terrorism launched after the 9/11 attacks, the so-called globalization of the world economy, along with increasing demands for collective security and human rights, pushed toward greater economic and legal cooperation. As a result, there emerged more supranational or transnational courts and quasi-judicial tribunals for resolving disputes. The European Union's Court of Justice (ECJ) and the European Court of Human Rights are, perhaps, the leading examples of supranational courts. Other increasingly important transnational courts are the World Court, the International Criminal Court, and the Organization of American States' Inter-American Court of Human Rights, among numerous other regional tribunals and transnational quasi-courts.

A less well-known transnational forum for the resolution of economic disputes is that under NAFTA. The principal institution of the NAFTA is the Free Trade Commission (FTC). It consists of the member states' trade ministers and oversees implementation of the NAFTA. Prior to the NAFTA there was no established forum or generally accepted process for resolving trade-related disputes between Canada, Mexico, and the United States. The NAFTA, however, provides for several dispute resolution mechanisms. They depend on the kind of economic dispute involved—whether dealing with financial services, labor disputes, or challenges to antidumping and countervailing duty determinations by member states. Instead of relying on the member states' national courts—the U.S. Court of International Trade (CIT) and the U.S. Court of Appeals for the Federal Circuit, for instance, or the Mexican Federal Tax Court (Tribunal Fiscal)—a NAFTA binational panel hears appeals from and challenges to decisions and determinations of the Canadian International Trade Tribunal (CITT), the Secretaria de Comercio y Fomento Industrial (SECOFI) in Mexico, and by the Department of Commerce and the U.S. International Trade Commission (USITC).

Although inviting the criticism that NAFTA undercuts member states' sovereignty by superimposing binational tribunals for each nation's courts, this transnational dispute resolution forum was agreed to for the following reasons: the costs and delays of antidumping and countervailing duty appeals in U.S. courts, Canadian and Mexican concerns that U.S. courts were and would be too deferential to the USITC, and the refusal of the U.S. to agree to an exemption for Canada from U.S. antidumping and countervailing duty laws.

When exercising jurisdiction over disputes, NAFTA panels apply, for example, the antidumping and countervailing duty laws of the nation challenged in the appeal. Significantly, they must also apply the standard of judicial review and the general legal principles "that a court of the importing party otherwise would apply to a review of a determination of" the CITT, the SECOFI, or the USITC. In other words, these binational panels apply the relevant domestic law of Canada, Mexico, and the United States.

Moreover, the tribunals do not have explicit authority to reverse or dismiss administrative decisions. Rather, technically, they may only either uphold an agencies' final determination or remand it for action not inconsistent with its decision. However, despite that restraint NAFTA panels have reversed agency decisions.[a] More typically, though, they vacate (and, thereby, effectively reverse) parts of, or the basis for, the decision below and remand the case for further action not inconsistent with the tribunal's decision.

Finally, a NAFTA tribunal panel's decision is deemed final and without the possibility of appeal except in cases alleging gross misconduct, bias, serious conflict of interests, disregard of fundamental rules of procedure, and for exceeding its authority and jurisdiction. In such an instance, an Extraordinary Challenge Procedure permits an appeal to a special three-person review panel or Extraordinary Challenge Committee. But only a NAFTA member state, not a private party to the dispute or any other interested parties, may initiate such appeals.

A closely related controversy to that over NAFTA's substitution of the binational panels for member states' national courts revolves around the process for composing the binational panels. The tribunals function as five-member panels chosen by the parties in a dispute from a standing roster of seventy-five experts designated by the member states' national NAFTA secretariat. They serve part time, with nominal per diem pay, for three-year terms, and are eligible for reappointment.

The selection and composition of the tribunal panelists has invited a number of criticisms and court challenges. Lawsuits filed in U.S. courts have challenged, albeit unsuccessfully, the appointment process and structure of the NAFTA panels on the grounds that provisions of the U.S. Constitution are violated. It has been argued, for example, that the panels include foreign nationals and that the panelists are not appointed either in accordance with the provisions of Article I of the U.S. Constitution, which provides for the creation of "legislative courts" such as the U.S. Court of Military Appeals, and Territorial Courts, or with the "advice and consent" of the U.S. Senate, as required for the appointment of federal judges under Article II. In addition, it has been argued that because most of the panelists lack judicial experience and are unaccountable, their appointments violate the stipulation in Article III that judges "shall hold their Offices during good Behaviour."[b]

Notably, a NAFTA's panel's report is not binding, only declaratory. Still, if a panel makes recommendations the disputing parties must immediately start consultations aimed at arriving at a "mutually satisfactory solution" within ninety days. If within nine months following the end of the consultations no changes in the amendment of a nation's laws are made or another agreement has been reached, then the complaining party may resort to "self-help" via enacting "comparable legislation or equivalent executive action" or, in the most extreme cases, terminate the NAFTA with the violating country.

More generally, a number of trends and features of the NAFTA panels' decisions and opinions are striking. First, in terms of what Martin Shapiro has called "the proto-type of courts"—that is, a triadic relationship between disputing parties and a third-party dispute resolution forum—the NAFTA binational panels, although constituted as quasi-courts, appear to strive to function and to appear like courts.[c] That is the case not only in the conduct of their quasi-judicial proceedings but also in the opinions handed down justifying or rationalizing their final decisions.

With few exceptions, the panels' opinions are highly detailed and lengthy, often running between 100 and 300 pages. They also read like U.S. federal district court opinions, providing detailed summaries of the disputing parties' arguments about the law and the facts, the standard of judicial review, and an analysis of the respective member state's agency's authority and factual determination. Precisely because NAFTA panels are required to apply the domestic law of the importing country in reviewing a trade dispute, substantial portions of the panels' opinions are devoted to the appropriate standard of judicial review.

Likewise, NAFTA panels reviewing duty disputes brought against the United States tend to adopt a deferential approach—though, a slightly less deferential approach than Canadian courts—to administrative agencies' interpretations and decisions. They rely primarily on the U.S. Supreme Court's decision in *Chevron v. Natural Resources Defense Council*.[d] Under the so-called *Chevron* doctrine, if a statute is "silent or ambiguous with respect to the specific issue, the question for the Court [and hence lower federal courts and NAFTA panels applying U.S. law] is whether the agency's answer is based on a permissible construction of the statute." As a result, the NAFTA panels are generally highly deferential in adopting standards of review and are therefore inclined to affirm the decisions of NAFTA member-states' administrative agencies, or alternatively to remand for reconsideration in light of their findings.

In sum, the NAFTA binational panels, no less than the ECJ and other supernational courts and tribunals, reflect the inexorable movement in the twenty-first century toward overlapping public and private spheres of governance (and hence dispute resolution processes) that transcend of national territories, boundaries, and old doctrines national sovereignty.[e]

Notes

[a] See, e.g., *Mexican Antidumping Investigation into Imports of Cut-to-Length Plate Products from the United States*, MEX-94-1904-02 (August 30, 1995).

[b] See, e.g., *American Coalition for Competitive Trade v. United States*, 128 F.3d 761 (D.C. Cir., 1997), dismissed for lack of standing.

[c] See Martin Shapiro, *Courts* (Chicago: University of Chicago Press, 1981), chapter 1.

[d] *Chevron v. Natural Resources Defense Council*, 467 U.S. 837 (1984).

[e] All decisions of NAFTA panels and more information may be found at the NAFTA Secretion's Web site at www.nafta-sec-alena.org

SELECTED READINGS

Haltom, William, and Michael McCann. *Distorting the Law: Politics, Media, and the Litigation Crisis.* Chicago: University of Chicago Press, 2004.

Kagan, Robert A. *Adversarial Legalism: The American Way of Law.* Cambridge: Harvard University Press, 2001.

Kritzer, Herbert M. *Risks, Reputations, and Rewards.* Stanford: Stanford University Press, 2004.

———————. *Let's Make a Deal: Understanding the Negotiation Process in Ordinary Litigation.* Madison: University of Wisconsin Press, 1991.

NOTES

1. American Tort Reform Foundation, *Judicial Hellholes 2004* (Washington, D.C.: American Tort Reform Foundation 2004), available from www.atra.org/reports/ hellholes/report.pdf (retrieved January 19, 2005).

2. Class Action Fairness Act of 2005, 109 P.L. 2 (February 18, 2005). See also Peter Baker, "Bush Campaigns to Curb Lawsuits: President Says 'Junk' Litigation is Driving Small-Town Doctors Out of Business," *Washington Post* (January 6, 2005), A06.

3. American Bar Association, "Perceptions of the U.S. Legal System," available from www.abanet.org/media/perception/perceptions.pdf (retrieved November 18, 2004) (Table 4), 115.

4. John C. Blakeman, "Activist Judges, Responsive Legislators, Frustrating Presidents: International Human Rights, National Security, and Civil Litigation Against Terrorist States," in *American National Security and Civil Liberties in an Era of Terrorism,* edited David B. Cohen and John W. Wells (New York: Palgrave, 2004), 89-104; Note, "The Paths of Civil Litigation" *Harvard Law Review* 113 (2000), 1752-1875.

5. William Haltom and Michael McCann, *Distorting the Law: Politics, Media, and the Litigation Crisis* (Chicago: University of Chicago Press, 2004), 179-81, 183-85.

6. See, e.g., Marc Galanter, "Reading the Landscape of Disputes: What We Know and Don't Know (and Think We Know) About our Allegedly Contentious and Litigious Society," *University of California Los Angeles Law Review* 31 (1983), 4; Lawrence M. Friedman, "The Day Before Trials Vanished," *Journal of Empirical Studies* (November, 2004), 689-703.

7. Marc Galanter, "The Vanishing Trial: An Examination of Trials and Related Matters in Federal and State Courts," *Journal of Empirical Legal Studies* (November, 2004), 459-570.

8. The composition of civil caseloads and a comparison of state and federal civil caseloads is found in National Center for State Courts, *Examining the Work of State Courts, 2004* (Williamsburg: National Center for State Courts, 2005),

21–30; Brian J. Ostrom, Shauna M. Strickland, and Paula L. Hannaford-Agor, "Examining Trial Trends in State Courts: 1976-2002," *Journal of Empirical Legal Studies* (November 2004), 755, 757 (Table 1); and Administrative Office of U.S. Courts, *Judicial Facts and Figures,* "Table 2.11, U.S. District Courts-Cases Filed, Terminated, Pending," available from www.uscourts.gov/judicialfactsfigures/table2.11.pdf (retrieved October 30, 2005).

9. National Center for State Courts, *Examining the Work of State Courts, 2003* (Williamsburg: National Center for State Courts, 2004), 22. See also National Center for State Courts, *Caseload Highlights* ("An Empirical Overview of Civil Litigation"), Volume 11, No. 1 (February, 2005), available from www.ncsconline.com (retrieved April 22, 2005).

10. Herbert M. Kritzer, *Risks, Reputations, and Rewards* (Stanford: Stanford University Press, 2004), 257.

11. See Robert E. Litan and Steven C. Salop, "Reforming the Lawyer-Client Relationship through Alternative Billing Methods," *Judicature* (January/February 1994), 191–97.

12. Herbert M. Kritzer, "Contingency Fee Lawyers as Gatekeepers in the Civil Justice System," *Judicature* (July/August 1997), 22. This argument is expanded in Kritzer, *Risks, Reputations, and Rewards.*

13. U.S. Senate, Committee on the Judiciary, "Contingency Fee Abuses," 104th Cong., 1st sess., 1995. S. Hrg. 104–828 (November 7, 1995), Washington, D.C.: U.S. Government Printing Office, 3, 37.

14. Judith Resnik, *Processes of the Law: Understanding Courts and Their Alternatives* (New York: Foundation Press, 2004), 5.

15. Rule 12(b) (6), *Federal Rules of Civil Procedure,* from Cornell University Law School, Legal Information Institute, available from www.law.cornell.edu/rules/frcp/ (retrieved May 1, 2005).

16. Rule 56, *Federal Rules of Civil Procedure,* from Cornell University Law School, Legal Information Institute, www.law.cornell.edu/rules/frcp/ (retrieved May 1, 2005).

17. Galanter, "The Vanishing Trial," 484. See also, ibid., 462–63, Table 1, 483–84.

18. Christopher Frost, "The Sound and the Fury, or the Sound of Silence: Evaluating the Pre-Amendment Predications and Post-Amendment Effects of the Discovery Scope-Narrowing Language in the 2000 Amendments to the Federal Rules of Civil Procedure," *Georgia Law Review* 37 (2003), 1039, 1040.

19. See Rule 26(b) (1), *Federal Rules of Civil Procedure,* from Cornell University Law School, Legal Information Institute, www.law.cornell.edu/rules/frcp/ (retrieved May 1, 2005).

20. See, e.g., Rule 36, *Federal Rules of Civil Procedure,* from Cornell University's Law School, Legal Information Institute, www.law.cornell.edu/rules/frcp/ (retrieved May 1, 2005).

21. See, e.g., Rules 27–32, *Federal Rules of Civil Procedure,* available from Cornell University's Law School, Legal Information Institute, at www.law.cornell.edu/rules/frcp/ (retrieved May 1, 2005).

22. See, e.g., Rule 35, *Federal Rules of Civil Procedure*, available from Cornell University's Law School, Legal Information Institute, at www.law.cornell. edu/rules/frcp/ (retrieved May 1, 2005).

23. John B. Oakley, "A Fresh Look at the Federal Rules in State Courts," *Nevada Law Journal* (Winter 2002/2003), 354, 355.

24. Seymour Moskowitz, "Rediscovering Discovery: State Procedural Rules and the Level Playing Field," *Rutgers Law Review* (Spring, 2002), 595, 613-17.

25. As reported in George L. Priest, "The Problems and Efforts to Understand It," in *Punitive Damages: How Juries Decide* Eds. Cass R. Sunstein, Reid Hastie, John W. Payne, David A. Schkade, and W. Kip Viscusi (Chicago: University of Chicago Press, 2002), 1.

26. *State Farm Mutual Automobile Insurance Co. v. Campbell*, 538 U.S. 408 (2003). See also *BMW of North America, Inc. v. Gore*, 517 U.S. 559, 575 (1999).

27. Chief Justice Burger's remarks are reported in "Mid-Year Meeting of the American Bar Association," 52 *United States Law Week* (February 28, 1984), 2471.

28. Jerome T. Barrett, and Joseph P. Barrett, *A History of Alternative Dispute Resolution: The Story of a Political, Cultural, and Social Movement* (San Francisco: Jossey-Bass, 2004), 149-52, 182-83, 214.

29. Thomas J. Stipanowich, "ADR and the 'Vanishing Trial': The Growth and Impact of 'Alternative Dispute Resolution,'" *Journal of Empirical Legal Studies* (November, 2004), 843, 849-50.

30. Stipanowich, "ADR and the 'Vanishing Trial,'" 849-50, 866-67, 898-900.

31. Richard Posner, "The Summary Jury Trial and Other Methods of Alternative Dispute Resolution: Some Cautionary Observations," *University of Chicago Law Review* (1986), 356, 372-75; but see Thomas D. Lambros, "The Summary Jury Trial: An Effective Aid to Settlement," *Judicature* (July/August 1993), 6-8. The strengths and weaknesses of ADR are summarized from a practitioner's perspective in Edward J. Costello, Jr., "Whether and When to Use Alternative Dispute Resolution," in *Alternative Dispute Resolution: The Litigator's Handbook*, edited by Nancy F. Atlas, Stephen K. Huber, and E. Wendy Trachte-Huber (Chicago: American Bar Association, 2000), 35-58.

32. William C. Smith, "Much to do about ADR," *American Bar Association Journal* (June, 2000), 62-68.

CHAPTER NINE

Judicial Decision Making and Behavior

Although her face was covered with duct tape, Mrs. Shirley Crook was alive and lucid when hog-tied with electrical wire and pushed off a railroad bridge into the Meramec River in Saint Louis County, Missouri in the early morning of September 8, 1993. Two fishermen later discovered her body. After bragging to an acquaintance that he killed Mrs. Crook, seventeen-year-old Christopher Simmons was arrested and subsequently sentenced to death. In 1997, the Supreme Court of Missouri affirmed Simmons's death sentence on appeal.[1]

Before 1997, Simmons could not legally claim that the Eighth Amendment's cruel and unusual punishment clause prevented the execution of juveniles because the U.S. Supreme Court upheld the practice in *Stanford v. Kentucky* (1989), which was the same day it upheld the execution of mentally retarded defendants in *Penry v. Lynaugh* (1989).[2] Relying on those cases, the State Supreme Court reasoned that Simmons's rights were not violated. However, while Simmons was on death row, the U.S. Supreme Court in *Atkins v. Virginia* (2002)[3] reversed course, holding that executions of mentally retarded defendants was unconstitutional because a new consensus had emerged since *Penry*. As a result, in a second appeal in 2003, the Supreme Court of Missouri ruled that a similar movement had emerged with regard to juvenile death sentences. The state court set aside the death penalty and resentenced Simmons to life imprisonment without the possibility of parole. That decision raised the issue of whether the nation's highest court would extend *Atkins's* rationale to bar juvenile executions in *Roper v. Simmons* (2005).[4]

In *Roper*, Justice Anthony Kennedy's opinion for a bare majority held that juvenile executions violate the Eighth Amendment. He reasoned that the amendment must be interpreted in light of the "evolving standards of decency that mark the progress of a maturing society." Justice Kennedy found that thirty states prohibited juvenile death sentences and that youthful offenders were rarely executed. In such cases, the death penalty was disproportionate because juveniles are too immature to understand fully the consequences of their acts. As a result, the Court established a categorical rule prohibiting capital punishment for juvenile offenders under the age of eighteen. While not authoritative, the Court also noted that foreign and international law demonstrated the "stark reality that the United States is the only country in the world that continues to give official sanction to the juvenile death penalty."[5]

In a scathing dissent, Justice Antonin Scalia objected that the decision was driven by the "subjective views of five Members of this Court and like-minded foreigners." Instead of looking to evolving standards of decency and speculating about how the Constitution changed over time, Scalia countered that the Court's obligation was to ascertain the original meaning of the Eighth Amendment. It was not the Court's place, Justice Scalia claimed, to substitute its own moral judgments for those of the states. In a separate opinion, Justice Sandra Day O'Connor agreed that the Court had authority to make moral judgments but dissented from the ruling because it deprived state legislatures from imposing the death penalty for serious crimes.[6]

The dissents in *Roper* underscore the rival views of the role of courts in interpreting law. Unlike trial courts, appellate courts are collegial institutions that ordinarily do not "find" the facts during the adversary process. Rather, they assume that the facts have been established by trial courts, and they apply the law to settle disputes. In so doing, appellate courts create public policy, and their principal function is not merely to correct legal errors but also to make uniform legal and public policy.

This chapter explores how appellate court judges influence legal policy change. It does so by outlining the appellate decision-making process and contrasting it with trial court adjudication. Four processes are highlighted: (1) agenda setting, (2) oral argument, (3) the judicial conference, and (4) judicial opinions. Because judicial policymaking is controversial and because the legal and the academic communities differ in their understanding of how appellate courts construe the law and formulate public policy, the next section analyzes different methodologies for explaining judicial behavior. Because appellate courts routinely declare and make law in statutory and constitutional cases, the concluding section examines the politics of judicial interpretation in both kinds of cases.

THE APPELLATE DECISION-MAKING PROCESS

State and federal appellate courts play a limited role in reviewing trial verdicts because the Constitution only guarantees "a fair trial, not a perfect one."[7] Studies confirm that only about twenty percent of federal trial court rulings are appealed annually and that most appeals are unsuccessful.[8] In addition, trial and appellate court behavior is largely indistinguishable from partisan affiliation, although there is evidence that Republican-nominees tend to favor "upperdogs," whereas Democratic-nominees support "lower dogs."[9] Still, there are basic differences between the principal functions of trial and appellate courts, and they significantly affect the role they play.

Because trial court judges and juries are in the best position to evaluate conflicting factual matters, appellate judges ordinarily defer to lower courts' findings of fact. Appeals courts review trial courts only if they are "clearly erroneous." Appellate review of questions of law is different and a *de novo* (considering facts and evidence in a fresh light) standard of review applies. Accordingly, the limited scope of appellate review gives trial courts virtually unbounded discretion, and they are generally the courts of first and last resort.[10]

Circuit Judge Richard A. Posner argues that trial court opinions are less important sources of law than appellate courts.[11] Unlike trial courts, appellate courts do not merely settle claims between conflicting parties in a single dispute. They render final judgments that set precedents within a specific state or federal geographical region.[12] Furthermore, appellate courts decide cases in randomly assigned panels of three judges or *en banc* (when all judges convene to make a ruling). As a consequence, appeals courts are collegial institutions that create final orders and precedents which broadly affect social policy.[13]

In light of rising caseloads, appellate judges spend less time hearing oral arguments, and instead research and write judicial opinions. They also must manage dockets and simultaneously supervise multiple support staff. For example, the legal staff per judge in state appellate courts usually consists of two or three law clerks and staff attorneys, plus secretaries. Furthermore, in appeals courts more emphasis is placed on clearing dockets through written judicial opinions. Consequently, in contrast to lower court judges, appellate judges must rely on their law clerks to do the research and write opinions. Clerks working for trial judges have different responsibilities, including drafting jury instructions, evaluating discovery motions, and acting as the judge's liaison in communicating with lawyers, other court personnel, and the public.[14]

The significance of the appellate courts is underscored by examining the critical stages of their decision-making process, including (1) how they set their agenda, (2) the influence of oral argument, (3) the role judicial conferences play, and, (4) the saliency and utility of writing judicial opinions.

Agenda Setting

Courts with discretionary jurisdiction, such as the U.S. Supreme Court and other state courts of last resort, have more flexibility to decide the cases they want to hear. Still, appeals courts that must hear mandatory appeals also set their agenda in accordance with governing statutes, the procedural rules, and judicial norms.

In all appeals courts, the clerk of court begins the appellate process once the losing party pays a fee and files notice of an appeal. Once an appeal is filed, the clerk assigns the appeal a docket number and puts the case on the court calendar. Typically, the assignment of cases is done by the random selection of three judge-court panels. Random selection prevents judges from picking the legal categories of the appeals they individually favor. Apart from panel assignment rules, the flow of appeals is controlled by the clerk of court, who serves as a kind of administrative "traffic cop" in communicating with counsel.[15]

After the preliminary case processing is finished, the appeals courts' staff attorneys and the judges' law clerks work on their assigned cases. They also continue to screen appeals with a view to determining whether they should receive plenary (full) consideration or not. Central staff attorneys, which are permanent staff, typically work for the court instead of specific judges. Among the legal staff, they have diversified duties, including screening cases for jurisdictional defects, setting cases for oral argument or summary disposition (without oral argument), researching substantive motions, and writing memoranda on whether to grant or deny relief in discretionary cases.[16]

Studies of federal and state appeals courts show that the central staff significantly influences a court's agenda. In an analysis of three federal appeals courts, legal scholar Jonathan Matthew Cohen found that central staff was the touchstone for deciding which appeals received "full-dressed" treatment and whether cases were granted oral arguments or given summary disposition. Likewise, in a study of 151 state appellate courts, court researchers Roger Hanson, Carol Flango, and Randall Hansen found that central staffers spent a significant portion of their time preparing legal memoranda for judges. The memos advised judges whether the appeal should stay on the docket for further consideration. They also assist judges by providing substantive legal analyses of cases granted full review. Both studies were consistent with the findings from an earlier study of the Michigan Court of Appeals that concluded central staff play an important role not only in dismissing cases, but also in reaching decisions on the merits.[17]

To a lesser degree, law clerks assigned to individual judges contribute to molding a court's agenda. Usually, less than three percent of the law clerks' time is spent handling procedural motions, regardless of whether they work in courts of last resort or intermediate appellate courts. Unless the court has discretionary authority, the rules governing the assignment of cases to panels, along with the judicial norms controlling the screening process, substantially dictate the workload and the legal types of cases appellate courts decide.[18]

Furthermore, procedural rules and norms affect case selection in federal and state courts of last resort. Rule 10, which guides the acceptance of *certiorari* petitions in the U.S. Supreme Court, states that the justices may opt to resolve conflicting interpretations of important questions of federal law originating from U.S. Courts of Appeals and state courts of last resort. The justices refer to these cases as involving *deep splits*—questions on which several lower courts have disagreed and are unlikely to resolve without the Supreme Court's intervention.[19]

Sidebar 9.1

The U.S. Solicitor General

The Office of Solicitor General (SG) was established by the Judiciary Act of 1870. It represents the government and the solicitor general is a presidential appointee confirmed by the U.S. Senate. In part because the act required that the SG help the Attorney General (AG) perform legal duties, the close connection between the offices gives the AG a large role in the SG's selection. The difficulty of separating the political and legal interests of the SG remains controversial. As one congressional subcommittee investigating the politicalization of the SG's Office put it: "Loyalty to the political interests of the administration may often require disloyalty to the goal of impartial justice."[a]

Several distinguished lawyers have served as SG, including John W. Davis, Robert H. Jackson, Archibald Cox, and Robert H. Bork. Many come from the nation's best law schools, clerked at the Supreme Court, and possess extensive political and professional credentials. The SG also enjoys a special relationship with the Supreme Court and is the only attorney to have an office in the Court's building. Because of the unique connection to the Court and allegiance to the political interests of the executive branch, the SG actually is loyal to two masters, the president and the Supreme Court. In fact, some scholars refer to the SG as the Court's "Tenth Justice."[b]

The SG performs a number of agenda-setting functions. The office is responsible for deciding which appeals merit filing a writ of *certiorari* petition; researching and writing appellate briefs supporting or opposing *certiorari* or, in cases adjudicating the merits, researching and writing briefs in which the government is a party; filing *amicus curiae* briefs if the U.S. is an interested party in the appeal; delivering oral arguments before the Court; and, on occasion and upon Court's request, conveying its views about whether to grant review or not, even in those cases when the SG is not a party.[c]

As a repeat player in litigation, the SG enjoys unparalleled success to the Supreme Court. One study found that the SG's overall success rate of wins and losses in all Supreme Court litigation (including access decisions, *amici* activity, and decisions on the merits) between 1959 and 1989 was a whopping ninety-six percent![d] Other empirical research makes similar findings regarding specific impacts on discrete policy areas. Political scientist Barbara Graham found that the SG's decision to file an *amicus curiae* brief expressing a liberal policy position (supporting minority rights) significantly increases the likelihood that the Court will issue a liberal ruling in race and ethnicity civil rights cases.[e]

That finding supported additional research demonstrating that the ideological attitudes and policy preferences of justices are highly correlated with support for positions taken by solicitor generals in *amici* briefs.[f] Not surprisingly, political scientist Richard Pacelle asserted that the SG "is arguably the most strategic actor in Washington," perhaps because it routinely participates in cases resting at the intersection of law and politics.[g]

Notes:

[a]As quoted in Rebecca Mae Salokar, *The Solicitor General: The Politics of Law* (Philadelphia: Temple University Press, 1992), 5. See also Salokar, *The Solicitor General*, 2, 11.

[b]Lincoln Caplan, *The Tenth Justice: The Solicitor General and the Rule of Law* (New York: Alfred A. Knopf, 1987). See also Salokar, *The Solicitor General*, 33–34.

[c]Ruth Bader Ginsburg, "Workways of the Supreme Court," *Thomas Jefferson Law Review* 2 (Summer, 2003), 519. See also Salokar, *The Solicitor General*, 12–13.

[d]Salokar, *The Solicitor General*, 27–28.

[e]Barbara L. Graham, "Explaining Supreme Court Policymaking in Civil Rights: The Influence of the Solicitor General, 1953–2002" *Policy Studies Journal* 31 (2003), 253–71.

[f]Rebecca E. Deen, Joseph Ignagni, and James Meernik, "Individual Justices and the Solicitor General: The Amicus Curiae Cases, 1953–2000," *Judicature* (September/October 2005), 68–77.

[g]Richard L. Pacelle, Jr. *Between Law & Politics: The Solicitor General and the Structuring of Race, Gender, and Reproductive Rights Litigation* (College Station: Texas A & M University Press, 2003), 5, 271.

Social science researchers have established that a combination of political and legal factors affect appellate courts' case selection. Seminal research by Sidney Ulmer concluded that the individual votes of Supreme Court justices in the final outcomes on the merits were strongly correlated with their initial votes to grant review. His key finding that justices pick cases in order to express preferred policy outcomes, is consistent with subsequent studies finding that judges act strategically in constructing their dockets. Judges strive to write their policy preferences into law with their agenda decisions but can only do so by taking into account the preferences of other judicial actors and the institutional context within which they operate.[20]

Strategic calculations at the access stage are closely linked to the institutional characteristics of courts and their social, economic, and political situations. Paul Brace and Melinda Gann Hall have shown that the availability of lawyers and the adequacy of resources (e.g., the number of clerks, central staff, and judges; salaries; docket size) significantly affect State Supreme Court agenda setting. "When lawyers are relatively plentiful and comparatively less costly, more have-nots [those with less money and legal resources to file lawsuits] reach state supreme courts, and they are more likely to win."[21] Likewise, other studies demonstrate that the Supreme Court's agenda is highly responsive to the policy initiatives of the president and Congress as well to public opinion.[22]

The agenda-setting stage is only the beginning of the appeals process, however. Once appeals are docketed and preliminarily screened, appellate courts may, though rarely, grant the litigants oral argument.

Oral Argument

In the early republic, attorneys in the United States built their reputations on the delivery of persuasive oral arguments. Some orations, especially those of famous advocates like Daniel Webster and Luther Martin, spanned several days. The norm of oral advocacy derived from the English common law tradition of barristers presenting their cases in open court. That tradition, however, has been reversed in contemporary legal practice. Attorneys now generally advance their arguments in written briefs. Although the movement away from oral advocacy is not new, oral arguments still play a vital role in appellate decision making. "Over the years, the time allotted for [oral] hearing has been shortened," as Justice Robert H. Jackson observed, "but its importance has not diminished." "The significance of the trend is that the shorter the time, the more precious is each minute."[23]

All appellate briefs identify the legal bases for convincing the court to accept jurisdiction and to entertain the appeal on the merits. Typically, they consist of a table of contents, a statement of legal issues, and a summary of the legal argument. As circuit Judge Frank Coffin observed, the brief's author and the identity of the lower court judge whose opinion is being appealed also informally determines whether a busy reviewing judge will spend the time to read it thoroughly. Accordingly, the quality of the brief writer's reputation may influence the recommendations of the central staff or law clerks to accept or decline review. In sum, the appellate brief is critical because it is directed at three distinct audiences: the central staff of attorneys; the panel of judges reviewing the case and their law clerks; and the judge assigned to write the opinion and his or her law clerks.[24]

If a case is set for oral argument, appellate judges usually ask their law clerks to write various memos, explaining the case and its merits. Some federal circuit judges use "chambers or mini-memoranda" to provide unedited thumbnail sketches of the major issues presented. Other memoranda critique those sent from other chambers and correct flaws in the analysis. Although the type of memo used is a function of the work habits of each chamber, most judges require clerks to construct *bench memorandum*—a detailed memo that may be shared with other chambers and that outlines the appeal's facts, legal issues, and legal authorities. Some judges describe bench memos as "road maps" to case specifics.[25]

Notably, the time spent preparing for oral hearings is increasingly designated for a smaller percentage of appellate court dockets. Although few courts of last resort have eliminated oral arguments, virtually all limit the amount of time given. In the Supreme Court, litigants receive only thirty minutes to argue their cases, unless there is an exception made under special circumstances. There is also a trend toward reserving plenary consideration for only those cases that absolutely require it, such as those presenting novel legal issues that have never been addressed and those creating a serious lack of uniformity in the law. The shift away from oral arguments is most conspicuous in the federal circuit courts. There, the percentage of appeals (see Table 9.1) decided without oral argument has been reduced by half since the 1980s, from sixty-three percent (1981) to thirty-one percent (2005).

The reduced opportunity for oral advocacy does not mean that it has become a lost art. Although some scholars and even some judges—such as Justice Oliver Wendell Holmes, who used to take catnaps on the bench, and Justice Clarence Thomas, who rarely asks questions during oral arguments—do not get much out of this stage of the appellate process, others are different. Justice Ruth Bader Ginsburg, for one, considers arguments not "an occasion. . .for grand speechmaking, but for an exchange of ideas about the case, a dialogue or discussion between knowledgeable counsel and judges who have done their homework, a 'hot bench,' as appellate advocates say." Unlike in appellate courts in civil law countries—in which the chief justice of a panel of judges assumes a primary role in deciding who among the brethren may speak or ask questions and, thus, controls the dialogue with counsel at the hearing, Justice Ginsburg characterizes oral arguments as the "last clear chance to convince the justices concerning points on which the decision may turn." Justice Ginsburg is not alone in that assessment. Not only do oral arguments provide a forum for exchange and persuasion, they personalize the case for the judges and give them key information that they may otherwise overlook shortly before they prepare to vote in judicial conferences, the next stage of the appellate process.[26]

TABLE 9.1 Appeals Terminated After Oral Hearing in U.S. Courts of Appeals

Year	Total Number of Appeals Terminated on Merits	Total Number of Appeals Terminated on Merits After Oral Hearing	Percentage of Appeals Terminated on Merits After Oral Hearing
1981	12,254	7,709	63
1988	18,977	9,692	51
1990	21,022	9,479	45
1995	27,772	11,080	40
2000	27,516	9,752	35
2005	27,354	8,573	31

Note. Data for the U.S. Court of Appeals for the Federal Circuit is unreported. Percentages are rounded off to nearest whole number.

Source: Administrative Office of U.S. Courts, *Judicial Facts and Figures: Multi-Year Statistical Compilations of Federal Court Caseload Through Fiscal Year 2004* (Compiled March 2004), available from www.uscourts.gov/judicialfactsfigures/contents.html (retrieved April 21, 2006), Table 1.8, (all years except 1981 and 2005). Data for 1981 are from Jonathan Matthew Cohen, *Inside Appellate Courts: The Impact of Court Organization on Judicial Decision Making in the United States Courts of Appeals* (Ann Arbor: University of Michigan Press, 2002), 62, Table 3; 2005 data are from Table B-1, at Administrative Office of U.S. Courts, "Federal Judicial Caseload Statistic, March 31, 2005," available from www.uscourts.gov/caseload2005/contents.html (retrieved April 21, 2006).

FIGURE 9.1 The Process of Appellate Decision Making.

Appeal Filed and Processed by Clerk of Court

- Appellate courts with mandatory jurisdiction must hear appeal
- Appellate courts with discretionary power set their docket agenda by selecting cases
- Clerk makes preliminary assessment whether procedural requirements for filing appeal are met
- Dates for applicable summary dispositions, preliminary hearings, civil settlement or mediation conferences, legal brief submission, and oral argument (if any) are tentatively calendared

Legal Brief Submission and Bench Memos Prepared

- Appellant/Petitioner (losing party at trial level) and Appellee/Respondent (winning party at trial level) file briefs summarizing respective legal arguments
- Third parties ("amicus curie") may intervene and file briefs with court's permission
- Law clerks and judges collaborate to prepare "bench memos" or legal analysis of issues on appeal as part of judge's preparation for oral argument and conference deliberations

Oral Argument

- Respective parties present synopsis of legal argument at court hearing in front of appellate judges during allotted time
- Judges frequently ask questions of counsel from bench about inconsistencies, omissions, strengths, and weaknesses of their case during oral argument

The Judicial Conference

- Judges discuss merits of appeal and cast preliminary votes to grant or deny requested relief
- If not assigned before oral argument, judges may be assigned the duty of writing majority, concurring, or dissenting opinions at conference

Preparation and Release of the Judicial Decision/Opinion

- Law clerks and judges write opinion and it is circulated to other justices for further editing and arriving at final outcome (in those cases in which judges do not switch votes)
- Final draft of opinion is prepared and released to parties and public through clerk of court or public information office of court

Judicial Conferences

All appellate courts have conferences, ostensibly for case disposition, but sometimes to determine who will write the controlling opinion, if another type of preconference or postconference opinion assignment practice is not used (see Figure 9.1). Judicial conferences also help with case management. The Supreme

Court, for instance, has an opening conference in the week before the beginning of each term in October in order to dispose of petitions for review that were filed over the summer recess. Conferences additionally permit judges to review appeals and cast preliminary votes "on the merits"—votes determining the core legal issues on appeal. Significantly, the votes are tentative because appellate judges may change their minds at any time prior to the court's final judgment. Although rising caseloads and limited judicial resources prevent conferences from becoming, as they once were, the principal forum for engaging in unrestricted debates about cases, they nonetheless foster judicial behavior that strategically affects the formation of voting coalitions and final decisions. Although appellate judges routinely negotiate with each other before and after conferences, judicial conferences serve as important venues for collectively debating competing legal claims.[27]

The different tactics judges use during conferences to build or strengthen voting coalitions vary with the court and its members. In part, the ability to persuade a colleague is dictated by institutional procedures and norms. Many appeals courts stick to the tradition of discussing cases by seniority, a practice that lets the chief judge, and then the most senior judge, speak and cast votes first. Other courts, however, use a reversed order of seniority, or simply let the chief justice assume control of the opinion assignment.

Judges announcing their positions first may have a powerful effect on the views of junior judges. They enjoy the advantage of informally shaping the court's final judgment if the voting blocs favoring their position hold. Still, though judges speaking last may be at a strategic disadvantage, it is offset in larger multimember courts, such as in the Supreme Court or in other appeals courts, in which the practice of going last has the advantage that it may determine the outcome in tied cases.[28]

The seniority tradition and the order in which judges speak may affect consensus-building on courts that allow the chief justice to assign opinions, either in conference or afterwards, provided the court's leader is part of the conference majority. Although in the Supreme Court the practice of opinion assignment has historically varied with the chief justice's style of leadership, such a general rule exists on the high court and sometimes it operates in conjunction with another norm that lets the justices "pass" when it is their turn to speak in conference. One study found that making the decision to pass was a strategy used by Chief Justice Warren Burger, and later by Chief Justice William Rehnquist, to control opinion assignment in cases in which they did not know how the rest of Court might vote. Taking a pass enhanced the chief justice's information about how the other justices would vote and, therefore, strategically enabled the chief justice to join the majority and control opinion assignment. As a result, Chief Justices Burger and Rehnquist passed when there was an uncertainty about the case's outcome or when there was a doubt they would be in the winning coalition. But, each chief justice also abstained from passing when they were sure that they would win or lose in cases decided on the merits. Such strategic behavior increased the chief justice's capacity to set the court's agenda and influence final outcomes.[29]

The dynamics of coalition building are not confined to the behavior of the chief justice, however. Although associate judges on the Supreme Court and other appeals courts may not hold opinion assignment power, they may still work to achieve their preferences in conference, or through writing with concurring (joining only in the result, but not the rationale) or dissenting opinions. Such opinions exert pressure on judges in the majority because they undermine the legal weight attached to the majority's view and also expose a court's disagreements by "go[ing] public."[30] Significantly, because most cases are "easy" and result in either unanimous or summary dispositions, individual threats to disrupt unanimity are only effective in cases that are most significant or difficult to resolve.

Opinion Writing

"It will come out in the writing," observed Justice Ginsburg about a colleague's perception of judicial decision making.[31] Judicial opinions evolve from the assimilation of information gathered from court pleadings, appellate briefs, the trial record and internal staff memoranda assembled by staff attorneys and judicial law clerks. They underscore Justice Lewis Powell's belief that appellate courts are similar to "small, independent law firms."[32] Justice Powell's analogy also accurately describes the in-chambers activities of judges and law clerks.

Because judges and clerks invest considerable time in producing judicial decisions, it is not surprising that Justice Clarence Thomas characterized the ordeal of hiring law clerks as "selecting mates in a foxhole."[33] In addition, several clerks of former Justice John Harlan II fondly recalled sharing drinks with him at his home and reading the justice documents in chambers when his eyesight was fading.[34] Such recollections reflect the deferential role clerks' play in relation to what judges ask them to do. "The tasks of the clerks," as John P. Frank once put it, are "very much the product of the whims of their Justices."

> In general, it is the job of the clerk to be the eyes and legs for his judge, finding and bringing in useful materials. This can involve an immense amount of work, depending upon how curious the Justice is. It is legend that Justice Brandeis once asked a clerk to look at every page of every volume in the United States Reports looking for a particular point. The clerks may also have semi-social duties, like those who visited with Holmes or took walks with Stone or played tennis with [Justice] Black, or superintended the circulation of the guests at the [Justice] Brandeis Sunday teas. All of this is in the spirit of an amiable relationship between a wise, elderly man and a young cub at the bar.[35]

A law clerk for Justice Powell echoed these sentiments, observing that the "ideal law clerk is both loyalist and critic—faithful to the judges's instructions, yet alert to any deficiencies of thought or expression."[36] In addition, law clerks earn the professional trust of their mentors by screening cases for review, conducting legal research, and writing draft legal opinions for analysis, comment, and interchamber circulation. Of these duties, assisting in writing judicial opinions is the primary function. In state appellate courts, career law clerks spend roughly sixty-five percent of their time preparing judicial opinions, and the same appears in federal courts. Specifically, such preparation includes reviewing the trial record, drafting opinions (most often compiling the facts in a case), consulting with judges regarding cases, *shepardizing* (checking the validity of legal citations and existing precedent) cases and, generally, checking footnotes or editing opinion drafts.[37]

The give-and-take normally associated with drafting opinions not only occurs between the clerk and the judge but also between judges in different chambers and their clerks. The circulation of draft memoranda and opinions is a critical aspect of the appellate court's deliberative process for old positions may shift and thereby create new alliances. The pressure to hold onto a majority may be extremely challenging because institutional opinions speak for the entire court.[38]

Judges expressing themselves individually in concurrence or dissent (see Table 9.2) do not symbolically or legally carry the same institutional weight as controlling "opinions for the court." Unlike majority opinions, they are not binding precedent. Still, the mere threat to issue a concurrence or a dissent may at times be an effective coalition building strategy by causing judges from different chambers to rethink their positions. Hence the threats, along with their execution, are bargaining tools.

The decision to issue a dissenting opinion or a concurrence registers dissensus. Under Chief Justice John Marshall's strong leadership in the formative years of the nation, the Supreme Court strove to reach unanimous outcomes and dissenting opinions were discouraged. But, that tradition gradually broke down and the decline of a "norm of consensus" has become a defining aspect of judicial behavior since the New Deal in the 1930s.[39]

A related issue to the rise of individual opinions concerns the growing but controversial practice of unpublished opinions (see the Controversies Over Courts

TABLE 9.2 Types of Judicial Opinions

Type	Characteristics
Majority	An opinion supported by a majority of participating judges
Plurality	An opinion agreeing in one result but supported by less than a majority
Per Curiam	An opinion "by the court" but unsigned; the author/judge is not identified
Concurring	An opinion agreeing with the result but not the legal rationale
Dissenting	An opinion disagreeing with the result and/or its legal rationale
Separate	An opinion in part concurring and dissenting

TABLE 9.3 Appeals Terminated Without Published Opinion in U.S. Courts of Appeals

Year	Total Number of Appeals Terminated on Merits	Total Number of Appeals Terminated on Merits Without Published Opinion	Percentage of Appeals Terminated on Merits Without Published Opinion
1989	19,322	12,497	65
1990	21,022	14,298	68
1995	27,772	21,083	76
2000	27,516	21,958	80
2005	29,913	24,411	82

Note. Data from 2005 are from Table S-3, at Administrative Office of U.S. Courts "Judicial Business of the U.S. Courts 2005," available from www.uscourts.gov/judbus2005/contents.html (retrieved April 21, 2006). Data for the U.S. Court of Appeals for the Federal Circuit are unreported. Percentages are rounded to nearest whole number.

Source: Administrative Office of U.S. Courts, *Judicial Facts and Figures: Multi-Year Statistical Compilations of Federal Court Caseload Through Fiscal Year 2004* (Compiled March 2004), available from www.uscourts.gov/judicialfactsfigures/contents.html (retrieved June 6, 2005) (Table 1.6).

box in this chapter). In the federal circuit courts, sixty-five percent of appeals are terminated without published opinions; and, in 2005, the rate jumped to eighty-two percent (see Table 9.3). Most courts decline to publish because doing so will not significantly contribute to the orderly development of the common law. Judges resolving appeals may conclude that a written opinion is not justified because (1) the appeal fails to raise an original or new legal question; (2) a written explanation will not have an important impact on public policy and, instead, benefits only the specific interests of the parties to the appeal; and, (3) the lower court has written a judicial opinion that can stand on its own. Advocates of the practice, therefore, ordinarily defend the shift toward summary dispositions on the grounds of economy: They avoid cluttering the law with inconsistent and contradictory precedents that are, on balance, relatively inconsequential to the public.[40]

Critics, on the other hand, find the tendency to use summary dispositions troubling because it undermines the basic principles of the adversary system of justice. "Too much of the appellate process is lost," asserts law professor Thomas Baker, "unless the artist is obligated to apply at least a few brushstrokes beyond the signature." For Baker, filing unpublished opinions compromises the "ultimate integrity" of appellate process that "requires that courts state their reasons" whenever they decide outcomes and create precedents.[41] Although Professor Baker's view is strengthened by considering that the public rarely has the opportunity to witness first hand what courts do except through reading opinions, it nonetheless remains an open question whether there is a constitutional basis for claiming that unpublished opinions have precedential effect.

Controversies over Courts

Should Unpublished Judicial Opinions Count as Precedents?

Over the past several decades, there has been a growing trend toward the nonpublication of federal appellate court opinions. As a result of rising caseloads and the costs of producing and publishing judicial opinions, the Judicial Conference of the United States and the Federal Judicial Center encouraged the nonpublication of some judicial opinions in order for courts to keep pace with workloads and to promote judicial efficiency.[a] All of the federal circuit courts adopted rules for the publication and citation of judicial opinions. Although most circuits at one time discouraged attorneys from citing unpublished opinions (even though they are available on Lexis and Westlaw), in April 2006 the Supreme Court approved an amendment to the Federal Rules of Appellate Procedure to permit the citation of opinions, orders, judgments, or other written dispositions that have been designated as "unpublished" or "nonprecedential" by federal courts.

Despite the rule change, the underlying debate over permitting the citation and use of unpublished opinions as precedent remains lively. Critics claim the nonpublication of opinions undermines judicial accountability and the development of law because the facts and reasoning in similar cases cannot be compared. Moreover, studies of unpublished opinions have found that many involve cases that are nonroutine, politically significant, and involve considerable judicial discretion.

THE CONSTITUTION REQUIRES UNPUBLISHED OPINIONS TO COUNT AS PRECEDENTS

The controversy over unpublished opinions intensified when Judge Richard S. Arnold held in *Anastasoff v. United States*[b] that the Eighth Circuit's rule that unpublished opinions may not be cited as precedents was unconstitutional and violated the "judicial power" conferred in Article III of the Constitution. Judge Arnold reasoned that, in establishing the "judicial power," Article III presumed that all judicial decisions were authoritative and precedential. In his words,

> [i]nherent in every judicial decision is a declaration and interpretation of a general principle or rule of law; *Marbury v. Madison*, 5 U.S. 137 (1803). This declaration of law is authoritative to the extent necessary for the decision and must be applied in subsequent cases to similarly situated parties. These principles, which form the doctrine of precedent, were well established and well regarded at the time this nation was founded. The framers of the constitution considered these principles to derive from the nature of judicial power, and intended that they would limit the judicial power delegated to the courts by Article III of the Constitution.

The doctrine of precedent was well established by the time the Framers gathered in Philadelphia. To the jurists of the late eighteenth century (and thus by and large to the framers), the doctrine seemed not just well established but an immemorial custom, the way judging had always been carried out, part of the course of the law. In addition, the framers had inherited a very favorable view of precedent from the seventeenth century, especially through the writings and reports of Sir Edward Coke; the assertion of the authority of precedent had been effective in past struggles of the English people against royal usurpations, and for the rule of law against the arbitrary power of government. In sum, the doctrine of precedent was not merely well established; it was the historic method of judicial decision-making, and well regarded as a bulwark of judicial independence in past struggles for liberty.

In addition to keeping the law stable, this doctrine is also essential, according to Blackstone, for the separation of legislative and judicial power. In his discussion of the separation of governmental powers, Blackstone identifies this limit on the "judicial power," that is, that judges must observe established laws, as that which separates it from the "legislative" power and in which "consists one main preservative of public liberty." If judges had the legislative power to "depart from" established legal principles, "the subject would be in the hands of arbitrary judges, whose decisions would be then regulated only by their own opinions. . . ."

The Framers accepted this understanding of judicial power (sometimes referred to as the *declaratory theory of adjudication*) and the doctrine of precedent implicit in it. Hamilton, like Blackstone, recognized that a court "pronounces the law" arising upon the facts of each case. . . . Like Blackstone, he thought that "the courts must declare the sense of the law" and that this fact means courts must exercise "judgment" about what the law is rather than "will" about what it should be. Like Blackstone, he recognized that this limit on judicial decision making is a crucial sign of the separation of the legislative and judicial power. Hamilton concludes that "to avoid an arbitrary discretion in the courts, it is indispensable that they should be bound down by strict rules and precedents, which serve to define and point out their duty in every particular case that comes before them. . . ."

We do not mean to suggest that the framers expected or intended the publication (in the sense of being printed in a book) of all opinions. For the framers, limited publication of judicial decisions was the rule, and they never drew that practice into question. Before the ratification of the Constitution, there was almost no private reporting and no official reporting at all in the American states. As we have seen, however, the framers did not regard this absence of a reporting system as an impediment to the precedential authority of a judicial decision. Although they lamented the problems associated with the lack of a reporting system and worked to ensure more systematic reporting, judges and lawyers of the day recognized the authority of unpublished decisions even when they were established only by memory or by a lawyer's unpublished memorandum.

NOT ALL UNPUBLISHED OPINIONS NEED OR SHOULD COUNT AS PRECEDENTS

Although some judges embrace the ruling and reasoning in *Anastasoff*,[c] other circuits have followed the Court of Appeals for the Ninth Circuit in rejecting its analysis of the practice of citing unpublished opinions.[d] Writing for the Ninth Circuit in *Hart v. Massanari*,[e] Judge Alex Kozinski maintained that the ruling in *Anastasoff* was misguided. Judge Kozinski reasoned that

> [t]he term "judicial Power" in Article III is more likely descriptive than prescriptive. If we nevertheless were to accept *Anastasoff*'s premise that the phrase "judicial Power" contains limitations separate from those contained elsewhere in the Constitution, we should exercise considerable caution in recognizing those limitations, lest we freeze the law into the mold cast in the eighteenth century. The law has changed in many respects since the time of the Framing, some superficial, others quite fundamental. ...
>
> One danger of giving constitutional status to practices that existed at common law, but have changed over time, is that it tends to freeze certain aspects of the law into place, even as other aspects change significantly.
>
> To accept *Anastasoff*'s argument, we would have to conclude that the generation of the framers had a much stronger view of precedent than we do. In fact, as we explain in the following paragraphs, our concept of precedent today is far stricter than that which prevailed at the time of the framing. The Constitution does not contain an express prohibition against issuing nonprecedential opinions because the framers would have seen nothing wrong with the practice.
>
> The modern concept of *binding precedent*—where a single opinion sets the course on a particular point of law and must be followed by courts at the same level and lower within a pyramidal judicial hierarchy—came about only gradually over the nineteenth and early twentieth centuries. Lawyers began to believe that judges made, not found, the law. This coincided with monumental improvements in the collection and reporting of case authorities. As the concept of law changed and a more comprehensive reporting system began to take hold, it became possible for judicial decisions to serve as binding authority.
>
> Early American reporters resembled their English ancestors—disorganized and meager—but the character of the reporting process began to change after the Constitution was adopted, with the emergence of official reporters in the late eighteenth century and the early nineteenth century. And, later in the nineteenth century, the West Company began to publish standardized case reporters, which were both accurate and comprehensive, "making it possible to publish in written form all of the decisions of courts." Case reports grew thicker, and the weight of precedent began to increase—weight, that is, in terms of volume.
>
> Although we agree with *Anastasoff* that the principle of precedent was well established in the common law courts by the time Article III of the Constitution was written, we do not agree that it was known and applied in the strict sense in which

we apply binding authority today. It may be true, as *Anastasoff* notes, that "judges and lawyers of the day recognized the authority of unpublished decisions even when they were established only by memory or by a lawyer's unpublished memorandum," but precedents brought to the attention of the court in that fashion obviously could not serve as the kind of rigid constraint that binding authority provides today. Unlike our practice today, a single case was not sufficient to establish a particular rule of law, and case reporters often filtered out cases that they considered wrong or inconsistent with their view of how the law should develop. The concept of binding case precedent, though it was known at common law, was used exceedingly sparingly. For the most part, common law courts felt free to depart from precedent in instances in which they considered the earlier-adopted rule to be no longer workable or appropriate.

A system of strict binding precedent also suffers from the defect that it gives undue weight to the first case to raise a particular issue. . . .

It goes without saying that few, if any, appellate courts have the resources to write precedential opinions in every case that comes before them. The Supreme Court certainly does not. Rather, it uses its discretionary review authority to limit its merits docket to a handful of opinions per justice, from the approximately 9,000 cases that seek review every term. Although federal courts of appeals generally lack discretionary review authority, they use their authority to decide cases by unpublished—and nonprecedential—dispositions to achieve the same end: They select a manageable number of cases in which to publish precedential opinions, and leave the rest to be decided by unpublished dispositions or judgment orders. In our circuit, published dispositions make up approximately sixteen percent of decided cases; in other circuits, the percentage ranges from ten to forty-four, the national average being twenty percent.

Increasing the number of opinions by a factor of five, as *Anastasoff* suggests, does not seem to us a sensible idea, even if we had the resources to do so. Adding endlessly to the body of precedent—especially binding precedent—can lead to confusion and unnecessary conflict.

Without entirely resolving the controversy over the precedential weight of unpublished opinions, in 2006 the Supreme Court announced that attorneys filing appeals must cite all relevant unpublished opinions in their briefs.

Notes

[a]See, e.g., *Federal Judicial Center, Standards for Publication of Judicial Opinions* (Washington, D.C.: Federal Judicial Center, 1973).

[b]*Anastasoff v. United States*, 223 F.3d 898 (2000).

[c]See Judge Jerry E. Smith's dissenting opinion in *Williams v. Dallas Area Rapid Transit*, 256 F.3d 260 (2001).

[d]See *Symbol Technologies, Inc. v. Lemelson Medical, Education, & Research Foundation*, 277 F.3d 1361 (2002).

[e]*Hart v. Massanari*, 266 F.3d 1155 (2001).

Once an appeal is decided, the parties are informed by an order affirming or reversing what the lower court did. Though the language of the order varies, courts may affirm, vacate, or reverse the lower court's ruling in its entirety, or opt instead to modify the result in part (thereby affirming and overturning different portions of the lower court's ruling). Moreover, it is not unusual for courts to issue detailed instructions directing the lower court to fix the error it committed and for remedial action.

STUDYING JUDICIAL DECISION MAKING

In his famous 1897 essay, "The Path of the Law," Oliver Wendell Holmes, Jr. declared that law is nothing more than "prophecies of what the courts will do in fact."[42] Holmes's prediction theory presumed that the discovery of facts is the key to understanding judicial behavior. As such, it was a forerunner to contemporary efforts to explain court outcomes. Scholars today routinely ask whether variables determine judicial decision making. They include the following: (1) do judges decide cases solely on the basis of law or do ideological considerations influence judicial outcomes as well?; (2) do institutional structures and norms play a significant role in explaining judicial decisions?; and (3) are judges strategic actors in making decisions that take into account legal or institutional constraints in reaching their policy goals?

The thrust of these studies are directed at identifying the underlying causes of judicial policymaking. Although the approaches they use vary, public law scholars exploring normative theory use historical analyses, the process of legal reasoning, and rival conceptions of judicial interpretation to study judicial politics. By contrast, researchers investigating empirical theory use quantitative or qualitative methods to generate data, test hypotheses, and discover relationships between variables.[43]

Some of the principal rival theories of judicial politics are outlined below. More specifically, three predominant approaches to modeling judicial behavior are detailed: (1) attitudinal model, (2) new institutionalism, and (3) strategic choice theory. A normative theory of legal reasoning is then analyzed.

See Table 9.4 for select categories of legal or political variables used to explain or predict judicial decisions.

The Attitudinal Model

C. Herman Pritchett's *The Roosevelt Court: A Study in Judicial Politics and Values, 1937-1947* (1948)[44] inspired scholars to seek "behavioral" explanations for judicial decisions. The so-called behavioral revolution of the 1940s and 1950s, led by Pritchett, Glendon Schubert, and S. Sidney Ulmer, stressed the "science" of politics and relied upon quantitative methods to explain judicial votes. In spite of Pritchett's rather ambiguous statement in *The Roosevelt Court* that "the Supreme Court inevitable acts in a political context," behavioralists gradually deemphasized the historical and institutional characteristics of courts and

TABLE 9.4 Select Categories of Legal or Political Variables Used to Explain or Predict Judicial Decisions

Variable Categories	What variable purports to explain or predict regarding judicial choices
Personal Preferences	The impact of personal policy preferences or ideological predispositions of judges on judicial decision making
	Examples include the following: past judicial votes of judges and the background and social characteristics of judges (e.g., partisan affiliation; prior judicial, legal, or political employment; judge's age; judge's race; judge's gender; judge's income; judge's education)
Legal Factors	The impact "law" has on judicial decision making
	Examples include the following: past judicial opinions ("precedent" or "*stare decisis*")
Case Characteristics	The impact of specific case facts in judicial opinions on judicial decision making
	Examples include the following: "Aggravating" or "mitigating" factors in death penalty cases (e.g., killing a police officer during a robbery; whether the defendant is mentally disabled); the presence of certain factors in Fourth Amendment search or seizure cases (e.g., if the search is conducted with a search warrant at a private residence)
Institutional Arrangements	The impact of formal rules, organizational structures, and norms on judicial decision making
	Examples include the following: methods governing judicial recruitment or retention (by partisan or nonpartisan elections or by executive appointment); presence or absence of an appellate court; the supply of lawyers in a jurisdiction; changing leadership styles of chief justice; judicial opinion assignment procedures; technological or staff changes affecting judicial operations
Environmental Characteristics	The impact of political, economic, or social environments on judicial decision making
	Examples include the following: electoral composition of legislative or executive branches; level of partisan electoral competition; level of budgetary support; urbanism

Source: Paul Brace and Melinda Gann Hall, "Integrated Models of Judicial Dissent," *Journal of Politics* (November, 1993), 914–35; David M. O'Brien, "Institutional Norms and Supreme Court Opinions: On Reconsidering the Rise of Individual Opinions," in *Supreme Court Decision Making: New Institutionalist Approaches,* edited by Cornell W. Clayton and Howard Gillman (Chicago: University of Chicago Press, 1999), 91–113; Harold J. Spaeth and Jeffrey A. Segal, *Majority Rule or Minority Will: Adherence to Precedent on the U.S. Supreme Court* (Cambridge: Cambridge University Press, 1999).

hypothesized that judicial votes are quantifiable expressions of individual policy preferences. As a result, for behavioralists the normative study of legal doctrine gave way to empirical studies seeking to discover which personal attitudes influenced judicial decision making.[45]

Although Pritchett is generally considered an attitudinal pioneer, his research incorporated qualitative evidence, such as doctrinal interpretations of judicial opinions, to demonstrate that attitudes are shaped by the justices' role conceptions about how to interpret the law. Even so, *The Roosevelt Court* was among the first attempts by scholars to investigate systematically the relationship between ideological attitudes and votes by arranging concurrences and dissents in nonunanimous cases into voting blocs. As a result, Pritchett "blazed a trail" for the next generation of judicial behavioralists, such as Glendon Schubert and Harold Spaeth.[46]

Schubert's scholarship, along with Spaeth and Jeffrey Segal's updating of the attitudinal model in *The Supreme Court and the Attitudinal Model* (1993) and *The Supreme Court and the Attitudinal Model Revisited* (2002), probably represent the most rigorous (but controversial) elaborations of attitudinal explanations for Supreme Court policymaking. In *Quantitative Analysis of Judicial Behavior* (1959), Schubert used scalogram analysis, a statistical method borrowed from psychological studies and also known as *Guttman scaling*, to test the theory that attitudes drive judicial behavior. Although the use of scales, which infer attitudes by counting votes and arranging them on ideological scales representing liberal and conservative values, was innovative, its shortcomings caused Schubert to test the attitudinal model in a different way by using a factor analysis of the justices' votes in another book, *The Judicial Mind* (1965), in terms of two ideological dimensions (scales), *political liberalism* and *economic liberalism*, in order to explain the justices' votes.[47]

In *The Judicial Mind Revisited* (1974), Schubert applied these techniques and others to not only confirm his earlier findings but also to introduce *game theory*—a theory positing that Supreme Court justices make strategic choices to grant *certiorari* and set the Court's agenda. Although Schubert's work generated much debate, it nonetheless established the attitudinal model.[48]

Although Schubert's theory was retested by others in subsequent years, the most complete analysis was done by Spaeth and Jeffrey Segal in *The Supreme Court and the Attitudinal Model*.[49] Segal and Spaeth used the statistical method of logistical regression to argue that the *attitudinal model*, which holds that decisions from the Court are based on the ideological attitudes and policy preferences of the justices, is the best and only empirically verifiable explanation for judicial policymaking. In contrast, they assert Supreme Court decisions cannot be explained by the so-called *legal model*—the model positing that legal factors ("the law"), such as precedent and the justices' interpretation of constitutional and statutory provisions, are the basis for judicial outcomes.

For Segal and Spaeth, the view that law determines judicial decision making is mistaken because interpreting precedent and constitutional or statutory text is inherently subjective. Consequently, legal factors may not be used as independent variables, thus defeating any attempt by researchers to test empirically the effects of a legal model. Hence, they declare that legal considerations have little impact on judicial outcome decisions, and law is "made" by judges, and not "discovered." This view is strengthened because the attitudinal model is capable of rigorous testing. Using observable data, such as justices' past votes, case facts, and the justices' ideological beliefs (as constructed through newspaper editorials), they concluded that the justices' attitudes are the best predictors of case outcomes. In their words, Chief Justice "Rehnquist votes the way he does because he is extremely conservative; [Associate Justice Thurgood] Marshall voted the way he did because he is extremely liberal."[50] See Table 9.5 and Table 9.6.

The success of the attitudinal model in explaining Supreme Court decisions is only matched by the critical response it received from the political science and legal academies. Critics have identified a number of inconsistencies in the model, and Spaeth and Segal responded in a revised edition, *The Supreme Court and the Attitudinal Model Revisited*.[51] The debate surrounding the attitudinal model nonetheless remains significant and illustrates the strengths and weaknesses of alternative approaches to explaining judicial policymaking. In general, three basic criticisms are as follows: (1) the attitudinal model does not adequately account for the role law plays in explaining judicial decision making; (2) the political and legal factors affecting judicial decision making cannot always be quantitatively reduced; and (3) the attitudinal model unduly minimizes the significant role institutions and judicial strategies play in influencing judicial policymaking. Moreover, Spaeth and Segal have been criticized for their coding of cases. *Bush v. Gore*, for instance, was coded as a "conservative" decision, even though a majority of justices ruled that there was a violation of voting rights on the basis of a "liberal" interpretation of the Fourteenth Amendment equal protection clause, and, paradoxically, the outcome effectively gave the 2000 presidential election to George W. Bush.[52]

Also, justices' votes are at times hard to code. For example, in two other widely watched cases, the Court revisited the controversy over the public display of the Ten Commandments and other religious symbols. In *Van Orden v. Perry*,[53] writing for a plurality Chief Justice Rehnquist held that the erection of a six-foot granite monument on which the Ten Commandments were chiseled did not violate the First Amendment (dis)establishment clause. Liberal Justices Stevens, O'Connor, Souter, and Ginsburg dissented. However, in *McCreary v. American Civil Liberties Union of Kentucky*,[54] Justice Souter ruled that two Kentucky counties violated the First Amendment by prominently displaying the Ten Commandments in their courthouses. Conservative Chief Justice Rehnquist and Justices Scalia, Kennedy, and Thomas dissented. In both cases, Justice Breyer cast the pivotal vote and formed bare majorities. He did so on pragmatic grounds, reasoning that the Texas monument had stood unchallenged for over forty years, whereas the Kentucky displays immediately sparked controversy and appeared to clearly aim at endorsing religion. These persistent criticisms have prompted political scientists to develop alternative methodologies for explaining judicial behavior, as discussed next (see Figure 9.2).

TABLE 9.5 Voting Alignments in the Rehnquist Court, 1986–2004

	Rehnquist	White	Blackmun	Stevens	O'Connor	Scalia	Kennedy	Souter	Thomas	Brennan	Marshall	Ginsburg	Breyer	Powell
Rehnquist	—	80.8	55.2	52.1	80.7	78.1	83.1	65.7	78.7	47.6	46.5	63.4	63.0	86.1
White	80.8	—	62.2	60.4	72.5	69.9	75.8	73.5	67.8	52.9	52.9	—	—	77.3
Blackmun	55.2	62.2	—	72	58.4	49.1	57.7	64.9	44.4	77.4	77.0	68.2	—	68.9
Stevens	52.1	60.4	72.0	—	56.9	46.3	57.7	72.3	44.6	69.9	71.6	77.8	75.5	56.7
O'Connor	80.7	72.5	58.4	56.9	—	70.5	78.1	71.7	69.0	49.5	47.9	66.4	71.6	83.3
Scalia	78.1	69.9	49.1	46.3	70.5	—	74.9	58.2	86.2	47.5	45.0	54.1	53.0	73.5
Kennedy	83.1	75.8	57.7	57.7	78.1	74.9	—	69.8	73.2	53.8	51.2	66.3	65.4	73.5
Souter	65.7	73.5	64.9	72.3	71.7	58.2	69.8	—	55.3	—	54.6	84.8	81.5	—
Thomas	78.7	67.8	44.4	44.6	69.0	86.2	73.2	55.3	—	—	—	52.1	50.8	56.3
Brennan	47.6	52.9	77.4	69.9	49.5	47.5	53.8	—	—	—	95.0	—	—	56.3
Marshall	46.5	52.9	77.0	71.6	47.9	45.0	51.2	54.6	—	95.0	—	—	—	55.0
Ginsburg	63.4	—	68.2	77.8	66.4	54.1	66.3	84.8	52.1	—	—	—	82.1	—
Breyer	63.0	—	—	75.5	71.6	53.0	65.4	81.5	50.8	—	—	82.1	—	—
Powell	86.1	77.3	68.9	56.7	83.3	73.5	—	—	56.3	56.3	55.0	—	—	—

Source: Table 1, *Harvard Law Review's* Annual Review of U.S. Supreme Court's term in Volumes 101–118 (1986–2004).

TABLE 9.6 Rehnquist Court Voting Blocs, By Natural Court, 1994–2004

	Rehnquist	Thomas	Scalia	Kennedy	O'Connor	Souter	Ginsburg	Breyer	Stevens
Rehnquist	–	79.3	78.0	84.8	81.4	63.6	63.0	63.0	51.7
Thomas	79.3	–	86.6	73.6	70.1	53.9	52.1	50.8	45.2
Scalia	78.0	86.6	–	72.9	70.0	55.1	53.4	53.0	44.2
Kennedy	84.8	73.6	72.9	–	78.4	67.7	66.5	65.4	58.6
O'Connor	81.4	70.1	70.0	78.4	–	71.3	66.1	71.6	57.0
Souter	63.6	53.9	55.1	67.7	71.3	–	85.6	81.5	76.3
Ginsburg	63.0	52.1	53.4	66.5	66.1	85.6	–	82.1	78.0
Breyer	63.0	50.8	53.0	65.4	71.6	81.5	82.1	–	75.5
Stevens	51.7	45.2	44.2	58.6	57.0	76.3	78.0	75.5	–

Note: Boxes were placed around agreement percentages equaling sixty-eight percent or more. The "natural court," or period of stable membership on the Court, began with Justice Stephen Breyer's ascension to the Court (1994) and ended with Chief Justice William Rehnquist's death (2005).

Source: Table 1, *Harvard Law Review's* Annual Review of U.S. Supreme Court's term in Volumes 109–118 (1994–2004).

New Institutionalism

New institutionalism studies embrace interdisciplinary (historical, sociological, or political study) approaches. Inspired by the work of Martin Shapiro on the significance of "political jurisprudence" and by that of Rogers Smith,[55] public law scholarship generally reflects two dominant strands: rational choice ("strategic") institutionalism and historical institutionalism. Rational choice research analyzes the extent to which judges, as strategic actors, achieve individual policy goals by making choices that are constrained by the actions of other participants. By contrast, historical institutionalism research theorizes that institutions, as structured by their historical and political contexts, are the basis for judicial decisions in that they help define the unique politics, values, identities, and interests of courts and judges.

New institutionalism stands in sharp contrast to attitudinal theory. But its basic premise, namely, that legal considerations affect judicial decisions, is not "new" and originates from traditional constitutional law study. An objective of historical institutionalism research is thus to connect, from an interpretative and historical perspective, normative conceptions of law and courts with the contemporary analysis of legal institutions and their political roles.[56]

Historical institutionalism contextualizes judicial decision making by situating it within the framework of institutional arrangements and practices, such as the structure of courts, judicial norms, and the makeup of law schools or bar associations, which are embedded in the legal culture. This conceptualization of

FIGURE 9.2   Research Methodologies for Studying Judicial Politics.

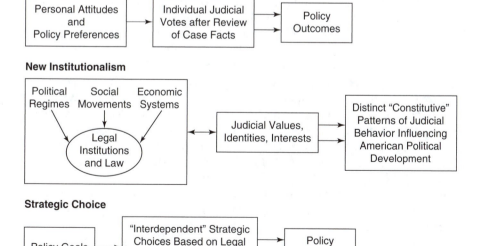

judicial politics, arguably, supplies a comprehensive explanation of "the motivational frame of mind of legal actors" striving to fulfill their legal obligations with a distinct sense of judicial purpose and commitment. In addition, its proponents maintain that the discovery of the institutional characteristics of judicial behavior offers a more nuanced and balanced view of the patterns of "purpose and meaning" that underlie American political development.[57]

Two books, *Supreme Court Decision-Making: New Institutionalist Approaches* (1999) and *The Supreme Court in American Politics: New Institutionalist Interpretations* (1999),[58] are illustrative. They analyze how courts are institutionally affected by the impact of judicial review and other legal principles; rights-based doctrines; judicial leadership styles; opinion assignment practices; judicial selection methods; the relationships courts have to bar associations; and the political dynamics courts share with other institutions, such as the presidency, Congress, or American political parties.

Still, critics of new institutionalism argue that its substantive claims and methodological approach are inherently flawed, principally because historical and interpretative findings are not prone to rigorous empirical analyses. Whereas, rational choice studies in new institutionalism tend to overestimate the role law plays as a constraint on the behavior of judges.[59]

Strategic Choice Theory

With the aid of the justices' private papers and court memoranda, Walter Murphy, in his classic *The Elements of Judicial Strategy* (1964), demonstrated that policy-minded Supreme Court justices construct a "grand strategy and particular strategies" to achieve their goals in their dealings with colleagues and other nonjudicial political actors.[60] Subsequent research analyzed the role strategic considerations play in producing judicial outcomes, ostensibly reconciling the attitudinal and institutionalist assumptions that personal attitudes and legal considerations affect judicial decision making. In addition, strategic or rational choice scholars tend to favor empirical methods. Thus, whereas strategic choice theorists share the institutionalist belief that law matters, their use of quantitative methods suggests that they may have more in common with those of the attitudinal perspective.

Strategic choice theory maintains that judges base their decisions on strategic calculations that are tempered by legal factors and institutional constraints. As two leading strategic choice scholars put it, "[j]ustices may be primarily seekers of legal policy, but they are not unsophisticated actors who make decisions based merely on their ideological attitudes. Instead," they explain, "justices are strategic actors who realize that their ability to achieve their goals depends on a consideration of the preferences of other actors, of the choices they expect others to make, and of the institutional context in which they act."[61] As strategic actors, judges seek to achieve their policy goals, but they only do so after weighing the risks and benefits of their actions. Judicial decision making is thus interdependent because, in order to maximize their own policy preferences, judges choose a course of action that takes into account the preferences of others in a given institutional context. Judges are also "sophisticated" decision makers: They may not be able to vote their true or "sincere" preferences because making such choices may not be the best ones to make under the circumstances. On this view, then, judges vote in accordance with policy positions that best approximate their sincere choices because to do otherwise might compromise their chance to achieve their most preferred goals.[62]

Research that has used strategic choice theory is exemplified by *The Choices Justices Make* (1998) and *Crafting Law on the Supreme Court: The Collegial Game* (2000).[63] Lee Epstein and Jack Knight in *The Choices Judges Make* used the private papers of justices and case analysis to illustrate that decisions during the Burger Court (1969–1985) were achieved through an extensive process of strategic negotiations, bargaining, and compromise. Using analogous data in roughly the same time period and an interactive model of decision making, Forrest Maltzman, James Spriggs, and Paul Wahlbeck in *Crafting Law on the Supreme Court* demonstrated that justices engage in a "collegial game" of strategic coalition building in opinion assignment and in drafting opinions in order in maximize their policy preferences. Although critics may not agree with whether the authors were successful, both books try to reconcile central themes found in the attitudinal and the new institutionalist perspectives. In other words, they try to overcome the attitudinal insistence that judicial decision making is only driven by political preferences, without regard to legal considerations; and the institutionalist claim that legal factors and institutional constraints are vital elements of judicial policymaking.

Legal Reasoning and Interpretative Approaches

The discovery of legal principles and their application to cases remains at the heart of the judicial function. Not surprisingly, judges are most comfortable deciding cases when the legal rule is clear and the facts are similar to those in past decisions. At least in those situations, it is not very difficult for judges to distill a common legal principle from past cases and then apply it to the case. But, when the facts are dissimilar, the task of judging and scholarly attempts to explain what the judge is doing, are more difficult. In those "hard" cases, the questions raised in political science about what is influencing the judicial decisions—the judge's attitudes, the impact of institutions, or the strategic calculations—gain the attention of the legal and social science academies.

Unlike political science, traditional legal studies do not emphasize the creative element in analyzing judicial decision making. As circuit Judge Harry Edwards once observed: "it is the law—and not the personal politics of individual judges—that controls decision making in most cases resolved by the courts of appeals." Although he later retreated from this view,[64] Edwards suggested that his socialization and training in law school reinforced his conviction that the decision making process is nothing more than "thinking like a lawyer," which typically means that the law is "found" in a mechanical fashion by analyzing past judicial opinions and applying legal rules to litigated controversies. Blackstone's declaratory theory of law (discussed in chapter 1) is perhaps the closest illustration of this myth, and one that characterizes judicial interpretation as essentially value free and virtually non discretionary. Rarely is the judicial decision-making process so simple, however. As a result, many lawyers and judges are trained to read appellate cases in order to uncover, and then to apply, controlling legal principles by a method of legal reasoning former Chicago Law School Dean Edward H. Levi called *reasoning by example*, or "reasoning from case to case."[65] Unlike the mechanical or declaratory approach, *reasoning by analogy* does not simply search for known legal rules. Instead, it culls legal principles from past cases that are factually similar to the one being decided.

Under Levi's framework, reasoning by example occurs in three stages. First, judges recognize the similarity between a past case and the case under review. Next, the judge discovers a rule of law from the first case. Finally, judges then apply the rule to the case at hand. Because the "rules arise out of a process which, while comparing facts situations, creates the rules and then applies them," for Levi the most crucial task of the judge is to determine the similarity or difference in facts between cases.[66]

Still, as Justice Benjamin Cardozo observed in his classic *The Nature of the Judicial Process*, the judiciary often confronts ambiguous cases and facts that encourage the creative exercise of discretion. "The rules and principles of case law," he explained, "have never been treated as final truths, but as working hypotheses, continually retested in those great laboratories of the law, the courts of justice." Cardozo understood that legal reasoning is a dynamic enterprise that sometimes necessitates subjective interpretation, or as Cardozo characterized it, a "method of free decision." Although he remained committed to discovering and applying the underlying principle, Cardozo acknowledged that the "directive force of a principle" is fashioned by the judge through the use of community traditions and methods of philosophy, history, and sociology.[67]

The Law and Politics of Legal Precedent

> We can now look forward to at least another Term with carts full of mail from the public, and streets full of demonstrators, urging us—their unelected and life-tenured judges who have been awarded those extraordinary, undemocratic characteristics precisely in order that we might follow the law despite the popular will—to follow the popular will. Indeed, I expect we can look forward to even more of that than before, given our indecisive decision today.

So Justice Scalia lamented in *Webster v. Reproductive Services* (1989), a ruling that upheld several abortion restrictions imposed by Missouri but that did not overturn *Roe v. Wade* (1973).[68] By 1992, and when Justices William J. Brennan and Thurgood Marshall had been replaced by the appointments of David Souter and Clarence Thomas, the Court again seemed poised to overrule *Roe* in *Planned Parenthood of Southeastern Pennsylvania v. Casey* (1992).[69] But, in an unusual joint opinion for the Court by Justices Sandra Day O'Connor, Souter, and Kennedy, the Court reaffirmed *Roe*. "Liberty finds no refuge in a jurisprudence of doubt," observed the majority, and the doctrine of *stare decisis* (legal precedent) commanded respect for *Roe's* place in the law. *Stare decisis* constrained the justices to:

> take care to speak and act in ways that allow people to accept its decisions on the terms the Court claims for them, as grounded truly in principle, [and] not as compromises with social and political pressures having, as such, no bearing on the principled choices that the Court is obliged to make.

To do anything less, the majority continued, would damage the rule of law as well as the Court's legitimacy because citizens relied upon *Roe* and its underlying right to personal autonomy.[70]

Casey reminds us that the judiciary is generally inclined to adhere to prior case law for several reasons. First, legal precedent promotes stability, certainty, and uniformity. Citizens, as well as judges and practicing lawyers, thus look to precedent to order their legal expectations and to resolve disputes in a pragmatic fashion. Second, adherence to precedent prevents arbitrary rule and facilitates the rule of law. Third, it instills public confidence that judicial decisions are based on established legal principles.

Casey and *Webster* also reinforce Justice William O. Douglas's observation that *stare decisis* is not "so fragile a thing as to bow before every wind," as well as that of Justice Louis Brandeis that respecting precedent is "usually the wise policy, because in most matters it is more important that the applicable rule of law be settled than it be settled right."[71] Hence the reversal of precedent is exceedingly rare in light of the total workload of policymaking appellate courts. According to estimates, the Supreme Court has overturned only 223 precedents in its entire history, which roughly amounts to about fewer than three cases per term.[72] Yet, sticking to precedent is by no means automatic, and overturning past law supplies judges with fresh opportunities to shape new legal policy. In the words of Chief Justice Rehnquist, "*stare decisis* is not an inexorable command; rather, it is a principle of policy and not a mechanical formula of adherence to the latest decision."[73]

A mix of legal and political factors allows appellate courts to make new policy by minimizing the force of precedent or, less often, by entirely disregarding it. In addition to ignoring precedent, judges may diminish the weight of precedents by *distinguishing, questioning,* or *limiting* them. Distinguishing cases avoids applying a precedent on the basis that its facts are different from those in the case being reviewed. It is also a useful technique to avoid the directive precedential force of an earlier case. As *Casey* suggests, questioning a precedent permits courts to change the law without actually overturning a prior ruling. *Roe* is still on the books, but it does not carry the same weight as it once did because the Court threw out the so-called trimester analysis which safeguarded the mother's privacy rights by preventing government from regulating abortion procedures until the last stages of pregnancy. In still other cases, appellate courts may choose to "limit" a precedent by confining its application in new cases to a very narrow set of circumstances which, in turn, restricts it as a controlling legal principle.

Although such decisions permit judges to adjust the scope and the application of precedent in light of changing facts and circumstances, they do little to shed light on the specific legal criteria or political factors that courts use to justify precedent reversals. Traditional *stare decisis* analysis usually dictates that courts will not overturn past cases unless there is a "special reason" to do so. Such reasons include the reviewing court's judgment that a precedent was wrongly decided; that the precedent's application has become unworkable in practice; or that changing law, facts, or circumstances, as measured from the time the precedent was originally handed down to the present, have rendered it obsolete or susceptible to misapplication and injustice.[74]

Still other factors influence the decision to overturn precedent: One is whether the court is deciding a constitutional or statutory case. Supreme courts are likely to show more respect to precedent involving statutory construction because legislatures may override their decisions and fix badly conceived laws. Courts, on the other hand, are in a better position to revise earlier interpretations of cases involving constitutional law. In addition, courts are reluctant to reverse precedents involving contracts or other commercial interests because such interests are vested and become more valuable over time. Moreover, whether the court creating the precedent was unanimous or divided in its outcome affects a controlling legal principle. Finally, courts are more likely to respect older precedents and to not disturb the stability of the law and social expectations.[75]

Often the decision to depart from past decisions results from changes in the composition of the bench and other institutional factors and legal norms. When an appellate court's membership rapidly changes, and new majorities coalesce in a short period of time, "constitutional law will be in flux," at least "until the new judges have taken their positions on constitutional doctrine" that they did not help to create. Conversely, in periods of stable membership, known as *natural courts*, there are fewer overturns and, concomitantly, less judicial conflict. To be sure, in periods of constitutional flux it is not unusual for judges to chastize publicly their new brethren for upsetting established precedents in high-profile cases. In his last dissent as a Supreme Court justice, for example, Justice Marshall accused the Court's majority of subverting the doctrine of *stare decisis* by overturning two recently decided cases that disallowed victim impact statements to be introduced at capital sentencing hearings. "Power, and not reason," he observed in his dissent, is the "new currency of [the] Court's decisionmaking," and emphasized that, "[n]either the law nor the facts supporting [the overturned precedents] underwent any change in the last four years. Only the personnel of [the] Court did."[76]

Although some scholars deny that legal influences constrain courts from overturning past decisions, the struggles on the bench over whether to adhere to or overturn precedent is also a byproduct of judicial selection. Researchers James Spriggs and Thomas Hansford, for example, underscore that the judiciary's respect for precedent depends on whether courts have ideological disagreements with the legal principles established in earlier cases. In their analysis of Supreme Court cases, they found that reversals of liberal precedents were more likely if the reviewing Court was conservative and, not surprisingly, that more overturns were likely if the precedents were conservative and the Court was liberal. They also reported that legal norms and institutional constraints were key overruling factors as well.[77]

STATUTORY INTERPRETATION

This section considers the significance of appellate judicial policymaking by examining the different ways courts interpret statutes and agency action within a constitutional framework. The growing importance of statutory construction is evaluated and, thereafter, various methods of constitutional interpretation and rival judicial philosophies are discussed.

Statutory Construction and Administrative Regulation

"In my view today's opinion," said dissenting Justice Scalia in *P.G.A. Tour, Inc. v. Martin*, "exercises a benevolent compassion that the law does not place it within our power to impose."[78] The main issue concerned whether the American with Disabilities Act (ADA) of 1990 should be interpreted to permit a disabled professional golfer, Casey Martin, to use a golf cart in tour-sponsored events. In writing for seven justices, Justice Stevens reasoned that the ADA's language and underlying legislative history supported the conclusion that Martin, who suffered from a degenerative circulatory blood disease, was entitled to reasonable accommodations in order to give him an equal chance to compete. Justice Scalia, joined by Justice Thomas, in dissent thought otherwise, claiming that the majority's interpretation of the statute "distorts the text of Title III, the structure of the ADA, and common sense."[79]

As Justice Scalia observed, the issue before the Court was not whether Martin ought to get a disability accommodation, but rather whether Congress required the P.G.A. to give him one on the basis of a common sense reading of the statute. Although they disagreed on the outcome, both justices construed the ADA according to "the plain meaning" of the statute. What divided the justices was what to do afterward. For Justice Scalia, who embraces a textualist approach to statutory construction (see Table 9.7), the ADA plainly reflected an intent that did not impose any legal obligation on the P.G.A. to accommodate Martin's disability.

For Justice Stevens, however, the text of the ADA was only the beginning and not the end of the analytical process: The statute's total structure had to be considered, as well as its overall purpose and supporting legislative history. Notably, though the interpretative approach Justice Stevens took might appear more compassionate (in the words of Justice Scalia, epitomizing a "decent, tolerant, and progressive judgment"), it was probably more of an attempt to bring some objectivity to an otherwise vexing process of figuring out how to apply a statute in a new context.[80]

TABLE 9.7 Interpretative Methods of Statutory Construction

Method	Main Characteristics	Underlying Rationale or Application
Public interest theory (legislative purpose)	Judge ascertains legislative purpose or objective in enacting statute	The search for the meaning of ambiguous statutes begins with an identification of the legislative purpose or policy the statute represents in order to deduce a result in the legal dispute at issue
Textualism	Judges construes plain meaning of statutory text in light of its overall structure and related parts	A formalistic approach that uses statutory text to discern the original intent of drafters in order to reflect outcomes that best respect the democratic policy choices of people's representatives in enacting the statute
Dynamic statutory interpretation	Judge interprets statute in light of how the original meaning of the law has evolved over time due to changing facts and circumstances	Pragmatic and normative approach that assumes statutory meaning is not fixed in time and changes dynamically in response to how the statute ought to be applied to concrete, contemporary problems in their present societal, political and legal context
Public choice theory	Judges must interpret statutes by understanding that legislators are political actors who bargain and negotiate with other legislators and special interest groups in order to maximize their self-interest	An approach emphasizing that judges must defer to the "bargains" struck by legislators, and which were created by the realities and "public choices" inherent in the operation of the political process, unless they are unreasonable; or the statute commands the judge to act a certain way in interpreting the statute

Legislative history	Judge looks to legislative history to help ascertain meaning or purpose of statute	Judges consult the underlying history behind the law's enactment as an aid to determine legislative purpose or intent Legislative history includes the following: ■ congressional committee reports ■ conference committee reports ■ statements made by legislative during floor debate ■ floor votes
Interpretative canons of statutory construction	Judge uses traditional "canons" of statutory interpretation as guide to aid in the process of interpreting statute or applying it	Canons are used as rules or guidelines to help ascertain statutory meaning or understand how statute apply to the facts of legal disputes Canons include the following: ■ the expression of one thing is the exclusion of another ■ repeals by implication are disfavored ■ every word of a statute must be given significance ■ if the language is plain and unambiguous, it must be given effect

Source: Robert A. Katzmann, *Courts and Congress* (Washington, D.C.: Brookings Institution Press, 1997); William N. Eskridge, Jr., *Dynamic Statutory Interpretation* (Cambridge: Harvard University Press, 1994).

The sticking point for the Court in the *P.G.A. Tour* case, as Justice Frankfurter may have observed, lies in "the determination of the extent to which extraneous documentation and external circumstances may be allowed to infiltrate the text on the theory that they were a part of it, written in ink discernible to the judicial eye."[81] All judges begin the process of statutory interpretation by reading the text. But, what is plain to some is not so to others. Justice Breyer illustrated the point by using the example of the sign that says, "No animals in the park." An "animal," he notes, could be a squirrel, a dog, or even an insect. If a New Yorker sees the sign above Central Park, the sign might refer to "dogs"; but Londoners may refer to "animals" as "insects" and might think something else if the sign is posted in a microbiologist's laboratory next to a shelf that "park" the scientist's test tubes.[82]

As a result, the ambiguity of statutory language often compels judges to look to extraneous sources and to the overall context to ascertain the legislature's "intent." Such extralegal sources include the statute's structure, its purpose, its history, and sometimes, what the statute means in light of contemporary circumstances.

None of the theories or methods of construction are free from criticism. The search for legislative intent might have the advantage of being contextual, but in the end judges make choices about what sources to consult and whose intent controls (a problem exacerbated by the self-interest of legislators and the fact that popular assemblies are an aggregation of many legislators and multiple conflicting intents). In referring to the futility of the use of interpretative canons, former federal appeals court Judge Abner Mikva once observed: "When I was in Congress, the only 'canons' we talked about were the ones the Pentagon bought that could not shoot straight."[83] His colleague on the D.C. Circuit Judge Harold Leventhal once quipped that using legislative history is like "looking over a crowd and picking out your friends."[84] In short, every method of statutory construction is value laden and remains a function of judicial discretion.

Similar interpretative problems arise when legislatures delegate its authority to administrative agencies. The task of statutory construction actually becomes more complicated when appellate courts have to make interpretative choices in weighing the legality of agency action. When agencies promulgate rules, they act as surrogate "policy experts" for the legislative branch. Hence, agencies are given broad statutory mandates: The Federal Trade Commission, for example, is vested with the power to eliminate "unfair methods of competition," and the Securities and Exchange Commission has authority to establish a "fair and orderly market."[85]

Thus, when agency action is challenged in court, reviewing courts may opt to defer to agencies or alternatively to use their power to overturn regulatory action. The significance of these issues is best understood in the context of 1930s New Deal politics, the birthplace of the so-called modern administrative state.

NEW DEAL POLITICS AND JUDICIAL DEFERENCE TO AGENCIES In a series of rulings, the Supreme Court confronted the New Deal head on and refused to ratify it by striking down parts of critical legislation, such as the National Industrial Recovery Act (NIRA). In *Panama Refining Co. v. Ryan* (1935), the Court used the *nondelegation doctrine* (prohibiting the redelegation of power from the legislature to agencies) to invalidate the president's authority under the NIRA to remove excess regulated oil from interstate commerce. In *Schechter Poultry Corporation v. United States* (1935), the Court used an identical rationale to reject the president's power under the NIRA to establish codes of fair competition regulating the poultry industry.[86]

In response, President Roosevelt threatened to change the composition of the Court with his so-called court-packing plan—legislation that would enlarge the size of the bench to fifteen and would secure a majority favoring progressive reforms. However, the Court shortly thereafter reversed course and upheld New Deal legislation, most notably in *West Coast Hotel Company v. Parrish* (1937) (upholding a state minimum wage law) and in *National Labor Relations Board v. Jones & Laughlin Steel Corporation* (1937) (sustaining the agency's power to adjudicate unfair labor practices under the National Labor Relations Act).[87] Thereafter, the Court buried the nondelegation doctrine. Its demise helped usher in an era of judicial deference to agencies that lasted until a new wave of regulatory reform in the 1960s and 1970s.

Beginning in the 1960s, Congress reasserted its regulatory powers by enacting social legislation expanding regulation over health, safety, and environmental protection. Such action-forcing legislation, when combined with the new powers it afforded federal agencies, was met with great resistance in the 1980s by the Reagan Administration, which favored deregulation. At roughly the same time, the D.C. Circuit Court of Appeals, which hears most challenges to administrative regulations, was in the midst of a political transformation of its jurisdiction due to court reforms.

The D.C. Circuit was also known for its activism and generated a rift between the Reagan Administration and its attempts to achieve deregulation. Moreover, the politics of the D.C. Circuit had an effect on Supreme Court jurisprudence, as the increasingly conservative Court found itself at odds with the D.C. Circuit's attempt to impose procedural requirements on agencies in order to fulfill their respective legislative mandates. Initially, in *Vermont Yankee Nuclear Power Corporation v. Natural Resources Defense Council* (1978), the Supreme Court endorsed a version of the so-called *hard look doctrine*—a D.C. Circuit-created standard of law insisting that agencies take a "hard look" at the regulatory decisions. But, several years later in a *Chevron v. Natural Resources Defense Council* (1984), the Supreme Court reigned in the D.C. Circuit and other federal courts exhibiting less deference to agencies by creating a new standard of appellate review that commanded judicial deference to agency decisions.[88]

In *Chevron*, the Court sent a signal indicating that it favored less judicial control over bureaucracies by establishing a *deference principle*: Agency decisions interpreting vague legislation must be upheld if they are reasonable and not contrary to specific legislative intent. Scholars, however, debate whether *Chevron* actually inspired more judicial deference to agencies or whether, instead, it produced the opposite effect because it left plenty of room for judicial creativity. Moreover, there is some evidence that judicial ideology is among a number factors affecting the degree of deference afforded agencies' interpretations. The D.C. Circuit, in particular, tends to support agencies if agency policy is ideologically consistent with that of judges reviewing agency action.[89] Consequently, not only is *Chevron* a landmark ruling controlling the disposition of most statutory construction cases in administrative law, its application is arguably a function of judicial politics.

CONSTITUTIONAL INTERPRETATION

In weighing the meaning of Congress's Article I power to enact laws that are "necessary and proper" to carry them into execution, Chief Justice John Marshall noted that the "provision is made in a constitution intended to endure for ages to come, and consequently, to be adapted to various crises of human affairs." In *McCulloch v. Maryland* (1819) he thus held that Congress had authority to create the Second Bank of the United States and that Maryland lacked the authority to impose a tax on it.[90]

McCulloch recognized Congress's broad powers over regulating the economy, even though the precise language of the Constitution said nothing about chartering a national bank. Chief Justice Marshall's expansive reading of the necessary and proper clause remains controversial because it implied that the Constitution is a "living document" that changes with the times. The ambiguity of the text did not prevent the Court from supplying its own meaning about the proper distribution of powers between the national government and the states.

In countless other examples, the Court has exercised the power of judicial review to limit governmental authority and to etch into law other previously undefined civil rights and liberties. In *Lochner v. New York* (1905),[91] for example, a "liberty of contract" right was fashioned out of the due process clause to strike down a state law restricting the number of hours an employee could work at a bakery. But, in *Buck v. Bell* (1927),[92] a Virginia law permitting the compulsory sterilization of feebleminded persons was upheld as a matter of due process, and Justice Holmes concluded that "three generations of imbeciles are enough." With *Brown v. Board of Education* (1954),[93] a state law requiring the separation of black and white children in public schools was nullified as a violation of basic equality. In *Roe v. Wade* (1973),[94] the Court used a judicially created right to privacy to afford women the right to choose to have an abortion.

What *McCulloch* and these other examples illustrate is that the underlying principles of the Constitution come to life through the judgments of appellate judges. Though it is critical to know who the judges are and when they occupy the bench, the legal sources judges use, in addition to their methodology or judicial philosophy, are also key factors regarding the constitutional choices judges make: Both determine the legitimacy and scope of constitutional meaning for the present and future.

The Methods of Constitutional Interpretation

Generally, judges use two broad methods of constitutional interpretation: Interpretivism and noninterpretivism (for further discussion, see the box on Controversies

Over Courts in chapter 2). The use of one or the other does not automatically create an outcome that is associated with a specific political philosophy. Even so, identifying the general method judges' use provides insight to their controlling *judicial philosophy*—the general guidelines or principles on which they decide cases.

Interpretivism holds that judges should construe constitutions by analyzing the text in light of historical context. One variant is *strict constructionism*, which holds that judges should examine the plain meaning of the words as they literally appear within the four corners of the document. Limiting interpretation to the text best preserves, and remains faithful to, the original intent of the framers. According to Edwin Meese III, President Reagan's attorney general, respecting framing intent is the "proper role of the Supreme Court in our constitutional system." He stated that

> [t]he intended role of the judiciary generally and the Supreme Court in particular was to serve as the 'bulwarks of a limited constitution.' .... As the 'faithful guardians of the Constitution,' the judges were expected to resist any political effort to depart from the literal provisions of the constitution. The text of the document and the original intention of those who framed it would be the judicial standard in giving effect to the Constitution.[95]

In theory, judges who use original intent favor *judicial restraint* in the sense that they neither stretch the meaning of the words beyond what the framers intended nor "legislate from the bench" and interject their own values.[96]

Judges endorsing *originalism*, "original meaning," or "original understanding," such as Justice Scalia, Robert Bork, and Chief Justice Rehnquist, take a slightly different view. In order to meet the objection that it is impossible to know what the framers intended, they conclude it is better to derive a general understanding of what the framers meant, as informed by historical context. "What I look for in the Constitution," in the words of Justice Scalia, "is precisely what I look for in a statute: the original meaning of the text, not what the original draftsmen intended."[97] Though imperfect, originalists defend the method as a better alternative to *noninterpretivism*.[98]

Noninterpretivists celebrate what originalist judges' scorn: a living constitution that adjusts to changing circumstances. Justice Kennedy's opinion in *Roper v. Simmons*, discussed earlier, relied on the "evolving standards of decency" to forbid the execution of juveniles convicted of murder. In other words, constitutional provisions must be interpreted in accord with contemporary principles and basic human values. Although text and history begins the analysis, they are incomplete guides. Justice Brennan explained that

> [w]e current justices read the Constitution in the only way that we can: as [twenty-first] century Americans. We look to the history of the time of framing and to the intervening history of interpretation. But the ultimate question must be, [w]hat do the words of the text mean in our time? For the genius of the Constitution rests not in any static meaning it might have had in a world that is dead and gone, but in the adaptability of its great principles to cope with current problems and current needs.[99]

The Sources of Constitutional Interpretation

The basic sources of common law adjudication are precedents, statutes, constitutions, and administrative regulations. Nonetheless, appellate judges resort to the use of extra legal sources, such as social science or scientific studies, public opinion polls, and sometimes law reviews, to support their decisions. *Roper*, again, is illustrative because the Court incorporated law reviews, international opinion, governmental studies, and social science evidence to support its holding.

Some of the Court's most important cases have relied upon extra legal sources. In *Lochner*, dissenting Justice Holmes argued that "the Fourteenth Amendment does not enact Mr. Herbert Spencer's *Social Statics*" in objecting to the judicial creation of a "liberty of contract" between employer and employees that general health, safety, and welfare legislation cannot disrupt.[100] In *Brown v. Board of Education*,[101] the Court looked to numerous sociopsychological studies to hold that the "separate but equal" doctrine fostered a sense of inferiority among public school children segregated by race. In *Miranda v. Arizona*,[102] the Warren Court referred to police training manuals in concluding that criminal suspects are entitled to advance warnings about their constitutional rights during custodial interrogations. More recently, in *Miller-El v. Dretke* (2005),[103] statistics showing prosecutorial abuse in making race-based determinations to exclude blacks during jury selection were the basis for overturning the defendant's death sentence.

These examples demonstrate that appellate courts use extra legal sources to sustain holdings. Consequently, the use of outside sources is controversial, and often criticized, as illustrated by Chief Justice Rehnquist and Justice Scalia's attacks on the use of international law and public opinion polls to support the Court's holdings in *Lawrence v. Texas* (striking down criminal prohibitions of consensual homosexual sodomy) and *Atkins v. Virginia* (nullifying the death penalty for mentally retarded defendants).[104]

SELECTED READINGS

Baum, Lawrence. *The Puzzle of Judicial Behavior.* Ann Arbor: University of Michigan Press, 2000.

Breyer, Stephen. *Active Liberty: Interpreting Our Democratic Constitution.* New York: Knopf, 2005.

Cardozo, Benjamin N. *The Nature of the Judicial Process.* New Haven: Yale University Press, 1921.

Clayton, Cornell W., and Howard Gillman, eds. *Supreme Court Decision-Making: New Institutionalist Approaches.* Chicago: University of Chicago Press, 1999.

Coffin, Frank M. *On Appeal: Courts, Lawyering, and Judging.* New York: W. W. Norton, 1994.

Cohen, Jonathan Matthew. *Inside Appellate Courts: The Impact of Court Organization on Judicial Decision Making in the United States Courts of Appeals.* Ann Arbor: University of Michigan Press, 2002.

Epstein, Lee, and Jack Knight. *The Choices Justices Make.* Washington, D.C.: CQ Press, 1998.

Epstein, Lee, and Joseph F. Kobylka. *The Supreme Court and Legal Change.* Chapel Hill: University of North Carolina, 1992.

Gillman, Howard, and Cornell Clayton, eds. *The Supreme Court in American Politics: New Institutionalist Interpretations.* Lawrence: University of Kansas Press, 1999.

Hammond, Thomas, Chris W. Bonnean, and Reginald Sheehan. *Strategic Behavior and Policy Choice on the U.S. Supreme Court.* Stanford: Stanford University Press, 2005.

Hansford, Thomas G., and Spriggs, James F., II. *The Politics of Precedent on the U.S. Supreme Court.* Princeton: Princeton University Press, 2006.

Hettinger, Virginia, Stephanie A. Lindquist, and Wendy L. Martinek. *Judging on a Collegial Court.* Charlottesville University of Virginia Press, 2006.

Levi, Edward H. *An Introduction to Legal Reasoning.* Chicago: University of Chicago Press, 1949.

Maltzman, Forrest, James F. Spriggs II, and Paul J. Wahlbeck. *Crafting Law on the Supreme Court: The Collegial Game.* Cambridge: Cambridge University Press, 2000.

Murphy, Walter. *Elements of Judicial Strategy.* Chicago: University of Chicago Press, 1964.

O'Brien, David M., ed. *Judges on Judging: Views from the Bench,* 2nd ed. Washington, D.C.: C.Q. Press, 2004.

Peppers, Todd. *Courtiers of the Marble Palace: The Rise and Influence of the Supreme Court Law Clerk.* Stanford: Stanford University Press, 2006.

Pritchett, Herman C. *The Roosevelt Court: A Study in Judicial Politics and Values, 1937-1947.* New York: MacMillan Co. 1948.

Rowland, C.K., and Robert Carp. *Politics & Judgement in Federal District Courts.* Lawrence: University Press of Kansas, 1996.

Scalia, Antonin, ed. *A Matter of Interpretation: Federal Courts and the Law.* Princeton: Princeton University Press, 1997.

Schubert, Glendon. *Judicial Behavior: A Reader in Theory and Research.* Chicago: Rand McNally & Co., 1964.

Segal, Jeffrey A., and Harold J. Spaeth. *The Supreme Court and the Attitudinal Model Revisited.* Cambridge: Cambridge University Press, 2002.

Spaeth, Harold J., and Jeffrey A. Segal. *Majority Rule or Minority Will: Adherence to Precedent on the U.S. Supreme Court.* Cambridge: Cambridge University Press, 1999.

Stearns, Maxwell, ed. *Public Choice and Public Law.* Cincinnati: Anderson, 1997.

Artemus, Ward, and David Weiden. *Sorcerers' Apprentices: 100 Years of Law Clerks at the United States Supreme Court.* New York: New York University Press, 2006.

NOTES

1. *Missouri v. Simmons*, 944 S.W.2d 165 (Mo. 1997).
2. *Penry v. Lynaugh*, 492 U.S. 302 (1989); *Stanford v. Kentucky*, 492 U.S. 361 (1989).
3. *Atkins v. Virginia*, 536 U.S. 304 (2002).
4. *Roper v. Simmons*, 543 U.S. 551 (2005). See also *Simmons v. Roper*, 112 S.W.3d 397 (Mo. 2003).
5. *Roper v. Simmons*, 574.
6. *Roper v. Simmons*, 587-88 (O'Connor, J., dissenting). See also ibid., 607 (Scalia, J., dissenting).
7. *Rose v. Clark*, 478 U.S. 570, 579 (1986).
8. C.K. Rowland and Robert A. Carp, *Politics and Judgment in Federal District Courts* (Lawrence: University Press of Kansas, 1996), 8.
9. Rowland and Carp, *Politics and Judgment in Federal District Courts*, 24-57.
10. Richard A. Posner, *The Federal Courts: Challenge and Reform* (Cambridge: Harvard University Press, 1996), 340. For an explanation of appellate standards of review, see Jonathan Matthew Cohen, *Inside Appellate Courts: The Impact of Court Organization on Judicial Decision Making in the United States Courts of Appeals* (Ann Arbor: University of Michigan Press, 2002), 46-48.
11. Posner, *The Federal Courts*, 158.
12. J. Woodford Howard, Jr., *Courts of Appeals in the Federal Judicial System: A Study of the Second, Fifth, and District of Columbia Circuits* (Princeton: Princeton University Press, 1981), *xvii*. See also Susan B. Haire, Stephanie A. Lindquist, and Donald R. Songer, "Appellate Court Supervision in the Federal Judiciary: A Hierarchical Perspective" *Law & Society Review* 37 (2003), 145.
13. Cohen, *Inside Appellate Courts*, 12-13, 27-34, 171-74.
14. Posner, *The Federal Courts*, 158, 348-49. Allocations of legal staff for state appellate judges are found in Roger A. Hanson, Carol R. Flango, and Randall M. Hansen, *The Work of Appellate Court Legal Staff* (Williamsburg: National Center for State Courts, 2000), 20-22.
15. See Hanson, Flango, and Hansen, *The Work of Appellate Court Legal Staff*, 8. Random panel selection is discussed in Cohen, *Inside Appellate Courts*, 72.
16. Hanson, Flango, and Hansen, *The Work of Appellate Court Legal Staff*, 19, 46-52, 54-55.
17. Mary Lou Stow and Harold J. Spaeth, "Centralized Research Staff: Is There A Monster in the Judicial Closet?" *Judicature* (December/January 1992), 216-21, 218-20. See also Hanson, Flango, and Hansen, *The Work of Appellate Court Legal Staff*, 54-55; Cohen, *Inside Appellate Courts*, 71.
18. Cohen, *Inside Appellate Courts*, 83-84. The time law clerks spend on procedural motions in state appeals courts is reported in Hanson, Flango, and Hansen, *The Work of Appellate Court Legal Staff*, 42.

19. Ruth Bader Ginsburg, "Workways of the Supreme Court," *Thomas Jefferson Law Review* (Summer, 2003), 517, 522.
20. H. W. Perry, *Deciding to Decide: Agenda Setting in the United States Supreme Court* (Cambridge: Harvard University Press, 1991), 272-77. See also S. Sidney Ulmer, "The Decision to Grant Certiorari as an Indicator to Decision 'On the Merits'" *Polity* 4 (1972), 429-47. See generally, Lee Epstein and Jack Knight, *The Choices Justices Make* (Washington, D.C.: CQ Press, 1998).
21. Paul Brace and Melinda Gann Hall, "'Haves' Versus 'Have Nots' in State Supreme Courts: Allocating Docket Space and Wins in Power Asymmetric Cases," *Law & Society Review* 35 (2001), 393, 409.
22. Jeff Yates, Andrew B. Whitford, and William Gillespie, "Agenda Setting, Issue Priorities and Organizational Maintenance: The U.S. Supreme Court, 1955 to 1994," *British Journal of Political Science* 35 (2005), 369-81.
23. Robert H. Jackson, "Advocacy Before the United States Supreme Court," *Cornell Law Quarterly* (Fall, 1951), 2. For an analysis of the legal norms of written and oral advocacy in the United States and England, see Suzanne Ehrenberg, "Embracing the Writing-Centered Legal Process," *Iowa Law Review* (April, 2004), 1159-99.
24. Frank M. Coffin, *On Appeal: Courts, Lawyering, and Judging* (New York: W. W. Norton, 1993), 107-08, 111-12.
25. Cohen, *Inside Appellate Courts*, 91-92, 101-05. See also Howard, *Courts of Appeals in the Federal Judicial System*, 198.
26. Ginsburg, "Workways of the Supreme Court," 522-25. See also Timothy R. Johnson, *Oral Arguments and Decision Making on the United States Supreme Court* (Albany: State University of New York Press, 2004).
27. David M. O'Brien, *Storm Center: The Supreme Court in American Politics,* 7th ed. (New York: W. W. Norton, 2005), 250-56. For an analysis of the dynamics underlying shifting judicial preferences, see J. Woodford Howard, Jr., "On the Fluidity of Judicial Choice," *American Political Science Review* (March, 1968), 43-56.
28. Ginsburg, "Workways of the Supreme Court," 526.
29. Timothy R. Johnson, James F. Spriggs II, and Paul J. Wahlbeck, "Passing and Strategic Voting on the U.S. Supreme Court," *Law & Society Review* (June 2005), 349-77.
30. Howard, *Courts of Appeals in the Federal Judicial System*, 208.
31. Ginsburg, "Workways of the Supreme Court," 526.
32. Lewis F. Powell, Jr., "What the Justices are Saying" *American Bar Association Journal* 62 (1976), 1454.
33. Justice Thomas is quoted in Corey Ditslear and Lawrence Baum, "Selection of Law Clerks and Polarization in the U.S. Supreme Court," *Journal of Politics* (August, 2001), 869, 883.
34. Normana Dorsen and Amelia Ames Newcomb, "John Marshall Harlan II, Associate Justice of the Supreme Court 1955-1971: Remembrances by his Law Clerks," *Journal of Supreme Court History* (July 2002), 138-75.

35. John P. Frank, *Marble Palace: The Supreme Court in American Life* (Westport: Greenwood Press, 1958), 116.

36. John C. Jeffries, Jr., *Justice Lewis F. Powell, Jr.* (New York: Charles Scribner's Sons, 1994), 294.

37. Hanson, Flango, and Hansen, *The Work of Appellate Court Legal Staff*, 39, 64–65. For a specific description of the various tasks law clerks perform, see Charles H. Sheldon, "Law Clerking with a State Supreme Court: Views from the Perspective of the Personal Assistants to the Judges," *Justice System Journal* 6 (1981), 346, 352 (Table 1).

38. David M. O'Brien, "The Dynamics of the Judicial Process," in *Judges on Judging: Views from the Bench,* 2nd ed. Edited by David M. O'Brien (Washington, D.C.: CQ Press, 2004), 45–46.

39. David M. O'Brien, "Institutional Norms and Supreme Court Opinions: On Reconsidering the Rise of Individual Opinions," in *Supreme Court Decision-Making: New Institutionalist Approaches,* edited Cornell W. Clayton and Howard Gillman (Chicago: University of Chicago Press, 1999), 113.

40. Cohen, *Inside Appellate Courts*, 74.

41. Thomas E. Baker, *Rationing Justice on Appeal: The Problems of the U.S. Courts of Appeals* (St. Paul: West's Publishing Co., 1994), 119.

42. Oliver Wendell Holmes, "The Path of the Law" *Harvard Law Review* 10 (1896), 43.

43. The distinction between normative and empirical theory is discussed in John B. Gates, "Theory, Methods, and the New Institutionalism in Judicial Research," in *The American Courts: A Critical Assessment,* edited by John B. Gates and Charles A. Johnson (Washington, D.C.: CQ Press, 1990), 469–70.

44. C. Herman Pritchett, *The Roosevelt Court: A Study in Judicial Politics and Values, 1937–1947* (New York: MacMillan Co., 1948).

45. See Nancy Maveety, "The Study of Judicial Behavior and the Discipline of Political Science," in *The Pioneers of Judicial Behavior,* edited by Nancy Maveety (Ann Arbor: University of Michigan Press, 2003), 9–17. See also Pritchett, *The Roosevelt Court*, xiii.

46. Jeffrey A. Segal, "Glendon Schubert: The Judicial Mind," in *The Pioneers of Judicial Behavior*, 80. See also Lawrence Baum, "C. Herman Pritchett: Innovator with an Ambiguous Legacy," in *The Pioneers of Judicial Behavior*, 57–77.

47. Segal, "Glendon Schubert," 80. See also Glendon A. Schubert, *The Judicial Mind: The Attitudes and Ideologies of Supreme Court Justices, 1946–1963* (Evanston: Northwestern University Press, 1965).

48. Segal, "Glendon Schubert," in *The Pioneers of Judicial Behavior*, 78–100. See also Glendon Schubert, *The Judicial Mind Revisited: Psychometric Analysis of Supreme Court Ideology* (New York: Oxford University Press, 1974).

49. Jeffrey A. Segal and Harold J. Spaeth, *The Supreme Court and the Attitudinal Model* (New York: Cambridge University Press, 1993).

50. Ibid., 65.
51. Jeffrey A. Segal and Harold J. Spaeth, *The Supreme Court and the Attitudinal Model Revisited* (Cambridge: Cambridge University Press, 2002). Various criticisms and rebuttals from political scientists and legal scholars concerning the merits and application of the attitudinal model are found in "Symposium: The Supreme Court and the Attitudinal Model," *Law and Courts Newsletter* (Spring, 1994), 3-12; "Symposium on the Supreme Court and the Attitudinal Model Revisited," *Law and Courts Newsletter* (Summer, 2003), 10-38.
52. Howard Gillman, "Separating the Wheat from the Chaff in the Supreme Court and the Attitudinal Model Revisited," *Law and Courts Newsletter* (Summer 2003), 14.
53. *Van Orden v. Perry*, 545 U.S. 677 (2005).
54. *McCreary v. American Civil Liberties Union of Kentucky*, 545 U.S. 844 (2005).
55. Rogers Smith M. "Political Jurisprudence, the 'New Institutionalism,' and the Future of Public Law," *American Political Science Review* 86 (1988), 89-108.
56. Cornell W. Clayton, "The Supreme Court and Political Jurisprudence: New and Old Institutionalisms," in *Supreme Court Decision-Making: New Institutionalist Approaches,* edited by Cornell W. Clayton and Howard Gillman (Chicago: University of Chicago Press, 1999), 15-41.
57. Clayton, "The Supreme Court and Political Jurisprudence," 35 ("patterns of purpose and meaning"); Rogers M. Smith, "Historical Institutionalism and Public Law," *Law and Courts Newsletter* (Summer 1998), 6-7.
58. *Supreme Court Decision-Making: New Institutionalist Approaches,* edited by Cornell W. Clayton and Howard Gillman (Chicago: University of Chicago Press, 1999); *The Supreme Court in American Politics: New Institutionalist Interpretations,* edited by Howard Gillman and Cornell Clayton (Lawrence: University Press of Kansas, 1999).
59. See Lee Epstein and Jack Knight, "The New Institutionalism, Part II," *Law and Courts Newsletter* (Spring 1997), 4-9; Howard Gillman, "Placing Judicial Motives in Context: A Response to Lee Epstein and Jack Knight," *Law and Courts Newsletter* (Spring, 1997), 10-13.
60. Walter Murphy, *The Elements of Judicial Strategy* (Chicago: University of Chicago Press, 1964), 207.
61. Lee Epstein and Jack Knight, "Toward a Strategic Revolution in Judicial Politics: A Look Back, A Look Ahead," *Political Research Quarterly* (September, 2000), 625-61.
62. Epstein and Knight, "The New Institutionalism, Part II," 4.
63. Forrest Maltzman, James F. Spriggs II, Paul J. Wahlbeck, *Crafting Law on the Supreme Court: The Collegial Game* (Cambridge: Cambridge University Press, 2000); Lee Epstein and Jack Knight, *The Choices Justices Make* (Washington, D.C.: CQ Press, 1998).
64. Harry T. Edwards, "The Judicial Function and the Elusive Goal of Principled Decisionmaking," *Wisconsin Law Review* (1991), 837, 838.

65. Edward H. Levi, *An Introduction to Legal Reasoning* (Chicago: University of Chicago Press, 1949), 1.

66. Levi, *An Introduction to Legal Reasoning*, 2, 4.

67. Benjamin N. Cardozo, *The Nature of the Judicial Process* (New Haven: Yale University Press, 1921), 16, 23, 28, 30-31.

68. *Roe v. Wade*, 410 U.S. 113 (1973). See also *Webster v. Reproductive Health Services*, 492 U.S. 490 (1989), 535 (Scalia, J., concurring in part).

69. *Planned Parenthood of Southeastern Pennsylvania v. Casey*, 505 U.S. 833 (1992).

70. Ibid., 846, 861, 866, 877-79.

71. *Burnett v. Coronado Oil and Gas Co.*, 285 U.S. 393, 406 (1932): (Brandeis, J., dissenting). See also William O. Douglas, "Stare Decisis," *Columbia Law Review* 49 (1949), 735.

72. Saul Brenner and Harold J. Spaeth, *Stare Indecisis: The Alteration of Precedent on the U.S. Supreme Court*, 1946-1992 (Cambridge: Cambridge University Press, 1995). See also David M. O'Brien, *Constitutional Law and Politics: Civil Rights and Civil Liberties (Volume Two)* 6th ed. (New York: W. W. Norton, 2005), 130.

73. *Payne v. Tennessee*, 501 U.S. 808 (1991), 828.

74. See, e.g., *Dickerson v. United States*, 530 U.S. 428 (2000), 443 ("special justification"); and *Planned Parenthood of Southeastern Pennsylvania v. Casey*, 864, "special reason." For a general statement of stare decisis principles, see *Planned Parenthood of Southeastern Pennsylvania v. Casey*, 854.

75. Cardozo, *The Nature of the Judicial Process*, 149; Robert C. Wigton, "What Does It Take to Overrule? An Analysis of Supreme Court Overrulings and the Doctrine of *Stare Decisis*," *Legal Studies Forum* 18 (1994), 3, 7-8.

76. *Payne v. Tennessee*, 501 U.S. 808 (1991), 844. See also See Christopher P. Banks, "The Supreme Court and Precedent: An Analysis of Natural Courts and Reversal Trends," *Judicature* (February/March 1992), 264-68, Tables 3, 4, 5; Douglas, "Stare Decisis," 736-37.

77. James F. Spriggs II and Thomas G. Hansford, "Explaining the Overruling of U.S. Supreme Court Precedent," *Journal of Politics* (November, 2001), 1091-1111.

78. *P.G.A. Tour, Inc. v. Martin*, 532 U.S. 661, 691 (2001) (Scalia, J., dissenting).

79. *P.G.A. Tour*, 691.

80. See John Paul Stevens, "The Shakespeare Canon of Statutory Construction," *University of Pennsylvania Law Review* 140 (1992), 1373-87.

81. Felix Frankfurter, "Some Reflections on the Reading of Statutes," in *Judges on Judging: Views from the Bench*, 2nd ed, edited by David M. O'Brien (Washington, D.C.: CQ Press, 2003), 248.

82. Stephen Breyer, "On the Uses of Legislative History in Interpreting Statutes," *Southern California Law Review* 65 (1992), 845, 848.

83. Abner J. Mikva, "Reading and Writing Statutes," *University of Pittsburg Law Review* (1987), 627, 629.

84. As quoted by Abner. J. Mikva, "Statutory Interpretation: Getting the Law to Be Less Common," *Ohio State Law Journal* 50 (1989), 979, 981.

85. O'Brien, "The Judiciary and Federal Regulation," in *Judges on Judging*, 242.

86. *Schechter Poultry Corporation v. United States*, 295 U.S. 495 (1935); *Panama Refining Co. v. Ryan*, 293 U.S. 388 (1935).

87. *National Labor Relations Board v. Jones & Laughlin Steel Corporation*, 301 U.S. 1 (1937); *West Coast Hotel Company v. Parrish*, 300 U.S. 379 (1937).

88. *Chevron v. Natural Resources Defense Council*, 467 U.S. 837 (1984); *Vermont Yankee Nuclear Power Corporation v. Natural Resources Defense Council*, 435 U.S. 519 (1978).

89. Christopher P. Banks. "Ideology and Judicial Deference in the D.C.. Circuit" *Southeastern Political Review* (December, 1998), 861-88. See also Kiki Caurson and J. Michael Bitzer, "At the Crossroads of Policymaking: Executive Politics, Administrative Action, and Judicial Deference by the D.C. Circuit Court of Appeals (1985-1996)," *Law & Policy* (October, 2004), 347-69.

90. *McCulloch v. Maryland*, 17 U.S. 316 (1819).

91. *Lochner v. New York*, 198 U.S. 45 (1905).

92. *Buck v. Bell*, 274 U.S. 200 (1927).

93. *Brown v. Board of Education*, 347 U.S. 483 (1954).

94. *Roe v. Wade*, 410 U.S. 113 (1973).

95. Edwin Meese III, "Speech Before the American Bar Association, July 9, 1985, Washington, D.C.," in *The Great Debate: Interpreting Our Written Constitution* (Washington, D.C.: The Federalist Society, 1986), 1.

96. Farber, Daniel A. and Suzanna Sherry, *Desperately Seeking Certainty: The Misguided Quest for Constitutional Foundations* (Chicago: University of Chicago Press, 2002), 11.

97. Antonin Scalia, "Common-Law Courts in a Civil-Law System," in *A Matter of Interpretation: Federal Courts and the Law* edited by Antonin Scalia (Princeton: Princeton University Press, 1997). 38.

98. William H. Rehnquist, "The Notion of a Living Constitution," *Texas Law Review* 54 (1976), 693, 699. Antonin Scalia, "Originalism: The Lesser Evil," *Cincinnati Law Review* 57 (1989), 849, 854-55, 862.

99. William J. Brennan, "The Constitution of the United States: Contemporary Ratification," in *Interpreting Law and Literature: A Hermeneutic Reader*, edited by Sanford Levinson and Steven Mailloux (Evanston: Northwestern University Press, 1988), 17-18.

100. *Lochner v. New York*, 198 U.S. 45 (1905) (Holmes, J., dissenting).

101. *Brown v. Board of Education*, 347 U.S. 483 (1954).

102. *Miranda v. Arizona*, 384 U.S. 436 (1966).

103. *Miller-El v. Dretke*, 545 U.S. 231 (2005).

104. *Atkins v. Virginia*, 536 U.S. 304 (2002); *Lawrence v. Texas*, 539 U.S. 558 (2003).

CHAPTER TEN

The Scope and Limits of Judicial Power

In *Federalist* No. 78 Alexander Hamilton defended judicial independence by arguing that courts are the least dangerous branch. In response to Anti-Federalists, opponents to the Constitution favoring states' rights, Hamilton countered that courts were less powerful than the executive or legislative institutions because the judiciary possessed "neither force nor will, but merely judgment."[1] Hamilton argued that judicial discretion was relatively harmless because its exercise was constrained by democratic politics and the judicial obligation to uphold the rule of law. As a result, the misuse of judicial authority was unlikely. In light of those checks, courts would, arguably, strike an appropriate balance between the competing demands of respecting majority will and protecting minority rights.

Still, judges are routinely attacked for legislating from the bench. The Supreme Court's reluctance to endorse school prayer, but upholding gay rights, affirmative action plans, and partial birth abortions have intensified the political drive to curb judicial power. For example, a state court's refusal to prevent the removal of the feeding tube sustaining Terri Schiavo's life in Florida in 2005 prompted some conservative politicians to lash out at the third branch. Senator Tom Coburn (R-Ok.), for one, embraced a radical approach to reduce judicial interference by bluntly declaring, "I'm in favor of mass impeachment if that's what it takes."[2] In the states, similar political opposition has led to reform proposals and new legislation seeking to diminish judicial influence over public policies favoring school vouchers, cutting funding to public schools, and preventing same-sex marriages.

On the federal level, repeated calls to increase legislative oversight over courts and judges have been made. In 2005, Representative James Sensenbrenner (R-WI.) sought to create an office of inspector general as a watchdog to keep judges in check and accountable to popular will. Other legislative solutions include diminishing court funding; stripping the courts of jurisdiction to hear certain cases, such as over abortion, pledge of allegiance, or religious displays; and, in addition to impeachment, expediting the removal of judges that are found guilty of violating their obligation to exhibit "good behavior" in office.[3] These attacks have been a part of a growing nationwide effort to block the implementation of majoritarian political preferences.

This chapter considers the scope and limitations of judicial authority by examining the political struggles over judicial policymaking. The first section provides a brief overview of judicial policymaking by illustrating how courts are agents of political change in state school funding and federal abortion cases. Next, the impact of judicial policymaking is considered in the context of homosexual rights in the aftermath of *Lawrence v. Texas*,[4] and the corresponding struggle to institute same-sex marriages. The concluding section outlines the internal and external restraints on judicial power and explores whether courts are institutionally capable of forging major social change.

JUDICIAL POLICYMAKING

Although Justice Benjamin Cardozo acknowledged that judges have discretion to make law, he nonetheless admonished that a judge "is not to innovate at pleasure" as "a knight-errant roaming at will in pursuit of his own ideal of beauty or of goodness."[5] Critics aiming to limit judicial power typically attack courts and their exercise of judicial review for the following interrelated reasons: (1) for making "unprincipled" decisions (those not based on established rules of law); (2) for making social policy decisions exceeding judicial capacity or competence; and (3) that, on the federal level, for "legislating from the bench" by functioning as *countermajoritarian institutions* (courts staffed by unelected judges serving life terms) that cannot be directly held accountable by the people.[6]

Courts have been attacked for being creative policymakers in certain areas of the law, such as school desegregation, prisoner rights, and freedom of speech cases. But defenders counter that courts are simply part of the policymaking process, not leaders of it. In effect, they perform as administrators of legal policy by generating and implementing solutions to problems after weighing different policy alternatives.[7] The debate over the scope of their authority is exemplified by two controversial topics of social policy: state school-funding cases and abortion rights' policy under federal law.

State Judicial Policymaking: Equality in Educational Financing Cases

In ruling that separate educational facilities are unconstitutional, *Brown v. Board of Education* (1954) stressed that "education is perhaps the most important function of state and local governments, ... [in part because] it is the very foundation of good citizenship." As Chief Justice Earl Warren explained, "it is doubtful that any child may reasonably be expected to succeed in life if he is denied the opportunity of an education, [and] such an opportunity, where the state has undertaken to provide it, is a right which must be made available to all on equal terms."[8] By the 1970s, state supreme courts began to test the scope of *Brown's* equality principle in school financing litigation.

In *Serrano v. Priest* (1971),[9] the Supreme Court of California struck down the state's system of public school funding on the grounds that it deprived students of a "fundamental right" of education based in the Fourteenth Amendment's equal protection clause. Specifically, the state overrelied on local property taxes to fund public schools and that policy created disparities in expenditures that discriminated against the poor living in underfunded school districts. In *Robinson v. Cahill* (1972), the New Jersey Supreme Court likewise nullified the state's financing scheme. But, unlike *Serrano*, the court reasoned that it did not satisfy the state constitution's obligation to provide for a "thorough and efficient" system of education for citizens.[10]

The movement toward reforming state public school funding on the basis of the federal constitution's equal protection guaranty was abruptly halted, however, by the Supreme Court's decision in *San Antonio Independent School District v. Rodriguez* (1973).[11] In a 5:4 ruling, the justices turned back the challenge of Hispanic students living in urban districts with a low property tax base. The equal protection clause, the Court declared, did not make education a "fundamental right." In reaching this conclusion, the Court used the *rational basis test* (determining whether the state had a rational, or reasonable, basis for funding state courts in the manner they chose) in deference to the states' interest in maintaining local control over educational policy.[12] In short, the Court exercised judicial restraint in refusing to make substantive choices about the proper direction of educational policy, a traditional province of the states.

Still, despite its holding, *Rodriguez* produced more litigation. Between 1973 and 2002, forty-four states faced legal challenges to their education finance systems. In several early cases, the state courts looked to the equal protection clauses in their state constitutions to invalidate inequitable school funding mechanisms. But they did not specify how to design plans that would overcome the constitutional problem. In other states, some popular assemblies struggled to equalize resources but found it impracticable to do so. As a result, the initially favorable rulings for challenges to state school-funding systems in the 1970s gave way to a series of defeats in the 1980s. By 1989, fifteen state supreme courts had denied relief, whereas only seven other high courts granted it.[13]

Yet, reformers continued to press through litigation to achieve equality in state financing for public schools on state constitutional grounds but by stressing the "adequacy" of educational resources instead of "equity." Whereas *equity lawsuits* pushed for the elimination of wealth disparities by equalizing the amount of resources distributed to all districts, *adequacy lawsuits* sought better opportunities on the basis of demonstrable standards of academic performance. In doing so, state courts interpreted state constitutions that range from guaranteeing a "system of free common schools" to providing a "thorough and efficient" or "adequate public education" as the basis for reform. Simply put, all students must have a reasonable chance to get an "adequate" education and whether they received one was measured by student achievement through performance standards. Although the state supreme courts in New Jersey, Washington, and West Virginia nullified state education financing systems on the basis of inadequacy, it was not until the Kentucky Supreme Court's decision in *Rose v. Council for Better Education* (1989) that the adequacy reform movement in state courts reached its full potential.[14]

Unlike most other high courts that struggled to define "adequacy" of educational resources, *Rose* established specific standards to measure if students were achieving an "efficient" education: whether, for example, they were taught effective oral and written communication skills or gained a sufficient understanding of government, the arts, or vocational skills. Significantly, the reliance on standards as a measure of adequacy was, in part, developed from the findings by various commissions and studies that were initiated in the federal government and states in the aftermath of *Rodriguez*. Once liability was determined, many of the guidelines originating from *Rose* resulted from the trial court judge's decision to "stay" judgment in the case for the purpose of conducting a thorough investigation about how to devise a remedy.[15]

During the six-month stay, the trial judge appointed a select committee to construct a remedy to fix the problem of insufficient school resources. After five highly publicized hearings across the state, the commission recommended standards that were ultimately adopted by the Kentucky Supreme Court. Thereafter, the legislature enacted the Kentucky Education Reform Act, prompting one commentator to hail *Rose* as the "starting point in what has become a significant dialogue among the public, the courts, and the legislature on standards-based reform."[16] The focus on adequacy and intergovernmental cooperation has had significant consequences for other jurisdictions. Between 1989 and 2002, plaintiffs won eighteen of twenty-eight of the school financing cases filed in state supreme courts. As of early 2005, The Education Commission of the States reported that thirty-two adequacy lawsuits were commenced and, of those claims, fourteen found violations of state constitutions, seven delivered judgments favoring defendants, four were settled out of court, six cases were still pending, and only one case was withdrawn.[17]

In all likelihood, state supreme courts will remain at the forefront of shaping local education financing policy for years to come. The trend has been fueled, in part, by the No Child Left Behind Act, performance-based federal legislation signed into law by President George W. Bush in January, 2002, and Congress's reauthorization of the Elementary and Secondary Act of 1965 shortly thereafter. New litigation testing the limits of judicial activism in educational policy was somewhat inevitable in light of the economic consequences of 9/11 and the resultant failure of local governments to meet their funding obligations under the new federal legislation, a problem exacerbated by overburdened fiscal economies experiencing budget shortfalls.

Sidebar 10.1

Judicial Activism and Restraint

Although the terms *judicial activism* and *judicial restraint* are often used to describe court behavior, their meaning fluctuates with the prevailing political climate.[a] Generally, an *activist court* means that its rulings are deviating or overturning established legal principles and "legislating from the bench." By contrast, a *restrained court* is thought of adhering to precedent and not engaging in social policymaking. Often, but mistakenly, "conservative" courts are viewed as exemplifying restraint, whereas "liberal" courts are branded "activist." Yet, history and contemporary examples show such labels are misleading. The liberal Roosevelt–New Deal Court of the 1930s–1940s favored judicial restraint in order to uphold progressive governmental reform. In contrast, the conservative Rehnquist Court (1986–2005) aggressively overturned or undercut long-established precedents in federalism, criminal procedure, and congressional power.

Although some legal scholars offer similar guidelines,[b] political scientist Bradley Canon created a framework to understand "judicial activism" by assigning it certain "dimensions." The six dimensions are as follows:[c]

1. *Majoritarianism:* the degree to which policies adopted through democratic processes are judicially negated;
2. *Interpretive Stability:* the degree to which earlier court decisions, doctrines, or interpretations, are altered;
3. *Interpretative Fidelity:* the degree to which constitutional provisions are interpreted contrary to the clear intentions of their drafters or the clear implications of the language used;
4. *Substance/Democratic Process Distinction:* the degree to which judicial decisions make substantive policy rather than affect the preservation of democratic political processes;
5. *Specificity of Policy:* the degree to which a judicial decision establishes policy itself as opposed to leaving discretion to other agencies or individuals;
6. *Availability of an Alternate Policymaker:* the degree to which a judicial decision supersedes serious consideration of the same problem by other governmental agencies.

Although Canon's framework is helpful, judicial activism is a "notoriously slippery"[d] term that cannot be easily applied to judicial practice. Virtually any act of judicial discretion can be described as activist, including those decisions striking down democratically enacted statutes, rulings departing from precedent, or specific results in cases that are politically unpopular. Although activism is often used as a term to attack a court's decision making, on occasion it is invoked to describe the judiciary's role in protecting fundamental civil rights and liberties.[e] What is activist, then, is uncertain because the act of judicial interpretation, and how it is perceived, are invariably ambiguous because the "words [a judge] must construe are empty vessels into which he can pour nearly anything he will."[f]

Notes

[a]See, e.g., Herman Schwartz and Bruce Fein, "The Supreme Court: Is the Rehnquist Court 'Activist'?" *American Bar Association Journal* (August, 1990), 32–33.

[b]Ernest A. Young, "Judicial Activism and Conservative Politics," *University of Colorado Law Review* (Fall, 2002), 1139, 1144.

[c]Bradley C. Canon, "Defining the Dimensions of Judicial Activism," *Judicature* (December/January 1983), 236, 239.

[d]Frank H. Easterbrook, "Do Liberals and Conservatives Differ in Judicial Activism?" *Colorado Law Review* (Fall, 2002), 1401.

[e]Keenan D. Kmiec, "The Origin and Current Meanings of 'Judicial Activism,'" *California Law Review* (October, 2004), 1441, 1463–77.

[f]Learned Hand, "Sources of Tolerance," *University of Pennsylvania Law Review* 79 (1930), 1, 11–12.

Federal Judicial Policymaking: Privacy Rights and Abortion Politics

Although it is often taken for granted as a basic freedom, the U.S. Constitution does not explicitly make reference to a right to privacy. Yet, in *Boyd v. United States* (1886),[18] a search and seizure case, the Supreme Court acknowledged privacy as part of the Fourth and Fifth Amendments. Thereafter, state courts began to recognize privacy as well. By 1960, the right to privacy was recognized in over thirty states.[19] By the midtwentieth century, the Supreme Court also extended the right under the Fourteenth Amendment's due process clause to protect against governmental interference in areas of child rearing and, later, to reproductive rights and marriage interests. In *Pierce v. Society of Sisters* (1925),[20] the Court struck down a state law requiring parents to send their children to public instead of private schools, reasoning that it restricted parental freedom to rear and educate offspring. Although *Buck v. Bell* (1927)[21] upheld a Virginia law authorizing the compulsory sterilization of mentally challenged individuals, in *Skinner v. Oklahoma* (1942)[22] the Court nullified a state law allowing for the sterilization of "habitual criminals." Several years later, interracial marriages were legally sanctioned by the reversal of a state miscegenation law in *Loving v. Virginia* (1967).[23]

Even though these precedents created a protected sphere of privacy interests in certain contexts, a constitutional right of privacy was not established until *Griswold v. Connecticut* (1965).[24] There, a physician and the executive director of the Planned Parenthood League of Connecticut were prosecuted for dispensing contraceptives to a married couple in violation of state law. In a 7:2 decision written by Justice William O. Douglas, the Court invalidated the state law and proclaimed a constitutional right to privacy based on the penumbras or shadows of several guarantees in the Bill of Rights. Justice Douglas explained that:

> [s]pecific guarantees in the Bill of Rights have penumbras, formed by emanations from those guarantees that help give them life and substance. . . . Various guarantees create zones of privacy. The right of association contained in the penumbra of the First Amendment is one. . . The Third Amendment in its prohibition against the quartering of soldiers 'in any house' in time of peace without the consent of the owner is another facet of that privacy. The Fourth Amendment explicitly affirms the 'right of the people to be secure in their persons, houses, papers, and effects, against unreasonable searches and seizures.' The Fifth Amendment in its Self-Incrimination Clause enables the citizen to create a zone of privacy which government may not force him to surrender to his detriment. The Ninth Amendment provides: 'The enumeration in the Constitution, of certain rights, shall not be construed to deny or disparage others retained by the people.'[25]

In dissent, however, Justices Hugo Black and Potter Stewart countered that the Court was acting like a superlegislature in creating a right to privacy and exercising "unbounded judicial authority would make of this Court's members a day-to-day constitutional convention."[26]

Griswold had implications for other areas of privacy and reproductive rights as well. *Eisenstadt v. Baird* (1972)[27] held that *Griswold* and the Fourteenth Amendment's equal protection guaranty applied in striking down a Massachusetts law outlawing the use of contraceptives by unmarried persons. In Justice William J. Brennan's words, "If the right to privacy means anything, it is the right of the *individual*, married or single, to be free from unwarranted governmental intrusion into matters so fundamentally affecting a person as the decision whether to bear or beget a child."[28] *Eisenstadt* helped set the stage for the Court's announcement in *Roe v. Wade* (1973)[29] that women have a constitutional right to have an abortion.[30]

The movement to liberalize abortion laws prior to *Roe*, ironically, was a return to earlier jurisprudence before the Civil War. By the midnineteenth century, most states permitted abortions until the first movement of the fetus, or "quickening"; and in jurisdictions criminalizing it, abortions were generally minor transgressions. In light of growing pressure by the medical profession and antiabortionists, states ratcheted up penalties and enforcement. By 1910, all states except Kentucky made abortions a felony, and a majority authorized them when it was necessary to save the mother's life. Still, in the 1960s and 1970s, the trend had begun to reverse itself as a minority of states condoned abortions in other circumstances, such as when the pregnancy was the result of a rape or incest, or when there was a likelihood of fetal abnormality. Four jurisdictions—Hawaii, Alaska, New York, and Washington—went so far as to abolish criminal penalties for abortions performed in the early stages of pregnancy.[31]

Roe struck down Texas's criminal abortion statute on the grounds that it violated a women's constitutional right to privacy. Specifically, it compromised a pregnant mother's "liberty" interest to have an abortion under the Fourteenth Amendment's due process clause. In writing for the majority, Justice Harry Blackmun reasoned that government did not have a sufficient "compelling interest" to completely ban abortions. Instead, it had the power to regulate abortions more intensively as the pregnancy progressed to term. As a result, under the so-called trimester approach, women and their physicians retained an absolute right to abort in the first three months of the pregnancy. In the second trimester, up to the point of viability (between twenty-four and twenty-eight weeks—the time a fetus could sustain life outside of the womb) states could regulate abortions in order to protect maternal health. After viability, or in the third and last stage of pregnancy, states had a compelling interest to preserve fetal life and, accordingly, retained the authority to limit or ban abortions, except when necessary to save a woman's life.

Although overshadowed by President Lyndon B. Johnson's death a day before *Roe* was announced, the ruling ignited a firestorm of controversy. A majority of states and the federal government rewrote their abortion laws in light of *Roe*. Some state jurisdictions tailored their legislation to conform to the Court's ruling, but many others either left their pre-*Roe* laws in place or began to restrict the availability of abortions severely. New laws were passed on the state or federal level restricting or eliminating abortion funding when the procedure was not medically necessary, prohibiting abortions in public hospitals, requiring spousal or parental (for a minor) informed consent before having abortions, requiring fetal lung and maturity tests, imposing mandatory waiting periods, and banning advertisements for abortion clinics.[32]

Anti-*Roe* sentiments framed the Christian evangelical movement and Republican platforms during the Reagan presidency as well as the administrations of George H. W. Bush and George W. Bush. In addition, abortion politics fueled battles over federal judicial appointments to the bench as manifested by the politicization of the President Reagan's 1987 nomination of D.C. Circuit appeals court judge Robert Bork. Bork, who was widely regarded as the new "swing vote" in replacing Justice Lewis Powell, generated intense interest group and media coverage because Bork had not only publicly denounced *Roe* but had also intimated that he would vote to overturn it. As a result, Bork and the abortion issue polarized the nation. In the end, the pro-choice groups mobilized faster and better than their conservative counterparts, and they were instrumental in defeating Bork's claim to the bench. Afterward, President Reagan appointed Anthony Kennedy, a more moderate Ninth Circuit appeals court judge, and he was easily confirmed by the Senate in 1987.[33] Ironically, Justice Kennedy would come to play a key role in voting to uphold *Roe* in a pivotal challenge to its holding several years later.

The changing composition of the bench and the shift to the right in the 1980s and 1990s led the Court to revisit *Roe* several times. But thus far a majority of the justices have elected to retain the basic right to have an abortion. An unusual joint opinion by Justices Sandra Day O'Connor, David Souter, and Anthony

Kennedy, in *Planned Parenthood of Southeastern Pennsylvania v. Casey* (1992),[34] reaffirmed *Roe's* "essential holding." Women still enjoyed the freedom to terminate a pregnancy up to the point of a fetus's viability. The ruling was based on two underlying factors. First, the Court feared its legitimacy would suffer if *Roe* was reversed under political pressure. Second, *Roe* was upheld as a legal precedent that citizens relied upon as an enduring principle of personal autonomy.

Still, *Roe* was considerably weakened because the Court jettisoned its trimester and *strict scrutiny analysis* and introduced a new, less rigorous standard, the *undue burden test*. Under the undue burden test, restrictive antiabortion legislation is upheld if it does not place a substantial obstacle in the path of women seeking to exercise the right. Consequently, although *Roe* remains the law of the land, *Casey* undermined it considerably since its effect is to allow for greater antiabortion limitations that substantially burden a woman's right to choose but that still pass constitutional muster.

Although the Court appeared to try to end the abortion controversy in *Casey*, the controversy remains hotly contested and politically explosive. As Yale law professor Jack Balkin observed, the Court's efforts to settle the question of abortion rights "has proved to be little more than wishful thinking."[35] A recurring issue, for example, is the constitutionality of parental notification laws for to minors seeking abortions. In majority of states, minors must notify their parents or obtain their consent before having one, though they may also go to court and receive a judge's permission. One state, New Hampshire, outlawed abortions for minors unless their parents were given notice in writing forty-eight hours in advance of the procedure. But the law was challenged because it did not explicitly permit a physician to perform an abortion in a medical emergency without parental notification. In *Ayotte v. Planned Parenthood of Northern New England* (2006),[36] a unanimous Roberts Court did not decide the matter but instead returned the case to the lower courts to reconsider whether the nullification of the law in its entirety was appropriate.

In addition, over one-half of the states have so-called late-term or partial-birth abortion bans on certain medical procedures; some apply through a pregnancy and at least eighteen have been judicially nullified.[37] By a 5:4 vote, the Court in *Stenberg v. Carhart* (2000)[38] overturned Nebraska's law. Yet, President Bush signed the Partial-Birth Abortion Ban Act of 2003, under which doctors are prohibited from performing partial birth abortions except when the mother's life, but not her health, is in jeopardy. That law was invalidated by federal appellate courts, but the administration appealed those decisions to the Supreme Court in *Gonzalez v. Carhart* and *Gonzalez v. Planned Parenthood Federation of America*, which were granted review in 2006.[39]

Finally, new reproductive technologies, such as RU486 (the abortion pill), cloning, and stem cell research, continue to keep the issue on national and judicial agendas. Abortion politics is now a central issue in the federal judicial nomination and confirmation process as well. The growing politicalization of the federal bench, along with the overarching issue of where new nominees stand on the abortion issue, will persist and intensify in light of Justice Sandra Day O'Connor's retirement and William Rehnquist's death, which led to the elevation of D.C. Circuit Judge John Roberts to chief justice and to circuit judge Samuel Alito's appointment as associate justice. New efforts to restrict or ban abortion rights will continue apace. In early 2006, for example, the South Dakota legislature enacted a law imposing a ban on all abortions except to save the life of the woman.[40] Challenges to the constitutionality of such restrictions are certain to fuel the controversy and return it to the Supreme Court.

In Comparative Perspective

The European Court of Justice and The Globalization of Judicial Power

The European Court of Justice (ECJ), formally known as the Court of Justice for the European Union, was created in 1957. Along with the Council of Ministers, the European Commission, the European Parliament, and later the Court of Auditors, the ECJ was created to promote the goal of economic integration in Western Europe. The ECJ's role is to create a uniform system of law—once referred to as European Community (EC) law and now as European Union (EU) law. Originally, only six countries—Belgium, France, West Germany, Italy, Luxembourg, and the Netherlands—participated. But subsequently, other countries joined. In 1973, Denmark, Ireland, and Britain became members, followed by Greece in 1981, and Portugal and Spain in 1986. In 1995, Austria, Finland, and Sweden joined, bringing the total number in the EU to fifteen. In 2004, then, the largest expansion occurred with the addition of ten other Central and East European countries—Cyprus (Greek Territory), the Czech Republic, Estonia, Hungary, Latvia, Lithuania, Malta, Poland, Slovakia, and Slovenia. The EU continues to debate the adoption of a treaty establishing a constitution for the European Union, melding and replacing prior treaties, which will likely to reinforce the role and supremacy of the ECJ.

The European Court of Justice, located in Luxembourg, is independent and composed of fifteen justices—one justice recommended by each country and appointed by unanimous approval of all member states. There are also six advocates general. The justices and advocates general serve six-year staggered and renewable terms. The justices also vow not to consider national interests in making their decisions. All decisions of the ECJ are unanimous, no dissenting opinions are issued, and even opinions announcing the decisions are not signed by individual justices.

Cases may be filed before the ECJ by other EU institutions, member states, or "directly affected" EU citizens. Most of the ECJ's caseload, though, come as reference

(Article 177) cases from member states' national courts that ask for preliminary rulings on EU law that the ECJ has not yet determined; the ECJ receives approximately 200 cases per year under its reference jurisdiction. Since its inception, the ECJ's caseload has grown steadily. As a result, in 1998 a court of first instance was created in order to ease the ECJ's workload and backlog of cases. Still, in the 1990s the ECJ annually handed down about 300 decisions and took, on average, two to three years to decide each case.

The ECJ has been compared with the U.S. Supreme Court in the early nineteenth century under Chief Justice John Marshall, whose rulings striking down state taxes, trade barriers, and other regulations under the interstate commerce clause promoted an economic common market and solidified the Court's power of judicial review. Some critics of the ECJ complain that it has become too activist, indeed even more activist than the Marshall Court, because it turned the Treaty of Rome into a kind of constitution that gives it the power of constitutional review. Notably, EU member states may overturn an ECJ decision interpreting a treaty provision but only by revising the treaty and that requires the unanimous consent of all member states.

During the 1960s and 1970s, the ECJ laid the groundwork with precedents promoting the value of European integration. By the 1980s and 1990s the ECJ had not only established its power of judicial review but also (1) the supremacy of EU law over that of member states' legislation, in holding that national courts of the EU must always interpret their own laws to be in conformity with EU laws; (2) the competence and superiority of EU institutions over areas, such as environmental protection and human rights, that the treaties were originally silent about; and (3) expanded the legal policy areas over which it exercises jurisdiction by expanding standing for private parties to sue on the basis of treaty provisions and acts of EU institutions that require implementing legislation. For instance, the ECJ ruled that national courts have the power to declare EU acts valid (but not invalid) within their countries.[a] The ECJ also held that a national court must refuse to enforce a national law or statute that contravenes EU laws while questions concerning the compatibility of the national law and EU law are pending before the ECJ, thereby mandating judicial review.[b]

In addition, initially EU law based on treaties contained few provisions for dealing with individual rights. Yet, the ECJ's decisions on citizens' standing to sue when "directly affected" by EU law expanded its jurisdiction over member states' legislation and power to strike down legislation contravening EU law and its decisions. As a result, the ECJ moved not only in the direction of promoting an economic common market but also toward developing human rights on the basis of the doctrines of the "direct effect"—the *direct effects doctrine*—and the supremacy of EU law. For example, in *J. Nord, Kohlen und Baustoffengroßhandlung v. Commission on the European Communities*,[c] the ECJ invoked an international treaty, the European Convention for the Protection of Human Rights, in addition to the constitutions of member states, as sources for its declaration of fundamental rights.

Paralleling the U.S. Supreme Court's incorporation of guarantees of the Bill of Rights into the Fourteenth Amendment and application of them to the states, the ECJ also "discovered" fundamental rights in the constitutions and treaties of member states.[d] As noted above, the ECJ also requires member states' national courts to always interpret their own laws in ways that conform to EU laws—the so-called *indirect effects doctrine*. Moreover, the ECJ has enforced human rights principles against not only member states but also corporations and private parties in the EU.[e]

Observers and scholars disagree over how to explain the expansion of the ECJ's power of judicial review and role in forging European legal integration. Some consider the expansion of the ECJ's power as inevitable given its treatment of EU treaties as though they are a "higher law" constitution. Others argue that the ECJ's role has grown as part of the so-called trend toward the globalization of judicial power in the latter half of the twentieth century as a result of pressures for greater economic and legal integration (see the In Comparative Perspective boxes in chapters 2, 4, and 6).

More specifically, legal scholars and political scientists have advanced the following four different and competing explanations for the expanding power of the ECJ: (1) a legalist explanation, (2) a neorealist explanation, (3) a neofunctionalist explanation, and (4) an intercourt competition explanation.

The legalist explanation for the ECJ's expanding power and role maintains that EU law, like other countries' supreme courts and constitutional law, has an inherent logic. It creates a kind of internal dynamic by building on precedents and expanding the role of the ECJ in promoting integration and compelling member states' courts to comply with and apply the ECJ's decisions. In other words, the ECJ's rulings have authoritative legal force and over time they have transformed the legal and political context of the integration of Europe.[f]

Political scientist Martin Shapiro and others, however, have criticized this legalist explanation of the ECJ's role in European integration as "constitutional law without politics" because the ECJ is presented "as a juristic concept; the written constitution (the treaty) as a sacred text; the professional commentary as a legal truth; the case law as the inevitable working out of the correct implications of the constitutional text; and the constitutional court (the ECJ) as the disembodied voice of right reason and constitutional teleology."[g] In short, critics of the legalist explanation argue that it amounts to legal formalism. It omits the role of politicians, the member states, and other political forces in complying with and reinforcing the ECJ's decisions through a series of successive treaties, legislation, and ultimately a constitution for the EU.

By contrast, *neorealists* argue that ECJ and the national courts' decisions are shaped by EU member states' national self-interests in economic integration. They underscore that courts are subject to external political pressures and reprisals if they go too far and too fast with their rulings; for example, courts may be manipulated through judicial appointments, changes in jurisdiction, overruling of their decisions by legislation and constitutional amendments, as well as noncompliance with their rulings. Both G. Garrett and Barry Weingast stated that[h]

> [e]mbedding a legal system in a broader political structure places direct constraints
> on the discretion of a court, even one with as much constitutional independence

as the United States Supreme Court. This conclusion holds even if the constitution makes no explicit provisions for altering a court's role. The reason is that political actors have a range of avenues through which they may alter or limit the role of courts. . . . The principal conclusion . . . is that the *possibility of such a reaction drives a court that wishes to preserve its independence and legitimacy to remain in the arena of acceptable latitude.*

Courts, to be sure, are constrained by external political pressures and by their environment. But all political institutions are subject to political and legal constraints and restraints, so it remains unclear whether neorealists explain that much. Moreover, critics of the neorealist theory counter that it fails to demonstrate precisely how national self-interests are constituted and how political pressures have influences on the ECJ's decisions. Neorealists also have been criticized for neglecting political opposition to the ECJ's and the national courts' decisions promoting integration. In addition, in contrast to the legalist theory, the neorealist position appears to amount to "politics without constitutional law."

A third, *neofunctionalist*, explanation emphasizes the self-interests of litigants, judges on national courts and the ECJ as well as other EU institutions in incrementally promoting integration and thereby reinforcing the ECJ's role and decisions. In other words, the ECJ and its rulings created incentive structures and a context for entrenching its role through economic and legal integration. EU citizens received new rights and the basis for pursuing their interests through litigation and EU integration; national courts enhanced their prestige by practicing judicial review and referring cases to the ECJ; and lawyers practicing EU law received more business through the continuing expansion of EU law. As A. M. Burley and Walter Mattli explained: "The Court . . . created . . . opportunities, providing incentives for individual litigants, their lawyers, and lower national courts to participate in the construction of the community legal system. In the process, it enhanced its own power and the professional interests of all parties participating directly or indirectly in its business."[i] In sum, like the legalists, neofunctionalists emphasize the role of the rule of law, but they—unlike the legalists—explain the political acquiescence in the ECJ's power in terms of a process of incremental legal integration that "upgrades common interests" of individuals and institutions in the EU. The EU's legal integration, however, has not been entirely mutually advantageous; the supremacy of national high courts, for instance, has been overridden by the ECJ and the supremacy of EU law.

Finally, a fourth and related explanation underscores the ECJ's and national courts' *intercourt competition* in promoting legal integration and thereby buttresses the role of the ECJ. A variant of the theory of bureaucratic politics, the intercourt competition explanation emphasizes that courts, like other bureaucracies, pursue their own interests within the constraints imposed by other political institutions, judicial hierarchies, and legal rules. Highlighting the different positions of member states' lower and higher courts in relation to the ECJ, Karen Alter argued that "The inter-court competition explanation claims that different courts have different interests *vis-a-vis* EC law, and that national courts use EC law in bureaucratic struggles between levels of the judiciary and between the judiciary and political bodies, thereby inadvertently facilitating the process of legal integration."[j] Alter further explains that[k]

> [b]ecause of the actions of lower courts, EC law expanded and EC law came to influence national jurisprudence.... [T]he actions of the lower courts came to actually shift the national legal context from under the high courts. Lower courts eventually ignored higher court attempts to limit the reach of EC law, making references to the ECJ anyway and applying EC law.... At a certain point it became clear that obstruction higher courts had failed to block the expansion and application of EC law within the national legal system, so that continued opposition created legal inconsistencies, and limited the high court's ability to influence legal interpretation at all....

Ultimately, each of these competing explanations provide insights, and they are not necessarily mutually exclusive. Together, they go a long way toward explaining different aspects of the expansion of the ECJ's power and legal integration in the EU. With the EU's new constitution, and specifically its charter for fundamental rights, the ECJ's constitution would appear likely to continue to grow and become further entrenched.

Notes

[a]*Firma Foto-Frost v. Hauptzollant Lubeck-Ost*, Case 314/85 ECR 4199, 53 CMLR 57 (1987).

[b] See *R. v. Secretary of State for Transport, ex parte Factortame*, A.C. 603 (1991).

[c] *J. Bord, Kohlen und BaustoffengroBhandlung v. Commission on the European Communities*, Case 4/73, 1974 ECR 491, 2 CMLR 338 (1974).

[d] See *Yvonne van Duyn v. Home Office*, Case 41/74, 1974 ECR 1337 (1974).

[e] See *Gabrielle Defenne v. Societe Anonyme Belge Navigation Aerienne Sabeana*, Case 43/75, 1976 ECR 455 (1976).

[f] See, e.g., Federico Mancini, "The Making of a Constitution for Europe," XXIV *Common Law Market Review* 595 (1989); Mauro Cappelletti, M. Seccombe, and J. H. H. Weiler, eds., *Integration Through Law: Europe and the American Federal Experience Book 1* (Berlin: Walter de Gruyter, 1986); and J. H. H. Weiler, "A Quiet Revolution—The European Court of Justice and its Interlocutors," *Comparative Political Studies* 26 (1994), 510.

[g] Martin Shapiro, "Comparative Law and Comparative Politics," *Southern California Law Review* 53 (1980).

[h] G. Garrett and Barry Weingast, "Ideas, Interests, and Institutions: Constructing the ECs Internal Market," in J. Goldstein and R. Keohane, eds., *Ideas and Foreign Policy* (Ithaca: Cornell University Press, 1993), 173, 201–02.

[i] A. M. Burley and W. Mattli, "Europe Before the Court," *International Organization* 47 (1993), 41, 60.

^{j}Karen Alter, "Explaining National Court Acceptance of European Court Jurisprudence: A Critical Evaluation of Theories of Legal Integration," in Anne-Marie Slaughter, Alec Stone Sweet, and J. H. H. Weiler, eds., *The European Court and National Courts—Doctrine and Jurisprudence* (Oxford: Hart Publishing, 1998), 228, 241.

^{k}Alter, op. cit., 242–43.

Sources: Karen Alter, *Establishing the Supremacy of European Law: The Making of an International Rule of Law in Europe* (New York: Oxford University Press, 2001); Sally Kenney, William M. Reisinger, and John C. Reitz, eds., *Constitutional Dialogues in Comparative Perspective* (New York: St. Martin's Press, 1999); Anne-Marie Slaughter, Alex Stone Sweet, and J. H. H. Weiler, eds., *The European Court and National Courts—Doctrine and Jurisprudence* (Oxford: Hart Publishing, 1998); Alec Stone Sweet, Wayne Sandholtz, and Neil Fligstein, eds., *The Institutionalization of Europe* (New York: Oxford University Press, 2001).

THE IMPACT OF JUDICIAL DECISIONS

The impact of judicial decisions concerns the effect they have in shaping public policy and social relations. On one level, judicial rulings only affect the specific parties to a lawsuit. Yet judicial rulings do not only affect specific parties. They influence discretionary choices of government officials and private entities that must, in turn, implement the legal rules or policies that decisions create. Similarly, litigation may broadly affect the public at large and the political choices citizens make in responding to judicial decrees, as well as ultimately whether judicial decisions will earn full respect and compliance.

In short, the concept of "judicial impact" is multifaceted, fluid, and complex. The "cause and effect" of judicial rulings is largely dependent upon how they are perceived, implemented, and followed. Though courts may dictate social policy, at the end of the day they must rely on other institutional actors to translate their rulings into action. Courts and judges cannot control whether the law's command will be administered properly or even accepted as being legitimate. As a result, "implementation" and "compliance" are analytically distinct from "impact"; and both underscore not only the practical consequences of judicial decision making but also their public policy effect.

Although all judicial decision making has some effect on different subpopulations, groups, or citizens,[41] the extent to which judicial decisions are properly administered is far from certain and is often controversial. The Supreme Court's holding in *Blakely v. Washington* (2004)[42] is illustrative. Though the ruling invalidated the state's criminal sentencing guidelines, the implications of the decision forced many state governments to revisit or rewrite their own guidelines in order to comply with the Court's ruling. Shortly thereafter, when the federal sentencing guidelines were struck down in *United States v. Booker* (2005),[43] the U.S. Sentencing Commission, as well as the federal judges, the law enforcement officials, and the defense counsels, had to adjust their policies, behavior, and advice to address the reality that the post-*Booker* federal sentencing guidelines were only given advisory, and not binding, force in subsequent criminal prosecutions.

A number of interrelated factors influence implementation of and compliance with judicial decisions and ultimately, judicial impact. Whether an appellate court speaks with one voice, or is fragmented or split by dissents and separate opinions, affects the weight of the precedent and whether it will be properly administered and obeyed. The nature of the dispute may make a difference as well, because controversial decisions are likely to provoke more hostility and opposition than more benign ones. The institutional prestige of the court, along with the dynamics associated with the prevailing political climate and public opinion, are important too.

All of these elements, as well as many other intangibles, may hinder enforcement and compliance, especially when the court is ahead of the prevailing public opinion. Although there are many high-profile examples of judicial impact in terms of implementation and compliance—ranging from the enforcement of affirmative action policies, the regulation of expenditures and contributions in political campaigns, the display of religious monuments in public forums, and the imposition of capital punishment—arguably the best introduction to the general difficulties courts face in achieving implementation and compliance with their rulings on major political controversies remains the politics of school desegregation and the Supreme Court's decision in *Brown v. Board of Education* (1954).[44]

In *Brown*, racial segregation in public schools was prohibited by implicitly ending, but not directly overruling, the so-called separate but equal principle of *Plessy v. Ferguson* (1896).[45] In a companion case, *Bolling v. Sharpe* (1954),[46] the segregation in the District of Columbia's public schools was invalidated on the basis of the Fifth Amendment's due process clause, a decision holding that the guarantee of equal protection applied against federal action as well as against state governments. The mandate for equality in both cases, however, met with stiff resistance in many local communities, a problem that was compounded by the Court's failure to issue any remedial orders to implement its decree until a year later in *Brown v. Board of Education* (1955) (*Brown II*).[47] Even then, the only remedy offered was the justices' insipid pronouncement that desegregation in schools should commence "with all deliberate speed."

The Court's inability to enforce its own rulings transformed *Brown's* mandate into little more than a "moral appeal and an invitation for delay."[48] Although a few states began to move toward desegregation even before the Court's rulings, *Brown II* encouraged defiance in the south instead of compliance. Immediately after *Brown*, white supremacist "citizen councils" were organized. Several popular assemblies enacted numerous resolutions disputing *Brown* and implicitly condemning the court that imposed it. In the U.S. Congress, a significant minority of Senators and Representatives issued the "Southern Manifesto," a proclamation denouncing *Brown* as an unconstitutional exercise of judicial authority. President Dwight Eisenhower reluctantly accepted *Brown* but refused to enforce it aggressively and defending the federal government's inaction by saying that "it is difficult through law and through force to change a man's heart."[49]

Because of mounting pressures of the civil rights movement and persistent litigation by the NAACP, the federal government began to act more decisively in the early 1960s. In 1961, the U.S. Civil Rights Commission recommended that all school districts file desegregation plans with the federal government and to deny fifty percent of federal funds for education from segregated districts. Subsequently, Congress passed the Civil Rights Act of 1964, the landmark civil rights legislation that guaranteed the right to vote and prohibited segregation and discrimination in public places as well as the workplace.[50] The Department of Justice then began to sue districts refusing to comply, thereby forcing them to desegregate or to lose millions of dollars in federal money.

Despite this progress, direct enforcement of *Brown* remained uncertain and piecemeal as the political climate and the composition of the judiciary changed, though the momentum of the civil rights movement also began to fade in the late 1970s. The Supreme Court, led by Chief Justice Warren Burger, reacted to lower court rulings authorizing gerrymandered school district lines and compulsory busing of school children by issuing key rulings prohibiting *de jure* (state-sponsored) segregation in public schools but permitting *de facto* segregation (resulting from demographic changes in housing patterns), unless there was evidence of intentional discrimination.[51]

Although hundreds of lawsuits were filed in the 1970s and 1980s to press local school boards to integrate fully, the judiciary had a difficult time enforcing *Brown* in local communities, and the Supreme Court became increasingly reluctant to commit its power to micromanaging efforts to achieve integration. Without firm guidance from the Supreme Court, the litigation involving desegregation floundered in the lower federal courts until William Rehnquist became chief justice in 1986. Thereafter, the Court revisited the controversy over school desegregation and began to disengage the federal judiciary from the task of superintending local school boards as they tried to work toward achieving integrated, or "unitary," school districts.

In *Missouri v. Jenkins* (1990),[52] the Court affirmed the power of federal judges to order a school board to levy taxes to implement desegregation plans. But, subsequently, the high court changed direction. In *Board of Education of Oklahoma City Public Schools v. Dowell* (1991),[53] and later in *Freeman v. Pitts* (1992),[54] the justices held that judicial supervision of segregated school districts could end if there was evidence that school boards made reasonable efforts to comply with desegregation plans and, to the extent practicable, they eliminated "the vestiges of past discrimination." In one scholar's view, *Dowell* and *Freeman* heralded a "new course, not a dramatic reversal, pointing to a new period of litigation—a period not unlike that immediately after *Brown* but one in which lower courts gradually moved to relinquish, rather than assert, control over public schools."[55]

For critics, *Brown* and its aftermath underscore the incompetence of the judiciary to force major social change through its rulings.[56] Though the Supreme Court could set the bar for equality in its case law, it could not fully implement it without the sustained cooperation of the political branches and, in the end, without full public support. Although total compliance with *Brown* has never been achieved, the Court's judicial policymaking did steer the country in the direction of significant public policy change toward ending racial discrimination in public schools and elsewhere. In this regard, *Brown* "dramatically and undeniably altered the course of American life."[57]

Nor is *Brown* an isolated case. *Lawrence v. Texas* (2003), the Court's controversial ruling striking down laws criminalizing homosexual sodomy, provoked similar responses by different institutional actors and segments of the population. Those reactions are considered in the next section in accordance with a model public law scholars use in evaluating judicial impact, implementation, and compliance.

The Politics of Gay Rights and Same-Sex Marriages: A Case Study

Political scientists Bradley Canon and Charles Johnson have analyzed the scope and application of judicial policymaking by conceptualizing how different populations in the legal culture interpret, implement, and comply with judicial decisions.[58] Their model emphasizes that judicial policies are not self-executing. Appellate courts must rely on other institutional actors, including lower courts, state attorney generals, prosecutors, the police, key agency officials, and municipal employees, to translate legal principles into policy action.

Hence, *judicial impact* (how court decisions affect society) is, by definition, a function of *judicial implementation* (how court decisions are implemented by government officials) and *judicial compliance* (whether judicial policies are followed or not by those interpreting or implementing them). See Figure 10.1. The underlying dynamics of implementation, compliance, and impact are not mutually exclusive or static; rather, they are fluid and situational. The politics of gay rights and the issue of whether same-sex couples may marry were greatly affected by *Lawrence v. Texas* (2003). Accordingly, that decision helps to illustrate the political dynamics of judicial policymaking and its aftermath.

In *Lawrence*, the Court accelerated the movement toward recognizing a broad range of homosexual rights by ruling against one facet of antihomosexual regulation—the criminal ban on sodomy—and overruling the precedent set in *Bowers v. Hardwick* (1986).[59] By 2001, almost one-half of the States had already repealed their criminal laws banning consensual sodomy. Before

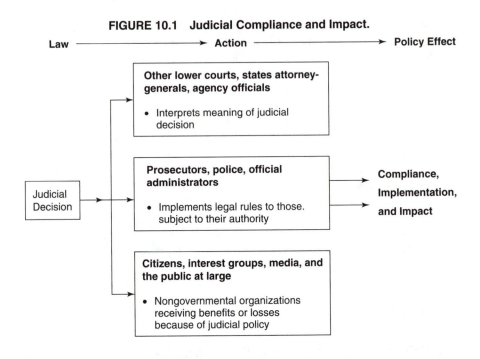

FIGURE 10.1   Judicial Compliance and Impact.

Law ⟶ Action ⟶ Policy Effect

Judicial Decision

Other lower courts, states attorney-generals, agency officials

- Interprets meaning of judicial decision

Prosecutors, police, official administrators

- Implements legal rules to those. subject to their authority

Citizens, interest groups, media, and the public at large

- Nongovernmental organizations receiving benefits or losses because of judicial policy

Compliance,
Implementation,
and Impact

Lawrence, some states had also whittled away at *Bowers* despite counter-vailing national and state pressure to ban homosexual marriages. In 1996, for example, President Bill Clinton signed the federal Defense of Marriage Act (DOMA), which defines marriage as a heterosexual relationship. The federal legislation prompted a majority of states to enact similar laws, called *junior DOMAs*. But in 2000, Vermont became the first State permitting homosexual "civil unions" (allowing same sex couples to enjoy legal rights given in heterosexual marriages).[60]

The cross-cutting movements within the political system to reaffirm het-erosexual marriage and yet recognize the legality of same-sex relationships greatly intensified after *Lawrence*. Although the Court's ruling only nullified criminal bans on sodomy, advocates and critics of homosexual rights perceived it as open-ing the door for full judicial recognition of same-sex marriages. In the words of dissenting Justice Antonin Scalia, *Lawrence*, "leaves on pretty shaky grounds state laws limiting marriage to opposite-sex couples."[61]

Different constituencies responded to *Lawrence* in diverse ways. Their reactions were based on the possibility that the judiciary would continue to play an active role in expanding homosexual rights. Homosexual rights activists saw new hope in *Lawrence*, but the decision caused an equally intense backlash against homosexuals, especially among religious and conservative groups. Significantly, *Lawrence* had the unintended effect of changing rights' discourse: Antigay animus was no longer necessarily rooted in moral objections to homosexuality, as it was before *Lawrence*. Rather, arguments for restricting same-sex unions were refashioned to stress that they undermined the traditional institution of marriage by causing harm to children.[62] The new parameters of the political debate about gay rights thereby redefined the strategies, responses, and burdens of political elites, such as legislators and well-organized special interest groups that were frequent litigators, to mount opposition against same-sex marriages in order to preserve the status quo.

Consequently, after *Lawrence*, the primary actors—lower courts, judges, and lawyers—began to adjudicate the basic question of whether the traditional conception of marriage should remain the legal norm. Before *Lawrence*, two state appellate courts, in Vermont and Hawaii, and a lower court in Alaska extended some legal protections to homosexual relationships. In both Hawaii and Alaska, however, the popular assembly subsequently amended their constitutions to limit marriage to opposite-sex couples.[63] Still, after *Lawrence*, the pace of reform picked up considerably as state and federal courts fielded challenges to laws restricting whether homosexuals enjoyed the right to marry.

With *Goodridge v. Department of Health* (2003)[64] and *Opinions of the Justices to the Senate* (2004),[65] Massachusetts became the first state to validate same-sex marriages, whereas Vermont and Connecticut ultimately recognized "civil unions." California sanctioned a comprehensive benefits regime for "domestic partnerships" (allowing unmarried partners to share in employment benefits)," and the legislatures in Hawaii, Maine, and New Jersey approved similar laws on a limited basis. Notably, though, Connecticut was the first jurisdiction to enact legislation without prompting from a court order.[66]

Still, despite these developments the landscape of judicially enforced marriage rights for same-sex couples remains in flux. State courts in California, New York, and Washington have reaffirmed some same-sex rights,[67] but similar judicial challenges in New Jersey and Arizona have failed.[68] In federal court, a district court in Nebraska struck down a state constitutional amendment recognizing only heterosexual marriages on the basis that it chilled speech and association rights under the federal First Amendment.[69] But, another district court in California upheld the federal Defense of Marriage Act and refused to recognize a fundamental right to marry for same-sex couples.[70]

These cases are not likely to be the last word. Several of the rulings have been appealed, and the courts will inexorably continue to hear cases involving whether there is a constitutional right to same-sex marriage as well as others that will test the rights of same-sex couples to adopt children, obtain divorces, and receive health or retirement benefits. It remains ambiguous, however, precisely how government officials and private corporations in the implementing population will apply legal policies because the decisions of post-*Lawrence* courts are conflicting and vary across the country.

Moreover, the different signals emerging from federal and state courts also undoubtedly complicated political reform efforts on the national and local level. Homosexual rights organizations have retooled their strategies to advance their cause. For many gay activists, the struggle to end criminalization of sodomy laws was only one part of the larger political struggle to win greater civil rights and liberties. Since the late 1960s, homosexuals have sought political and judicial solutions to ease legal restrictions against the Lesbian, Gay, Bisexual, Transsexual (LGBT) community, including the enactment of hate crime legislation, comprehensive health resources for AIDS victims, antidiscrimination employment laws, and domestic partner benefits. Grassroots campaigns pushing for the recognition of state-sanctioned marriages were simply not on the mainstream LGBT agenda because many homosexuals thought that asserting marriage equality would be counterproductive and might possibly lead to political backlash and recrimination. Consequently, *Lawrence* and *Goodridge* unexpectedly became the vehicles to revitalize the issue of marriage equality and also to reassert and possibly extend existing priorities on the national LBGT political agenda.[71]

Lawrence and *Goodridge* thus galvanized the LBGT community to reassert their legal claims. Shortly after *Goodridge* was handed down, over 6,100 gay and lesbian couples were married in jurisdictions outlawing the practice. But, subsequently, the courts stepped in and voided them in San Francisco, California; Sandoval County, New Mexico; New Paltz, New York; and, Multnomah County, Oregon. For their part, these judicial decisions caused opponents of homosexual rights to use the ballot box and legislative pressure to protect against any further erosion of traditional family values by the courts, mainly through the amendment process. On Election Day in 2004, eleven states approved of antigay marriage amendments to their state constitutions, joining two others that did so earlier in the year. Until that point, only four states had constitutional bans on homosexual marriages.[72]

Moreover, in 2005 Kansas and Texas adopted antigay amendments, as did Alabama in 2006, and similar constitutional bans went into effect in accordance with regional election results, thus bringing the total number of state bans on same-sex marriages to twenty.[73] Several other states passed nonbinding resolutions demanding Congress enact a constitutional amendment to prohibit homosexual marriages. The Federal Marriage Amendment was introduced by Congress, but it was defeated in 2004 because it did not garner enough votes in the House of Representatives. Furthermore, even in Massachusetts, after *Goodridge* a "compromise" constitutional amendment was tentatively approved (subject to the voters' ratification in 2006) banning same-sex marriage but approving civil unions. Because the same-sex issue remains salient and politically volatile, the pressure to amend the federal and other state constitutions is likely to persist, especially if the courts expand homosexual rights in a conservative political environment. In short, the politics of homosexual rights underscores that the capacity of the judiciary to forge social change is contingent upon whether its decisions are in line or out of step with prevailing dominant political coalitions and public opinion (See The Controversies over Courts box in this chapter).[74]

THE LIMITATIONS OF JUDICIAL POWER

Major controversies involving the scope and application of state or federal public policy do not originate from courts. Yet, as the abortion, school desegregation, and same-sex marriage disputes reveal, courts are often asked by litigants to forge political and social change. They may do so, but with mixed results. As these controversies illustrate, the exercise of judicial power is subject to a variety of internal and external constraints that limit the impact of judicial policymaking.

Internal Constraints

A number of informal norms and professional constraints limit judicial policymaking. These "internal" constraints, which generally originate from the personal values of judges, shared conceptions of collegiality, and informal traditions defining proper judicial behavior, temper judicial decision making. A basic maxim, for example, is the faithful adherence to the judicial oath. As Chief Justice John Marshall put it, the Constitution was thought of by the framers as "a rule for the government of courts."[75] As a result, on assuming office all judges vow to uphold the constitution and the rule of law. Thus, all judges have a strong obligation to follow what the founding document says in discharging their official duties, notwithstanding their personal feelings about a case and its public policy implications.

Similarly, ingrained conceptions of judicial philosophy, as well as deference to court-generated norms, procedures, and traditions, may lead judges to avoid the temptation to "yield to spasmodic sentiment, to vague and unregulated benevolence" and, instead, compel them to "draw ... inspiration from consecrated principles."[76] The urge to follow the law and respect certain conceptions of the judicial role results from believing in time-honored values of judicial restraint: those that bolster basic notions of judicial integrity and equality; show deference to duly enacted statutes and institutional rules; and promote faithful adherence to precedent.[77]

Those vested with the power of judicial review understand these restrictions and consider them seriously in performing the task of judging. "Judges have to look in the mirror at least once a day, just like everyone else," federal circuit Judge Alex Kozinski mused, and "they have to like what they see."[78] In other words, self-respect is another powerful constraint on judicial behavior because it forces judges to base their decisions on legal reasons that must withstand scrutiny from peers as well as the test of time. Self-respect thus works in tandem with the fear of being chastised by colleagues on the bench, either internally or by appellate judges who have the power to reverse legal errors on appeal. Consequently, judges deviating too far from the law or established principles invite criticism and scorn, and doing so may also damage professional reputations.[79] In short, the effort to foster collegial relationships and the attempt to maintain high standards of professionalism, are compelling incentives that curb the tendency to make arbitrary or "unprincipled" decisions.

External Restraints

Besides internal constraints, the structural politics of constitutionalism, including the principle of separation of powers, operate as broad "external" limitations on judicial decision making. Judicial authority, in other words, is subject to an array of checks imposed on courts by legislatures, the executive branch, interest groups, and public opinion. One federal court of appeals judge perceived Congress's enactment of the Civil Rights Act of 1991 as such a check because it overturned twelve Supreme Court opinions relating to the scope of employment discrimination. Another example was the decision of California voters to oust at least three state supreme court justices in judicial elections in the 1990s.[80] In 2005, a group known as the South Dakota Judicial Accountability pushed for a ballot initiative that would amend the state constitution by eliminating judicial immunity for state judges and permit citizens to sue and criminally prosecute judges that deliberate violate the law when they rendered decisions.[81] These illustrations, and countless others, disclose that federal and state judiciaries are ultimately accountable to politicians and the public for the opinions they write, especially in controversial areas of public policy.

RESTRAINTS IMPOSED BY LEGISLATURES Legislators unhappy with judicial decisions have a variety of options that can be used to curb courts that stray too far from majoritarian preferences. They may (1) use the political process to amend their constitutions to reverse unpopular judicial decisions, (2) change the court's size or jurisdiction by legislation, (3) enact legislation that "overturns" unpopular judicial opinions, and, (4) ignore judicial rulings and not comply with them. They may also use more subtle tactics to pressure courts into compliance, such as attempting to influence judicial appointments or, in states that use elections, impose term limits on judicial service. Or, legislatures may reduce judicial funding or limit the distribution of institutional resources, such as cutting back on personnel, supplies, or office technology; or, they may refuse to provide salary increases. In extreme instances of political retribution, legislatures may opt to begin unwarranted impeachment proceedings or, more commonly, threaten to institute them against particular judges.

The political responses to judicial rulings favoring desegregation, abortion, and gay rights indicate that the impact of controversial decisions may be moderated by using any or all of these legislative weapons. Still, of the tactics, the constitutional amendment is the most effective court-curbing method, although it is a cumbersome and lengthy process to implement. Although amendments have been filed in order to reverse or revise court decisions relating to hot-button topics such as abortion, flag burning, busing, and same-sex marriages, only a small percentage actually get ratified and put into effect.

Amending the constitution has the symbolic effect of representing the people's will while also reigning in courts that threaten to go too far ahead of prevailing public opinion in local or national political communities. Though Massachusetts legislators were able to reach a compromise amendment to the state constitution that would ban same-sex marriage but allow civil unions in the aftermath of *Goodridge*, the deal was struck on the heels of an earlier failure to enact an amendment outlawing homosexual marriages; and, before it can go into effect, a second vote is required. Even so, by 2006 nearly one-half of the states had put amendments on the ballots, and none were rejected by the voters. On the federal level, however, there is less success in the use of, either directly or indirectly, constitutional amendments to overturn judicial rulings (see Table 10.1): It has happened with the passage of the Eleventh, Thirteenth, Fourteenth, Sixteenth, Nineteenth, Twenty-Fourth, and Twenty-Sixth Amendments.

TABLE 10.1   Constitutional Amendments Overturning Unpopular U.S. Supreme Court Decisions

Supreme Court Opinion	Opinion's Impact	Constitutional Amendment(s) and Effect
Chisholm v. Georgia, 2 U.S. 419 (1793)	Allowed citizens to sue state governments in federal courts	Eleventh Amendment (1795) provided sovereign immunity for states in lawsuits commenced in federal court by state citizens
Dred Scott v. Sandford, 60 U.S. 693 (1857)	Denied emancipated blacks full citizenship rights	Thirteenth (1865) and Fourteenth Amendments (1868) abolishing slavery and giving blacks full citizenship rights
Pollack v. Farmers' Loan and Trust Company, 157 U.S. 429 (1895)	Disallowed imposition of a federal income tax	Sixteenth Amendment (1913) enacted federal income tax
Minor v. Happersett, 88 U.S. 162 (1874)	Denied women the right to vote under state law	Nineteenth Amendment (1922) allowed women the right to vote in state and federal elections
Breedlove v. Suttles, 302 U.S. 77 (1937)	Permitted use of poll tax in elections under state law	Twenty-Fourth Amendment (1964) barred use of poll tax in state and federal elections
Oregon v. Mitchell, 400 U.S. 112 (1970)	Allowed Congress to lower the voting age to eighteen for federal, but not state, elections	Twenty-Sixth Amendment (1971) allowed voting age to be lowered to eighteen in state and federal elections

Source: David M. O'Brien, *Storm Center: The Supreme Court in American Politics,* 7th ed, (New York: W.W. Norton & Company, 2005), 350–51.

Besides amending constitutions, legislatures limit judicial power by altering the size of courts, changing the court's jurisdiction, or redrawing circuit boundaries. Each method may restrict the ability of courts to make social policy in contentious areas of the law. Changing the court's size may deny presidents the opportunity to pack courts. For example, during the New Deal, President Roosevelt unsuccessfully attempted to push through Congress legislation that would have unseated anti-New Deal justices that were nearing retirement age and ultimately have them replaced with sympathetic New Dealers. If FDR's court-packing plan had been successful, it would have expanded the president's ability to enact progressive reform without judicial interference.

Altering the court's jurisdiction is also a viable option and may reduce judicial influence. In the 1970s, the Nixon administration convinced conservatives in Congress to contest the liberal decision making of the U.S. Court of Appeals for the D.C. Circuit by taking away its authority to act as a *de facto* "state" supreme court in criminal appeals, principally because the D.C. Circuit was perceived to coddle criminal defendants with expansive rulings giving them constitutional rights. Under the pretext of court reform, Congress thus enacted the "D.C. Circuit Crime Bill," legislation that removed criminal appeals from the docket and, in turn, replaced that jurisdiction with judicial authority to hear federal agency appeals.[82]

Likewise, in the 1980s, the Fifth Circuit, which then spanned a number of southern states, was split in two, in part because federal judges in that region were sympathetic to black civil rights. As a result, a new circuit, the Eleventh, was created in an attempt to defuse the old Fifth Circuit's authority.[83] Circuit-splitting, or the process of reconfiguring judicial boundaries, remains a popular court-curbing tool in the new millennium as well because conservatives in Congress have reignited legislation to divide the Ninth Circuit in late 2005, the nation's largest appellate court covering several western states. As in the cases of the D.C. and the Fifth Circuits, splitting the Ninth is purportedly justified by claims that the division would streamline judicial operations; but, studies have shown that the proposal is driven by potent political constituencies seeking to diminish the power of liberal California judges to decide cases favoring criminal defendants' rights and broadening environmental protection, and others that strike down the pledge of allegiance on the grounds of religious freedom.[84]

Another method to restrict judicial authority is passing legislation that effectively overturns judicial rulings. Although it is far more common for the legislature to ratify judicial opinions by silence or indifference, sometimes legislatures are impelled to pass laws that counter judicial rulings that interpret federal statutes and that are thought to be ill-conceived or unpopular. Congress's enactment of the Detainee Treatment Act of 2005[85] (a law that severely restricts access to federal courts in Guantanamo Bay detainee cases and, in effect, that override *Rasul v. Bush* (2004), discussed in chapter 7), is but one illustration of this power.

However, on occasion, the attempt to reign in courts by using statutory overrides may not succeed, especially if they threaten the power of courts to be the final arbiter of constitutional disputes. In the aftermath of *Employment Division, Department of Human Resources of Oregon v. Smith* (1990) (*Oregon*),[86] a ruling that arguably stultified the First Amendment right of religious expression in certain cases on the grounds of neutrality, Congress enacted the Religious Freedom Restoration Act (RFRA), a law that reinstated the preexisting, and more religious-friendly, legal standard that governed the constitutionality of religious freedom cases before *Oregon*. Shortly thereafter, the Court ruled in *City of Boerne v. Flores* (1997)[87] that Congress exceeded its authority to "enforce," by "appropriate legislation" under Section 5 of the Fourteenth Amendment (the RFRA), the First Amendment freedom of religious expression. The Court defended its ruling on the grounds of judicial supremacy, declaring that it was the Court's responsibility, and not Congress's, to determine the scope and meaning of constitutional law. Thus *Boerne* is an example of the judiciary rebuffing a bold attempt by the legislature to restrict the basic judicial prerogative to interpret constitutional law.

The historic struggle between legislative and judicial supremacy accentuates that courts and legislatures are engaged in on an ongoing, and sometimes strategic,[88] constitutional dialogue to establish the contours of public policy. Although data from the states and many federal sources is lacking, empirical research relating to the exercise of the Supreme Court's authority estimates that the Court has struck down between 159 to 173 congressional acts in whole or in part between 1789 and 2004.[89] However, other reports show that Congress has overridden 121 Supreme Court statutory construction decisions between 1967 and 1991.[90] The overriding behavior of Congress demonstrates that overrides are part of a dynamic, open, and fluid political process, and one that results from the signals sent by interest groups and the justices themselves that the rulings might need legislative correction because of the controversial nature of the judicial decision or the fact that Court was less than unanimous and ideologically divided in reaching outcomes.[91]

Finally, apart from statutory reversals, the political branches may limit court power by simply ignoring rulings from the judiciary. As passive institutions, courts have little power to enforce their own decisions. Perhaps the most famous example of this principle is President Andrew Jackson's refusal to abide by *Worcester v. Georgia* (1832),[92] a Supreme Court decision favoring the rights of Cherokee Indians over the sovereign rights of Georgia under federal law. President Jackson reportedly rebuked the Court by saying, "John Marshall made his decision—now let him enforce it!"[93] The strain of such interbranch relations still exists today, and it is felt on all levels of the judiciary. Apathy or indifference to judicial mandates extends to legislatures as well, and sometimes it puts an abrupt halt to disfavored judicial intervention. In Ohio, for instance, the state supreme court ruled in *DeRolph v. Ohio* (1997)[94] that Ohio's method of funding public schools violated the state constitution because it overrelied on local property taxes, thus creating an unequal disparity between rich and poor school districts. Yet, despite a number of attempts to do so, the judicial decree has never been enforced by the legislature because of fierce political resistance and partisan changes in the court's composition (see Sidebar 10.2).

Sidebar 10.2

The Battle over School Funding in the States

The protracted nature of state school financing litigation highlights the question of enforcement of judicial decrees. Although there are a multitude of funding lawsuits in the states,[a] litigation in Kansas and Ohio illustrates the difficulty of enforcing judicial decrees favoring reform and that force legislatures to increase funding or devise new plans to remedy the inadequate distribution of state monies.

In Kansas, in *Montoy v. State* (2005),[b] the state supreme court ordered the legislature to devise a funding method that met the constitutional mandate to "make suitable provision for finance" of public schools. After complying the court's April 2005 deadline for compliance by increasing funding by $142 million, in June the court ruled it was insufficient and set a July deadline for compliance.[c] If it was not met, the court might have ordered that the schools be closed. After a special session, the legislature increased funding to $285 million, but only after a proposed constitutional amendment preventing the courts from closing the schools failed by ten votes in the assembly after passing in the senate. Shortly thereafter, the court declared the additional funding passed constitutional muster and dismissed the lawsuit; but it retained jurisdiction to ensure further compliance.[d]

The Ohio litigation and its impact stand in stark contrast to what happened in Kansas. Starting in 1991, plaintiffs filed a funding inadequacy lawsuit, alleging that the state was not providing a "thorough and efficient" system of public schooling. In *DeRolph v. State of Ohio* (1997)[e] the Ohio Supreme Court agreed and ordered the legislature to undertake a "complete systematic overhaul" of the state's funding system but without specifying how. The court also retained jurisdiction to ensure compliance. Despite continuous efforts by the legislature over several years to reform funding, none met the court's constitutional mandate.[f] In 2001, the court gave specific guidance to the assembly on how it could satisfy the judicial decree, but in the next year the court terminated its jurisdiction and ended its involvement in the case once it became clear that the court's mandate would not be fulfilled.[g] The inability of the court to implement its decree was due to key changes in the court's composition and increased political resistance in the general assembly in the aftermath of the 2002 elections. Shortly thereafter, and even though the funding system was still unconstitutional, the court declared that "the duty now lies with the General Assembly to remedy an educational system," and, accordingly, the supreme court ordered the trial court hearing the matter to stop any further enforcement proceedings.[h]

The Kansas and Ohio school funding cases underscore that courts have had mixed success in micromanaging contentious areas of social and public policy legislation. The difficulty arises because school funding lawsuits are invariably political questions that raise fundamental concerns about whether courts have exceeded their authority in issuing decrees that must be enforced with the cooperation of the legislative branch.[i]

Notes

[a]Michael Griffith and Molly Burke, "School Funding Adequacy Cases," *ECS State Notes (February 2005), Education Commission of the States*, available from www.esc.org (retrieved August 21, 2005).

[b]*Montoy v. State of Kansas*, 102 P.3d 1160 (Kansas 2005).

[c]*Montoy v. State of Kansas*, 112 P.3d 923 (Kansas 2005).

[d]Tim Carpenter, "Courts Rings Schools Open," *Topeka Capital-Journal* (July 9, 2005), A1.

[e]*DeRolph v. State of Ohio*, 677 N.E.2d 733 (Ohio 1997) (*DeRolph*).

[f]*DeRolph v. State of Ohio*, 728 N.E.2d 993 (Ohio 2000) (*DeRolph II*); and *DeRolph v. State of Ohio*, 754 N.E.2d 1184 (Ohio 2001) (*DeRolph III*).

[g]*DeRolph v. State of Ohio*, 780 N.E.2d 529 (Ohio 2002) (*DeRolph IV*).

[h]*State v. Lewis*, 789 N.E.2d 195 (Ohio 2003).

[i]See Larry J. Obhof, "DeRolph v. State and Ohio's Long Road to an Adequate Education," *Brigham Young University Education and Law Journal* 2005 (2005), 83–149.

RESTRAINTS IMPOSED BY THE EXECUTIVE BRANCH   Although state and federal executives (governors and the president) and their subordinates (attorneys general, agency counsel, and cabinet officials) have limited authority to curb courts, the main device to do so remains judicial recruitment in the states and the federal appointment process (discussed in chapter 4). The pervasive impact of state judicial elections diminishes executive control over the judiciary, although governors may influence the composition of the bench by making recess appointments during vacancies or, conversely, by affecting decisions about who serves on judicial nomination commissions. Likewise, with few exceptions, presidents have not been successful in entirely transforming the federal courts. In the beginning of the republic, Presidents George Washington and John Adams were able to entrench the bench with Federalist appointments; and President Franklin D. Roosevelt's long tenure in the Oval Office over four terms in the 1930s and 1940s gave him the unprecedented chance to fill eight vacancies on the Supreme Court.[95] Still, presidents, especially those serving two terms, generally enjoy more triumphs in packing lower courts because they have more opportunities to fill them with a large cadre of ideologically like-minded judges.

Besides appointments, presidents and governors can undermine judicial policymaking in subtle ways by using litigation to advance majoritarian political agendas or, conversely, to resist certain unpopular rulings. Political support for the president's agenda may come from the use of a sympathetic judiciary that is allied with the many of the same litigation goals as the prevailing administration.[96] Similarly, government lawyers appointed by the president and serving in the Department of Justice, most notably the solicitor general and the attorney general, have a pervasive impact in expanding or retarding the president's policies as frequent "repeat players" in the judicial process. As such, it is not an overstatement to claim that the president, either directly or indirectly, controls litigation policy in the administrative bureaucracy[97] and, accordingly, greatly influences judicial decision making over vast areas of law, including abortion, affirmative action, the death penalty, religious freedom, environmental protection, consumer rights, government securities, tax, and antitrust law.

RESTRAINTS IMPOSED BY PUBLIC OPINION In conjunction with the political pressure put on courts to conform to legislative or executive policy directives, the judiciary is always accountable to the people. Scholars have demonstrated that courts are sensitive to public opinion in different ways. On the one hand, strategic judges are responsive to public views as part of the information courts gather in choosing to make policy choices when they decide cases.[98] On the other hand, public opinion may generate resistance to judicial policymaking, especially during times of political upheaval, such as partisan realignments or during critical elections.[99] At those moments in history, courts with stable membership over time are likely to be out of step with the prevailing political mood of the country and, accordingly, might risk their legitimacy with unpopular rulings. However, during all other times courts are most inclined to follow the election returns and to dispense justice in accordance with the policy preferences of dominant national coalitions. In this sense, courts are simply one element of an ongoing "constitutional dialogue" in American democratic politics.[100] Even so, scholars remain divided on the related question of whether courts are responsible for and institutionally capable of creating major social change (see Controversies over Courts: Do Courts Forge Major Social Change? below).

Controversies over Courts

Do Courts Forge Major Social Change?

In his January 2005 annual report on the state of the federal judiciary, Chief Justice William H. Rehnquist focused "on the recently mounting criticism of judges for engaging in what is often referred to as 'judicial activism,'" though he also emphasized that "criticism of judges and judicial decisions is as old as our republic."[a] The Marshall Court (1801–1835) was sharply criticized and, as the chief justice noted, it took a generation for the Court's reputation to recover after its infamous ruling on slavery in *Dred Scott v. Sandford*.[b] The Court's invalidation of early New Deal and other progressive legislation culminated in President Franklin D. Roosevelt's court-packing plan and the "constitutional crisis" of 1937.[c] Over fifty years ago, the landmark school desegregation decision, *Brown v. Board of Education of Topeka, Kansas*,[d] sparked massive resistance and a long-running controversy over the implementation of its mandate.

Recent judicial rulings on abortion, the death penalty, the separation of church and state, and homosexual rights have intensified the controversy over the role of courts. Scholars, jurists, politicians, and citizens disagree about whether the judiciary is an "imperial" institution in overturning federal, state, and local laws; or leading a "vital national seminar" that engages the country in a constitutional dialogue within a pluralistic political system; or usually "behind the times" and reinforces the dominant national coalition; or a "hollow hope" in terms of ensuring minority rights and bringing about major social changes.

AN "IMPERIAL JUDICIARY"?

Whereas liberals criticized a conservative Court for invalidating progressive legislation before 1937, afterward conservatives turned the table and attacked courts during the last fifty years for "activist" liberal rulings on individual rights, due process, and the equal protection of the law. In a very influential article, "Towards an Imperial Judiciary?," Harvard University sociologist Nathan Glazer argued that "American courts, the most powerful in the world ... are now far more powerful than ever before.... And courts, through interpretation of the Constitution and the laws, now reach into the lives of the people, against the will of the people, deeper than they had in American history."[e]

Subsequently, conservative scholars, jurists, and politicians expanded and advanced Glazer's argument in two different directions. On the one hand, many conservatives contending that we have "an imperial judiciary" follow Judge Robert H. Bork in claiming that courts have forged major social changes with their rulings on desegregation, abortion, affirmative action, school prayer, the rights of the accused, and equal protection for women and homosexuals. In their view, over the last fifty years unelected judges have increasingly functioned antidemocratically and their rulings are countermajoritarian in thwarting popular opinion.[f] Moreover, in light of the Court's and federal judiciary's move in more conservation directions since the 1980s, even some liberal scholars agree and have lamented recent conservative "judicial activism" and the judiciary's anti-democratic role.[g]

On the other hand, some conservatives and scholars argue that the judiciary lacks the resources and managerial expertise to forge significant social change in, for example, overseeing the supervision of public school desegregation, improving the conditions of prisons, and reforming law enforcement policies. In short, courts lack not only the legitimacy but also the institutional capacity, expertise, and resources to bring about coherent social change.[h]

A "VITAL NATIONAL SEMINAR," "BEHIND THE TIMES," OR A "HOLLOW HOPE"?

By contrast, writing in the 1960s at the height of massive resistance to *Brown v. Board of Education*, Yale law school professor Eugene V. Rostow countered conservative criticisms of the judiciary by arguing that the Court engages the country in a "vital national seminar" over constitutional values. In his words "[t]he Supreme Court is, among other things, an educational body, and the Justices are inevitably teachers in a vital national seminar."[i] Rostow highlighted the fact that,

> [t]he process of forming public opinion in the United States is a continuous one with many participants—Congress, the President, the press, political parties, scholars, pressure groups, and so on. . . . The reciprocal relation between the Court and the community in the formulation of policy may be a paradox to those who believe that there is something undemocratic in the power of judicial review. But the work of the Court can have, and when wisely exercised does have, the effect not of inhibiting but of releasing and encouraging the dominantly democratic forces of American life.[j]

Other scholars have further developed the argument that the Court's rulings, along with those of state and federal judiciaries, engage other political branches and the country in a constitutional dialogue over the direction of law and public policy. They underscore the often neglected but important role of state legislatures, Congress, the executive branch, and other political institutions and organizations within a pluralistic political system in determining the direction of law and social change.[k]

Yet, Yale University political scientist Robert Dahl took a different direction in charging that the Supreme Court is generally in tune with the dominant national political coalition, and hence it is not as countermajoritarian as conservatives claim. "By itself," he concluded, "the Court is almost powerless to affect the course of national policy."[l] On the basis of an examination of the Court's invalidation of congressional legislation, Dahl found that Congress ultimately prevailed seventy percent of the time. Congress was able to do so by reenacting legislation and because of changes in the composition and direction of the Court. In other words, on major issues of public policy, Congress is likely to prevail or at least temper the impact of the Court's rulings.

However, the Court forges public policy not only when invalidating federal legislation but also when overturning state and local laws, and Dahl failed to consider that important fact. The continuing controversies over decisions invalidating state and local laws on abortion, school prayer, and against homosexual rights are a measure of how the Court's striking down state and local laws may elevate issues to the national political agenda.

Nonetheless, a number of scholars have recently followed Dahl in maintaining that, contrary to conservatives who charge that we have an "imperial judiciary," the Court largely reinforces the policy preferences of dominant national political coalitions rather than forging major social change. Put differently, the Court usually only reaches out to bring "outliers" into line with an emerging or the dominant national consensus. Among others,[m] for one, law school professor Michael J. Klarman contended that the Court has not brought about major social changes. Instead of forging "countermajoritarian revolutions" with its rulings on civil rights and liberties, the Court has largely followed social changes in tune with an emerging national consensus. Klarman stated that[n]

> [t]he modern Court's individual rights jurisprudence can be usefully distilled into two general categories. First, ... frequently ... the [court seizes] upon a dominant national consensus and impos[es] it on resisting local outliers. Cases illustrating this pattern include *Griswold v. Connecticut* .... Second, ... the Court intervenes ... where the nation is narrowly divided—racial segregation in 1954, the death penalty in 1972, abortion in 1973, affirmative action in 1978, and ... sexual orientation in 1986. On these occasions, the justices seem, whether consciously or not, to be endeavoring to predict the future....

Still other scholars, such as Gerald N. Rosenberg, in his book *The Hollow Hope: Can Courts Bring About Social Change?*,[o] go even further in claiming that "courts can *almost never* be effective producers of significant social reform." *Brown's* failure to achieve widespread desegregation in the following decades, for instance, remains instructive, Rosenberg contended, in developing a model of judicial policymaking based on two opposing theories of judicial power. On the one hand, a "*constrained court*" theory posits that three institutional factors limit judicial policymaking: "[t]he limited nature of constitutional rights," "[t]he lack of judicial independence," and "[t]he judiciary's lack of powers of implementation." On the other hand, a "*dynamic court theory*" emphasizes the judiciary's freedom "from electoral constraints and [other] institutional arrangements that stymie change" and thus enable the courts to take on issues that other political institutions might not or cannot. But neither theory is completely satisfactory, according to Rosenberg, because occasionally the Court does bring about social change. The Court may do so when the three institutional restraints identified with the constrained court theory are absent and at least one of the following conditions exists to support judicial policymaking when other political institutions and actors offer either (1) incentives, (2) costs to induce compliance, (3) "when judicial decisions can be implemented by the market," or (4) when the Court's ruling serves as "a shield, cover, or excuse, for persons crucial to implementation who are *willing to act.*" On the basis of the resistance to *Brown's* mandate, Rosenberg concluded that "*Brown* and its progeny stand for the proposition that courts are impotent to produce significant social reform." In sum, conservatives' charges of "an imperial judiciary" are sometimes exaggerated, whereas liberals may be misguided in looking to the courts to bring about major social changes.

Notes

[a]Chief Justice William H. Rehnquist, "2004 Year-End Report on the Federal Judiciary," January 1, 2005, available from www.uscourts.gov/newsroom/2004YearEndReport.pdf (retrieved November 20, 2005).

[b]*Dred Scott v. Sandford*, 19 How. (60 U.S.) 393 (1857).

[c]See William E. Leuchtenburg, *The Supreme Court Reborn: The Constitutional Revolution in the Age of Roosevelt* (New York: Oxford University Press, 1995).

[d]*Brown v. Board of Education of Topeka, Kansas*, 347 U.S. 483 (1954).

[e]Nathan Glazer, "Towards an Imperial Judiciary?" *The Public Interest* 104 (1975), 106.

[f]See Robert H. Bork, *The Tempting of America: The Political Seduction of the Law* (New York: Free Press, 1990); and Robert H. Bork, *Coercing Virtue: The World Wide Rule of Judges* (Washington, D.C.: American Enterprise Institute, 2003). For an overview of the literature and "imperial judiciary" criticism, Mark Kozlowski, *The Myth of the Imperial Judiciary: Why the Right is Wrong about the Courts* (New York: New York University Press, 2003).

[g]See, e.g., Mark Tushnet, *Taking the Constitution Away from The Courts* (Princeton: Princeton University Press, 1999); and Jamin B. Raskin, *Overruling Democracy* (New York: Routledge, 2003).

[h]See, e.g., Donald L. Horowitz, *The Courts and Social Policy* (Washington, D.C.: The Brookings Institution, 1977); and Lino A. Gralia, *Disaster by Decree* (Ithaca, New York: Cornell University Press, 1976).

[i]Eugene V. Rostow, *The Sovereign Prerogative: The Supreme Court and the Quest for Law* (New Haven: Yale University Press, 1962), 167.

[j]Ibid., 167, 170.

[k]See, e.g., Louis Fisher, *Constitutional Dialogues: Interpretation as Political Process* (Princeton: Princeton University Press, 1988); Louis Fisher and Neal Devins, eds., *Political Dynamics of Constitutional Law*, 3rd ed. (St. Paul: West Group, 2001); and Neal Devins and Louis Fisher, *The Democratic Constitution* (New York: Oxford University Press, 2004).

[l]Robert Dahl, "Decision-Making in a Democracy: The Supreme Court as a National Policy-Maker," *Journal of Public Law* 6 (1957), 279, 293.

[m]See, e.g., Lucas A. Powe, Jr., *The Warren Court and American Politics* (Cambridge: Belknap/Harvard University Press, 2000).

[n]Michael J. Klarman, "Rethinking the Civil Rights and Civil Liberties Revolution," *Virginia Law Review* 82 (1996), 1. See also Michael J. Klarman, *From Jim Crow to Civil Rights: The Supreme Court and the Struggle for Racial Equality* (New York: Oxford University Press, 2004).

[o]Gerald N. Rosenberg, *The Hollow Hope: Can Courts Bring About Social Change?* (Chicago: University of Chicago Press, 1991).

SELECTED READINGS

Canon, Bradley C., and Charles A. Johnson. *Judicial Policies: Implementation and Impact*, 2nd ed. Washington, D.C.: CQ Press, 1999.

Dahl, Robert. "Decision-Making in a Democracy: The Supreme Court as a National Policy-Maker," *Journal of Public Law* 6 (1957), 279.

Fisher, Louis. *Constitutional Dialogues: Interpretation as Political Process.* Princeton: Princeton University Press, 1988.

Horowitz, Donald L. *The Courts and Social Policy.* Washington, D.C.: The Brookings Institution, 1977.

Ivers, Greg, and Kevin T. McGuire, eds. *Creating Constitutional Change: Clashes Over Power and Liberty in the Supreme Court.* Charlottesville: University of Virginia Press, 2004.

Kahn, Ronald, and Ken I. Kersch, eds. *The Supreme Court and American Political Development.* Lawrence; University Press of Kansas, 2006.

Keck, Thomas M. *The Most Activist Supreme Court in History: The Road to Modern Judicial Conservatism.* Chicago: University of Chicago Press, 2004.

Kersch, Ken I. *Constructing Civil Liberties: Discontinuities in the Development of American Constitutional Law.* New York: Cambridge University Press, 2004.

Klarman, Michael J. *From Jim Crow to Civil Rights: The Supreme Court and the Struggle for Racial Equality.* New York: Oxford University Press, 2004.

Peretti, Terri Jennings. *In Defense of a Political Court.* Princeton: Princeton University Press, 1999.

Rosen, Jeffrey. *The Most Democratic Branch: How the Courts Serve America.* New York: Oxford University Press, 2006.

Rosenberg, Gerald N. *The Hollow Hope: Can Courts Bring About Social Change?* Chicago: University of Chicago Press, 1991.

Tate. C. Neal, and Torbjorn Vallinder, eds., *The Global Expansion of Judicial Power.* New York: New York University Press, 1995.

Urofsky, Melvin, ed. *The Public Debate Over Controversial Supreme Court Decisions.* Washington, D.C.: C.Q. Press, 2006.

NOTES

1. Alexander Hamilton, "Federalist No. 78," in *The Federalist Papers*, edited by Clinton Rossiter (New York: Mentor, 1961), 465.
2. Ruth Marcus, "Booting the Bench," *Washington Post* (April 11, 2005), A19.
3. Marcus, "Booting the Bench," A19.
4. *Lawrence v. Texas*, 539 U.S. 558 (2003).
5. Benjamin Cardozo, *The Nature of the Judicial Process* (New Haven: Yale University Press, 1921), 141.

6. See, e.g., Herbert Weschler, "Toward Neutral Principles of Constitutional Law," *Harvard Law Review* 73 (1959), 1–35.
7. Malcolm M. Feeley and Edward L. Rubin, *Judicial Policy Making and the Modern State: How the Court Reformed America's Prisons* (New York: Cambridge University Press, 1997).
8. *Brown v. Board of Education*, 347 U.S. 483 (1954), 493.
9. *Serrano v. Priest*, 487 P.2d 1241 (1971).
10. *Robinson v. Cahill*, 287 A.2d 187 (1972).
11. *San Antonio Independent School District v. Rodriguez*, 411 U.S. 1 (1973).
12. *San Antonio Independent School District*, 24, 31, 33, 40.
13. Michael A. Rebell, "Educational Adequacy, Democracy, and the Courts," in *Achieving High Educational Standards for All: Conference Summary (2002)*, available from www.schoolfunding.info/resource_center/research/adequacychapter.pdf (retrieved August 20, 2005), 226–27.
14. Rebell, "Educational Adequacy, Democracy, and the Courts," 229–34. See also, *Rose v. Council for Better Education*, 790 S.W.2d 186 (1989).
15. Rebell, "Educational Adequacy, Democracy, and the Courts," 229–30, 235.
16. Ibid., 235.
17. Michael Griffith and Molly Burke, "School Funding Adequacy Cases" *ECS State Notes (February 2005), Education Commission of the States*, available from www.esc.org (retrieved August 21, 2005).
18. *Boyd v. United States*, 116 U.S. 616 (1886).
19. David M. O'Brien, *Constitutional Law and Politics: Civil Rights and Civil Liberties (Volume 2)*, 6th ed. (New York: W.W. Norton, 2005), 1222–23.
20. *Pierce v. Society of Sisters*, 268 U.S. 510 (1925).
21. *Buck v. Bell*, 274 U.S. 200 (1927).
22. *Skinner v. Oklahoma*, 316 U.S. 535 (1942).
23. *Loving v. Virginia*, 388 U.S. 1 (1967).
24. *Griswold v. Connecticut*, 381 U.S. 479 (1963).
25. Ibid., 484.
26. Ibid., 537 (Black, J. dissenting).
27. *Eisenstadt v. Baird*, 405 U.S. 438 (1972).
28. Ibid., 453 (Brennan, J.).
29. *Roe v. Wade*, 410 U.S. 113 (1973).
30. Barbara Hinkson Craig and David M. O'Brien, *Abortion and American Politics* (Chatham, N.J.: Chatham House Publishers, 1993), 9.
31. Craig and O'Brien, *Abortion and American Politics*, 9–10.
32. O'Brien, *Constitutional Law and Politics: Civil Rights and Civil Liberties*, 1229–30.
33. Jack M. Balkin, "Roe v. Wade: An Engine of Controversy," in *What Roe v. Wade Should Have Said: The Nation's Top Legal Experts Rewrite America's Most Controversial Decision*, edited by Jack M. Balkin (New York: New York University Press, 2005), 11–13.

34. *Planned Parenthood of Southeastern Pennsylvania v. Casey*, 505 U.S 833 (1992).

35. Balkin, "*Roe v. Wade*: An Engine of Controversy," in *What Roe v. Wade Should Have Said*, 17.

36. *Ayotte v. Planned Parenthood of Northern New England*, 126 S.Ct. 961 (2006).

37. The Alan Guttmacher Institute, "Bans on Partial Birth Abortion," (April 1, 2006), available from www.guttmacher.org/statecenter/spibs/spib_BPBA.pdf (retrieved April 21, 2006).

38. *Stenberg v. Carhart*, 530 U.S. 914 (2000).

39. *Gonzalez v. Carhart*, 126 S. Ct. 1314 (2006); *Carhart v. Gonzalez*, 413 F.3d 791 (8th Cir. 2005). See also *Gonzalez v. Planned Parenthood Federation of America*, 74 U.S.L.W. 3702 (2006); *Planned Parenthood Federation of America v. Gonzalez*, 435 F. 3d 1163 (9th Cir. 2006).

40. The Alan Guttmacher Institute, "Monthly State Update: Major Developments in 2006" (April 1, 2006), available from www.guttmacher.org/statecenter/updates/index.html#bans (retrieved April 21, 2006).

41. See Bradley C. Canon and Charles A. Johnson, *Judicial Policies: Implementation and Impact*, 2nd ed. (Washington, D.C.: CQ Press, 1999), 2-3.

42. *Blakely v. Washington*, 542 U.S. 296 (2004). The Court based its holding on the principles first announced in *Apprendi v. New Jersey*, 530 U.S. 466 (2000).

43. *U.S. v. Booker*, 543 U.S. 220 (2005).

44. *Brown v. Board of Education*, 347 U.S. 483 (1954).

45. *Plessy v. Ferguson*, 163 U.S. 537 (1896).

46. *Bolling v. Sharpe*, 347 U.S. 497 (1954).

47. *Brown v. Board of Education*, 349 U.S. 294 (1955), Brown II.

48. O'Brien, *Constitutional Law and Politics: Civil Rights and Civil Liberties*, 1386.

49. As quoted in Michael J. Klarman, *From Jim Crow to Civil Rights: The Supreme Court and the Struggle for Racial Equality* (New York: Oxford University Press, 2004), 324. See also Klarman, *From Jim Crow to Civil Rights*, 320, 344-45.

50. Klarman, *From Jim Crow to Civil Rights*, 362-63.

51. *Swann v. Charlotte-Mecklenburg Board of Education*, 402 U.S. 1 (1971); *Milliken v. Bradley*, 418 U.S. 717 (1974).

52. *Missouri v. Jenkins*, 495 U.S. 33 (1990).

53. *Board of Education of Oklahoma City Public Schools v. Dowell*, 498 U.S. 237 (1991).

54. *Freeman v. Pitts*, 503 U.S. 467 (1992).

55. O'Brien, *Constitutional Law and Politics: Civil Rights and Civil Liberties*, 1392.

56. See, e.g., Gerald N. Rosenberg, *The Hollow Hope: Can Courts Bring About Social Change?* (Chicago: University of Chicago Press, 1991).

57. David M. O'Brien, *Storm Center: The Supreme Court in American Politics*, 7th ed. (New York: W.W. Norton, 2005), 326.

58. Canon and Johnson, *Judicial Policies: Implementation and Impact.*

59. *Bowers v. Hardwick*, 478 U.S. 186 (1986).

60. See William N. Eskridge, Jr., *Equality Practice: Civil Unions and the Future of Gay Rights* (New York: Routledge, 2002), 16–82.

61. *Lawrence*, 540–41 (Scalia, J. dissenting).

62. Frederick Liu and Stephen Macedo, "The Federal Marriage Amendment and the Strange Evolution of the Conservative Case against Gay Marriage," *PS: Political Science & Politics* (April 2005), 211–15.

63. *See Baehr v. Lewin*, 852 P.2d 44 (Haw. 1993): *Brause v. Bureau of Vital Statistics*, 21 P.3d 357 (Alaska 2001). See also *Baker v. Vermont*, 744 A.2d 864 (Vermont 1999).

64. *Goodridge v. Department of Health*, 798 N.E.2d 941 (Mass. 2003).

65. *Opinions of the Justices to the Senate*, 802 N.E.2d 565 (2004).

66. Kavan Peterson, "Same-sex unions—A constitutional race," available from www.stateline.org (retrieved August 30, 2005).

67. *Andersen v. King County*, Superior Court of Washington, King County No. 4-2-04964-4 (August 4, 2004), Downing, J.; *Castle v. Washington* Superior Court of Washington, Thurston County No. 4-2-00614-4 (September 7, 2004), (Hicks, J.); *Hernandez v. Robles*, Supreme Court of New York, New York County, Part 62 No. 1003434/2004 (February 4, 2005) (Ling-Cohan, J.); *Coordination Proceeding No. 4365 (Woo v. Lockyer)*, Superior Court of California, County of San Francisco (March 14, 2005) (Kramer, J).

68. *Lewis v. Harris*, 875 A.2d 259 (N. J. Super. App. Div. 2005); *Stanhardt v. Superior Court*, 77 P.3d 451 (Az. App. Ct. 2003).

69. *Citizens for Equal Protection v. Bruning*, 368 F. Supp. 2d 980 (D. Neb. 2005).

70. *Smelt v. County of Orange*, 374 F. Supp. 2d 861 (Calif. C.D., S.D. 2005).

71. Patrick J. Egan and Kenneth Sherrill, "Marriage and the Shifting Priorities of a New Generation of Lesbians and Gays," *PS: Political Science & Politics* (April 2005), 229–32.

72. Kavan Peterson, "Same-sex unions—A constitutional race," available from www.stateline.org (retrieved August 30, 2005).

73. David Crary, "Texas Voters Approve Ban on Gay Marriage," *Guardian Unlimited* (November 9, 2005), available from www.guardian.co.uk (retrieved November 9, 2005).

74. Robert Dahl, "Decision-Making in a Democracy: The Supreme Court as a National Policy-maker," *Journal of Public Law* (1957), 279, 293. See also Kavan Peterson, "Same-sex unions—A constitutional race," available from www.stateline.org (retrieved August 30, 2005).

75. *Marbury v. Madison*, 5 U.S. 137 (1803), 180.

76. Cardozo, *The Nature of the Judicial Process*, 141.

77. Henry J. Abraham, *The Judicial Process*, 7th ed. (New York: Oxford University Press, 1998), 359–60.

78. Alex Kozinski, "What I Ate for Breakfast and Other Mysteries of Judicial Decision-Making," *Loyola of Los Angeles Law Review* (Summer, 1993), 993, 994.

79. Kozinski, "What I Ate for Breakfast and Other Mysteries of Judicial Decision-Making," 994–95.

80. Ibid., 995–96. The twelve Supreme Court rulings overridden by Congress are listed in William N. Eskridge, Jr., "Overriding Supreme Court Statutory Interpretation Decisions," *Yale Law Journal* (November, 1991), 331, 332 n. 4.

81. Associated Press, "Judges in S.D. May Lose Lawsuit Immunity," *The New York Times* (November 14, 2005), available from www.nytimes.com (November 15, 2005).

82. Christopher P. Banks, *Judicial Politics in the D.C. Circuit Court* (Baltimore: John Hopkins University Press, 1999), 26–32.

83. Deborah J. Barrow and Thomas G. Walker, *A Court Divided: The Fifth Circuit Court of Appeals and the Politics of Judicial Reform* (New Haven: Yale University Press, 1988), 68.

84. Christopher P. Banks, "The Politics of Court Reform in the U.S. Courts of Appeals," *Judicature* 84 (2000), 34–43.

85. Section 1005 of the Department of Defense Appropriations Act of 2006, Pub. L. No. 109–148 (2005). See also *Rasul v. Bush*, 542 U.S. 466 (2004).

86. *Employment Division, Department of Human Resources of Oregon v. Smith*, 494 U.S. 872 (1990).

87. *City of Boerne v. Flores*, 521 U.S. 507 (1997).

88. Pablo T. Spiller and Emerson H. Tiller, "Invitations to Override: Congressional Reversals of Supreme Court Decisions," *International Review of Law and Economics* 16 (1996), 503–21.

89. Congressional Research Service, *The Constitution of the United States of America: Analysis and Interpretation* (2004 Supplement), (Washington, D.C.: U.S. Government Printing Office, 2004), 59 (listing 159 acts of Congress overturned up to 2003); David M. O'Brien, *Constitutional Law and Politics: Struggles for Power and Governmental Accountability* (Volume One) 6th ed. (New York: W.W. Norton., 2005), 36 (listing 173 acts of Congress overturned up to 2004); Jed Handelsman Shugerman, "A Six-Three Rule: Reviving Consensus and Deference on the Supreme Court," *Georgia Law Review* (Spring, 2003), 893–1019 (listing 167 acts of Congress overturned up to 2002).

90. Eskridge, "Overriding Supreme Court Statutory Interpretation Decisions," 331–424.

91. See Jeb Barnes, *Overruled?: Legislative Overrides, Pluralism, and Contemporary Court-Congress Relations* (Stanford: Stanford University Press, 2004).

92. *Worcester v. Georgia*, 31 U.S. 515 (1832).

93. Abraham, *The Judicial Process*, 370.

94. *DeRolph v. Ohio*, 677 N.E.2d 733 (Ohio 1997).

95. R. Shep Melnick, "The Courts, Jurisprudence, and the Executive Branch," in *The Executive Branch*, edited by Joel D. Aberbach and Mark A. Peterson (New York: Oxford University Press, 2005), 470.

96. Keith E. Whittington, "'Interpose Your Friendly Hand': Political Supports for the Exercise of Judicial Review by the United States Supreme Court," *American Political Science Review* (November, 2005), 583–96.

97. Melnick, "The Courts, Jurisprudence, and the Executive Branch," 476–79.

98. Kevin T. McGuire and James A. Stimson, "The Least Dangerous Branch Revisited: New Evidence on Supreme Court Responsiveness to Public Preferences," *Journal of Politics* (November, 2004), 1018–35.

99. Richard Funston, "The Supreme Court and Critical Elections," *American Political Science Review* (September, 1975), 795–811; Dahl, "Decision-Making in a Democracy," 279.

100. Louis Fisher, *Constitutional Dialogues: Interpretation as Political Process* (Princeton: Princeton University Press, 1988).

Case Index

Index